This Book Comes With a Website

Nolo's award-winning website has a page dedicated just to this book, where you can:

DOWNLOAD FORMS – All the forms and worksheets in the book are accessible online

KEEP UP TO DATE – When there are important changes to the information in this book, we'll post updates

READ BLOGS – Get the latest info from Nolo authors' blogs

LISTEN TO PODCASTS – Listen to authors discuss timely issues on topics that interest you

WATCH VIDEOS – Get a quick introduction to a legal topic with our short videos

You'll find the link in the appendix.

And that's not all.
Nolo.com contains thousands of articles on everyday legal and business issues, plus a plain-English law dictionary, all written by Nolo experts and available for free. You'll also find more useful **books, software, online services,** and **downloadable forms.**

Get forms and more at
www.nolo.com

DOWNLOAD FORMS
at nolo.com

16th edition

A Legal Guide for

Lesbian and Gay Couples

Attorneys Frederick Hertz

and Emily Doskow

Sixteenth Edition	APRIL 2012
Editor	EMILY DOSKOW
Production & Cover Design	SUSAN PUTNEY
Proofreading	SUSAN CARLSON GREENE
Index	SONGBIRD INDEXING
Printing	BANG PRINTING

Clifford, Denis.
  A legal guide for lesbian and gay couples / Frederick Hertz and Emily Doskow.
— 16th ed.
    p. cm.
  Rev. ed. of: A legal guide for lesbian and gay couples / by Denis Clifford, Frederick
Hertz, and Emily Doskow. 15th ed. 2010.
  Includes index.
  Summary: "Provides legal information to help same-sex couples exercise their rights
and make sound decisions together"—Provided by publisher.
  ISBN 978-1-4133-1681-0 (pbk.) — ISBN 978-1-4133-1694-0 (epub ebook)
  1. Gay couples—Legal status, laws, etc.—United States. 2. Lesbian couples—Legal
status, laws, etc.—United States. 3. Homosexuality—Law and legislation—United States.
I. Hertz, Frederick. II. Doskow, Emily. III. Title.
  KF539.C58 2012
  346.7301'68—dc23

                               2011039667

Please note

We believe accurate, plain-English legal information should help you solve many
of your own legal problems. But this text is not a substitute for personalized
advice from a knowledgeable lawyer. If you want the help of a trained
professional—and we'll always point out situations in which we think that's a
good idea—consult an attorney licensed to practice in your state.

Note From the Publisher

More than thirty years ago, Nolo published the first edition of *A Legal Guide for Lesbian and Gay Couples*. It was the fifteenth title issued by Nolo, which was then a new company breaking ground in the area of legal do-it-yourself publishing. Two years before, we had published *The Living Together Kit*, a legal workbook for heterosexual couples, and had begun to get requests for a book geared to same-sex couples. My first reaction was that since lesbian and gay couples have very few legal rights, it would barely amount to a pamphlet. But Denis Clifford and the late Hayden Curry begged to differ and produced a detailed proposal focusing on couple-related contract issues such as sharing income or co-owning a house and other valuable property. Thanks to their creative energy, Nolo decided to go ahead. Over the years we have redone *A Legal Guide for Lesbian and Gay Couples* many times, with each edition reflecting the (mostly positive) changes in the law affecting LGBT couples. In the process, we have sold over 200,000 copies and educated at least that many couples about their legal rights.

I'm very proud of the *Legal Guide*, but I look forward to the day when in all 50 states same-sex couples enjoy exactly the same legal rights as heterosexual couples, and we can finally begin to shrink this fat book.

Ralph Warner
Nolo Cofounder

Acknowledgments

We thank all those friends, new and old, who worked with us on this book; their assistance has been truly invaluable and working with them was fun. Special thanks to those people who read and critiqued the original manuscript back in 1980: Roberta Achtenberg, Gloria Bosque, Kay Clifford, Jim Duerr, Patrick Ferruccio, Michael Fuchs, Linda Graham, Pamela Gray, Linda Gryczan, Linda Guthrie, Donna J. Hitchens, Floyd S. Irvin, Keith Kelgman, Phyllis Lyon, Terri Lyons, Mary Morgan, Joseph Nieberding, Zona Sage, Sue Saperstein, Kim Storch, and Michael Thistel.

Special thanks to Kate Kendell, Executive Director of the National Center for Lesbian Rights, for insights and assistance regarding the recent developments involving the children of lesbian and gay parents. Much appreciation is due to William Singer of Singer and Fedun, whose contributions to the new information on New Jersey civil unions were significant, and to Deb Kinney, whose review of the estate planning and health care information was invaluable. We would also like to thank Stefen Johnson of Lambda Legal Defense and Education Fund, Los Angeles.

Finally, with this 16th edition, Denis Clifford departs as a named author, for business-related reasons. His contribution to creating this wonderful book will never be forgotten—he was one of two original authors whose vision and dedication made the first-ever book about the law for lesbian and gay couples a reality. Thank you, Denis.

Dedication

To HAYDEN CURRY, 1940–1991

Hayden was one of the original authors of this book, with Denis Clifford. The two met in 1967, later worked together in a legal services office in East Oakland, then became law partners with another poverty law colleague. Their experiences convinced them that the conventional legal system was (at best) generally unsympathetic to the lesbian and gay community. Preventive law—people creating their own legal arrangement and avoiding lawyers and courts—was both practical and long overdue. Thus arose their commitment to *A Legal Guide for Lesbian and Gay Couples,* first published in 1980.

Hayden died of AIDS on September 30, 1991. Until his death, he continued to be an invaluable contributor to this book. Denis wrote the following memorial upon Hayden's death: "Hayden and I were soul mates and shared much. He was a seeker, adventurer, philosopher, lover of the arts and bon vivant extraordinaire. A proud participant in gay life in the Bay Area, he publicly presented himself as gay in the early 1970s. Fully accepting himself, he opened his loving heart and flamboyant spirit to his many, many friends. When Hayden became seriously ill, he bore his afflictions with such grace and courage that he truly transcended his disease, becoming increasingly luminous in spirit until his death."

Nolo misses you, Hayden.

About the Authors

Frederick Hertz

For the tenth edition, attorney Frederick Hertz joined the effort. Frederick Hertz is a practicing attorney and mediator in Oakland, California, and is the author of *Making It Legal: A Guide to Same-Sex Marriage, Domestic Partnerships, and Civil Unions* (Nolo), *Legal Affairs: Essential Advice for Same-Sex Couples* (Owl Books), and coauthor of Nolo's *Living Together* and *A Legal Guide for Lesbian and Gay Couples.* His practice focuses on the formation and dissolution of nonmarital partnerships, both gay and straight, and he also serves as a mediator and arbitrator of nonmarital dissolutions. More information about his work can be found at his website, www.samesexlaw.com. Fred was a friend and colleague of Hayden Curry's, which does much to ensure that Hayden's spirit lives on in this book.

Emily Doskow

Emily Doskow is an author and editor for Nolo and a practicing attorney and mediator who has been working with LGBT families in the Bay Area for more than 20 years. She specializes in family law, including adoption, parentage issues, domestic partnership formation and dissolution, and divorce. She is a graduate of Boalt Hall School of Law at the University of California at Berkeley and currently lives in Oakland.

Table of Contents

Your LGBT Family Companion..1

How We See Our Relationships..3

How This Book Can Help...4

Using the Forms in This Book...6

1 Defining Family: Basics of Marriage, Domestic Partnership, and More..7

Defining Family 9

Domestic Partnership..15

Employee Benefits for Domestic Partners.......................................17

Other Benefits 20

Marriage and Marriage-Like Relationships in the United States:
   An Overview...21

Can You Get Married?...23

Creating Marriage-Like Relationships by Contract.........................27

Ending a Relationship..31

Keeping Up With Legal Changes 32

2 Marriage and Marriage-Equivalent Relationships...............33

Same-Sex Marriage in the Marriage Equality States.......................37

Marriage Equivalent: California's Domestic Partnership Law............41

Other Marriage-Equivalent Laws...48

Pre- and Postpartnership Agreements...52

Marriage Lite: Relationship Recognition in Wisconsin, Colorado,
   and Maine..53

Is Marriage (or Its Equivalent) Right for You?..................................55

3 Money, Insurance, Name Changes, and Immigration Issues 59

Cash and Credit 60

Insurance 70

Name Changes.. 74

Foreign Lovers: Visits and Immigration...................................... 77

4 Renting a Home Together... 85

If a Landlord Discriminates Against You 86

Sharing a Rental 88

Sharing One Partner's Rented Home 92

Renter's Insurance.. 96

Moving On.. 97

Public Benefits and Living Together.. 98

5 I'm Mom, She's Mommy(or I'm Daddy, He's Papa)..............101

Legal Parents and the Second-Parent Trap 102

Having a Child.. 121

Adopting a Child.. 138

Foster Parenting... 149

Becoming a Guardian 153

Agreements With Teenagers 158

6 Medical and Financial Matters: Delegating Authority... 161

Health Care Decisions 164

Physician-Assisted Suicide... 176

Burial and Body Disposition 177

Estate Planning Note.. 180

Durable Power of Attorney for Finances...................................... 181

7 Looking Ahead: Estate Planning...197

Death and Living Together Contracts... 199

Wills... 200

Estate Planning Beyond a Will.. 227

8 Living Together Contracts for Lesbian
and Gay Couples..247

Living Together Contracts Are Legal.. 250

When You Need a Living Together Contract................................. 252

What to Include in a Living Together Contract............................. 253

Sample Living Together Contracts.. 260

Contracts for Jointly Acquired Items.. 265

Modifying Your Agreement.. 285

Beware the Tax Man!... 285

9 Buying a Home Together
(and Other Real Estate Ventures)......................................287

Finding a House 289

How Much House Can You Afford?.. 292

Proceeding With Your Purchase.. 300

Taking Title to Your New Home.. 305

Contracts for Home Purchase and Ownership............................. 309

10 Going Separate Ways:
Issues at the End of a Relationship....................................335

Breaking Up: An Overview.. 336

The Separation Process: What to Do.. 338

Getting to Yes: How to Work Toward Resolution......................... 343

Ideas for Solving Some Common Problems.................................353

Breaking Up When There's No Legal Relationship.......................371

Dissolving a Same-Sex Marriage... 373

Dissolving a Straight Marriage 387

Domestic Violence in Same-Sex Relationships.. 392

11 **Help Beyond the Book**.. 393

Hiring a Lawyer.. 394

Doing Your Own Legal Research 398

Legal Organizations 403

A **Using the Interactive Forms**.. 407

Editing RTFs... 408

List of Forms 409

Index.. 411

Your LGBT Family Companion

How We See Our Relationships 3

How This Book Can Help 4

Using the Forms in This Book 6

This is a book about family values, and about the value of family. It's about the importance—especially to couples and families whose rights aren't necessarily protected by the law—of taking steps to ensure that your family life proceeds according to your wishes. Its purpose is to explain your alternatives when it comes to legal matters such as how to structure your relationship, whether to marry or register as domestic partners or civil union partners, how to deal with joint property ownership, and how to become parents if you want to. It's intended to give you the tools to create a harmonious and productive life together. Discussing and planning the financial, practical, and legal aspects of a relationship can lead to greater understanding and trust—and can help you avoid the surprising and often dire consequences you might suffer if you let your state's laws decide these issues for you.

This is a practical book. We're often asked such questions as, "Is it possible for a court to remove my child from my home because I live with my lover?" "If I die, can my partner inherit my car and my house?" "Can a hospital legally prevent me from visiting my lover in intensive care?" We answer these specific questions. We also supply sample legal documents and forms, such as living together agreements, wills, parenting agreements, and the like, so you can design and prepare your own documents. These are available online on a page dedicated to this book. See the Appendix for the link. You'll find other useful information there, too, including author blogs, podcasts, and videos.

The Legal Guide focuses mainly on the nitty-gritty of daily life, and not on broader political concerns—although the book is inherently political in that it reflects the essential struggle of LGBT people to obtain equal rights and eliminate antigay prejudice from the laws and culture of America.

Each time we update this book, we pause to reflect on the gains, losses, and near misses celebrated and suffered by the lesbian and gay community in the interim.

The past few years have been a period of extraordinary change and legal activity. The LGBT community and the struggle for full equality under the law remain a major part of the social and political landscape, and the closet door has opened in a major way. Sixteen states have now passed laws granting same-sex couples marital rights or family rights equivalent to marriage, while numerous other states have passed laws or constitutional amendments limiting marriage to a legal relationship between one man and one woman. Children and issues of parentage continued to dominate the court proceedings involving same-sex families, with the courts again going every which way in making decisions about the rights of gay and lesbian parents.

A Few Words About Words

It's surprisingly hard to figure out what words to use in a book like this. Words have often helped to perpetuate homophobia and hate—"faggot," for instance, is derived from the French word for the bundles of sticks used at one time to burn homosexuals at the stake. And as Truman Capote said, "A fag is a homosexual gentleman who has left the room."

In the end, we've chosen to keep it simple. "Partner," "lover," "lesbian," and "gay" are the words we use most often, and we will refer throughout the book to "same-sex couples." When full legal marriage is the subject, the word "spouse" may also be appropriate. We also use "LGBT" to refer to the lesbian, gay, bisexual, and transgender community.

How We See Our Relationships

The LGBT community is not a monolith, and there is still some lingering debate over whether marriage rights should be our highest priority. For many, the right to marry is a basic civil right, and as long as society offers benefits based on marital status then lesbian and gay couples want the same rights that others have to participate in that institution. To others— especially those concerned with what is perceived as the "assimilationist" tendencies of our movement—marriage remains a hetero-normative and patriarchal institution, and rather than seeking to enter into it, same-sex couples should create alternative versions of family and community. We don't express any opinion on that debate here, but note it for the record.

With the changing legal landscape for lesbian and gay couples, many of us are finding it necessary to sit back and consider just what we are doing in our relationships. Do we think of ourselves as married, as a family unit? Or do we consider ourselves unmarried and more separate, sharing our emotional lives but remaining legally independent in many ways? Do we think of our fates as entirely intertwined, or do we believe that each of us is autonomous and responsible for our own welfare? When we entered into a relationship, did we intend to become responsible for our partner's debts, or to support our partner after a breakup? What about parenting?

Many couples, especially in states where marriage or marriage-equivalent registration is available, are now considering these questions. All our intentions upon entering into a relationship are called into question by these new legal structures. For some of us, entering into a legal relationship by registering as domestic partners, entering a civil union, or even marrying, may not be the best option from a practical standpoint, or may not reflect how we see our intimate relationships at all.

For many of us, making a legal commitment is the ultimate expression of our emotional commitment. This was demonstrated in 2004 in San Francisco, where thousands of couples lined up for hours (in the rain) to demonstrate their devotion to each other by entering into the state of legal matrimony, and it's been demonstrated thousands of times over by all the couples who have legally married in the last eight years. However, it's important that we understand the consequences of tying the knot. (For a much more in-depth discussion of these subjects, see *Making It Legal: A Guide to Same-Sex Marriage, Domestic Partnerships, and Civil Unions*, by Frederick Hertz with Emily Doskow (Nolo).)

How This Book Can Help

Here at Nolo, we believe that everyone should know their legal rights and be active participants in structuring their legal affairs. This is particularly important for same-sex couples because of the current state of marriage and family laws in this country. Married couples' relationships are closely regulated by each state's family law rules, which give spouses certain rights, determine how property will be divided and custody issues worked out if the couple splits up, and dictate who will be responsible for the couples' debts, among many other things. This isn't so for same-sex couples, however.

As of January 2012, lesbian and gay couples can legally marry in six states and the District of Columbia and can register for marriage-equivalent relationships in nine others—but the implications of same-sex marriage have yet to be fully tested. In most other states, LGBT relationships are governed by the rules of contract law—the same rules that apply when you hire someone to repair your car or paint your home.

Because of the continuing lack of federal recognition, same-sex couples suffer plenty of negative consequences: higher estate tax and property tax bills, higher insurance payments, difficulties in making end-of-life health care decisions for their partners, and significant obstacles in adopting children. But we also have the freedom to create our own legal relationships, without the limitations that state marriage laws impose. And even in the states in which marriage or marriage-like relationships are possible, it may work better for some couples to structure their relationships outside of those legal rules.

That's where this book comes in—it provides all of the information and forms you need to make your own agreements about property, family issues, and more. Making these decisions and using these written agreements will help you think about the responsibilities you want to accept—and the commitments you want to make—toward each other. This book will show you how to create a marriage-like relationship—even in the absence of legal marriage—if that's what you want, and will explain how that will affect your relationship on the most practical level. It will also explain how to tailor your relationship to your specific agreements, whether or not those agreements resemble marriage.

Transgender people often find themselves in particularly complex legal situations. Oftentimes their birth certificates, driver's licenses, and other identification documents create confusion and uncertainty. Their legal rights and duties with respect to their unmarried partners, however, are the same as anyone else's. Special issues involving transgender individuals are discussed throughout the book where the issues are relevant.

Using the Forms in This Book

Throughout this book you will find sample agreements covering topics such as living together, raising children, buying a home together, and splitting up. As you will see, each of these agreements is tailored to the individualized circumstances of the (fictional) partners involved in the example.

You'll find blank copies of these sample agreements on the book's companion page. See the Appendix for the link. You'll find other useful information there, too, including author blogs, podcasts, and videos. We encourage you to use our sample agreements as starting points for your own documents. Use the language and structure as they fit your needs, and delete and add material as you think it is required. If it would make you more comfortable to have a lawyer draft your documents, by all means do so—possibly after looking at some of our agreements and using them as a framework for discussing the issues. As a less expensive alternative, you can have a lawyer review the documents that you write yourselves using the forms provided online. (Chapter 11 discusses finding an attorney who will help you in one of these ways.)

Defining Family: Basics of Marriage, Domestic Partnership, and More

Defining Family...9

    Government Benefits...10

    Court Cases and Legislative Action...12

Domestic Partnership..15

    Who Are Domestic Partners?..15

Employee Benefits for Domestic Partners 17

Other Benefits..20

Marriage and Marriage-Like Relationships in the United States:

    An Overview 21

Can You Get Married?.. 23

    The Fight for Same-Sex Marriage in the United States.................... 23

    Same-Sex Marriage in Canada and Around the World 26

Creating Marriage-Like Relationships by Contract 27

    Special Issues When One Partner Is Transgender........................ 28

    Adopting Your Partner 30

Ending a Relationship 31

Keeping Up With Legal Changes...32

I n February 2004, America turned on its televisions and saw something that had never been seen before in this country: same-sex couples taking marriage vows. Two blushing brides or dashing grooms smiled at the cameras as history was made, complete with flowers, beaming families and friends, and legal marriage licenses. Despite the later invalidation of these same-sex marriages and all of the gyrations by the California voters and Supreme Court, the marriage debate will never be the same.

And not only because of what happened in San Francisco and other cities in early 2004. Even before the San Francisco weddings, same-sex marriages were legal in some provinces in Canada—and were being performed regularly. In May 2004, Massachusetts became the first U.S. state to legalize same-sex marriage, and now five other states and the District of Columbia have followed suit, with Washington state poised to join them in June 2012. Nine other states now have laws creating relationships for same-sex couples that are equivalent to marriage. Colorado, Maine, and Wisconsin have all taken steps in that direction, and other states are beginning to recognize domestic partnerships from elsewhere.

In all, an estimated 40% of same-sex couples now live in states where marriage or its functional equivalent is available. And over 140,000 same-sex couples—approximately 20% of all those in the United States—have finalized their legal relationships under state law.

This chapter gives an overview of all these developments, including:
- the legal definition of "family," and court decisions affecting it
- state benefits (such as unemployment insurance) for partners in same-sex couples
- domestic partnership and similar programs
- same-sex marriage
- how to structure your relationship with a contract
- adult adoptions, and
- how to keep up with fast-moving legal developments.

In Chapter 2, we describe in detail the laws and procedures in each of the states offering marriage or a marriage equivalent.

Thirty Years Later: An Historical Perspective on Family

The first edition of this book (published in 1980) addressed the issue of marriage only by noting that it wasn't available to same-sex couples, and discussing what that meant. The first chapter was about legal and political strategies for fighting discrimination, and about legal rules governing sexual conduct throughout the United States. It was only in the 12th edition, published in 2004, that we deleted the chart listing state laws prohibiting consensual sexual conduct—it took the 2003 United States Supreme Court decision in *Lawrence v. Texas* to make sodomy laws obsolete.

In 1980, there was no such thing as "domestic partnership." No state offered any benefits to nonmarital partners, straight or gay, and the only way for same-sex couples to protect their rights in relationships was to write contracts defining how they wanted to deal with their money and assets. These contracts were the focus of the first edition, and they are still a primary focus 30 years later. While there have been major changes in some states, the need for same-sex couples to take control of their legal relationships has not changed. We still need to educate ourselves, communicate about how we want to structure our relationships, and take the time to put our arrangements in writing.

Defining Family

According to *Webster's New Collegiate Dictionary*, a family is "the basic unit in society having as its nucleus two or more adults living together and cooperating in the care and rearing of their own or adopted children." Despite this inclusive (and sexual-orientation-neutral) definition, a lesbian or gay couple—with or without children—is not the picture that many people see when they think of a family.

As a result, government benefits traditionally awarded to spouses—such as unemployment insurance for spouses who relocate to accommodate their partner's job change, and workers' compensation benefits for spouses of injured workers—have historically been denied to same-sex partners.

And because they are often not considered "immediate family," partners of lesbians and gay men have been denied the right to sue for emotional distress over the death of a partner or to stay in an apartment after their lover dies when their name isn't on the lease. Along the same lines, until recently, same-sex couples have generally not been treated as spouses when their relationships ended, leading to confusion over how to divide assets.

Finally, however, things seem to be changing. Many courts are beginning to treat same-sex partners like spouses, even many same-sex couples who cannot marry or even register as domestic partners. This section gives some examples in which public entities have treated same-sex relationships as families in the eyes of the law. Such cases are not the norm, but they seem to represent the beginning of a trend toward greater flexibility and inclusiveness in official definitions of family. And in those states that recognize legal partnerships, full equality on a local level is now available.

Government Benefits

Most of the examples in this section come from California cases (yes, there are reasons so many gay men and lesbians flock to the Golden State), but other states' agencies are coping with the same issues, and in some instances, making similar decisions.

Unemployment benefits for caretakers. For years, married partners have received unemployment insurance benefits if they quit their jobs to care for terminally ill spouses. Several years ago, a gay man in California who left his job to care for his lover who had AIDS successfully sought unemployment benefits. The Unemployment Appeals Board acknowledged that gay relationships can be as serious, loving, and committed as marriages.

Unemployment benefits for relocation. A woman was awarded unemployment insurance benefits after she quit her job to move with her lover, who was beginning a medical residency in Pennsylvania. The Unemployment Appeals Board judge who decided the case stated that benefits are available when a person leaves a job to move with a spouse to a place from which it is impractical to commute. In this case, the applicant's "spouse was accepted into residency and this certainly provided good cause for the couple to move." The judge knew the couple was lesbian, but chose to refer to them as spouses.

Workers' compensation death benefits. A gay man won benefits when his lover, a county district attorney, committed suicide because of job-related stress. The Workers' Compensation Appeals Board found that the surviving partner had depended on the deceased man for support, and said that the homosexual relationship of the two men shouldn't preclude the survivor's rights to benefits.

Pension benefits. New York State's public employee pension fund will recognize marriages of same-sex couples just as they do marriages of opposite-sex couples for purposes of providing death benefits and cost of living adjustments to surviving spouses.

Partner benefits for diplomats. As of May 2009, partners of American foreign service officers must be treated the same as opposite-sex spouses for purposes of various departmental policies. Although the policy arguably violates the Defense of Marriage Act, Secretary of State Hilary Clinton stated it was necessary for recruitment purposes as well as being "the right thing to do."

Social Security benefits. The United States Justice Department granted Social Security disability benefits to the child of a disabled lesbian, even though the parent-child relationship was based on the nonbiological mom's civil union relationship with the biological mom. The DOJ found that the benefits were payable because they're based on the parent-child relationship, not the relationship between the two parents, and therefore paying benefits doesn't violate the DOMA.

Paid family leave. In California, Washington, and New Jersey, same-sex partners in registered domestic partnerships and civil unions, respectively, are included among employees entitled to paid family leave under state law.

Court Cases and Legislative Action

Courts, legislatures, and public agencies have also begun to grant recognition to same-sex partnerships in some circumstances, sometimes treating partners just as they would spouses even where formal recognition is not yet in place. Here are some examples:

- The federal Office of Personnel Management updated its definition of "family member" and "immediate relative" for leave purposes, to include same-sex domestic partners in the broad category of "individual[s] related by blood or affinity whose close association with the employee is the equivalent of a family relationship."

- In New York City, where affordable and decent housing is very hard to find, a domestic partnership law gives a surviving domestic partner the right to keep an apartment after the death of the leaseholder even if the couple is unmarried. Before this law was enacted, a surviving partner risked sudden homelessness when the leaseholding partner died and the survivor's name was not on the lease.

- Also in New York, a state court ruled that New York City must actively enforce its Equal Benefits Law, which requires city contractors to provide domestic partners the same employment benefits they provide to spouses. The Pennsylvania Supreme Court upheld a similar ordinance in Philadelphia. (San Francisco and Los Angeles have similar laws.)

- In Denver, a city worker who took three days off to care for her seriously injured lover was granted sick leave by a hearing officer who declared that the policy allowing workers to take sick leave to care for family members was applicable to all city employees regardless of sexual orientation.

- In Washington, DC, a woman was allowed to file a claim under the district's Wrongful Death Act after her lover died, because a court found that the surviving partner qualified as her deceased lover's "next of kin." (This was before the District of Columbia got marriage in 2011.)

- A New Mexico court ruled that an unmarried cohabitant can make a claim for "loss of consortium"—usually defined as the loss of the companionship of a spouse as a result of injury. The court ruled that factors to be considered in determining whether an unmarried partner's claim should be granted include the length of the relationship and the degree to which the partners' lives are intertwined. (*Lozoya v. Sanchez*, 133 N.M. 579, 66 P.3d 948 (2003).) On the other hand, the Massachusetts Supreme Court ruled in 2008 that an unmarried same-sex partner could not state a loss of consortium claim even though marriage wasn't available to the couple at the time of the accident and the couple was clearly committed, and a loss of consortium claim was also denied in New Jersey, for the same reasons.

- In a Pennsylvania case, two men who had lived together for 18 years were both convicted of possession and sale of methamphetamine. Both had the same probation officer after being released from prison; the officer refused to grant permission for the two to associate with each other because of the standard prohibition on parolees associating with felons. The federal court ruled that the two had a constitutionally protected right to continue their intimate relationship.

- In California, a surviving unmarried partner of a man who died from AIDS was awarded $175,000 by a court for emotional distress experienced after a funeral company mishandled the deceased man's ashes. Previously, such recoveries were limited to spouses.

- A New York trial court ruled a few years ago that a property settlement entered into by a gay couple married in Massachusetts would be enforced in New York even though at the same time, the state wouldn't recognize the marriage.

- Again in New York, the New York City Department of Homeless Services changed its policies and agreed to recognize domestic partners for purposes of providing shelter to homeless families.

- Even before the state began offering civil union registration, the Rhode Island attorney general issued an opinion stating that Rhode Island would recognize marriages performed in any other state, including same-sex marriages in Massachusetts, and that such recognition was not against Rhode Island public policy.

- The Virginia Supreme Court ruled that the Department of Vital Records must issue new birth certificates listing both same-sex parents following the adoption of children born in Virginia.
- The Alaska Supreme Court held that public employers in that state could not deny same-sex domestic partners the benefits that were provided to spouses of married employees.
- In June 2004, two lesbians reached a settlement with a Presbyterian retirement community that had denied them admission based on a policy against accepting any unmarried, nonrelated couples. The settlement allowed the women to join the retirement community, and the facility changed its policy to allow equal access to all qualified applicants.
- In a mixed result, the California Supreme Court held that a country club discriminated under state and local laws by denying a lesbian member's partner the right to spousal privileges at the club, based on its policy that only legally married spouses could enjoy these privileges. (*Koebke v. Bernardo Heights Country Club*, 36 Cal.4th 824.) But in Minnesota, an appeals court supported an athletic club that refused a family membership to a lesbian couple and their child, on the basis that family memberships required marriage, which is not available to same-sex couples there.

And in a high-level legal shift that was a preview of more changes on the way, in 2002 the American Law Institute, a prestigious organization made up of judges, lawyers, and legal scholars, issued a report recommending sweeping changes in domestic relations law. The report recommended that all unmarried partnerships be subject to the same rights and responsibilities upon breakup as spouses in a marriage.

To be sure, not all cases have resolved in favor of same-sex partners:

- In Florida, a state pension board denied a petition filed by the surviving partner of a Tampa police officer killed in the line of duty who sought pension rights that would automatically have gone to her if she and her partner had been able to marry. The circuit court upheld the pension board's decision, and the case is now pending in the state Court of Appeals.

- An appeals court in Michigan ruled that because the state constitution was amended to refuse to recognize nonmarital unions, public employers may not offer domestic partner benefits to same-sex partners of employees.

- A Florida appeals court ruled that a Tampa hospital did not discriminate when it refused a lesbian access to her dying partner in the hospital's emergency room and intensive care unit and wouldn't update her on her partner's condition, even after the woman presented the hospital with a power of attorney granting her access to medical information and the right to make medical decisions for her partner.

Domestic Partnership

Because lesbian and gay couples historically have not been allowed to marry, the idea of domestic partnership developed as an alternative that would be less threatening to the established social system while still providing same-sex couples some societal—and later, legal—recognition.

But the term "domestic partnership" doesn't always mean the same thing. This section discusses the varying meanings of domestic partnership and explains some of the benefits and consequences of domestic partnership relationships.

Who Are Domestic Partners?

The concept of domestic partnership has undergone an evolution, and the term now can have various levels of legal significance depending on its context.

Informal arrangements. Many couples call themselves "domestic partners" because they live together in a committed relationship. There are no legal consequences to simply referring to yourselves this way, but if you live in a state where legal domestic partnership is available, just considering yourself domestic partners and referring to yourselves that way isn't enough—you must register formally with the state in order to be eligible for any benefits your state offers. If you don't, you're technically not domestic partners—"cohabitants" would be a more accurate term.

Domestic Partnership Milestones
1982: *The Village Voice* newspaper in New York is the first private company to offer its employees domestic partnership benefits.
1984: Berkeley, California, is the first city to do so.
1995: Vermont becomes the first state to extend domestic partnership benefits to its public employees.
1997: Hawaii is the first state to extend domestic partnership benefits to all registered same-sex couples throughout the state.
2003: New Jersey enacts domestic partner legislation.
2004: Maine enacts domestic partner legislation.
2005: California registered domestic partners become subject to almost all state marital laws.
2006: The District of Columbia enacts domestic partner legislation.
2008: Maine and Oregon enact domestic partnership legislation.
2009: Washington State enacts domestic partnership legislation.
2011: Delaware, Hawaii, Illinois, and Rhode Island all enact civil union registration.

Partnerships recognized by employers. Many employers—government and private—now treat cohabiting partners of employees the same way they treat employees' spouses. For example, domestic partners may be eligible for coverage on the employee's health insurance policy. It's up to the employer to determine who qualifies as a domestic partner and what proof it requires. Not all employers require formal registration documents to confer benefits, but in states where marriage or official registration is available, employers are more likely to require partners to take that step in order to receive employer-provided benefits.

In most of the marriage-equivalent states, employers are required to treat registered domestic partners or partners in a civil union exactly the same as they treat heterosexual married couples.

Local registration. Some cities and counties allow residents to register locally as domestic partners, but these registrations do not impose marital rights or duties. Often, a county transfer tax exemption for property transfers between partners—saving anywhere from a few hundred to a few thousand dollars in taxes when a house is transferred or sold—is the most meaningful benefit offered by local entities.

State registration. In California, Washington State, the District of Columbia, Oregon, and Nevada, the term has a very specific legal meaning: Only couples who have registered with the state are legally domestic partners, and as a result they have a slew of rights and responsibilities that are almost identical to those that come with marriage. So are similar programs that go by the name civil unions in New Jersey, Delaware, Illinois, Hawaii, and Rhode Island. Chapter 2 has details about all of these relationship options.

Employee Benefits for Domestic Partners

For many in the LGBT community, domestic partnership seems like "half a loaf" of bread, while married folks get the entire package. Although the whole loaf of bread remains unavailable to most same-sex couples, hundreds of government entities and private businesses offer valuable benefits to the domestic partners of their employees.

Who Provides Benefits

Hundreds of employers, including more than a dozen states and many Fortune 500 companies, now provide domestic partner benefits to their employees. In fact, in 2006, the number of Fortune 500 companies offering domestic partner benefits passed the halfway point. This means that the employer treats the employee's registered domestic partner the same as it treats the spouse of a married employee—sometimes for all purposes, sometimes for only some. Some companies offer benefits to both straight and gay couples, while others offer them only to same-sex partners because heterosexual couples have the option of marrying legally.

States That Offer Domestic Partner Benefits to State Employees		
California	Iowa	New York
Connecticut	Maine	Oregon
Delaware	Montana	Rhode Island
District of Columbia	New Hampshire	Vermont
Hawaii	New Jersey	Washington
Illinois	New Mexico	Wisconsin

In addition to these states, hundreds of municipalities and counties all over the country offer domestic partnership benefits to employees, along with 60% of the top colleges and universities.

Finding companies that provide benefits. For useful links and information on domestic partnership benefits, including a list of major companies that provide domestic partnership benefits and a guide to getting your employer to offer domestic partner benefits, check out the Alternatives to Marriage project website at www.unmarried.org.

Working for domestic partner benefits. If you are interested in working with your employer to establish domestic partnership benefits, get a copy of *The Domestic Partnership Organizing Manual for Employee Benefits*, published by the Policy Institute of the National Gay and Lesbian Task Force. You can download it from the NGLTF website at www.thetaskforce.org/reports_and_research/dp_manual.

Finding public employers that provide benefits. For a list of states, municipalities, and other entities offering domestic partnership benefits, as well as updates on related litigation, go to the domestic partnership section of the Lambda Legal Defense and Education Fund's website at www.lambdalegal.org. At the Human Rights Campaign's website at www.hrc.org, you can check out the Corporate Equality Index to see how well private employers are doing in providing benefits.

Kinds of Benefits

Different employers offer very different benefits. Some offer only sick or bereavement leave when a domestic partner becomes ill or dies. Others provide benefits that are extensive—and expensive. They may include:
- health, dental, and vision insurance
- accident and life insurance, and
- parental leave (for a child you coparent).

There is no legal right to domestic partner benefits, even if the employer provides benefits for spouses, unless you live in a state with marriage or a marriage equivalent or in a city that requires employers doing business there to treat spouses and domestic partners equally, and you are married or registered. Otherwise, it is up to the employer to decide what benefits it offers, and at what cost. In some instances, domestic partnership benefits are being phased out if full legal marriage is available.

Even if an employer treats domestic partners just like spouses, the benefit may be less valuable to domestic partners because of the way tax laws are currently written. If the employer foots the bill for the partner's health benefits, for example, the employee must pay federal taxes on the value of the benefit—while an employee whose spouse received these benefits would not be taxed. This is because the IRS considers benefits awarded to an unmarried partner as part of the employee's taxable compensation (in contrast to benefits for spouses). An employer can compensate for this inequality by boosting the gross pay of workers who have to pay taxes on their domestic partners' benefits, in order to make their net pay equal to that of their married counterparts.

Qualifying for Benefits

To qualify for domestic partner benefits, you must put your domestic partnership on record with the employer. Commonly, the employer provides a simple form (usually a sworn statement) for the employee and partner to sign. Usually, partners must state that they live together in an exclusive relationship and share the basic necessities of life, and that neither is married to or in a domestic partnership with someone else.

If your relationship ends, you will need to file whatever documents are required to notify your employer that the domestic partnership no longer exists.

Employer forms aren't binding contracts. Employer-provided domestic partnership forms often require that you and your partner state your intention to provide mutual support. But even if you sign an employer-provided application that says you promise to support each other, it's generally not considered a legally binding commitment. In other words, your partner can't sue you for failing to provide support as promised.

No COBRA Coverage for Domestic Partners

If you work for a company with more than 20 employees and you leave your job, you are entitled to continue your health benefits, at your own expense, under the federal law called COBRA. If the company has fewer than 20 employees, you may still be entitled to continuation coverage under similar state laws. Under COBRA, employers are required to offer continuation coverage to spouses of employees who have health coverage, so if a married person leaves a job, the employee's spouse is entitled to buy COBRA coverage. However, because the federal government still does not recognize same-sex relationships, a same-sex spouse or domestic partner is not entitled to federal COBRA continuation coverage even if covered under the employer-provided policy. The only exception is in states with marriage-equivalent registration, where state-registered domestic partners can qualify for state COBRA coverage.

If your state law requires employers to treat registered same-sex partners the same as spouses, or if your city has a domestic partner ordinance, you could try to challenge your employer and the insurer under that law, but you may not get far. Until the federal government changes its approach to same-sex unions, discrimination under federal law will continue to be perfectly legal.

Other Benefits

Even if your employer doesn't have domestic partner benefits, other organizations with which you do business might. For example, airlines that used to let frequent flyers share accumulated miles only with their spouses now usually let you bring your domestic partner. Some airlines also will give discount bereavement fares to domestic partners. Many auto insurance companies offer discounted rates to cohabitants, especially if you share ownership of your automobiles.

Several kinds of institutions that used to offer membership discounts only to married couples, such as museums, health clubs, and public television stations, now offer them to any household, regardless of marital status or the gender of the partners.

Hundreds of colleges and universities now offer some type of domestic partnership benefits to students, staff, or both. For example, domestic partners may get the same housing rights and tuition reduction as do married students or employees.

Marriage and Marriage-Like Relationships in the United States: An Overview

There are now 19 states in which same-sex couples can enter into committed legal relationships through state-recognized procedures. The range of rights provided is broad, from full legal marriage in six states and the District of Columbia to a relationship called "designated beneficiaries," providing little in the way of benefits to registrants, in Colorado. But whatever the specifics may be, each of these states now provides for some solemnization of same-sex relationships and offers some level of rights and responsibilities along with the legal status.

These states are:
- California (domestic partnership)
- Colorado (designated beneficiaries)
- Connecticut (marriage)
- Delaware (civil union)
- District of Columbia (domestic partnership and marriage)
- Hawaii (civil union)
- Illinois (civil union)
- Iowa (marriage)

- Massachusetts (marriage)
- Maine (domestic partnership)
- Nevada (domestic partnership)
- New Hampshire (marriage)
- New Jersey (civil union)
- New York (marriage)
- Oregon (domestic partnership)
- Rhode Island (civil union)
- Vermont (marriage)
- Washington (domestic partnership/marriage–see below)
- Wisconsin (domestic partnership).

As this book goes to press, Washington State is in an uncertain status. The legislature passed a marriage equality law, which the governor signed on February 14, 2012. In the absence of any intervening events, the act would become law on June 7, 2012. However, opponents of the law have until June 6 to gather more than 120,000 signatures in favor of putting the issue on the November ballot for a vote. If they succeed, the law will be on hold until the results of the election are certified in December 2012. Most observers consider it likely that the opponents will gather the necessary signatures, so Washington State's marriage equality law will likely remain in limbo until the end of 2012. In the meantime, same-sex couples can still register as domestic partners.

In all six states that allow marriage, domestic partnership and civil unions are no longer available, but the District of Columbia offers both options. Nine other states confer on couples the same rights and responsibilities that come with marriage in those states. The federal government does not recognize these relationships for the purpose of any federal law, a conflict that gives rise to a number of complex issues that will be discussed in more detail in Chapter 2.

The rest of this chapter deals with the history of same-sex marriage in the United States and abroad and with general marriage-related matters. For detailed information about each of the states that offer marriage and marriage-like relationships, and a discussion of whether marriage or a marriage-equivalent relationship is right for you, turn to Chapter 2.

Can You Get Married?

The United States Supreme Court has declared marriage to be "of fundamental importance to all individuals," "one of the 'basic civil rights,'" and "the most important relation in life." The court also noted that "the right to marry is part of the fundamental 'right to privacy'" contained in the U.S. Constitution. (*Zablocki v. Redhail*, 434 U.S. 374, 98 S.Ct. 673 (1978).) All of this elegant language notwithstanding, the fundamental right described by our nation's highest court is still denied to same-sex couples in the great majority of the 50 United States.

The Fight for Same-Sex Marriage in the United States

If you just want to know the details about same-sex marriage currently, turn to Chapter 2. If you want the historical details, read on.

In 1971, two Minnesota men sued, claiming that they were entitled to marry under the state's marriage statute. That case was unsuccessful, but in the last 14 years several other important cases, especially in Hawaii, Vermont, and Massachusetts, have changed the legal landscape for same-sex couples that want to marry.

In *Baehr v. Miike*, 80 Hawai'i 341, 910 P.2d 112 (1996), three same-sex couples sued the state of Hawaii, arguing that its failure to issue them marriage licenses violated the Equal Rights Amendment to the state constitution. A trial judge ruled that the state's same-sex marriage ban was invalid, but while an appeal was pending, Hawaii voters passed a constitutional amendment banning same-sex marriage. The legislature, however, to avoid granting full marriage rights, provided for a new class of partners called "reciprocal beneficiaries," which is discussed in Chapter 2. This new law effectively ended the case.

Although not quite the victory that the same-sex marriage movement had hoped for, it was still groundbreaking at the time because it was the first statewide domestic partnership law passed in the United States. Worried legislatures in other states passed laws banning same-sex marriage, called "defense of marriage acts," or "DOMAs". The federal government joined the fight against same-sex marriage, passing a federal

Same-Sex Marriage (and Legal Partnership) Around the Globe

Americans aren't the only ones wrestling with the issue of legal rights for same-sex couples. In addition to Canada, same-sex couples can marry in Argentina, Belgium, Iceland, Mexico City, the Netherlands, Norway, Portugal, Spain, Sweden, and South Africa. There are strict residency requirements, however, so American travelers cannot marry in those countries while on vacation. Many other countries around the world are also moving to recognize same-sex relationships:

Andorra. Same-sex couples can enter into registered partnerships that carry a few of the rights of marriage. No adoption or other parenting rights are granted.

Australia. As of 2008, Australia offers same-sex couples the same rights as unmarried heterosexual couples who can prove they are in a de facto relationship; these couples have most of the rights of married couples.

Austria. Same-sex couples can enter into registered partnerships that carry a few of the rights of marriage. No adoption or other parenting rights are granted.

Colombia. Registered same-sex couples have the same pension, social security and property rights as registered heterosexual couples.

Croatia: Same-sex couples can enter into registered partnerships that carry a few of the rights of marriage. No adoption or other parenting rights are granted.

Czech Republic. Same-sex partners can enter into civil partnerships that carry many of the rights of marriage.

Denmark. Denmark was the first country, in 1989, to allow same-sex couples to form "registered partnerships," giving them a status and benefits similar to marriage. The Danish law extends to Greenland, which is a territory of Denmark.

Ecuador. Same-sex civil union partners have most of the same rights as heterosexual married couples and opposite-sex civil union partners, with the exception of adoption rights.

Finland. In 2001, Finland passed a same-sex partnership law similar to Denmark's; same-sex partners cannot adopt children, however.

Same-Sex Marriage (and Legal Partnership) Around the Globe (cont'd)

France. Registered partnerships (called Civil Solidarity Pacts or PACs) are available and include tax benefits, public insurance and pension benefits, inheritance and lease protections, and even the right to demand employers offer them concurrent vacation schedules.

Germany. Gay and lesbian couples may register same-sex partnerships. Registered partners have the same inheritance rights as married couples, and may adopt the same last name, but they do not have the same tax advantages and rights to adopt that married couples have.

Hungary. Same-sex couples finally won the right to register as partners in 2009, giving them most marital rights.

Ireland. Same-sex civil partnerships are legal in Northern Ireland only.

Italy. Pisa and Florence allow same-sex couples to register as domestic partners, but there is no countrywide recognition of domestic partnerships.

Luxembourg. Same-sex partners may register for some of the rights of marriage.

Mexico. Beginning in 2007, residents in two of Mexico's districts are able to enter into same-sex civil unions.

New Zealand. Registered partners are recognized nationwide.

Norway. Registered partnerships similar to those in Denmark are available to same-sex couples.

Slovenia. Provides cohabiting same-sex couples the right of inheritance and some other rights.

Spain. The Spanish Parliament voted to legalize same-sex marriage in 2005.

Sweden. As of 2009, registered same-sex partners have the same rights as married couples.

Switzerland. Registered partnership for same-sex couples grants limited rights.

United Kingdom. Couples in the UK can register as civil partners and be subject to just about all the rights and duties of marriage.

Uruguay. A 2008 law provides certain rights to partners of any sex who cohabit for longer than five years; if the partners register, they can establish community property.

DOMA in 1996. The federal law prohibits the federal government from recognizing same-sex marriages and denies federal benefits (such as joint income tax filing, immigration, and Social Security) to spouses in same-sex marriages (should any exist).

Furthermore, in anticipation of a time when some forward-thinking state might allow full legal marriage for a same-sex couple, the federal DOMA permits states to ignore a same-sex marriage entered into in another state. This provision has become much more relevant now that a number of states allow same-sex marriage.

Soon after the *Baehr* decision in Hawaii, across the country, the Vermont Supreme Court ruled that prohibiting same-sex marriage violated the provision of the Vermont constitution guaranteeing equal rights to all citizens, because it denied same-sex couples the rights to which straight couples were entitled. (*Baker v. State*, 170 Vt. 194, 744 A.2d 864 (1999).) But instead of ordering the government to issue marriage licenses to gay and lesbian couples, the court left it up to the state legislature to remedy the situation. In response, the legislature passed a law creating the civil union registration system. Under this system, until 2009, same-sex couples could only enter into a civil union ceremony and were then subject to all state laws applying to married couples.

Then in 2003, the Massachusetts Supreme Court ruled that the state's DOMA law violated the Massachusetts constitution. (*Goodrige v. Dept. of Public Health*, 440 Mass. 309, 798 N.E.2d 941 (2003).) In *Goodridge*, again the plaintiffs were same-sex couples who had been denied marriage licenses. Since then, courts and legislatures in five other states and the District of Columbia have opened the marriage doors to same-sex couples. However, DOMA continues to keep the federal doors closed. There's more about that in later chapters.

Same-Sex Marriage in Canada and Around the World

Same-sex couples can legally marry throughout Canada. There are no residency requirements, so American citizens can also travel to Canada to get married. There are no medical tests, either—you need only get a marriage license, find an authorized person to perform the ceremony, and bring two witnesses.

Some American governmental entities will recognize the marriage, and some will not. Watch for this issue to reach the courts soon, along with the issue of recognizing marriages (as well as domestic partnerships and civil unions) from other states.

If you are married in Canada and you live in a U.S. state that recognizes your marriage, you should also be able to get divorced in that state using the same court procedures that opposite-sex spouses use. However, if you live in a state that does not recognize your marriage, you probably won't be able to divorce there either. To get a divorce in Canada, at least one partner has to live there for a year before filing a divorce request.

Creating Marriage-Like Relationships by Contract

Even if you live in one of the many states where you cannot get married, register as domestic partners, or enter into a civil union—or if you live in one of those states and choose not to do any of those things— there are ways that you can protect and affirm your relationship. By creating an agreement tailored to your wishes, you can create a relationship with many of the same rights and obligations that married couples have toward each other, if that's what you want. You can pick and choose which benefits and obligations you want to take on, rather than being forced to accept the whole package as you would be if you entered into one of the available legal relationships.

For example, if you want to follow marriage rules when it comes to managing your assets and property, you can prepare a written contract stating that you agree to be bound by the laws of your state that govern legal marriages, and share your income and property just as married couples do. You can agree to provide for postseparation support by contract, or provide for an equal division of property. It's up to you. Properly drafted and signed, these agreements are enforceable in court.

SEE AN EXPERT

Consult an attorney about which legal documents you need.
Depending on your financial situation and where you live, there may be some
documents you can prepare yourself, but you should get a lawyer's advice in any
event. Some lawyers will prefer to spell out all the provisions in a comprehensive
contract, and other lawyers may choose to put your agreement in general
terms and then refer to your state's marital law rules to cover any unforeseen
circumstances. Because the federal tax rules for married couples won't apply to
your relationship, customized provisions on that subject will need to be included.

RESOURCE

You can learn more about prenuptial agreements in *Prenuptial
Agreements: How to Write a Fair & Lasting Contract*, by Katherine E. Stoner and
Shae Irving (Nolo).

Some of the agreements you might choose are included in Chapters 7
and 8. Others are beyond the scope of this book, including complex wills
and trusts.

Special Issues When One Partner Is Transgender

For transgender folks, legal recognition of relationships can be a thorny
issue. For example, if an opposite-sex couple marries, and one partner
later transitions to the other sex, the partners are now of the same sex. Is
their marriage still valid? Or, if a same-sex couple registers as domestic
partners in California, where opposite-sex couples cannot register
(unless one partner is 62 or older), and then one partner later transitions
to the other sex, the partners are now an opposite-sex couple. Is their
registration still valid? Can they legally marry, and if so, must they end
their domestic partnership first?

The issues are complicated by the very nature of transitioning from one
gender to another—at what point in the transition does a person become
legally the other gender? Is it necessary to have sex reassignment surgery
to legally change gender? What identity documents are necessary to
confirm the gender change? How does the stage of the person's transition

affect the issue of relationship recognition? Legal rules about these questions differ from state to state.

Many married couples in which one partner is transgender live quietly without any outside interference in their relationships. Legal problems tend to arise when an employer challenges the marriage in order to exclude one partner from a health insurance plan, or when one partner dies and the other tries to collect survivor benefits or claim inheritance rights.

As far as we know, there are no court cases deciding whether a marriage is valid after one person transitions to the other sex during the marriage. But in many states, the validity of a marriage is determined at the time the marriage is created—so if the spouses were different genders when they married, their marriage should still be legal even if one party transitions.

The Transgender Law Center recommends that couples in which a partner is transgender take a few additional steps beyond getting a marriage license. These include writing up and signing a Memorandum of Understanding before the marriage—stating clearly that the partners are aware of each other's gender history and identity, and intend to be bound by all marriage rules and laws, including those relating to parenting—and prior to the birth of any children, creating a will or trust in favor of the partner, and preparing reciprocal powers of attorney for health care.

A few courts have addressed the question of whether a marriage is valid when one of the spouses has had a sex change before the marriage. The results have been mixed: In California, New Jersey, and Louisiana, courts have ruled that marriages where one party is transgender are valid. (*M.T. v. J.T.*, 355 A.2d 204 (1976)) (citations for the California and Louisiana cases are not available).) At least one court in Australia has reached the same decision. But in Florida, Illinois, Kansas, Ohio, and Texas, courts have ruled the other way, finding that a person's sex is determined at birth, and the marriages were void because the partners were actually of the same sex. (*Kantaras v. Kantaras*, (Fla. Dist. Ct. App., No. 2D03-1377, 7/23/04, reversing 2003 decision to the contrary); *In re the Marriage of Sterling Simmons*, No. 98 D 13738 (Cir. Ct., Cook County, 2003); *In re Estate of Gardiner*, 42 P.3d 120 (Kansas 2002); *Littleton v. Prange*, 9 S.W.3d 223 (Texas 1999).)

The case of *Littlejohn*, however, was called into question by a recent trial court case in Texas. In a divorce between a woman and a transgender man, the wife tried to deprive the husband of his share of marital property on the basis that their marriage was void. The judge dismissed this claim, because the wife was aware of the husband's transgender status, and because he had completed his gender reassignment and had a birth certificate and passport stating his male gender, both in place at the time of the marriage.

In an Ohio case, a Court of Appeals upheld the state's denial of a marriage license to a couple because one partner was a female-to-male transsexual. The court refused to honor the would-be husband's amended Massachusetts birth certificate showing his sex as male. (*In re Application of Nash and Barr,* Ohio Ct. App., No. 2002-T-1049, 12/13/03.) And the U.S. Citizenship and Immigration Services has denied legal residency to a Filipino man who married a legal U.S. resident, because the wife is transsexual—despite the fact that her citizenship documents list her sex as female.

RESOURCE

If you are a transgender person with a relationship recognition problem, you will need further information and assistance. The Transgender Law Center (www.transgenderlawcenter.org) can provide information and referrals to knowledgeable attorneys.

Adopting Your Partner

A handful of couples, unable to marry, have used adoption to create a legally recognized relationship for themselves. The primary purpose for doing this is to guarantee inheritance rights between the parties.

Courts have allowed some adult adoptions between same-sex partners. For example, courts in New York, California, and Delaware have allowed same-sex adult adoptions in a few instances. A New York court, however, has also denied a same-sex adult adoption application, holding that "the evasion of existing inheritance laws" was a main purpose of the adoption. (*In re Adoption of Robert Paul P.,* 63 N.Y.2d 233, 471 N.E.2d 424 (1984).)

And in Maine, a lesbian was unsuccessful in her attempt to void her 1991 adoption of her ex-partner. With the adoption intact, the partner can inherit through a family trust.

As domestic partnership registration and even marriage become more widely available, adoption—never a particularly desirable option—becomes even less attractive. You will likely face many barriers if you try to adopt your lover, including:

- state laws barring adult adoptions—Alabama, Michigan, Nebraska, and Ohio all have such laws
- state laws barring gays and lesbians from adopting at all—currently, Colorado, Florida, Mississippi, and Utah have such laws
- incest statutes that prohibit sexual relations between an adoptive parent and child, and
- laws specifying a minimum age difference between the adoptive parent and child.

In addition, many other factors should give you pause. As lesbians and gay men seek the right to raise children, adopting a lover may seem inappropriate—adoption connotes parent and child; to allow lovers to use it to confer legal status upon themselves is repugnant to some people. Also, adoption is permanent in most instances, removing the option of ending the relationship. (In rare instances, there may be grounds for rescinding an adoption decree.) Finally, adoption means that the court must terminate the parent-child relationship between the person to be adopted and his or her legal parents. For a lesbian or gay man with a positive relationship with parents, this could be destructive and insulting.

Ending a Relationship

Ending a relationship can often be harder than starting one. If you have kids, we suggest you read Chapter 5 and the pertinent parts of Chapter 10. For help dividing your property, take a close look at Chapters 8, 9, and 10. This section discusses only how to end your "family" status.

If you went through some kind of union, commitment, or marriage ceremony that was not legally sanctioned by the state, you are not required to take any legal steps to end the relationship—remember, you are not legally married. Some people go back to whomever officiated at their ceremony and seek help in splitting up.

If you registered as domestic partners through a municipality, an employer, a school, or another entity, be sure to terminate the partnership formally, by submitting a written document to the entity. Some have forms of their own; if they don't, prepare a letter signed by both partners, have it notarized, and submit it.

If you were legally married in the United States or overseas, or registered in a domestic partnership or civil union in a marriage-equivalent state, see Chapter 2, where we discuss how to terminate those relationships.

Keeping Up With Legal Changes

If the last few years are any indication, legal issues for same-sex couples will continue to make news, and more change is inevitable. The new laws nationwide are causing backlash.

At the same time, we seem to be closer than ever to the repeal of DOMA and other discriminatory laws and regulations. Here are some ways you can stay on top of current developments:

- Check the Nolo website at www.nolo.com for updates to this book, and also check FAQs and articles on LGBT issues.
- For general information on issues affecting LGBT families, check these websites:
  - The National Center for Lesbian Rights at www.nclrights.org
  - Lambda Legal Defense and Education fund at www.lambdalegal. org, and
  - The Human Rights Campaign at www.hrc.org.
- For information on same-sex marriage, check the website for Marriage Equality USA at www.marriageequality.org.

Marriage and Marriage-Equivalent Relationships

Same-Sex Marriage in the Marriage Equality States..37

    Requirements for a Marriage License...37

    Rights and Responsibilities..38

    Ending a Legal Marriage 39

Marriage Equivalent: California's Domestic Partnership Law 41

    Requirements for Registration...41

    Rights and Responsibilities of California Registered Domestic Partners.......44

    Ending a California Domestic Partnership 45

Other Marriage Equivalent Laws...48

    Requirements for a Civil Union or Domestic Partnership 49

    Rights and Responsibilities of a Civil Union or Domestic Partnership.......49

    Ending a Domestic Partnership or Civil Union 50

    The Status of "Outdated" Civil Unions..52

Pre- and Postpartnership Agreements 52

**Marriage Lite: Relationship Recognition in Wisconsin,
    Colorado, and Maine**..53

    Colorado's Reciprocal Beneficiaries Law..54

    Wisconsin's Domestic Partnership Law 54

    Domestic Partnership in Maine 55

Is Marriage (or Its Equivalent) Right for You?...55

E very year for centuries, heterosexual couples have married without giving a second thought to the legal ramifications of their decision. Most likely they assumed they would share finances, and often one partner supported the other financially. They often owned property together, and often one partner owned property before the marriage and added the new spouse to the title after they married. They gave each other gifts, sometimes very expensive ones. Most typically, they had children and no one questioned either spouse's legal relationship with those children. If they divorced, they assumed the court system would accommodate their legal needs, and they transferred property between themselves to settle the divorce without any concern about tax consequences.

As of 2012, when this edition of this book is being published, same-sex couples in more than 15 states can sign up for marriage or its equivalent, two more states have marriage equality laws pending, and an estimated 80,000 couples now come under the umbrella of state marital rules. But unlike their straight friends and relatives, these couples cannot afford to enter into legal relationships without considering the financial and legal consequences.

While your state's law may give you the same rights and responsibilities enjoyed by heterosexual married couples, the lack of recognition across state lines—and most crucially, the discriminatory nonrecognition by the federal government—is a distinction that makes all the difference. For example, let's say that you and your partner live in Connecticut. You now have the right to legally marry, but it's not clear what that really means. If you do it, will you be responsible for each other's debts? Will you have to share your income? Will you file joint tax returns? If you have children, will you both be legal parents? If you break up, who gets what, and who decides? Your partner is gung-ho about becoming legal partners, believing that it would demonstrate your commitment to each other, make a political statement about same-sex relationships, and make your lives better. You're completely committed to the relationship, but you wonder about the details of making it legal—and you're not sure it's the best option for the two of you.

What should you do? First, review the material below to learn the basics about how your state law treats same-sex couples who enter into legal relationships, whether full marriage or a marriage equivalent. Next, if you're not prepared to sign up for the complete package of marital rules, talk to a lawyer about how the rules would apply to your particular circumstances. Find out whether a written agreement signed before your marriage or legal partnership would allow you to opt out of the elements that you don't want, while allowing you the benefits that would work for your relationship. Talk with your partner about what you learn, and make an informed decision about what you want to do.

This chapter discusses the states with marriage or marriage-equivalent relationships, beginning with the ones that allow same-sex couples to marry. The chapter also covers marriage-like relationships in nine other states, and briefly summarizes where things stand in some of the "in-between" and "marriage-lite" states.

There are some basic principles you should keep in mind no matter where you live:

Having the same rights as married couples in your state does not translate over to federal rights. The federal government does not recognize same-sex marriage, domestic partner registration, or civil union. This means that none of the 1,000-plus federal rights that go along with marriage apply to same-sex couples, regardless of the status of the relationship under state law. For example, same-sex couples cannot take advantage of Social Security benefits, immigration privileges, or exemptions from gift tax and federal estate tax.

RESOURCE

For more about why federal marriage rights matter, see www. freedomtomarry.org or www.marriageequality.org.

If you want to marry or register but don't want all of your state's marriage rules to apply to you, you may be able to enter into a prenuptial or pre-partnership agreement—and you'll need a lawyer's help. Every state that recognizes same-sex relationships also permits prenuptial or preregistration agreements. You can use a preregistration agreement to define your financial relationship by stating what property is separate and what is shared and providing for a customized division of property and payment of support should you separate. Each state has its own rules about preregistration agreements, and it's crucial that you see a lawyer before preparing an agreement—otherwise the agreement may not be enforceable.

RESOURCE

If you want to learn more about preregistration agreements, see *Prenuptial Agreements: How to Write a Fair & Lasting Contract,* by Katherine E. Stoner and Shae Irving (Nolo).

Military service members still face challenges. In 2011, the discriminatory "Don't Ask, Don't Tell" policy was repealed, and lesbians and gay men can now serve openly in the U.S. military. However, service members continue to face discrimination. The Defense of Marriage Act (DOMA) means that the military, as a branch of the federal government, won't provide the same benefits—for example, health care—to the spouses of gay and lesbian service members as they do to opposite-sex spouses. Other benefits available to opposite-sex but not same-sex partners and spouses include family housing, assistance with relocating a spouse, and various types of practical and social assistance offered by the military to service members' families.

Immigration issues and public benefits are also red flags that may mean it's better not to register. If one partner is not a U.S. citizen and is either undocumented or here on a nonimmigrant visa, it's probably not a good idea to register as domestic partners. Registering might be considered evidence of an impermissible intent to stay permanently in the United States. In addition, if either partner receives public benefits, legal registration could cause more trouble than it's worth. If you're in any of these situations, talk to a lawyer before you register.

Parentage isn't necessarily secure under federal law. In most marriage-equality and marriage-equivalent states, a child born into a marriage or registered domestic partnership or civil union is legally the child of both partners under state law. Both parents' names can go on the birth certificate immediately, and the nonbiological or "second" parent has equal rights with the biological parent. However, the federal government may not recognize the second parent with regard to Social Security, COBRA coverage, or other federal purposes, so it's still important that the second parent use a legal adoption procedure to ensure that the parent-child relationship is protected. There's more about parentage in Chapter 5.

Use a court procedure to change your name. Although all states allow married people to change their names upon marriage without a court proceeding, there is still discrimination against same-sex couples when it comes to name changes. If you want to be sure that your name change is legal, use a court procedure.

Same-Sex Marriage in the Marriage Equality States

Marriage equality came first to Massachusetts when the Massachusetts Supreme Court ruled in November 2003 that the state's ban on same-sex marriage violated the state constitution. The ruling took effect on May 27, 2004. In the five and a half years that the law has been in effect, more than 16,000 same-sex couples have married. In the last four years, full marriage equality has been extended to same-sex couples in Vermont, New Hampshire, New York, Connecticut, Iowa, and the District of Columbia— quite a dramatic change in the landscape. In addition, both Washington State and Maryland have passed marriage equality laws that will take effect in late 2012 and early 2013, respectively, unless voter referendums interfere. While the specifics for each state are slightly different, the general requirements and procedures for marriage are fairly standard.

Requirements for a Marriage License

To get a marriage license in any marriage-equality state, you must be 18 or older, not married to anyone else, not related by blood to your intended spouse, and in a few remaining states, have taken a blood test showing that you do not have communicable syphilis. When Massachusetts first allowed same-sex marriage, you had to be a Masschusetts resident unless you lived in a state that would recognize your Massachusetts marriage—

but this is no longer the rule. None of the other states have residency requirements either (nor does Canada, which legalized same-sex marriage some years ago). But don't forget that in each of these states, there is a residency requirement to divorce—see below.

Rights and Responsibilities

Once married, same-sex couples who live in a marriage-equality state have all the rights and responsibilities granted to all married couples in the state. But the federal government continues to refuse to acknowledge same-sex marriages, so the federal benefits of marriage are still unavailable. If you don't live in a marriage-equality state and you travel to get married, then depending on the precise law of your home state, your marriage may or may not be recognized. Your marriage is still valid, in the sense that you will be treated as married in any marriage-equality state, but it probably won't be recognized in the state where you live.

The ramifications to the emergence of full marriage equality in a handful of states are enormous, and will continue to affect couples nationally for many years. Undoubtedly, some couples will marry in their marriage-equality home state, then move for business or personal reasons and attempt to enforce their marriage in their new home state. This raises the constitutional issues called "comity" and "full faith and credit." The United States Constitution generally says that marriages in one state must be recognized by all other states. But in some instances, states are granted the right to disregard a marriage of another state based on so-called "public policy" concerns. And the federal Defense of Marriage Act (DOMA) says that same-sex marriages in one state do not have to be recognized in other states, or by federal agencies. Many states have passed their own DOMAs banning recognition of same-sex marriages from out of state, and a depressing number of states have passed constitutional amendments prohibiting the state from recognizing same-sex relationships of any kind from other states.

Thus, unless you are living in a full marriage-equality or marriage-equivalent state that explicitly recognizes same-sex marriages, it may be years before your legal status is recognized where you actually live, and you may encounter a patchwork of uneven responses. In other words, one employer or state agency may treat you as married, while another views you as two single unrelated adults. As unfair as this disparate treatment is, it is going to be our reality during this time of legal transition and social evolution.

Ending a Legal Marriage

Another important issue is how couples married in a marriage-equality state can end their relationships if they no longer live in that state (or ever lived there), or in another marriage-equality state. The only way to end a marriage is through divorce, and because some states will not recognize a same-sex marriage, it may be difficult to get courts in those states to grant a divorce. (Texas and Oklahoma have refused to entertain divorce cases for same-sex couples. In Texas, the two men appealed and eventually were allowed to get their divorce, but in Oklahoma the decision stands, so far.)

You may think you can just return or move to a marriage-equality state to get a divorce, but it's not that simple. Most states have a residency requirement for divorce, meaning that before you can even file for divorce you must have lived in the state for a certain period of time, usually six months to a year. (A few states have no residency requirements to start a divorce action, but they have special rules that you should consult before filing.) And once you file for a court divorce, it typically takes at least six months, and probably longer, for a divorce to become final.

And it's not just a question of having access to the court for a divorce. There is often the bigger quandary of whether you are treated as married when it comes to issues of parentage, money, and assets. In a divorce process, it may be in the financial or personal interest of one spouse to have the marriage go unrecognized, so they can avoid sharing assets or parentage with their now-despised partner. It's an unfortunate truth that some same-sex partners will ask courts not to recognize the marriage for that reason.

There are really no certain answers to these questions as yet—but see below for ways that you can keep up to date on what is happening in this quickly changing area of the law—and manage your personal lives in the meantime.

Relationship Recognition in the Workplace

Marriage raises a whole set of issues for employment-related issues. Most pension and retirement benefits are governed by federal law, but employers sometimes have to look to state rules about benefits. Employers in marriage-equality states must offer nonfederal benefits for all married couples, whether they are of the same or opposite sex.

The conflict between state marriage laws and the federal Defense of Marriage Act has already led to litigation, and it's likely some employers' refusal to provide marital benefits to same-sex spouses will lead to more. Among other cases, a federal court in California recently ruled that the federal government had to provide spousal benefits to the wife of a female court employee after the couple married in 2008. The office of Personnel Management refused to comply with the order, and both sides filed new arguments in 2011 challenging the constitutionality of the DOMA itself. The case will be decided in 2012, but more litigation on this issue is likely.

Employee benefits can be complex, and there's no way for us to cover all the workplace issues that might arise. If your employer won't recognize your relationship, contact a local attorney, the National Center for Lesbian Rights at www.nclrights.org, the Human Rights Campaign at www.hrc.org, or Gay & Lesbian Advocates & Defenders, at www.glad.org.

CAUTION

Don't be a bigamist. If you are married or have registered for a marriage-equivalent civil union or domestic partnership, check with a lawyer before trying to get married again anywhere else—to the same person or to someone else. If you have a marriage certificate, you are legally married and any marriage you enter into later will probably be considered invalid. If you have a marriage-equivalent civil union or domestic partnership, you have a legal status that is equivalent to marriage and you may also be guilty of bigamy if you marry someone else while the other legal relationship is still intact. It's unclear what the legal consequences might be of marrying the same person with whom you have the previous marriage, domestic partnership, or civil union. At best, it won't matter. At worst, you could find yourself in a complicated fight if you and your partner separate and end up in a dispute about which relationship is valid and what was your "date of marriage," and which state's laws you'll use to end your relationship.

RELATED TOPIC

Chapter 3 has information about tax filing status if you are legally married, and also addresses other practical issues about recognition of your marriage. Chapter 5 explains the effect of marriage on your status as parents, if you have kids.

Marriage Equivalent: California's Domestic Partnership Law

California's domestic partnership law has evolved from providing some limited rights, such as hospital visitation, when it was first enacted in 2000, to offering a comprehensive scheme that gives domestic partners essentially all of the same rights and responsibilities as spouses under state law. The new law went into effect on January 1, 2005, with some of its provisions having a retroactive effect, as discussed below. We're treating California separately from the other marriage-equivalent states because it has the largest number of legally registered couples and some of the most settled rules.

Requirements for Registration

Same-sex partners must register with the California Secretary of State (www.ss.ca.gov) to be eligible for rights and benefits under the domestic partnership laws. Registering with a California city, county, or private employer that also offers domestic partner registration is not enough to get the benefits and obligations provided for in the state law, even if you believed in good faith that you were obtaining all those rights.

The requirements for state registration, which costs $33, are:

- Both partners must be 18 or older and capable of consent (if you are reading and understanding this book, you are capable of consent).

- Neither partner may be married to, or in a registered domestic partnership with, someone else.
- The partners must live together (but it's okay for one or both partners to own another house that they use part time, and you don't have to both own the house you live in). You don't need to live in California in order to register, but many other states won't recognize your domestic partnership, so as a practical matter there's not much point in coming in from out of state to register unless you plan on sticking around.
- The partners must not be related by blood.
- The registration form must be notarized.

In addition, the partners must both be of the same sex, or one partner must be over the age of 62. Opposite-sex couples in which neither partner is 62 or over are not eligible to register as domestic partners. (The 62-or-over exception exists because for many people in that age bracket, marriage can have a negative effect on Social Security and other benefit entitlements. Allowing people in this situation to register as domestic partnerships means they can take advantage of the benefits of marriage without the potential downsides.)

When you register, you must attest that you meet the above requirements. You also have to agree that if your relationship ends when you live somewhere else, you can use a California court to divorce. This means the California court can process the legal paperwork involved in ending your relationship and decide how your property will be divided if you and your partner can't reach your own agreement. If the state you're living in when you separate won't dissolve your relationship in its courts, this provision will allow you to use a California court to officially terminate your domestic partnership.

The Domestic Partner Rights and Responsibilities Act went into effect on January 1, 2005. If you registered before that date, all of the new rules apply to you—you don't need to reregister. And the provisions of the law are retroactive to the date of your registration, a rule which undoubtedly will give rise to litigation as couples break up and argue about who owned how much of what, and when.

We Left Our Hearts in San Francisco: The Fight for Same-Sex Marriage in California

On February 12, 2004, San Francisco Mayor Gavin Newsom made history when he ordered the city to begin issuing marriage licenses to same-sex couples. Phyllis Lyon and the late Del Martin, pioneers in the gay rights movement who had been together 50 years, were the first couple to take their vows. After that, thousands of couples wed—before the state Supreme Court put a stop to the marriages in March, and in June issued an opinion voiding all of the marriages that had been performed.

But Mayor Newsom and all the couples who married during the brief window of opportunity started something. A lawsuit on behalf of some of the couples who married and then had their marriages voided resulted in an historic victory in 2008 when the California Supreme Court ruled that the ban on same-sex marriage was unconstitutional. Unfortunately, that victory was short-lived—in November, the voters passed a constitutional amendment that reinstated the ban, and the amendment itself was upheld by the state court as constitutional. While we have grave doubts as to the legal wisdom of that decision, it remains the law. A federal court decision in San Francisco declared the initiative unconstitutional, and in early February, 2012, the ninth Circuit Court of Appeals Upheld that decision. However, the losing side in that case is preparing to appeal the decision. Legislation confirmed the continuing validity of marriages performed between June and November, 2008, but after November 5, 2008, only the marriage-equivalent domestic partnership has been available to same-sex couples in the Golden State.

RESOURCE

Visit the California Secretary of State's website. For more information about domestic partnership, or to download the registration form, go to www.ss.ca.gov.

Rights and Responsibilities of California Registered Domestic Partners

Domestic partnership in California now carries with it a wide range of rights and responsibilities. All of these rights and responsibilities also apply to same-sex couples married during the June to November window in 2008. All of these couples are subject to the following rules:

- Domestic partners have community property rights, meaning that unless the partners agree otherwise in writing all income earned or property acquired by either partner during the partnership belongs to both partners equally, regardless of who earned or acquired it. This rule is retroactive to the date of registration, even though you might not have known when you registered that these rights would be involved.

- Each domestic partner has an equal right to manage and control community property (the income and property acquired by either spouse during the partnership), and an obligation to deal with the property in ways that will benefit both partners.

- The couple's community property is liable for community debts (those incurred during the partnership), and each partner may be responsible for debts incurred by the other partner during the partnership.

- A child born into a registered domestic partnership will be considered the legal child of both partners. Technically, no adoption proceeding should be necessary—but legal experts consider it wise to do an adoption to ensure that the second parent's rights are fully protected. Chapter 5 has more about this.

- Registered domestic partners must receive the same employee benefits as spouses, under a 2007 law that requires even employers with out-of-state home offices to provide the same level of benefits.

- Transfers of real property between domestic partners, whether in the course of the relationship or when the relationship ends, do not result in property tax reassessment (this applies to California state property tax only, not to federal tax questions of any kind).

- Domestic partners have the same privilege as spouses to refuse to testify against each other in court.

- Domestic partners have the same rights as married couples to family student housing, senior citizen housing, and other housing benefits.
- A surviving domestic partner has the right to make anatomical gifts, consent to an autopsy, and make funeral arrangements for a deceased partner.
- Upon separation, an economically dependent partner has the right to seek spousal support from his or her former partner.
- As of tax year 2007, registered domestic partners must use the same filing status as married couples.

In addition, domestic partners and spouses have the rights to:
- sue for the wrongful death of a partner
- make health care decisions for a partner who becomes incapacitated
- inherit just what a spouse would if the partner dies without a will
- use sick leave to care for an ill domestic partner or the child of a domestic partner
- relocate with a partner without losing eligibility for unemployment benefits
- apply for disability benefits on behalf of an injured or incapacitated partner, and
- deduct from taxable income the cost of a domestic partner's health insurance or another benefit for state income tax purposes.

Under a related law, all types of insurers in California—health, life, disability, automobile, and soon—must provide identical coverage to domestic partners and spouses. So if your employer offers health insurance benefits to spouses of employees, your domestic partner is entitled to those same benefits. The same goes for an auto insurance company that gives lower rates to spouses who jointly own their cars and share the same insurance policy.

Ending a California Domestic Partnership

The rules for terminating a domestic partnership changed dramatically with the new law in 2005. Before that, it took only a one-page form—signed by only one partner—to end a domestic partner relationship. Now, almost all registered domestic partners will need to file a formal dissolution proceeding in court, just as heterosexual married couples do. You'll have to exchange financial information and enter into a formal settlement agreement to divide your property and, if you have kids, to set out a plan for coparenting.

This involves quite a bit of paperwork—but it doesn't mean you have to go through a knock-down, drag-out divorce. The court will have to approve the termination of your partnership, but you and your partner can still agree on how you want to divide your property and debts, and deal with custody and visitation of your kids. Mediation is a great option for making these decisions together. There's more about mediation, and about what to do when a relationship ends, in Chapter 10.

If you registered in California and you live in another state when you break up, you can still terminate your domestic partnership in California if the courts in your new home state won't recognize your partnership. But if neither of you ever lived in California, it's unclear whether California law applies to your divorce—for example, whether community property rules apply. And if you have children, the divorce might be complicated by special laws about where custody cases can be heard. You'll probably want to talk to a lawyer if you are registered as California domestic partners but are living in another state.

Domestic Partners and Taxes

The advent of joint tax filing for domestic partners in California (and the other marriage and marriage-equivalent states) brings with it a host of complicated questions. For example, if your domestic partner receives insurance benefits through your employment, your employer is responsible for tracking benefits for domestic partners and letting you know what was paid on behalf of your partner, and—unlike those of married spouses—those benefits are taxable. Also, in the community property states, you may treat your total income as community property for state tax purposes, but not federal. It's important that you consult a tax professional for advice about filing status and how to deal with income, employee benefits, exemptions, and the like.

Do I Have to Go to Court?

A few domestic partnerships can be terminated in California without court approval, but you must both agree to the termination, and all of the following things must be true:

- There are no children of the partnership, and neither partner is pregnant.
- You have been domestic partners for five years or less.
- Neither of you owns any real property, either in California or anywhere else, and if you have a lease, it is not longer than a year and doesn't include an option to purchase the property.
- You don't have debts of more than $4,000 that were incurred during the domestic partnership (not counting car loans).
- You don't have jointly owned assets (other than cars) that are worth more than $32,000, and neither of you has separate assets worth more than $32,000.
- You and your partner have a written agreement about how you will divide your assets and debts, and you have signed any documents needed to accomplish the division.
- You both give up any right to get support from each other.
- You both have read and understood a brochure prepared by the California Secretary of State relating to the termination of your partnership.

If you meet all of these requirements, you can file a one-page form, called Notice of Termination of Domestic Partnership, to terminate your domestic partnership, and the termination will become final six months after you file the form with the Secretary of State. Otherwise, you will need to use a court process, as described in the main text.

A termination that is completed this way can be canceled by a court later if the court finds that all of the requirements listed above were not met. Either party can ask for a revocation of the termination within the six-month period after the notice of termination is filed, using a separate form called Revocation of Termination of Domestic Partnership. Usually, you would seek a revocation of the termination if you decided to get back together, or if one of you decided that you wanted a court to decide how to divide your assets.

Do I Have to Go to Court? (continued)
If only one partner wants to revoke the termination, he or she must file a form called Notice of Revocation of Termination of Domestic Partnership with the Secretary of State, and send a copy to his or her partner in the mail. When you terminate your partnership by filing the one-page form with the Secretary of State, you don't have the right to have a court make decisions about your property, and you can't go back later and challenge the division or any other element of your agreement with your former partner—though you can sue to enforce agreements you and your partner made, if he or she is not following through on them.

RESOURCE

You'll need more information about dealing with assets and debts at the end of a relationship. Take a look at *Nolo's Essential Guide to Divorce*, by Emily Doskow, and *Divorce & Money*, by Violet Woodhouse with Dale Fetherling (Nolo), for detailed information about all aspects of divorce. The California Judicial Council website also has a great deal of information and advice in its self-help section, at www.courtinfo.ca.gov.

Other Marriage-Equivalent Laws

In eight other states (Washington, Oregon, Nevada, New Jersey, Delaware, Illinois, Hawaii, and Rhode Island), same-sex couples can enter into a civil union or domestic partnership. If they live in any of these marriage-equivalent states (and maybe in some other states as well, see below), the civil union or state-registered domestic partnership will give them just about all of the legal rights of marriage under state law. As with marriage, the federal agencies don't currently recognize the legal partnership bestowed by state law.

Requirements for a Civil Union or Domestic Partnership

To enter a civil union or state-registered domestic partnership, typically both parties must be at least 18 years old, of sound mind, not related, and not already in a marriage or another legal partnership. A civil union license or domestic partnership registration is required. There is no residency requirement for entering into a civil union or state-registered domestic partnership. In most states you simply fill out the form and mail it in to the appropriate government office, but in some states, like Vermont, the civil union must be certified by a judge, a justice of the peace, or a clergy member who lives in Vermont (or has a special certification from the Vermont probate court).

Rights and Responsibilities of a Civil Union or Domestic Partnership

Parties to a civil union or state-registered domestic partnership generally accept responsibility to support each other just as spouses do, and the rights that come with a civil union or domestic partnership are the same as those granted to spouses in a marriage in whatever state you registered in. These most typically include:

- use of family laws that cover annulment, divorce, child custody, child support, alimony, domestic violence, adoption, and property division, according to the marital property laws of your state
- the right to sue for wrongful death, loss of consortium, and any other tort (personal injury) or legal claim related to spousal relationships
- medical rights such as hospital visitation, notification, and durable power of attorney (allowing partners to make health care decisions for each other)
- family leave benefits and public assistance benefits
- the right to hold property as tenants by the entirety
- the right to adopt a partner's child under stepparent procedures
- immunity from being compelled to testify against a partner, and the same marital communication privileges as a spouse

- the right to file joint state tax returns (and typically the duty to file your state tax returns as a married couple), and
- the right to inherit from each other without a will.

Although couples from other states can enter into a legal relationship in these states, many of their home states will not acknowledge an out-of-state registration for any purpose, including ending the relationship (see below). Only a few states have recognized domestic partnerships and civil unions for various purposes.

One of the oddest corners of uncertainty involves the issue of domestic partnership or civil union registration in the marriage-equality states. It would seem logical that if a state allows gay folks to marry, it would also recognize a marriage-equivalent registration from another state. But that's not always the case, and the rules for interstate recognition have not been fully resolved. If you move across state lines you should check with an attorney to determine whether you also should register or marry in your new home state.

Ending a Domestic Partnership or Civil Union

To end a civil union or marriage-equivalent domestic partnership you must go to court, just as if you were married. Most states have residency requirements: At least one party must have lived in the filing state for a specified period of time, usually between six months and a year before filing the petition for dissolution.

As we've discussed, whether other state courts will process the dissolution of a domestic partnership or civil union is an open question. So far, one Connecticut court refused to consider the Vermont civil union of two Connecticut residents a contract for purposes of awarding support and dividing property, and a Texas judge refused to grant a divorce to two men married in Massachusetts. But in West Virginia and Iowa, judges have granted divorces to couples who entered into civil unions in Vermont.

The New Jersey Civil Union Law and the Status of New Jersey Domestic Partnerships

Since 2004, New Jersey has offered same-sex couples some legal protections through domestic partnership registration. But in response to a New Jersey Supreme Court order that same-sex couples be treated the same as heterosexual couples under New Jersey law, the legislature enacted a civil union law similar to that in Vermont, which took effect in February 2007.

Partners in civil unions in New Jersey have all of the same state rights and obligations as married couples under state law. New Jersey law also forbids both individuals and businesses from discriminating against civil union partners.

If you were registered as domestic partners in New Jersey before February 2007, you can retain that status and the rights and responsibilities that came with it, which are significant but not as extensive as those attached to the new civil union status. For example, domestic partners don't have the right to sue for wrongful death, while civil union partners do. Unlike married couples and those in civil unions, domestic partners will not be responsible for each other's debts (unless, of course, the debt was undertaken jointly). Finally, while the domestic partnership law allows domestic partners to ask for alimony or property sharing when a relationship ends, a judge does not have to rule on these questions—even though it does require that the relationship be ended formally through the courts. In contrast, civil union partners have the right to an equitable distribution of property through the courts, like married couples.

If you enter into a civil union, your previous domestic partnership is automatically terminated. And as of February 19, 2007, the only couples eligible for domestic partnership registration in New Jersey are those in which both partners are 62 years old or older (they can be of the same sex or opposite sexes).

The Status of "Outdated" Civil Unions

In New England, the arrival of marriage means that states must deal with their marriage-equivalent systems. Now that Connecticut offers full legal marriage, the state has phased out civil unions, which are no longer allowed. All existing civil unions have been "upgraded" automatically to marriages—except for those already in the midst of a dissolution. Previously registered civil union partners need not do anything to obtain the upgraded status, but should consider themselves lawfully wedded.

A similar protocol has been worked out for New Hampshire: Domestic partners were upgraded to married spouses as of January 1, 2011, unless they had already married on their own or have initiated a dissolution proceeding.

Vermont has taken a slightly different path. There, existing civil unions remain as such, with all the rights and duties of marriage. Civil union partners may voluntarily upgrade to marriage by formally marrying, but otherwise they will remain civil union partners.

Pre- and Postpartnership Agreements

Just as with the rules of full legal marriage, the legal responsibilities created by the new domestic partner law are not for everyone. Some couples may want to enter into written agreements defining their financial relationship, just as couples planning to marry do when they make prenuptial contracts. These agreements allow couples to set out their specific wishes about how they will share property and income, as well as how they will divide assets and debts if the relationship ends.

Making a prepartnership agreement isn't as simple as just sitting down and writing out your agreements, though. There are special rules that apply to prenuptial agreements, and the same rules apply to same-sex couples who want to opt out of some or all of the marital laws. For example, each party must disclose to the other party all assets owned and debts owed. And although it's not technically required, it's strongly recommended that each partner have a separate attorney during the process of preparing a prepartnership agreement.

Also, although you can use a prepartnership agreement to divide property and money, and even define support obligations toward each other, you can't make agreements in advance about child support, and you can't make an agreement that releases either partner from the obligation to pay support for a child for whom the person is legally responsible.

RESOURCE

You can get a head start on your prepartnership agreement. You and your partner can sit down together and think about what you would want in an agreement, and even do a first draft of the agreement yourselves, before taking it to separate attorneys for review and finalization. Check out *Prenuptial Agreements: How to Write a Fair & Lasting Contract*, by Katherine E. Stoner and Shae Irving. This book will help you figure out whether you need an agreement, take you through the steps of deciding what you might want in it, and help you figure out how to find and work with lawyers.

If you are already registered but are concerned that you might not want all of the provisions of the new law to apply to you, you can try preparing a postpartnership agreement. However, be particularly careful to find an attorney who is knowledgeable in this area. Postnuptial agreements are strongly disfavored by courts, and have even stricter rules than prepartnership agreements.

Marriage Lite: Relationship Recognition in Wisconsin, Colorado, and Maine

Colorado was one of the most recent states to come on board with some form of relationship recognition for same-sex couples, opting also for a watered-down version. And Maine is the most heartbreaking story, beginning with its initial passage of a limited form of domestic partnership, then briefly flirting with a legislatively imposed marriage law, overturned by the voters, putting the state back at square one—a limited form of domestic partnership. Wisconsin has a similarly limited domestic partnership law.

Colorado's Reciprocal Beneficiaries Law

As of July 2009, Colorado has a reciprocal beneficiaries law, allowing couples to designate each other as beneficiaries and to choose from a list of rights by initialing an agreement form that's set out in the law. This creates a permanent record of what the partners have agreed to. (This is an exception to the rule that we keep reminding you of, that in most states you must meet rigorous standards for a prenuptial agreement that sets out your choices about these rights. It's also different from a prenuptial agreement in that it's part of the public record once you file it with the county clerk.) You can choose among the following rights: avoiding probate through trusts; designating beneficiaries under public employee benefits plans or, in some cases, private plans; owning property in the same joint form used by married couples; having priority as a conservator or the like; hospital visitation and the right to make anatomical gifts and decide on body disposition after death; inheritance if one partner dies without a will; workers' compensation; and rights to bring an action for the wrongful death of a partner. You can terminate your reciprocal beneficiary relationship by using a form provided by the state.

Wisconsin's Domestic Partnership Law

In Wisconsin, domestic partnership is limited to same-sex couples, and requires only that the partners both be over 18, live together, and not be closely related or married (or domestically partnered) to anyone else. Domestic partners don't have all the same rights as married couples in Wisconsin, but the rights they do have aren't insignificant—they include inheritance rights, a presumption that partners hold property as joint tenants, and the ability to sue for wrongful death of a partner, along with a number of other rights.

Domestic Partnership in Maine

Maine has a program similar to Wisconsin's, in that it includes inheritance and other rights but doesn't approach the marriage equivalent relationships available in other states. Partners have the right to inherit each other's property and are considered next of kin for purposes of making funeral and burial arrangements. They have the right to serve as guardian or conservator if the other partner becomes incapacitated, and to visit the other partner in the hospital, as well as other rights.

Is Marriage (or Its Equivalent) Right for You?

Now that same-sex couples in a significant minority of states actually have the opportunity to enter into legal relationships that include important rights and responsibilities, you will have to decide whether marriage or a marriage-equivalent domestic partnership or civil union is the best thing for you. Getting married or registering under new laws is like sitting in the emergency exit row of an airplane: You need to receive special warnings and be prepared for some real uncertainties, legally speaking.

One of the most important complications that comes with marriage or legal partnership is that it remains unclear whether other states will recognize your relationship, or how the federal government will treat your partnership. And it may take quite a few years for the courts to unscramble all of these complexities. Ironic as it seems, it's possible that the federal government will see the light before some states do. This could mean that your relationship could enjoy federal recognition without local or state validation—the reverse situation of where things stand today.

The key lesson to remember, given all these gyrations, is that the actual legal status of your relationship may change from region to region, and from one government agency to another and one situation to another. Don't make any assumptions about what the rules are—instead, learn where things stand in your state and then take appropriate action, especially if you live in a state where full legal recognition is not the law of the land.

In addition to the uncertainties that go with getting married under untested laws, you should consider the same pros and cons that every couple considering marriage should contemplate. For example, depending on your economic situation, marriage might be a positive or a negative move—remember, marriage means not just sharing assets, but also joint liability for debts and potentially the obligation to pay alimony if you break up. Also, marriage and divorce records are public, so there's no staying closeted once you tie the knot.

Marrying may cause you or your partner to lose state-provided public benefits, because your partner's income will be counted along with yours.

Every marriage requires a formal ceremony, and every marital separation requires some kind of formal court action—quite often with the help of a lawyer. Usually, there is a residency requirement for divorce, so if you intend to marry, register, or enter a civil union in a state other than the one in which you live, consider the ramifications if your relationship does not last. In contrast, unmarried couples can break up informally, and without the state requiring them to live there for a certain period of time.

In most states, assets acquired during marriage must be divided equally if the marriage ends; in community property states the partners' earnings during the marriage are considered community property unless you agree otherwise in writing. By contrast, if you are unmarried, your property is co-owned only if you have an agreement to make it so and have titled it jointly; and the same is true for debts and obligations. Transfers of property when a relationship ends are tax free for legally married couples, but not for unmarrieds, and probably not for most couples in domestic partnerships (although your state's law may provide certain tax exemptions).

If you don't marry, you will need to make sure that you write a will, create a trust, or designate your partner as beneficiary on your IRAs and other holdings, in order to pass assets at your death in the same way that spouses can (without any written documents). And certain tax benefits are forever denied to unmarried couples. For example, a surviving spouse generally inherits all the property if the other spouse dies without a will and has no children; this would be true for marriage-equivalent relationships

How Do You Want to Structure Your Relationship?

Even though many LGBT activists have worked for decades for the kind of social and legal legitimacy that marriage confers, plenty of people have mixed feelings about it. Some reject domestic partnership and civil unions as a "second class" legal status. Others believe that marriage as an institution should be abolished, and the state should stay out of people's private lives. There are also a great number of people who agree that marriage should be available to all, but they themselves would not marry—either because they prefer the freedom to make their own agreements about how to share their lives, without the encumbrance of the state's requirements, or because marriage is not in their economic interest. Whether or not you feel ready to take on the responsibilities of marriage, you now have options that earlier generations of same-sex couples could only dream of. Explore these choices, learn about them, talk about them—and then make the decision that's best for your family.

RESOURCE

For an in-depth analysis of all the personal, financial, and legal ramifications of legally partnering or marrying, we encourage you to read Nolo's newest book for lesbians and gay men, and those who advise and befriend them: *Making It Legal: A Guide to Same-Sex Marriage, Domestic Partnership & Civil Unions*, by Frederick Hertz, with Emily Doskow. For up-to-date information on the marriage equality battle, check out the authors' blogs, www.MakingItLegal.net and www. QueerJustice.com.

as well. However, at death, a bequest from one spouse to another is free from federal estate tax, regardless of its size. Because this is a federal law, it does not apply to same-sex couples, regardless of the legal status of their relationship. In some states, you can't disinherit a spouse unless you have a prepartnership agreement that addresses the issue specifically.

If you have children or hope to raise a family, marriage is probably the right option. Married couples by law have equal rights to raise their children, as well as equal obligations of support. If the relationship breaks up, both parents can seek visitation and custody, and if one parent dies, the other steps right in as the primary legal parent. The same is true for unmarried couples only if both are legal parents of the children. Otherwise, the second parent may be left out in the cold (see Chapter 10).

Money, Insurance, Name Changes, and Immigration Issues

Cash and Credit.. 60

    Joint Accounts—Dos and Don'ts 61

    Buying and Investing Together 67

    Tax Matters 68

Insurance 70

    Health Insurance 71

    Disability Insurance 71

    Life Insurance 71

    Homeowner's Insurance 72

    Automobile Insurance 72

Name Changes.. 74

Foreign Lovers: Visits and Immigration 77

    Visiting the United States.. 77

    Moving to the United States 79

When you and your partner decide to live together, you are probably acting on romantic impulses. But as we all know, practical problems do tend to tag along in the wake of romance. Most of these problems aren't legal and don't involve lawyers—all the barristers in the world can't help you when the two of you discuss your monthly budget or decide whose family you will visit next.

Many day-to-day hassles, however, are connected with law. This chapter discusses commonly encountered financial issues like credit cards and insurance, tax filing, insurance of all kinds, name changes, and immigration questions.

Cash and Credit

Although most of us aspire to rise above nickel-and-dime money issues when dealing with our partners, that doesn't mean we can ignore the financial aspects of our relationships. Every couple—even those who have registered or married—will benefit from having clear agreements about who pays the rent, makes the car payments, and buys the groceries. It's enormously helpful to have a written agreement regarding your finances. A contract won't keep two people in love or prevent them from splitting up, but it can prevent misunderstandings and arguments. If times get hard, a written agreement can do wonders to reduce paranoia and confusion, and help people deal with each other fairly. And if you do split up, a written document stating who gets what can save you untold hours of misery and thousands of dollars.

RELATED TOPIC

Chapter 8 has sample living together agreements. The agreements in Chapter 8 cover situations where you want to share money and assets, and situations where you want to keep your property separate—and options somewhere in between.

Joint Accounts—Dos and Don'ts

When a couple moves in together, questions come up about whether to pool money and property or keep it all separate. Just because you live with someone doesn't mean your financial lives have to be merged. If you want to combine finances, be sure you really know and trust your partner. Don't feel pressured to combine everything when you're just starting out simply because the lesbian couple upstairs—who have been together 22 years—have only one bank account.

Most lesbian and gay couples choose to handle their finances according to one of the following models.

Traditional marriage model. Property owned by each person before entering into the relationship remains the owner's separate property. Money that either person earns, and property acquired during the relationship, is considered to belong to both partners equally. You put most or all of your bank accounts, credit cards, and investments in both names. If you split up, the property acquired during the relationship is divided equally. This is the model that is typically imposed on you by the state if you register or marry.

Socialist model. You open joint accounts and pay joint bills out of these accounts, to which you contribute according to your financial abilities, such as three-fourths from one partner and one-fourth from the other.

Business partnership model. You open joint accounts for limited purposes, such as paying household expenses or to fund a distinct project—for example, renovating a house, saving for a vacation, or investing. For all other purposes, you keep your income and expenses separate.

 TIP

If you open a joint account for a specific purpose, identify it as such. Ask the bank if you can name the account—for example, "The Anderson-Henry Vacation Account." If you don't have equal shares, you can supplement your accounts with a living together contract specifying the percentages each of you owns. (See Chapter 8 for sample contracts.)

Splitsies model. Each partner agrees to be absolutely self-reliant. Each separately pays for food, clothes, entertainment, and everything else, including a share of household expenses. This couple has no joint accounts. This arrangement can be kept fairly rigid with vigilant accounting or can be worked out in a fairly easygoing, commonsense, "I-paid-for-breakfast, you-pay-for-lunch" way.

Joint Bank Accounts

Many lesbian and gay couples peacefully maintain joint bank accounts, but opening a joint account is taking a risk. Each person is responsible for all the activity that takes place with the account, and the funds are generally considered owned equally by the two of you. You're both equally liable for bounced checks, overdrafts, and all the rest. It's even possible that one partner could withdraw all the money without the other's consent, without any obligation to repay half of it.

If, on the other hand, you keep your property and debts separate and you don't register or marry, you'll have no financial obligation if your partner runs up debts. This means your paycheck cannot be garnished and your property cannot be taken to satisfy your partner's overdue bills.

SPECIAL ISSUES

If you are legally married or state-registered as domestic partners or in a civil union in a marriage-equivalent state, keeping your property separate may not protect you from financial obligations for your partner. In each of those relationships, partners have some level of financial responsibility for each other, even out of separately earned or saved assets. Any agreement you sign saying otherwise must be prepared according to the strict standards governing prenuptial and postnuptial agreements.

Another problem with joint accounts is record keeping. It can be hard to know how much money is in an account if you both write checks, use a debit card and make withdrawals. This is less of a problem these days, with instant access to banking information online.

If you decide that you can work these things out, obtaining a joint account isn't a problem. Financial institutions are happy to have your money under any name or names. You'll just have to decide whether both signatures will be necessary to write a check or make a withdrawal, or only one. It's easier to require only one signature, but it's riskier, too.

TIP
Joint accounts may help you avoid probate. When accounts are held in joint tenancy or there is a payable-on-death beneficiary, and one partner dies, the account passes to the other partner automatically, without probate.

CAUTION
Joint accounts may imply a contract to share income. As we discuss later in the book, in some states, including California, courts will sometimes imply a contract between unmarried people to share earnings and other property. Sharing bank or credit accounts might be a factor a court would consider in deciding whether a couple had an implied contract to share income and property. If you want to make sure this doesn't happen, it's best not to open joint accounts, or if you do, to sign an agreement about the accounts (and your other assets as well), such as the Agreement to Keep Income and Accumulations Separate in Chapter 8.

Joint Credit Accounts

Joint credit card accounts are riskier than joint bank accounts—each of you is individually liable for the entire amount owed on a joint credit account, and a lover who goes nuts financially can potentially do damage to your credit rating. (Here's an area where banks treat you as "family" whether you want it or not.)

It's fairly easy to put two names on a credit card. Creditors will generally open joint credit accounts—and why shouldn't they? A joint account means more people are responsible for a debt. For example, if Roger and James have a joint credit card, and Roger lets his sister Fiona charge $2,500 on it, Roger and James are both legally obligated to pay the bill, even if James didn't know about it or even told Roger not to do it. Similarly, if James retaliates by leaving Roger and going on a buying binge, Roger is legally responsible for all the charges James makes.

If one of you has a poor credit history, you may be denied a joint card, even if the other's credit is great. The partner with better credit may have to reapply alone. The partner who gets the credit card can have a second card issued on the account in the other partner's name—but this will only give the second partner the right to charge things on the credit card, not the responsibility to pay for it.

If you want to be generous, you are better off being generous with cash, not credit. Indeed, when living with someone who has debt problems, you should sign a contract keeping everything separate to avoid possible confusion.

> **CAUTION**
>
> **If a credit application has a blank for "spouse" instead of "co-applicant/spouse," cross off the word "spouse" and write in "co-applicant."** Don't present yourself as spouses—the term has specific legal meaning (having to do with liability and responsibility), and lying on the application is fraud. (Of course, if you are legally married or state registered, you can go ahead and list yourselves that way on the application.)

> **CAUTION**
>
> **If you break up, immediately close all joint accounts.** All too often, one person feels depressed during the breakup and tries to feel better through "retail therapy." Don't just allot the accounts so that each of you keeps some of them. You're both still liable for all accounts—and you could get stuck paying the "therapy" bill your ex ran up if you don't close the account.

Credit Discrimination

Discrimination against lesbians and gays in the area of credit is no longer very common. Ability to pay, not sexual orientation, seems to be the criterion used. If you believe you were discriminated against when requesting credit, check to see whether your state or local municipality has a law barring sexual orientation discrimination in credit transactions (not common, but possible in some places). If it does, report the creditor to the agency that oversees the law.

Beyond this, there is probably little you can do. A federal law called the Equal Credit Opportunity Act bars creditors from discriminating on account of race, color, religion, national origin, sex, marital status, age, or because all or part of a person's income derives from public assistance. Courts have declined to extend the law to include sexual orientation.

Checking Your Credit

When a bank, department store, landlord, or collection agency wants information about a person, they can get it by paying a small fee to a credit bureau. Credit bureaus are companies that collect information related to your creditworthiness, including your bank and credit card accounts, loans (such as mortgages, car loans, or student loans), payment history on those loans and accounts, delinquencies on accounts, bankruptcy filings, criminal arrests and convictions, current and previous employers, lawsuits and judgments against you, and tax or other liens.

You have the right to examine your credit file under the federal Fair Credit Reporting Act. If the file contains inaccurate or outdated information, the credit bureau is required to correct it, or at least to include your version of the dispute in your file.

Unfortunately, many credit reports do contain inaccurate or outdated information. If you have some joint accounts with your partner or have been living together for a long time, the credit bureaus may have included information on your credit record about your partner's separate accounts. Information about separate accounts should only appear on the report of the responsible partner. Information about joint accounts should appear on both reports.

To make sure your credit reports are accurate, request a copy of your credit report and review it for errors or outdated information. It's a good idea to do this every year. New credit reporting rules entitle you to one free credit report per year.

You can order a copy of your report by phone, online, or by mail:

- Phone: 877-322-8228
- Online: www.annualcreditreport.com
- By mail: Annual Credit Report Service, P.O. Box 105283, Atlanta, Georgia 30348-5283.

You must provide your name, address, Social Security number, and date of birth when you order. You also may be required to provide information that only you would know, such as the amount of your monthly mortgage payment.

If you want additional copies of your credit report within a year, or you need to correct information in your credit report, you'll probably need to contact a credit bureau directly.

How to Contact Credit Bureaus

If you find errors on your report (for example, a car loan for which your partner is the only signatory) or outdated information, notify the credit bureau in writing. The bureau is required by law to correct your report. If the bureau investigates the item and disagrees with you, at the very least you can include a brief explanation on your report about the disputed item.

The three major national credit bureaus are:

- Equifax, P.O. Box 740241, Atlanta, GA 30374; 800-685-1111; www.equifax.com
- Experian, National Consumer Assistance Center, P.O. Box 2002, Allen, TX 75013; 888-397-3742; www.experian.com
- Trans Union, Consumer Disclosure Center, P.O. Box 2000, Chester, PA 19022, 800-888-4213; www.transunion.com.

RESOURCE

Take control of your credit report. For more information on what can appear on your credit report and for how long, how to correct errors, and how to repair credit after a financial setback, see *Credit Repair*, by Robin Leonard and John Lamb (Nolo).

Buying and Investing Together

Many couples make investments and other purchases, such as a house or car, together. Shared home ownership is covered in Chapter 8. Here we discuss other assets and investments.

It's not difficult to make joint purchases or investments. Salespeople are used to seeing all combinations of people buying and investing together. In major urban areas, you will be able to find gay and lesbian investment brokers, car brokers, loan brokers, and the like. Just ask a friend or take a look at the classified section of a local LGBT newspaper.

If you make a shared purchase or investment, you should prepare an agreement reflecting who owns what percentage, especially if your contributions are unequal. Samples are in Chapter 8. Even if only one of you takes out a loan to finance the purchase or uses separate money to invest or buy, you can both be legal owners, if that's what you want.

Certain property items come with title documents—common examples are motor vehicles and stocks. The purpose of a title document is to document ownership and show the type of ownership you have. Stock certificates and other documents showing how investments are held are prepared by investment brokers or by the company in which you invest. Title documents for motor vehicles are prepared by your state motor vehicle department at your direction.

In most states, there are two possible ways to share ownership and register property with title certificates. The information given here is general. Different states have somewhat different terminology. (For motor vehicle purchases, check with your state's department of motor vehicles for details.)

- **Tenants in common.** With this type of ownership, you and your partner each own a specific percentage interest in the property, and can do with it whatever you like. Ownership of tenancy-in-common property may be divided however the owners choose. You can own equal shares, one owner can own 90% and the other 10%, or anything in between.

- **Joint tenancy with right of survivorship.** With this form of ownership, you and your partner each own the entire property along with the other. When one owner dies, the surviving owner automatically inherits the deceased owner's share.

Joint tenancy ownership must be spelled out in the ownership document. Generally, if no type of ownership is specified on a title document of jointly owned property, it is owned as a tenancy in common.

CAUTION

Take special care when you register your car. In some states, either owner can sell the car without the other's consent if you own it in joint tenancy.

As with so many other issues, if you are married or in a marriage-equivalent registration, marital rules will most likely trump the way you title your property.

RELATED TOPIC

Chapter 9 discusses types of ownership in the context of owning real property.

Tax Matters

Filing Joint Returns

Only couples who are legally married or in a marriage-equivalent relationship on December 31 of the tax year can file joint state income tax returns. If you are not legally married, you will have to file separately.

If you and your partner are married or registered in a marriage-equivalent state, you are in a dilemma. You are legally married, and the IRS (theoretically) requires married couples to file as married, even if each partner files a separate return—it is against the law for you to file as a single person. On the other hand, the federal DOMA says that the federal government does not recognize same-sex marriages. Complicating things further, some states require that you file your state taxes using the same status you used on your federal taxes—so even if you live in a state that recognizes your marriage, you may not be able to file as married with the state and as single on your federal taxes.

So, what should you do? The National Center for Lesbian Rights website (www.nclrights.org) offers a few possible options for same-sex couples who are legally married. In most states married and registered couples file as married, either jointly or separately, on their state tax returns. If you live in a community property state (California, Washington, or Nevada), you each report 50% of the community property income, meaning the combination of your two incomes, on your federal tax return, even though you continue to file your federal return separately as single taxpayers. Another option is to file as single (or head of household if appropriate) but include with the tax return a cover letter explaining the situation. Another is to file two sets of tax returns—one as married, one as single—and pay the higher tax, again including a cover letter explaining that you have made an effort to do what is legally required. Other advisers say simply file state returns as married and the federal returns as single.

SEE AN EXPERT

Consult an expert. Before making a decision about tax filing status, talk to a lawyer or an accountant who has expertise in the area of same-sex relationships. And make sure you keep up to date on current developments (see "Keeping Up With Legal Changes," Chapter 1).

Claiming Your Partner as a Dependent and Filing as Head of Household

Even though you cannot file joint returns, your partner may qualify as a dependent if you provide over one-half of your partner's total support (for food, shelter, clothing, medical and dental care, education, and the like) during the year. Other requirements are that your partner must have earned less than $3,650 in 2011 (not including tax-exempt income, such as welfare or Social Security benefits) and must be a U.S. resident or citizen who has lived with you the entire year. In addition, your partner cannot file a joint return with someone else (for example, with a spouse if he or she is still legally married to someone else). For more details on these requirements, see IRS Publication 501, *Exemptions, Standard Deductions and Filing Information*. To get this publication, contact the IRS at 800-829-1040 or visit its website at www.irs.gov.

The California Franchise Tax Board ruled recently that a lesbian supporting her partner and their child can file her state income tax return as a head of household. She had been denied head-of-household filing status because she was not legally or biologically related to the child, who was born to her partner through donor insemination during their relationship. If you are the sole or primary support for your family, check into whether head-of-household status is appropriate for you.

RESOURCE

If you claim your lover as a dependent and the IRS objects, or you have a problem with head-of-household status or any other dispute with the IRS, see *Stand Up to the IRS*, by Frederick W. Daily (Nolo).

SPECIAL ISSUES

Pay attention to property tax issues. In addition to issues related to income tax filing, marriage and marriage-like relationships can create confusion about property and transfer taxes. Many rules are in flux as states try to decide how to treat marital and marriage-like relationships between same-sex couples. If you own property and are married, registered as domestic partners, or in a civil union, you should talk to a lawyer or tax professional before transferring property to or from your partner.

Insurance

Same-sex couples will have no problem getting many types of insurance together. As with credit applications, make sure you don't represent yourselves as married, because fraudulent applications can lead to a loss of coverage when you most need it.

Health Insurance

As discussed in Chapter 1, many public and private employers now offer health insurance coverage for employees' domestic partners and children. For a list of major companies that provide benefits to domestic partners, visit the Alternatives to Marriage Project website at www.unmarried.com. Also, you can find a "Corporate Equality Index" at www.hrc.org. Some companies extend benefits to all cohabitants; others require marriage or formal registration.

If you don't have insurance benefits through your employer, you can buy a private health insurance policy. In some areas, you may be able to get a family rate for coverage that includes your domestic partner or children.

Disability Insurance

Disability insurance is intended to provide income if you are unable to work because of a disability. Some employers provide disability benefits for their employees, but many people must make do with public benefits or private plans that they pay for themselves. Where employers provide disability insurance, coverage generally is offered only to employees, not to spouses or domestic partners.

Life Insurance

Life insurance is another benefit that employers frequently offer. Even when coverage is available through work, some couples also purchase private life insurance policies. If you are in a couple, buying life insurance makes sense if:

- you have minor children and there would be insufficient money for them to live on if you die without insurance (remember any Social Security they might receive)
- life insurance is part of your estate plan—an asset you plan to leave to your partner that will not have to go through probate. This especially makes sense if your lover is dependent on you or you

rely heavily on each other's incomes—for example, you need both paychecks to make your mortgage payments, or

- you are close to retirement, and insurance serves as a special kind of savings to help out the partner who outlives the other.

If you have a life insurance policy, you can name your partner as the beneficiary. When asked the nature of the relationship, you may have to state "friend" or "business partner," which is true if you own any significant property together, or if you share some other financial interest such as an actual business.

Generally speaking, you cannot buy a policy on your partner's life and name yourself as the beneficiary unless you own real estate or a business together or are married or registered domestic partners. Insurance companies don't believe that nonmarried partners have an "insurable interest" in each other, and limit buying insurance on another person to spouses, business partners, and joint homeowners. But if you are able to do so, owning a policy on your partner's life can save on estate taxes for higher-asset couples, so be sure to investigate this option.

Homeowner's Insurance

If you and your partner buy a house together, you'll have to get home-owner's insurance, which insures the house against fire and other acts of destruction (for floods and earthquakes, you usually need additional coverage). You shouldn't have any trouble getting a joint policy. If only one of you owns the house, you'll need to get a rider covering the nonowner or be sure the other partner has renter's insurance. (Chapter 4 has more information about renter's insurance.)

Automobile Insurance

In most states, car owners are legally required to carry a minimum amount of auto insurance. If you and your lover each own a car separately, you may have trouble getting a single insurance policy for both cars. Some insurers won't insure you and your cars as if you were married, but rather, will write you each a separate policy, and name the other as secondary driver. Of course, this costs more.

If you really want one policy and you can't find an insurer who will write one, your only option is to change your title slips (you have to call the motor vehicles department), putting both cars in one person's name or both in both partners' names. Of course, you'll need a separate written agreement stating your actual ownership interests if you don't both own both cars in their entirety. And be careful not to do anything fraudulent that the insurance company could use as a basis to deny benefits if you make a claim.

SPECIAL ISSUES

In states where same-sex couples may marry or legally register, they must be treated like spouses and insurance companies are no longer permitted to discriminate against same-sex couples in providing insurance.

Some insurance companies refuse any secondary coverage to unrelated people who co-own a car. This means that you and your lover would be insured for accidents that occur when you're driving or riding in the car you own, but not while driving or riding in other cars, such as a rental car, or while you are a pedestrian. And some companies require that you designate just one person the "primary owner"—the company then provides secondary insurance for that person only. You may have to talk with a number of insurance agents before you find a policy that will provide complete coverage for both you and your lover.

If you have significant assets, you should also buy an umbrella policy, which provides additional coverage if you get into a major accident and your policy limits are exhausted. An umbrella policy doesn't kick in until you have used up all your other insurance benefits. As an unmarried couple, you may each have to purchase your own umbrella policy, but you should push to try to get a joint policy whenever possible.

Name Changes

Lots of lesbians and gay men change their names. Sometimes a woman who changed her name in a heterosexual marriage wants to return to her premarital name. Sometimes partners hyphenate their names or choose a name that's the combination of the two. (Audrey Berman and Sheila Gander become Audrey and Sheila Bergan.) And then there are couples where one partner simply takes the other's last name.

Changing your name is perfectly legal and usually quite simple. You cannot change your name to defraud creditors, for any illegal purpose, or to benefit economically by the use of another person's name—that is, you probably can't become Rachel Maddow or Oscar Wilde. You also cannot change your name to a racial epithet or another offensive word. Aside from these limitations, you can change your name for any reason and assume any new name you wish.

In some of the states where marriage or domestic partnership is available, one partner can change to the other partner's last name at the time of marriage or registration, without the necessity of a court order. You can't change both of your names to something new this way, though. And some people have had a hard time getting their name changes processed this way. If you are hoping to change your name after your marriage or registration, check with a local LGBT organization or an attorney in your area to find out whether this option is available and how high the hassle factor is.

If you can't change your name automatically, you'll need to get an order from a court. Getting a court order for a name change is usually pretty simple: You fill out a short petition and file it at the courthouse, publish legal notice of your intention to change your name in a local legal newspaper (which no one reads), and attend a routine court hearing.

Unfortunately, some LGBT individuals have had problems with name changes. For example, a Pennsylvania judge denied a woman's request to change her last name to that of her life partner, on the basis that the name change was against public policy because it created the appearance of a marriage when the parties were not in fact married. The woman appealed, and the court of appeals allowed the name change.

Also, a New Jersey appeals court upheld the statutory right of a lesbian to change her last name to that of her lover. In that case, the court reversed the lower court judge, who had refused to approve the name change based on the theory that granting the name change would show approval for same-sex marriage. The appellate court declared that a judge had no authority to deny a name change based on his "personal view of what is or should be the public policy of this state." California now allows registered domestic partners to take a partner's name after registration without having to go through a court petition process, and you should be able to get a passport with your new name as well.

Changing Your Name Without Going to Court

In days past, you could change your name by the so-called "usage" method. You could just use your new name in all circumstances, and write to official agencies advising them of the change. Eventually, your new name became your legal name. Technically, the usage method is still available in many states. But governmental regulations, created to combat modern types of fraud such as identity theft, are quickly making it more difficult to have a new name accepted without a court order. You can't just walk into a government office, tell the clerk you've changed your name, and have your name changed in the records. This is especially true since the terrorist attacks of September 11, 2001. If your state doesn't allow name changes automatically after marriage, the best way to change your name is to go to court and get a court order that serves as proof of your new name.

Transgender persons have also had problems with name changes in some states, and also with changing their gender designation on a birth certificate—a prerequisite for marrying an opposite-sex partner in all states. Forty-seven states now have laws or regulations that allow modification of birth records to reflect a gender change. Only Idaho, Ohio, and Tennessee have statutes or rules that allow them to refuse to change gender designation on a birth certificate. These laws might also support a court's refusal of a name change, but most state laws on name changes are extremely liberal. An exception to this recently occurred in New York, where a Manhattan judge refused to grant name changes for transgender petitioners because they had not documented their sex-reassignment surgery. Following a request for reconsideration, the judge backed down, but insisted that the name change orders state that they did not affect the petitioners' legal gender designation.

RESOURCE

Name and gender changes sometimes require a lawyer's help. If you are having trouble with a name change because you are transgender, or if you are having problems getting the gender designation on your birth certificate changed, contact the Transgender Law Center at www.transgenderlawcenter.org for information and lawyer referrals.

TIP

If you live in a state where you must give a reason for the change and you'd rather not tell the judge that you're changing your name to your partner's, you don't have to. You can state that your new name will make it more convenient for business or simply state that you like the new name better.

Once you obtain the court order changing your name, you must still change your records, identity cards, and documents. All you need to do is show the various bureaucrats the judge's order. Important entities that you should contact to change your records include the Social Security Administration, the Department of Motor Vehicles, the Internal Revenue Service and state tax authorities, the U.S. Department of State (to change your passport), employers, credit card issuers, insurance companies, health care providers, banks, issuers of stocks and bonds, utility companies, and the post office. It's particularly important to change your automobile and boat registration, real estate deeds, and estate planning documents, such as wills or trusts (including if you are a beneficiary of someone else's will or trust).

While married women generally don't need a court order for the federal government (or any state or local entity) to recognize a name change after marriage, men and same-sex partners in some states may be required to go through a court process and get a court order before they can obtain a new passport or Social Security card. But there's no reason not to try for the automatic postmarriage name change if you are married or in a domestic partnership.

RESOURCE

If you live in California, you can use the forms and step-by-step instructions in *How to Change Your Name in California*, by Lisa Sedano and Emily Doskow (Nolo). This book also includes a chapter on getting court recognition of gender changes.

Foreign Lovers: Visits and Immigration

Suppose a fantasy comes true: You take a trip abroad and meet the person of your dreams, who just happens to be a citizen of that distant land. You come home and go back to work to earn money to take your next vacation. In the meantime, your new lover wants to know the legal rules about visiting you in America. More optimistically, what about immigration rules if the sparks still fly once you're together again?

Or suppose you are just going about your daily business at home, and you meet and fall in love with someone who is a noncitizen, perhaps here on a student visa. The same questions arise.

Visiting the United States

No law currently restricts lesbians and gay men from entering the United States. To come as a tourist, your new lover would have two choices: to arrive without a visa, which is permissible if he or she is from a country that participates in the Visa Waiver Program (VWP), or to apply for a tourist visa, which is available from overseas U.S. consulates.

To find out which countries are part of the Visa Waiver Program, check the U.S. State Department's website at www.state.gov (click "Travel" then "Visa Waiver Program"). Most of the countries listed are Western ones, such as the United Kingdom, Denmark, France, and Germany. People from these countries can basically pack their bags, grab their passports, and head for the United States. Assuming they pass the border inspection, they'll be allowed in for a maximum 90-day stay. Despite the ease of this option, you should warn your new lover of its disadvantages: People who enter on visa waivers are very easy to kick out of the United States, because they have no right to a court hearing if U.S. immigration authorities take steps to deport them. (Exceptions are made for people with dire needs such as medical emergencies or fear of persecution overseas.)

The tourist visa option is the only choice for many applicants. This involves filing an application form and meeting briefly with an official at a U.S. consulate. With any luck, your new lover will be granted a multiple entry visa, which can be used many times for visits of up to six months, until the visa's expiration date (usually ten years away). Unfortunately, if your new lover indicates to the consulate or any border official an intent to live permanently in the United States, or comes often enough to be, in effect, living here, entry will be denied and the visa will be cancelled.

Some categories of people are never allowed into the United States for any reason—in legal terminology, they are "inadmissible." The U.S. immigration laws contain a long list of grounds for inadmissibility. For example, people with criminal records, terrorist links, or involvement in drug trafficking are inadmissible. This can be an issue if your lover is from a country that criminalizes homosexuality. Until recently, HIV was among the communicable diseases of public health significance that made a person inadmissible, and the tourist visa application form asks about communicable diseases (although the application process doesn't include a medical exam). Fortunately, in late 2009, the bigoted HIV rule was lifted.

Moving to the United States

Moving to the United States permanently is a trickier business. Gone are the days when a U.S. citizen could simply "sponsor" an immigrant—that is, vouch for the person's good character and issue an invitation. Now the would-be immigrant must fit into one of various categories of visas allowing either a temporary stay of a few years or permanent residence (a green card). A complete rundown of every U.S. visa is beyond the scope of this book. However, below we list some of the visa types most commonly used—or asked about—by gay and lesbian couples.

> TIP
>
> **Once in the United States, it is often possible to apply for a different type of temporary visa just before the expiration of the visa that the person used to enter.** In that case, though, the immigrant must prove that there have been no violations of the terms of the visa, and that there's an intention to go home at the end.

Marriage-based visa. Unfortunately, immigration laws still draw a sharp line between heterosexual and homosexual marriages. U.S. citizens and green card holders with heterosexual spouses can petition for them to immigrate, but until DOMA is repealed, those with homosexual spouses cannot—even if they've found a state or country that will legally marry them. The Justice Department (DOJ) instigated a major policy shift in early 2011, however, when it stopped defending DOMA in court. Now, DOJ actually files briefs arguing against DOMA's constitutionality. The Supreme Court is eventually expected to address this issue, though experts estimate that we shouldn't expect a Supreme Court decision before 2013. In the meantime, there's still no concrete way for a U.S. citizen to petition for a same-sex spouse to receive a green card.

However, in the meantime, U.S. Immigration and Customs Enforcement (ICE) has offered an interim solution, providing same-sex partners of U.S. citizens at least some minimal immigration rights. New guidelines allow ICE agents to use "prosecutorial discretion" when deciding whom to deport (remove) from the United States. Agents are to give special consideration to students and other upstanding immigrants who have strong or longstanding ties to the United States and make contributions to the community, especially when their removal from the country would divide a family into pieces. Although the relevant memo did not specifically allude to same-sex couples, subsequent actions and statements by the Department of Homeland Security, ICE, and the White House, as well as various decisions by immigration judges, have made clear that a same-sex marriage will be treated as a family tie for purposes of this exercise of discretion.

In literal terms, what does this exercise of prosecutorial discretion mean? An immigrant who is arrested and threatened with deportation can request an exercise of prosecutorial discretion from ICE (even before the matter gets to Immigration Court), by showing upstanding behavior and family ties. If the request is granted, the person would essentially be put into legal limbo—not deported, but not granted permanent status, either. If the request were not granted, the case would be referred to immigration court, where the immigrant should be able to renew the request for prosecutorial discretion. (The procedural details are still being worked out.) If granted, the case would be administratively closed—which means put on a pending, inactive status.

If you wish to marry a transgender person who is now of the opposite sex, there's good news: If your state recognizes the marriage, the immigration authorities will too, and should grant a marriage-based green card.

"Marriage of convenience" to a U.S. citizen. Yes, some people find a willing U.S. citizen of the opposite sex—perhaps even a close friend—to marry the immigrant and go through the paperwork and interviews required to get a green card. However, we can't recommend this illegal course or advise you on it. A sham marriage can land both parties in big trouble—including prison time, hefty fines (up to $250,000), and deportation of the immigrant, with little chance of returning to the United States. In one case, a lesbian immigrant married a U.S. citizen and got caught because she couldn't tell the immigration officer what kind of contraception she and her husband were using—having never had to worry about preventing pregnancy!

RESOURCE

For more information on marriage-based visas, see *Fiancé & Marriage Visas: A Couple's Guide to U.S. Immigration,* by Ilona Bray (Nolo).

Political asylum. If your lover comes from a country where persecution of homosexuals is a real fear, perhaps because of sexual orientation, an HIV diagnosis, or political activities, applying for political asylum is a possibility. (An application for asylum can be submitted only after your lover is in the United States, however. People who are still overseas can apply for refugee status, but it's more difficult to get.) The persecution may take various forms, such as harassment, violence, forced psychiatric treatment, or prosecution for homosexuality or a trumped-up crime such as "hooliganism." It does not need to have come directly from the government. For example, gays and lesbians from various countries have won asylum by showing that their government failed to protect them from antihomosexual street violence. Lesbians and gay men from Bangladesh, Brazil, China, Cuba, El Salvador, Eritrea, Ethiopia, India, Iran, Mexico, Nicaragua, Syria, Turkey, and other countries have been granted asylum.

After coming to the United States—perhaps on a visa waiver or tourist visa—your lover would need to apply for asylum quickly, because applications for asylum are accepted for only one year after a person enters the United States or the visa stay expires. We recommend that you get a lawyer's help for this. If money is a problem, many organizations offer free or low-cost help with asylum applications. Winning political asylum would give your lover a right to remain in the United States for as long as the situation is risky overseas—or permanently, if he or she applies for a green card one year after the asylum application is approved.

Adoption. Could you adopt your lover and apply for a green card on that basis? It's a creative idea, but doomed even before you get to the fraud problem. Children must be 16 or under to qualify for a green card based on adoption.

Visa lottery. Officially named the Diversity Immigrant Visa Lottery, this program offers green cards, by random drawing, to people from countries that in recent years have sent the fewest numbers of immigrants to the United States. Anyone can enter the lottery if they are a native of one of these countries and have either a high school diploma or a minimum of two years' experience in a job that normally requires at least two years of training or experience. One of the latest requirements is purely technological: Applicants now must submit their applications via the Internet and attach a digital photo. There are 50,000 winners selected per year.

One of the unpleasant secrets of the lottery program, however, is that many people "win" but are unable to collect on their green card, owing purely to U.S. government delays. If winners don't complete the application process by a certain deadline, including providing additional forms and documents and attending an interview with a U.S. immigration official, they lose their chance, period.

RESOURCE
For more information on entering the lottery, see the U.S. State Department website at www.travel.state.gov. Click "Diversity Visa (DV) Program."

Employment-based green card. If your new lover has job skills that are in short supply in the United States, an employer may act as a green card sponsor. Your best bet is a large employer that has dealt with immigration matters before and has ongoing contact with an immigration attorney. This is a long and difficult process, but the end result is the permanent right to live in the United States.

Temporary employment visa. Someone who has high-level job skills and can find an employer willing to make a job offer may qualify for one of a variety of temporary work visas. The most well-known of these visas is the H-1B, for workers in specialty occupations requiring at least a bachelor's degree or its equivalent. Another visa, known as the O-1, authorizes entry to persons of extraordinary ability in the sciences, arts, education, business, or athletics. The P visa authorizes entry for internationally recognized athletes and entertainers. For a full list, see the Immigration section of Nolo's website at www.nolo.com. Unfortunately, laborers, domestic workers, and other nonprofessionals won't find any helpful possibilities on this list.

Student visa. Anyone admitted to a U.S. vocational or academic school—which shouldn't be hard to arrange—can apply for a student visa (F-1 or M-1) that will cover the entire length of the school program. The difficult parts about this are usually proving to the U.S. government that the immigrant has enough money to fund the entire stay and plans to go home at the end.

Exchange visitor visa. If your partner finds a program organizing exchange visits, usually for academic or research purposes, a J-1 visa is a possibility. The primary disadvantage to this visa is that it often comes with a requirement that the immigrant go back home for two years before applying for any other visa or a green card.

Countries With Residency Rights for Same-Sex Partners

The rest of the world is moving much faster than the United States in offering immigration rights to same-sex partners. A number of countries, predominantly in Europe, now allow the noncitizen or nonresident partner to apply for permanent residency based on the relationship. Typically, the couple must have first entered into a civil union or lived together for a set period of time (usually two years).

Here are the countries that currently allow permanent residency or other significant immigration benefits through a same-sex partner. However, this is a rapidly changing legal area, so for details on a particular country, or to see whether a country has joined the list, contact a local gay rights organization.

Australia	France	Norway
Belgium	Germany	Portugal
Brazil	Iceland	South Africa
Canada	Israel	Spain
Denmark	Netherlands	Sweden
Finland	New Zealand	United Kingdom

SEE AN EXPERT

Immigration law is highly complex and the USCIS policies are in flux currently. After doing your own research, you may want to seek help from a gay-sensitive immigration attorney. For information and referrals, contact one of the lesbian and gay legal organizations listed in Chapter 11, or Immigration Equality at www.immigrationequality.org—check out their FAQs. Other good resources are the Transgender Law Center at www.transgenderlaw.org and the Immigration Project at The National Center for Lesbian Rights at www.nclrights.org.

Renting a Home Together

If a Landlord Discriminates Against You.. 86

Sharing a Rental... 88

    Your Legal Obligations to the Landlord...89

    Your Obligations to Each Other 90

Sharing One Partner's Rented Home 92

    The Rights and Responsibilities of Your New Housemate 93

    Making Your New Housemate a Subtenant... 94

    Putting Your Agreement in Writing 94

Renter's Insurance.. 96

Moving On 97

Public Benefits and Living Together.. 98

O ne first and favorite act of togetherness for many couples is living together. Sometimes, a couple rents a new apartment or house, making a fresh start, and often one person moves into a place already occupied by the other partner. This chapter discusses how you go about living together in a rental place, as well as discrimination you may face from landlords.

RESOURCE

If you are buying a house together or moving into a home that your partner already owns, look at Chapter 9.

If a Landlord Discriminates Against You

Some states, counties, and cities have laws or regulations that forbid landlords from discriminating against people on the basis of sexual orientation. To find out whether you live in one of these locations, contact the nearest LGBT organization or tenants' rights organization. (Check your local phone book or the Internet to find these groups.)

Even if you're protected by a nondiscrimination ordinance, some landlords may still argue that they don't have to rent to you. One argument a landlord might make is that being forced to rent to a certain type of person—gay men, lesbians, or any unmarried couples—violates their protected religious beliefs. While some state supreme courts have ruled that a nondiscrimination law takes precedence, at least one federal court has ruled otherwise, saying religious convictions prevail and allowing landlords to refuse to rent to gay and lesbian couples. The law that applies to you will depend on where you live, so you will probably need to consult a lawyer or a tenants' rights or gay rights organization to find out what your rights are.

CAUTION

Landlords are allowed to discriminate for legitimate business reasons. Even if you live in a state or city that prohibits discrimination, landlords may reject you if a reasonable landlord would conclude that you're a poor risk—for example, if you have a bad credit history or negative references from other landlords.

If you live in a place with no antidiscrimination ordinance, and a landlord discriminates against you on the basis of your sexual orientation, there's usually not much you can do, short of filing suit and hoping to make some good new law. So the question becomes whether to inform a prospective landlord that you're gay. Your sexual orientation is not the landlord's business, and nothing legally requires you to volunteer the information, so the question is tactical, not legal. Most landlords are concerned with getting the rent on time and having responsible tenants, not with your private life. But if the landlord lives downstairs and is almost sure to figure it out, it may make sense to be candid. (On the other hand, you may want to first get into the place, demonstrate that you are a great tenant, and later share your news, having shown by your actions that sexual orientation doesn't matter.) If the landlord lives halfway across the country, why bother?

Once you're living in your new place, you might be concerned about being evicted if the landlord discovers your relationship. If you rent under a month-to-month tenancy in an area where you have no antidiscrimination protection and there is no rent control, in most places your landlord can simply give you a 30-day notice to get out. If you have a lease for a fixed time or live in a place that requires landlords to have a "just cause" to evict someone, the landlord cannot terminate your tenancy midlease unless you have not paid the rent, have broken another important term of the lease, or are engaging in illegal activity on or near the premises. In addition, you can be evicted if you make too much noise (disturbing the "quiet enjoyment" of your neighbors), damage the apartment and refuse to pay for repairs, or get a pet in violation of a "no pets" clause. Being gay or lesbian is not a "just cause" for eviction.

> ⚠ CAUTION
>
> **Watch out for illegal provisions in your lease or rental agreement.**
> Before signing a lease or rental agreement, ask the landlord to cross off any illegal
> clauses, such as one giving the landlord the right to remove your belongings from
> the premises if you're late with the rent. And even though they may not be illegal,
> watch for clauses prohibiting "immoral behavior" or "association with undesirable
> people." Ask your landlord to cross out the offending language and make sure the
> landlord initials the change.

If your landlord tries to evict you because you're gay and you want
to fight it, you'll have to go to court and file a written response to the
eviction papers and raise the defense of illegal discrimination. Again,
contact a local tenants' rights organization or an LGBT advocacy
organization for help. Keep in mind that when an ordinance prohibits
sexual orientation discrimination in housing, a smart landlord will
probably give a phony nondiscriminatory reason for evicting you.

Sharing a Rental

Whatever relationship you establish with your landlord, for you and
your partner the crux of living together will be the understandings you
work out between yourselves. Don't underestimate the need to be clear.
Renting a place to live isn't only a monetary investment; it should also
provide you with a haven of relaxation and refuge. It's worth a little effort
to ensure that you both will feel secure and protected.

It's vital that you and your partner agree in writing on the basics of
how you'll share your place. Most importantly, make sure that you are
clear about whether you are both renting the place (as cotenants) or only
one of you is the tenant and the other is a subtenant (someone who rents
from the tenant). Your obligations to the landlord and to each other will
be different depending on the setup you choose. ("Sharing One Partner's
Rented Home," below, covers the tenant/subtenant situation.) Also, if you
are married or legally partnered, in some states you may both be on the
hook financially even if only one partner signed the lease.

Your Legal Obligations to the Landlord

If both of you enter into a lease or rental agreement with the landlord, it doesn't matter to the landlord how you split the rent—each of you is independently liable for all the rent and for any damage to the rental, and for complying with all terms of the lease or rental agreement. (Landlords often state this obligation by inserting into the lease a bit of legalese that says that all tenants are "jointly and severally" liable for paying rent and complying with the terms of the agreement.) This means that if one tenant can't pay the agreed-upon share of the rent one month, or simply moves out, the other tenant must still pay the full rent.

As an example, imagine that Sarah and Julie sign a month-to-month rental agreement for $1,500 a month. They agree between themselves to each pay half of the rent. Now, suppose Sarah moves out and stops paying her share. The landlord can demand the full rent from Julie.

TIP

A written agreement can protect you if your partner leaves. If you are left high and dry by a partner in an apartment that you both rented and you end up paying more than your fair share of the rent, you can get your ex-partner to pay you back only if you had an agreement that you would pay rent equally, and that agreement is provable (either because it is in writing or because you can testify to it and show evidence that you each paid half while you lived there). If you did have an agreement, try small claims court to get your ex to pay back what he or she owes you. (You can read about small claims court in *Everybody's Guide to Small Claims Court*, by Ralph Warner (Nolo).) However, it usually doesn't make sense to sue unless you are pretty sure you can collect the money that you win—so if your ex is a determined deadbeat, getting a small claims court judgment may not be worth the effort.

Cotenants' joint and several liability applies to more than just rent. If one partner damages the property or violates a term of the lease, the landlord can evict both tenants.

Your Obligations to Each Other

People sharing a rental unit usually have certain expectations of each other as roommates, even in a romantic relationship. We recommend that you write them down. After all, you sign an agreement with a landlord as a matter of course—why not do the same with each other? If your relationship does end down the line, a written agreement is much more useful than blurry memories about ambiguous discussions. To avoid later problems, write down your understandings when you first move in together.

Below is an example of an agreement covering moving into a newly (jointly) rented living space. A blank version of this form is also included on the companion page (for details see Appendix B). Edit this agreement as you see fit—for example, you can add paragraphs about food expenses, cleaning responsibilities, or anything else that is important to either of you. Be careful, though, if you are married or legally partnered, because there may be marital obligations in your state that trump private contracts.

Some people adopt an approach other than flipping a coin to decide who gets to stay in the event there is a conflict. They have a neutral third person decide, basing the decision on proximity to work, needs of any children, relative financial status, and other relevant facts. This approach can work well, but be careful that if you pick a close friend, you choose someone who can really be neutral, and not end up a friend of only one of you.

Happy Anniversary Candice and Audrey

Like many of the (completely fictional) couples in this book, Candice Dunk and Audrey Rabinowitz have been living together since 1980, when the *Legal Guide for Lesbian and Gay Couples* was first published. We're a little bit surprised that they haven't moved on to a house in Scarsdale, but with rent control, they are probably getting a pretty sweet deal on the Avenue B apartment. In any event, we're happy for them, and we like to think that the clarity they achieved by putting their agreements in writing may have contributed in some small way to the longevity of their relationship.

Sample Renting Together Agreement

Audrey Rabinowitz and Candice Dunk, an unmarried couple, have jointly rented Apartment 6B at 1500 Avenue B, New York, New York. We have both signed a month-to-month rental agreement with the landlord, Sharon Ellis, and have each paid $1,000 toward the security deposit of $2,000.

We agree as follows:

1. We will each pay one-half of the rent directly to the landlord and one-half of the gas, electricity, water, and fixed telephone charge. Each person will pay for her long-distance calls. Our rent will be paid on time and the electricity, gas, water, garbage, and telephone bills will be paid within ten days of receipt.

2. If either wants to leave, she will give the other partner and the landlord at least 30 days' written notice. The person moving agrees to pay her share of the rent (before she moves) for the entire 30-day period, even if she leaves sooner, and to forfeit her share of the security deposit. If the other one stays, she'll be liable for the entire rent as of the next month.

3. We intend to live as a couple, and neither of us wants a large number of houseguests. Therefore, neither of us will invite someone to stay overnight unless we have both agreed to it.

4. If we want to stop living together but both want to remain at this address, a third party will flip a coin to decide who stays. The loser of the coin flip will move out within 30 days and will pay all her obligations for rent, utilities, and any damage to the apartment before moving out, and the other one can stay but will be solely liable for the future rent and must reimburse the other party for her share of the security deposit.

5. Any dispute arising out of this agreement will be mediated by a third person mutually acceptable to both of us. The mediator's role will be to help us arrive at a solution, not to impose one on us.

This agreement is our complete understanding about our living together and replaces any agreements we made before, whether written or oral. It can be modified, but only in a writing signed by both of us.

_1/13/1980_	_Audrey Rabinowitz_
Date	Audrey Rabinowitz
_1/13/1980_	_Candice Dunk_
Date	Candice Dunk

Sharing One Partner's Rented Home

Almost as common as two people looking for a rental home together is one person moving in with the other. This can be simple and smooth where the landlord is reasonable, but can raise tricky problems if the landlord disapproves of same-sex relationships or doesn't want another person to move in for whatever reason. Don't try to argue with someone you know you can't convince. Better to spend your time and energy looking for a place where the landlord is pleasant and accepting.

Sometimes, especially if the landlord lives far away or isn't likely to make waves, it might seem to make more sense to just have your partner move in and worry about the consequences later. However, if your lease or rental agreement requires you to notify your landlord of any plans to add an occupant or limits the number of people who can occupy your unit, you are legally required to advise the landlord that another person plans to move in. Moving in an unauthorized occupant in violation of a lease clause will be grounds for eviction.

Even without such a requirement, it's normally wise to notify your landlord, who will almost surely figure it out anyway. It's especially important to avoid looking sneaky if you have a month-to-month tenancy in a non-rent-control area, where the landlord can evict you for any reason. Whether you tell the landlord that you're lovers or merely roommates is entirely up to you.

Often, landlords want more rent for an additional person. Unless a local rent control law prohibits it or the amount is exorbitant, it's probably better to accept a rent increase than to start apartment hunting. However, you can counteroffer a lower amount, letting the landlord know that the two of you may look elsewhere or you might even move out yourself, if you can't reach an acceptable compromise.

In most jurisdictions, the landlord also has a legal right to change other conditions of the tenancy when a tenant adds a roommate and they sign a new agreement. One change that is particularly likely is an increase in the security deposit. However, this is an area where the sky is not the limit. Many states limit the amount of security deposits, usually to a multiple of the monthly rent.

The Rights and Responsibilities of Your New Housemate

If Jason moves into Peter's apartment, does Jason have a legal relationship with Peter's landlord? More specifically, does Jason have a legal duty to pay rent if Peter fails to? If Peter moves out, does Jason have the right to stay? If Peter damages the kitchen counter or lets his dog scratch the door, does Jason have a legal obligation to pay the landlord for the damage?

Jason can become a full-fledged cotenant and have all the legal rights and responsibilities that go with tenant status, by doing any of the following:

- having the landlord prepare a new lease or rental agreement that includes both Jason and Peter as cotenants
- talking to the landlord and agreeing orally that Jason will become a cotenant. Jason must be careful, however—if the landlord reneges, Jason may have a hard time proving there was an agreement.
- paying rent directly to the landlord or property manager. If Jason does this, especially for a while, an "implied contract," as it is known in legalese, is formed. Nothing formal has been said or written down, but the conduct of both Jason and the landlord creates a landlord-tenant relationship.

TIP

The landlord can't accept rent and then protest. Even if your lease prohibits someone else from moving in, once your landlord accepts rent knowing that you live with someone, many courts will refuse to let the landlord enforce the lease prohibition.

There may be special laws about this where you live. For example, in New York City, landlords are prohibited from evicting a living-together partner if the couple have lived together for at least two years and can show "an emotional and financial commitment and interdependence."

Making Your New Housemate a Subtenant

In some situations, you may not want your new housemate to become a full-fledged tenant with all the same rights and responsibilities that you have. Instead, you may want to set up a tenant-subtenant situation, in which the newcomer becomes your tenant. The subtenant pays rent to you, and has no direct relationship with the landlord. The crucial difference between this arrangement and a cotenant arrangement is that in a tenant-subtenant situation, you have the right to end the subtenancy. When the two of you are cotenants, only the landlord can terminate the tenancy of either or both of you.

This may sound attractive to you because it means you won't lose your apartment if the relationship doesn't work out, but you'll find that most savvy landlords will not allow it. From their point of view, it's always better to have direct relationships with all residents, which allows them to demand the entire rent from any resident. They are also leery of allowing a new resident on their property when they haven't had the opportunity to screen that new person. Don't be surprised if your request to sublet your space is met with a firm "No," and an offer to screen the proposed new resident and—if the screening results are positive—add the new person as a tenant to your lease or rental agreement.

Putting Your Agreement in Writing

Just as you should when you rent a place together, when one partner moves into an apartment or house already rented by the other, it's a good idea to write down your understanding. Most important, make it clear whether you're entering a cotenant or tenant-subtenant arrangement. If you fall into tough times, a question like, "Whose apartment is this?" can come up. If you write down your understanding when you begin living together, you are forced to clarify the issues while you're both loving, not combative. Below is a sample that may help.

The agreement below will work only if the partner who lives in the apartment has already talked to the landlord. For example, in this agreement, Peter promises to sign a new lease with the landlord that includes Roger as a tenant. If Peter hadn't discussed this with his

Sample Moving-In Agreement

Roger Rappan and Peter Majors agree as follows:

1. Roger will move into the apartment that Peter rents at 111 Prairie Street, Chicago, Illinois, on March 1, 20xx. Beginning on that date, Roger will pay Peter one-half of the monthly rent, currently $1,400, on the first of each month. Peter will continue to pay the landlord the entire rental amount on the first of each month for the remainder of the lease term (six months).

2. Peter will continue to pay the electric, gas, water, garbage, and monthly telephone service charges, and Roger will reimburse Peter for one-half of all these expenses, immediately upon Peter's submitting the bills to him.

3. For the first six months, Peter will have the first right to stay in the apartment should he and Roger separate. If either person decides that Roger should move out during this period, he will give (or be given) 30 days' written notice and will be responsible for his share of the rent and all utilities during the 30 days. The partner who remains will be solely liable for any subsequent rent due.

4. After the initial six-month period, if Peter and Roger decide to continue living together, they will both sign a new lease with the landlord.
From this point forward, if they break up but both want to stay in the apartment, a third party chosen by both will flip a coin to determine who gets to stay.

_3/1/20xx_
Date

Roger Rappan
Roger Rappan

_3/1/20xx_
Date

Peter Majors
Peter Majors

landlord and allowed the landlord to screen Roger as a tenant, this is a promise he might not necessarily be able to keep. And he should get the landlord's approval for the initial six-month period, as well—Roger will be a subtenant during that time, and most leases require the landlord to approve any sublease arrangement. (Note that the moving-in agreement might not be valid for a married couple.)

Sometimes getting the landlord's approval for a new lease isn't as easy as it sounds. In New York, for example, a gay couple went to court when their landlord refused to add the second partner's name to the lease, despite the fact that the men had registered with New York City as domestic partners. The State Division of Housing and Community Renewal supported the landlord, and the Court of Appeal supported the agency.

Renter's Insurance

Renter's insurance protects tenants against the loss of their property due to theft or destruction. It's important for you to have this coverage because the landlord's policy covers only the building structure and the landlord's personal property in it, such as appliances—not the tenants' possessions.

Renter's insurance also includes liability coverage, protecting you, for example, if your carelessness causes a fire that damages the building. Landlords are increasingly requiring tenants to carry renter's insurance. (In some states it's unclear whether this requirement is legal, so if your landlord is requiring it and you don't want to pay for it, check with a lawyer or tenants' rights organization.)

You shouldn't have a problem getting a joint renter's insurance policy, but you may not want one. If you are married or legally partnered a joint policy probably makes sense. Under a joint policy, if your personal property is stolen or damaged, the insurance company will write you just one check for the value of the property. It will be up to you and your partner to divide it in a way that's consistent with who owned what, and that can be difficult if you haven't kept careful records.

On the other hand, if you have separate policies, the insurance company will pay each of you only for the property that is yours. If you own property jointly, you can ask for reimbursement for the value of your ownership share of that property (you'll have to show documentation of your ownership percentage).

Having just one policy is cheaper—and means there's only one deductible if you do have a loss—but having two is probably easier in the long run. Renter's insurance is inexpensive, so you won't have to pay that much for a separate policy.

Either way, whether you get a joint policy or each buy an individual policy, you absolutely must keep clear records of what belongs to whom.

> **TIP**
>
> **If you do have to buy two separate insurance policies, use the same insurance company.** Two giant companies asked to settle a claim may each try to shift responsibility to the other, rather than simply pay your claim for stolen or damaged property.

Moving On

What do you do if you decide to go separate ways, and you never made a written agreement specifying who gets the place? If you aren't married or otherwise legally partnered, all you can do is make the best effort to compromise. Here are a few suggestions that may help you through the process.

- If you are in a tenant-subtenant situation, the tenant has the superior claim to the apartment. But the tenant must give the other person the legally required amount of notice—usually 30 days—to move out.
- If you are cotenants—you both pay rent directly to the landlord or both signed a lease or rental agreement—you have equal rights to stay. This is true even if one of you lived there first. Flip a coin or have a third person mediate to help you reach a decision, or decide for you, to settle the dispute. Avoid court action if you can.

- If the rent is a bargain or is protected from dramatic increases by a rent control ordinance, the partner who stays should consider compensating the one who moves for the higher rent the moving partner will have to pay in a new place, at least for a short time.

Public Benefits and Living Together

People who receive public benefits sometimes worry that they will lose those benefits if their partner moves in. The rules vary from state to state, but in many places, having a partner move in can cause problems. This is especially true if you're married, registered as domestic partners, or have entered a civil union.

If you get benefits based on your financial situation and a physical or mental condition—aid to the aged, blind, or disabled, for example—you don't risk any loss. These programs function like Social Security—once you qualify, you're left alone, other than when the agency does routine reviews of recipients.

Welfare and food stamp programs, however, are based on your financial condition only. These programs are often the subject of political attack. As a result, you may be scrutinized in an effort to weed out "welfare cheats."

As a welfare recipient, you are legally required to tell the welfare department of all changes in your circumstances that could affect your grant. This includes living with a partner who may be paying some bills. If you don't report your partner's presence and the department discovers it, you can be penalized, or even have your grant terminated.

If you do report that you're living with a partner, however, you'll face other problems. If the welfare department determines that the other person is contributing money to you, your grant will be reduced, normally by the amount contributed. A person is considered to be contributing whether, for example, she gives $100 a month cash, pays $100 of the rent, pays for food, or buys the kids $100 worth of clothing. Moreover, some state regulations presume that a live-in lover contributes a set amount per month to the family, whether that's actually true or not. And if the partner moves in with you and doesn't contribute toward rent and utilities (or claims that's the case), then the partner may be committing the crime of living off a welfare grant without qualifying for the benefit. This situation is even trickier if you are married or legally partnered. If your benefits come from a state-funded program, your spouse's income may well disqualify you from receiving benefits. But if your benefits are federally funded, then DOMA gives you an "advantage" in that the feds won't recognize your relationship, so your partner's income probably won't disqualify you. Of course, if DOMA is repealed or declared unconstitutional, this won't be true any longer.

The best advice is to treat your lover as a roommate. Under welfare rules, a roommate is not presumed to contribute anything to a welfare recipient. In some counties, welfare officials may require a sworn statement by the roommate that she does not contribute to the recipient's support. Here are some steps to take to back up your statements.

If your total rent exceeds the maximum amount allowed by welfare officials, be sure that your roommate pays at least enough to cover the difference. And make sure the bigger room belongs to your partner.

Keep all finances separate. Make sure you don't have any access to or control over any of your partner's money—or the welfare department will conclude your lover is contributing to the family. Also make sure your partner doesn't have access to your money or the welfare department will conclude your partner is living off your grant.

Buy and store food separately. Keep cupboards marked with each person's name in case of a home visit by the social worker.

Keep a receipt book or ledger. It should show that each of you is paying only one person's share of expenses such as rent and utilities.

Your partner should keep car registration in sole ownership. Yes, all this is quite a hassle, but worth it. Welfare crackdowns come unpredictably and can lead to jail sentences, not just the termination of benefits.

If possible, discuss your situation with a sympathetic caseworker before you set up housekeeping or apply for benefits. Most welfare departments can be a bit easier to deal with if you use a little planning.

If one of you is receiving public assistance or benefits, be very careful how you take title to property or hold your financial assets. It can seem tempting to put or buy all property in the name of the partner who is not receiving public aid. But doing so can cause two serious problems. First, you may be exposing yourselves to claims of welfare fraud. Second, if you separate, the person whose name is "off title" will have a very hard time convincing any judge or jury that the property was jointly owned. In sum, even though we frequently question what passes for the "morality" of government policy, it's bad karma, as well as a bad idea, to lie in order to get or keep public funds.

RESOURCE

All the information you might need to know about your rights as a tenant can be found in *Every Tenant's Legal Guide,* **by Janet Portman and Marcia Stewart.** Californians should take a look at *California Tenants' Rights,* by Janet Portman and David Brown. Both books are published by Nolo.

I'm Mom, She's Mommy (or I'm Daddy, He's Papa)

Legal Parents and the Second-Parent Trap 102

    Legal Parentage 104

    Becoming Parents Together 105

    Protections for Second Parents 107

Having a Child 121

    Donor Insemination 121

    Egg Donation/Ovum Sharing 132

    Surrogacy 133

    When You Have a Child 134

    Lesbians and Gay Men Parenting Together 136

Adopting a Child 138

    Overview of Adoption 139

    Methods of Adoption 140

Foster Parenting 149

    Applying to Become a Foster Parent 150

    Placing Gay Kids (and Kids of Gays) in Gay Homes 152

Becoming a Guardian 153

    Informal Guardianships 154

    Court-Appointed Guardianships 158

Agreements With Teenagers 158

A quiet revolution has been taking place in the realm of lesbian and gay parenting during the last two decades. It is now commonplace for LGBT couples to have and raise children, and courts and legislatures all over the country have been busy making decisions (some good, some bad) about the rights of lesbian and gay couples to adopt their partners' children, adopt children as a couple, and serve as foster parents or legal guardians for minors.

This chapter outlines the various ways that LGBT couples bring children into their lives and establish and protect their legal relationships with those children. Chapter 10, about breakups, deals with what happens when a couple breaks up and there's a dispute about child support, custody, or visitation.

> ⓘ **CAUTION**
>
> **Always make sure you have the most current information on parenting issues.** The law in this area is constantly evolving, and there's not enough space here to provide specifics on every issue for each state. The book contains current information as it goes to press, but you should always check to make sure nothing has changed, and talk to a lawyer about the current law in your state and how it applies to your family. Chapter 11 tells you how to find a lawyer.

Legal Parents and the Second-Parent Trap

For gay and lesbian couples who are planning to have children or are already raising a child together, the question of who the child's legal parents are can be the most important question in the couple's relationship—as well as having great importance to the child. How the partners answer this question, and what steps they take to establish legal parentage, can make all the difference in the world—both when they are together, and if the relationship ends—because only the child's legal parents are entitled to custody and visitation, and only they are responsible for the child's care and support. How the courts define legal parentage also has enormous impact—both on the family that has a question or a dispute about it, and on the larger community.

This section gives an overview of legal parentage, but the entire chapter deals with the parentage question, because it comes into play no matter how children are brought into an LGBT relationship.

Parenting Back in the Day

Perhaps no area of the law relating to the LGBT community has changed more than parenting. A few quotes from the first edition of this book, with notes about what's true now, demonstrate that:

"… In almost all cases, only one of you will be able to have legal custody [of your child]." Now, second-parent adoptions are legally permitted or occur regularly in the majority of states, and are explicitly prohibited in only a few. There are thousands of same-sex couples parenting together in which both partners have equal parental rights.

"While there are no laws prohibiting lesbians or gays from adopting a child, in practice it is very rare." Not so anymore! Single lesbians and gay men, and same-sex couples all over the country, adopt children these days. Of course, there are still some states where it is difficult, if not impossible. But overall, adoption has gone from being "very rare" to being extremely common. Even Florida's long-standing ban on gays' and lesbians' adopting children was overturned in 2010.

"We hope that in a few years, as lesbian/gay adoptions become more common and prejudice diminishes, forms will be developed so that homo-sexuals can routinely handle their own legal work." While many same-sex couples choose to hire a lawyer, it is finally starting to be possible for parents to handle adoptions themselves in some places.

"Recently, there have been reports in the newspapers about men who advertise for a woman to bear their child …." In 1980, when the first edition was published, the term "surrogacy" did not even exist. Now, it's not at all uncommon for gay men to contract with a surrogate to bear a child for them. It's not legal in all states, but where it is, gay men are definitely taking advantage of their opportunity to have a child who is biologically related to at least one partner.

And, new law on the rights of lesbian and gay parents is being created regularly.

Legal Parentage

A legal parent is a person who has the right to live with a child and make decisions about the child's health, education, and well-being. Legal parents have a legal obligation to care for the child and support the child financially.

When a heterosexual married couple has a child or adopts a child together, both spouses are automatically considered legal parents. As a result, both have all the rights and responsibilities of legal parents. And if they split up, they both remain legal parents and each has a right to visitation and an obligation of support. Parentage ends only if a court terminates a mother or father's parental rights. A court will terminate parental rights only if a parent consents to the adoption of the child by the other parent's new spouse (or, in some states, new same-sex partner), a parent abandons a child and someone else wants to adopt the child, or the child becomes a ward of the court because of abuse or neglect.

In the states that offer marriage or marriage-equivalent registration, same-sex parents are supposed to be treated like married parents in relation to children born into the marriage, domestic partnership, or civil union. In addition, the law in the District of Columbia provides that when a woman bears a child conceived by artificial insemination and her spouse, unmarried partner, or chosen second parent consents in writing to the insemination, the consenting spouse or partner is a legal parent and that person's name will appear as a parent on the child's birth certificate. However, because the federal government—and many other states—don't recognize the same-sex relationship or any of the benefits the state attaches to that relationship, it's still wise for same-sex parents to see an attorney for advice and to complete an adoption on behalf of the nonbiological or nonlegal parent. And outside of the marriage-equality and marriage-equivalent states, there is no automatic presumption that both partners in a same-sex couple are legal parents—but there are ways that LGBT couples can become parents together at the same time. These are described below. If you don't become parents together, then only the biological or original adoptive parent is considered a legal parent unless and until you take steps to establish a legal relationship between the child and the other parent. These steps are described in "Protections for Second Parents," below.

That other parent is often called a "second parent" because there is often no automatic legal relationship between that parent and the child, as there is with the biological or adoptive parent, who is a legal parent from the beginning of her relationship with the child. And the hard reality is that in this situation, the legal parent has a great deal of legal power. In every state, courts give enormous deference to legal parents in allowing them to make decisions about their children, including who will have contact with those children in the event the relationship ends.

For the most part, if your relationship with a child is not acknowledged through a marriage, domestic partnership, or civil union, through a second-parent or stepparent adoption, or through a Uniform Parentage Act action, then you are a legal stranger to the child and you don't have any right to share custody or seek visitation. Moreover, your child won't have any right to inherit from you or to receive Social Security or other benefits upon your death. This is true even if you have parented a child for many years, the child considers you a parent, and you are prepared to accept all of the responsibilities of parenting.

There may be a slight trend in the other direction as some states allow arguments that second parents are, but overall, there's no doubt that second parents are second-class citizens.

Because of this, it's tremendously important that you take every available step to cement a legal relationship between the child and the second parent wherever possible. If you live in a state where that is not possible, then do everything else you can do to support and protect the relationship. That's what this section is all about.

Becoming Parents Together

There are a few ways that both parents can be legal parents from the beginning and so avoid ending up in the second-parent trap:

- **Enter into a marriage or a marriage-like relationship.** If you live in a marriage or marriage-equivalent state, you generally can secure the same rights as married couples when it comes to children who are born while you are in the legal relationship. In these states, both partners are considered legal parents of any child born into the marriage.

CAUTION

Even in states where there is a presumption of parentage, it's a good idea to do an adoption to protect the second parent's rights. In marriage-equality and marriage-equivalent states, the law presumes that both partners are parents of a child born after the date of marriage, registration, or civil union. However, many legal experts feel this presumption—and therefore, your status as a parent—may not apply outside of the home state. If you travel across state lines, a birth certificate showing both partners as legal parents may not be respected in some of the states that currently refuse to recognize same-sex relationships, or by the federal government. Because an adoption decree is much more likely to command another state's respect, we recommend that the second parent proceed with an adoption, even if your home state grants parental status automatically.

- **Adopt a child jointly—if your state allows it.** In some locations, social services agencies welcome same-sex couples willing to adopt hard-to-place children, and courts are just as happy to grant these adoptions. But other courts and legislatures have blocked joint adoptions by lesbian and gay couples—and in some states, what is allowed one year or in one particular county may not be okay in a different time or place. "Adopting a Child," below, covers ways to adopt a child, including joint adoption.
- **Use egg donation to conceive a child.** With egg (ovum) donation, an option that for obvious reasons is available only to lesbian couples, one partner contributes the egg, which is then fertilized and implanted in the other partner's womb. Because one partner has a genetic connection with the child, and the other gives birth, in many states both are considered legal parents. Even in those states there is some paperwork required to have a court confirm that both partners are legal parents. But this paperwork can often

be done before the child is born, so that from the moment of birth, it's clear that both partners are parents. However, if the egg donor mom doesn't get some kind of legal validation of her role, parentage questions can remain. Ovum donation is quite expensive and medically rather invasive, but it is an option some families are using successfully.

Protections for Second Parents

The following sections cover court procedures—like adoption and Uniform Parentage Act procedures—through which you can establish a legal relationship between a second parent and a child, and other steps you can take to protect the relationship between the second parent and the child.

Second-Parent Adoption, Domestic Partner Adoption, and Other Court Methods

In a second-parent or domestic partner adoption, the nonbiological or nonlegal second parent adopts a partner's biological or adoptive child. The adoption does not change the rights of the original parent, except that legal parental rights are shared equally between the two parents after the adoption. Through this process, both partners become legal parents with exactly the same rights and responsibilities toward the child.

The process protects both parents and child. After the adoption, the original parent can rely on the second parent's legal duty to support and care for the child, even if the relationship ends. The second parent can feel secure in the parent-child relationship because he or she is entitled to make parenting decisions along with his or her partner and will be able to maintain a relationship with the child even if the couple's relationship ends. And the child gains the security and stability of having two legal parents, who will both have legal rights even if the couple breaks up.

Below is a chart that shows how each state in the United States treats second-parent adoption. In the states where second-parent adoption is allowed in *all* courts, either the legislature has passed a law expressly allowing second-parent adoption or a court with the authority to bind other courts has ruled that the adoptions are legal. In the states where second-parent adoption is allowed in *some* courts, there are no binding laws or court decisions, but individual judges have granted adoptions in certain counties. Only four states have expressly prohibited second-parent adoption, but some of the remaining states that have no laws or court decisions addressing the issue are not exactly friendly venues for same-sex parents.

> CAUTION
>
> **Remember, things change quickly in this area of the law.** Make sure you check the National Center for Lesbian Rights website (www.nclrights.org) for up-to-date information, or contact a lawyer in your local area to find out the status of second-parent adoption where you live.

The procedures for second-parent adoptions vary from state to state, but in general, the process is very similar to that for any other adoption— with the important exception that the first legal parent's rights are not terminated when the adoption becomes final.

The adoption almost always involves a home visit by a social worker, who evaluates the adopting parent's fitness. In some states, there is also a requirement that the legal parent agreeing to the adoption attend a counseling session with a therapist to make sure he or she has considered the decision carefully. There is usually a substantial amount of paperwork required by the social services agency, giving them your personal, employment, and health history. At the end of the process you must make a trip to court, where a judge asks some questions and signs an order granting the adoption and making the second parent a full legal parent. In most states, the state registrar will issue a new birth certificate showing both partners as the child's legal parents. (See "Getting a New Birth Certificate After a Second-Parent Adoption," below.)

In some states, second-parent adoptions are done using the same process that the courts use for stepparent adoptions—adoptions done by the spouse of a legal parent. Stepparent adoptions usually are much simpler and less expensive than other adoptions, because of the privileged status of marriage in our society. In California, registered domestic partners can adopt their partners' kids under stepparent procedures—making the adoption significantly cheaper and six months faster than it was before. Even now, with domestic partnership rules offering a presumption of parentage, we recommend that California parents complete a stepparent adoption. In Washington, the courts also handle second-parent adoptions under stepparent adoption laws.

TIP

Even if you've broken up, it's sometimes still possible to do an adoption. If you and your partner aren't together anymore, but still want the second parent to have a legal relationship with the child, in some places you can go ahead with the adoption. Talk to a lawyer in your area.

The Internal Revenue Code provides for a tax credit for adoption expenses that most same-sex couples can take advantage of. It's not a deduction, but a dollar-for-dollar credit that offsets any tax liability that you would otherwise have (but you don't get a refund if you wouldn't otherwise owe anything). The maximum credit amount for 2010 was $13,170, and your adjusted gross income had to be less than $182,520 to qualify for the full credit. If its higher, you can get a partial credit. Check out www.irs.gov and search for "adoption" or for Form 8839 and its accompanying instructions for more information about the tax credit.

Challenges to Second-Parent Adoptions

As time passes and some couples who completed stepparent and second-parent adoptions end their relationships, inevitably some biological/legal parents challenge their partner's adoption. Rulings on these cases are remarkably consistent, with challenges to second-parent adoptions being rejected even in states as unfriendly as Oklahoma, North Carolina, and, in a landmark decision in 2009, Florida.

Second-Parent Adoption in the United States				
State	Second-Parent Adoption Allowed in All Courts	Second-Parent Adoption Allowed in Some Courts	Second-Parent Adoption Prohibited	No Specific Laws or Court Decisions
Alabama		X		
Alaska		X		
Arizona				X
Arkansas			X	
California	X			
Colorado	X			
Connecticut	X			
Delaware	X			
D.C.	X			
Florida	X			
Georgia		X		
Hawaii		X		
Idaho				X
Illinois	X			
Indiana	X			
Iowa	X			
Kansas				X
Kentucky				X
Louisiana		X		
Maine	X			
Maryland		X		
Massachusetts	X			
Michigan		X		
Minnesota		X		
Mississippi				X

Second-Parent Adoption in the United States (continued)				
State	Second-Parent Adoption Allowed in All Courts	Second-Parent Adoption Allowed in Some Courts	Second-Parent Adoption Prohibited	No Specific Laws or Court Decisions
Missouri				X
Montana		X		
Nebraska			X	
Nevada	X			
New Hampshire	X			
New Jersey	X			
New Mexico		X		
New York	X			
North Carolina			X	
North Dakota				X
Ohio			X	
Oklahoma				X
Oregon	X			
Pennsylvania	X			
Rhode Island		X		
South Carolina				X
South Dakota				X
Tennessee			X	
Texas		X		
Utah			X	
Vermont	X			
Virginia				X
Washington	X			
West Virginia				X
Wisconsin			X	
Wyoming				X

SEE AN EXPERT

In most states, you should have a lawyer's help with an adoption. There are a few places where same-sex adoptions are so routine that you can represent yourselves, including some counties in California. But in most states, a lawyer's help will be required.

Getting a New Birth Certificate After a Second-Parent Adoption

After a second-parent adoption is complete, in most cases you can amend the child's birth certificate to show both partners as legal parents. The birth certificate is an important legal document that you will use to register the child for school, get the child a passport, and for many other purposes. In most states, the registrar in the county where your adoption was granted will send the adoption decree to the vital statistics department of your state, and the state will automatically issue a new birth certificate.

However, if your child was born in a state that doesn't recognize same-sex parents, you may have a problem. Some of those states simply refuse to issue a new birth certificate showing two parents of the same sex, and there is no law that says that they have to. A couple of recent cases offer a glimmer of hope, though—in 2005, the Virginia Supreme Court ruled that the state had to issue a new birth certificate for children adopted by same-sex parents. Likewise, a federal court ruled that the Oklahoma State Department of Health must prepare new birth certificates for children born there and adopted by same-sex parents.

A Louisiana District Court Judge ordered state officials to issue a new birth certificate for a Louisiana-born child adopted in New York State by two gay men, but that decision was later reversed by appeals courts.

If your child was born in a state where two parents of the same sex can be listed on the birth certificate at the child's birth, you won't need to make a change after the adoption.

CAUTION

Don't try putting a second parent's name on the birth certificate at birth if you don't live in a state where that's allowed. It's fraud, for one, and it will also cause delays when you file for a second-parent adoption.

In some states where second-parent adoption is not an option, lesbian and gay couples have sought recognition for second parents under a law called the Uniform Parentage Act (UPA). The UPA is a way that states are trying to provide some consistency from state to state in how parentage is determined.

The UPA is being developed and revised by a group called the National Conference of Commissioners of Uniform State Laws. It provides a framework for states to conform with the federal law that requires them to provide for parentage proceedings, but states don't have to adopt all the provisions of the UPA, and most don't—they set up their own rules about parentage. The most recent version of the UPA came out in 2002. No state has adopted it verbatim, but quite a few states have enacted a version that's pretty close.

In a few of these states, courts have recognized second parents under the UPA. The law says that a person who treats a child as his or her own child, including holding the child out as his or her child and receiving the child into the person's home, can be considered a legal parent. Some trial courts have accepted this as a basis for considering a same-sex second parent a legal parent—and a case challenging a UPA judgment in California failed, so that the court order was secure.

There are some important court decisions that relate to heterosexual relationships, holding that a person who intends to be a parent and/or acts like a parent should be considered a legal parent, even if they don't have a biological connection to the child. Some of these cases are *In re Marriage of Buzzanca*, 61 Cal.App.4th 1410 (1998); *In re Nicholas H.*, 28 Cal.4th 56 (2002); *N.A.H. v. S.L.S.*, 9 P.3d 354 (Colo. 2000); *Ohning v. Driskill*, 739 N.E. 161 (Ind. 2000); and *Stitham v. Henderson*, 768 A.2d 598 (Me. 2001).

The other situation where the UPA is relevant is for gay men who conceive a child using a surrogate. The section called "Surrogacy," below, discusses the UPA in that context.

Third and Fourth Parents

For lesbian couples coparenting with a known donor, there is a difficult bind: Usually, only two of the three (or four, if the donor has a partner) people involved in parenting the child can actually be legal parents.

Either the donor or the lesbian second parent must live in a legal limbo, taking full responsibility for the child's upbringing but enjoying little protection for that relationship.

In a few instances, courts have granted adoptions to third parents—usually the lesbian partner of the biological mother, where the biological mother and the sperm donor are named on the child's original birth certificate. In this case, an addendum is attached to the birth certificate showing that the child has three legal parents. Most of these third-parent adoptions have been granted in the San Francisco Bay Area, where courts are fairly open-minded, although in early 2007, the Ontario, Canada, Court of Appeals ruled that a child can have three parents—a lesbian mother, her partner, and the sperm donor. Other California courts, and courts elsewhere, have refused to even consider the possibility of a child having more than two parents, often because the social workers and judges believe that the more parents there are, the more likely it is that there will be litigation over custody or visitation if the family structure dissolves. And ironically, as marriage and marriage-like relationships make LGBT families a bit more mainstream, courts are becoming reluctant to create relationships that are outside of the standard structure of two parents and children. This means that extended or blended families will have a harder time gaining recognition for parent-child relationships.

If you are in a family with more than two fully participating parents, and you want to test the waters, consult an attorney who has expertise in this area. (See Chapter 11 for advice on finding an attorney.)

Private Agreements

You may live in a state where you can't go to court to get legal acknowledgment for the second parent. Or you may have other reasons for not establishing a legal relationship between the second parent and the child—for example, if the child already has two legal parents because one partner was in a heterosexual marriage or the sperm donor is a legal parent. Even if you can't create a legal parent-child relationship, there are still steps you can take to support and protect the second parent's relationship with the child.

One way to do this is for the legal parent to make a will nominating the second parent as personal guardian for the child. If the legal parent dies, and a court needs to appoint a guardian to raise the child, the court will look at what the will says. The court is not bound to follow the nomination, but in most cases the parent's wishes will be followed. (Chapter 7 has more about nominating a guardian, and a sample will.) This can protect a second parent from losing a child to the legal parent's family members when a legal parent dies. In addition to the will, the legal parent should prepare and sign two other documents:

- a nomination of guardian form, stating his or her wishes about who should care for the child if he or she can't because of physical or mental incapacity (a sample nomination of guardian form is shown below), and

- an authorization to consent to medical treatment for the child, so that the second parent can legally make medical decisions in the legal parent's absence. A sample form is below, in the section on guardianships.

You can also make written agreements with your partner about your intentions to parent together. In most cases, these agreements won't be enforceable if one person fails to abide by the terms, because courts will allow the legal parent to call the shots. A legal parent who really wants to keep the second parent away from a child will be able to in most states. (Chapter 10 has more about this.)

But the agreement may serve to remind you later of your intent to parent together, and in some situations a judge might give it some attention as evidence of a parent-child relationship. It encourages you to think more clearly about your plans, and it provides a basis for making decisions later if your relationship ends. Most importantly, it provides the occasion for talking out your concerns and reaching agreement on the key issues about how you will parent together, which by itself may reduce the chances of a conflict later on.

Two sample coparenting agreements and a sample guardian nomination form are below. Blank versions of the agreements and guardian nomination are included on the companion page. Insert the appropriate names and delete unused options and instructions to create forms that you can use.

Agreement to Jointly Raise Our Child

We, Erica Lang and Maria Ramos, make this agreement to set out our rights and obligations regarding our child, Chloe, who is Erica's biological child but whom we parent together. We realize that our power to contract, as far as a child is concerned, is limited by state law. We also understand that current law recognizes Erica as the only mother of the child. With this knowledge, and in a spirit of cooperation and mutual respect, we agree that:

1. It's our intention to parent jointly and equally, with both of us providing support and guidance to our child. We will do our best to jointly share the responsibilities involved in feeding, clothing, loving, raising, and disciplining Chloe.

2. Erica has signed a consent for medical authorization giving Maria equal power to make medical decisions she thinks are necessary for Chloe. She agrees not to revoke the authorization.

3. We are both responsible for Chloe's financial support until she turns 18 or finishes college. We will each contribute to Chloe's support equally. This agreement to provide support is intended to be binding whether or not we live together.

4. Our child has been given the last name "Ramos-Lang."

5. Erica agrees to nominate Maria as executor of Erica's estate and as guardian of Chloe in her will and in a guardianship nomination form. We understand that designating Maria as the legal guardian of the child will not be legally effective until affirmed by the appropriate court. Erica is making this nomination because Maria is Erica's coparent, and because of Maria's long-standing, close relationship with Chloe.

6. Because of the possible trauma our separation might cause Chloe, we agree to participate in a jointly agreed-upon program of counseling if either of us considers separating from the other.

7. If we separate, we will both do our best to see that Chloe grows up in a healthy environment. Specifically, we agree that:

   a. We will do our best to see that Chloe maintains a close and loving relationship with each of us.

   b. We will do our best to shield Chloe from any conflict between us.

   c. We will share in Chloe's upbringing, and will share in her support, depending on our needs, Chloe's needs, and on our respective abilities to pay.

   d. We will make a good-faith effort to jointly make all major decisions affecting Chloe's health and welfare.

   e. We will base all decisions upon the best interests of Chloe.

   f. Should Chloe spend a greater portion of the year living with one of us, the person who has actual physical custody will take all steps necessary to maximize the other's visitation, and help make visitation as easy as possible.

   g. If either of us dies, Chloe will be cared for and raised by the other, whether or not we were living together at the time of the death. We will each state this in our wills.

8. Should any dispute arise between us regarding this agreement, we agree to submit the dispute first to mediation. If mediation is not successful, we agree to submit to binding arbitration, sharing the cost equally. In the event of such dispute, the arbitrator will be _____ . [See Chapter 10 for more detailed information on arbitration and mediation.]

9. We agree that if any court finds any portion of this contract illegal or otherwise unenforceable, the rest of the contract is still valid and in full force.

1/14/20xx	*Erica Lang*
Date	Erica Lang
1/14/20xx	*Maria Ramos*
Date	Maria Ramos

Here is a more formal version of a parenting agreement.

Parenting Agreement

This Agreement is made on August 1, 20xx, between Janice Borne ("Janice") and Joanne Amore ("Joanne") of Ann Arbor, Michigan, regarding the parenting of the minor child Nina Christine Borne ("Nina").

The parties agree as follows:

1. This agreement concerns the parenting of Nina, who was born to Janice on May 1, 20xx. Nina is being raised in the home of Janice and Joanne and is equally bonded to both women in mother-child relationships. Janice is the sole legal parent of Nina. The parties intend, however, that Nina shall continue to be raised by both Janice and Joanne until she is an adult.

2. Nina will be raised by both Janice and Joanne in their shared home.

3. Even though Joanne is not Nina's biological parent, she has participated in Nina's upbringing since birth, and she and Janice made the decision together to have a child. Joanne has attained the status of psychological and/or de facto parent to Nina. It is in Nina's best interests to maintain a parent-child relationship with both Joanne and Janice. Joanne shall have the same rights and obligations as if she were Nina's biological parent. Should any dispute arise between the parties, Janice will not assert that Joanne is not Nina's parent or that she has any lesser parental status because she is not a legal parent.

4. Joanne and Janice will be equally responsible for supporting Nina financially. They may agree from time to time to contribute unequal amounts to Nina's support.

5. If Janice and Joanne separate and no longer live together, their separation will not alter their relationships to Nina. The parties will continue to share parenting responsibilities and each will have a right to legal custody and visitation. The parties will work cooperatively to make arrangements for physical custody and/or visitation by each party, and shall continue to share equally in financial responsibility for Nina.

6. In the event of any dispute between Janice and Joanne regarding the custody, care, financial support, or upbringing of Nina, they will attend mediation sessions to resolve the dispute. They will participate in at least four mediation sessions, to be held weekly, with the cost of the mediation

to be shared equally by the parties. The parties will select the mediator together and if they can't agree, they will ask their friend, Daphne Wood, to choose a mediator.

7. The District Court of the State of Michigan shall have jurisdiction to resolve all matters regarding Nina's custody, visitation, and support. Each party will allow the participation of the other party in any court proceeding to determine parentage, custody, visitation, and/or support of Nina, without any jurisdictional objection.

8. If either party incurs any attorneys' fees or costs in a court proceeding regarding Nina, then the court will have the right to award attorneys' fees and costs as provided by this state's family code, even though the proceedings may be in a parentage or another action rather than in a dissolution or separation proceeding.

9. Janice nominates Joanne as the personal and property guardian of Nina in the event that Janice becomes unable to care for Nina, to serve without bond. If Joanne cannot serve as Nina's guardian, then Janice's mother, Hermine Borne, shall serve as personal and property guardian.

10. This agreement is the only agreement between the parties with respect to Nina. It may be waived, altered, or modified only with the written consent of both parties. In the event that any part of this agreement is held to be invalid, the remainder of the agreement shall be in full force and effect.

IN WITNESS THEREOF, the parties to this agreement have executed this agreement on the date and year written below.

_8/1/20xx_
Date

Janice Borne
Janice Borne

_8/1/20xx_
Date

Joanne Amore
Joanne Amore

Nomination of Guardian for a Minor

1. I, Sara Wilson, the biological parent of the minor child Jacob Fong-Wilson, who was born on July 15, 20xx, declare my wishes as to the individuals to be appointed the legal guardian of the person and property of my son in the event that I am unable, physically or mentally, to care for my child.

2. I nominate Andrea Fong, currently residing at 220 Main Street, Springfield, California, to be the legal guardian of Jacob's person and property. This nomination is based on the fact that a loving and parental relationship exists between Andrea and Jacob. My son has lived with Andrea his whole life and looks to her for guidance, support, and affection. It would be detrimental to deprive him of this established relationship at a time when I am unable to provide the security and care necessary to his healthy development.

3. If Andrea Fong is unable to serve as a guardian or is disqualified by a court of law from serving, I nominate Mona Wasserman to serve as the guardian of the person and property of the minor child Jacob Fong-Wilson.

4. Both the identity and whereabouts of the minor child's natural father are unknown to me. [Or The minor child was conceived through alternative insemination by donor and has no natural father.] [Or The minor child was conceived through donor insemination, and the donor waived, in writing, any and all rights he may have to object to my nomination of a guardian.]

5. I have purposefully not nominated my parents or siblings to be the guardians of my child in the event of my disability because they lack an established, close, and warm relationship with my child, and I believe it would be detrimental to Jacob to remove him from Andrea and place him with adults who are, for all practical purposes, strangers.

Executed this 4th day of May, 20xx, at Springfield, California.

_____

Sara Wilson

Witnesses:

_____   _____
Name   Signature

_____
Home address and telephone number

_____   _____
Name   Signature

_____
Home address and telephone number

Guardian Nomination form by the National Center for Lesbian Rights, www.nclrights.org. Reprinted with permission.

TIP

Honor your agreements. A coparenting agreement should specify that although only one of you is the legal parent, both of you consider yourselves parents. Include a mandatory mediation clause in your agreement to express your commitment not to run right off to court if your relationship ends and you are in conflict. And if your relationship does end, honor the agreement, whether or not a judge orders you to do so. Remember that at one time you loved and trusted each other, and felt strongly enough that you could parent together that you went ahead and had a child. If you get in a lengthy battle over your child, the person who will be hurt the most is that child. Take the time to read—and be sure you honor—the standards proposed by Gay & Lesbian Advocates & Defenders (GLAD) in Boston, called "Protecting Families: Standards for LGBT Families." You can download the guide at www.glad.org/protecting_families.

Having a Child

Lesbians and gay men have a number of options if they want to conceive children. Lesbians can use donor insemination, from a donor they know or an anonymous donor. Lesbian couples also have the option of egg (ovum) donation, where one partner contributes the egg and the other partner gestates the child. In many states, gay men can ask—and sometimes pay—a surrogate to carry a child who will be biologically related to one of the partners. Each of these scenarios has legal ramifications.

Donor Insemination

Donor insemination is probably the most common way that lesbians conceive children. In donor insemination, fresh or previously frozen donor sperm is injected into a woman's uterus to try to fertilize an egg and establish a pregnancy. There are many advantages to conceiving this way—first and foremost, the child conceived has a biological connection with at least one partner in the couple. Donor insemination can often be accomplished without medical personnel or any great expertise—although from a legal point of view, using a physician is normally advisable (see "Using a Known Donor," below, for more). If the couple uses a sperm bank, they can choose not to know the donor's identity, and thus be sure that no one outside of the relationship will claim parentage of the child.

If you decide to have a child by donor insemination, you must make a critical decision: whether to use a donor who is known to you or purchase sperm from a sperm bank without knowing the identity of the donor.

Insemination or Discrimination?

A California lesbian filed suit after a fertility clinic denied her treatment because of her sexual orientation. The doctors claimed that their refusal to treat the woman was because of religious objections to treating unmarried women, not because of homophobia. The California Supreme Court held that physicians cannot deny medical treatment to patients on the basis of sexual orientation. (*Benitez v. North Coast Medical Center*, 44 Cal.4th 1145 (2008).)

Using an Anonymous Donor

In every state, choosing an anonymous donor is the only way to absolutely guarantee that you will never have to face the issue of the donor seeking parental rights or visitation with your child. As you'll read below, using a known donor and making sure a physician is involved is also a way to protect yourselves, but it isn't foolproof.

If you use an anonymous donor, you can choose based on any criteria, including race, religion, and even height. Most sperm banks and physicians providing insemination services require that donors provide a thorough medical history (including illnesses of parents and grandparents) and be tested for diseases—both acquired (such as syphilis and AIDS) and hereditary (such as sickle-cell anemia).

Some women object to using an anonymous donor because choosing a donor through a sperm bank feels too impersonal, because they don't want medical intervention, or because they are afraid that if the child develops a genetic disease it might be impossible to find the donor to get medical information. All of these concerns are important, and would-be parents simply have to weigh these risks and negatives against the risks of using a known donor, discussed below.

One option to alleviate concern about never knowing the donor's identity is to choose an anonymous donor who agrees to be identified when the child becomes an adult. In many states, sperm banks give donors the option to allow disclosure of their personal information to a child conceived by use of their sperm at the time the child turns 18. If this is something you want, check to see whether sperm banks in your area offer this option, and ask for a donor who has agreed to the disclosure. Many women feel this is a good compromise, allowing the child to learn about the donor while still protecting the couple's parental rights.

Landmark District of Columbia Law Goes Into Effect

As of July 2009, the District of Columbia has a new law that states that a person who consents—in writing—to a woman's insemination with the intent to be a parent of the resulting child is a parent of the child. The law is important because it means lesbian couples intending to parent together can ensure that both of them are treated as parents from the moment of the child's birth. The law is also unique because it is neutral as to both gender and marital status—in other words, it doesn't matter whether the person consenting is male or female, or whether the two parents are married, domestically partnered, or have no legal relationship at all.

If there is no written consent, it is still possible to prove the consent and the intent to parent by the behavior of the couple holding the child out as their own. Until this law was adopted, the birth mother's partner could become a parent only through a second-parent adoption. Under the law, a semen donor is not a parent unless he and the birth mother have an agreement in writing saying that he is.

A similar law went into effect in New Mexico on January 1, 2010, and an appellate court decision in Oregon essentially reached the same result by interpreting a statute.

Using a Known Donor

Many lesbians ask someone they know to donate sperm. There are lots of good reasons for this. You will have access to medical information whenever you need it; you can see the person's physical, emotional, and intellectual characteristics first-hand, rather than on a piece of paper; and you have the option of involving the donor in the child's life to whatever extent you and the donor agree is desirable. Some couples ask a brother or another relative of the nonbiological mom to be the donor, so that the child has a genetic relationship to both parents. Some ask a trusted friend. Another option is to have a friend select the donor, so that the parents and the donor don't know each other, but the friend knows both identities.

If you use a donor whose identity is known to you (or a friend has permission to disclose it to you if necessary), you will have another important choice to make: whether to involve a doctor in the insemination process. This is an enormously significant choice from a legal perspective, because if a doctor or a doctor-supervised sperm bank is not involved, the sperm donor may be considered your child's legal father.

Some lesbian couples want to conduct the insemination process without any involvement by a doctor. The main advantages to this are that you are able to preserve the intimacy of the conception process, and you can use fresh sperm, which increases the chances of conception—but which most doctors are no longer willing to do because of the risk of latent illness in the semen and strict regulation of semen handling by the FDA.

But if you do a home insemination with a known donor, in most states the donor will then be the legal father of any child born from the insemination. In order for the second parent to complete an adoption, the donor will have to consent to termination of his parental rights. And if he refuses to do so, in most states you will have an uphill battle to terminate his rights. (Some states do offer you some protection. In Oregon, for example, a man who donates sperm for use in donor insemination with a woman other than his wife loses all parental rights unless he and the woman make an agreement giving him those rights. (*McIntyre v. Crouch*, 98 Or.App. 462, 780 P.2d 239 (1989).)

If, however, you involve a doctor in the process, the donor probably will not have any parental rights. In a number of states, including California, Colorado, and Illinois, the law says that if a donor provides sperm to a doctor for use in an artificial insemination with a woman who is not the donor's wife, the donor is not considered the legal father. So, even if you use a known donor, if you involve a doctor in the process the donor won't be considered the father. Several other states have similar laws—however, those states insert the word "married" before the word "woman," leaving open the questions of the effect of the law on unmarried women.

"Licensed physician" means a medical doctor, not a nurse, nurse practitioner, or midwife. In Georgia and Idaho, only a licensed physician can perform an insemination—otherwise it's considered practicing medicine without a license. And in one California case, a court held that where a licensed physician hadn't been used, the known donor was the legal father of the child and was entitled to full parental rights and responsibilities, over the mother's objections. (*Jhordan C. v. Mary K.*, 179 Cal.App.3d 386 (1986).)

Using a doctor doesn't always mean you will have to do the insemination at the doctor's office. Many state laws refer to semen "provided to a licensed physician for use in insemination," but don't specify that the doctor actually must perform the insemination. If your donor deposits sperm with the sperm bank, you can pick it up later and do the insemination yourselves, at home. Sperm banks are generally under the supervision of licensed physicians, so this process should meet the legal requirements. But make sure that the sperm bank will provide you with a letter saying that the semen was provided to a doctor even if you do the insemination at home—you need such a letter for purposes of an adoption or to show that the donor is not a legal father.

Recent Cases Involving Sperm Donors

In recent years, there has been a spate of cases involving sperm donors, not all involving lesbians but all potentially affecting same-sex partners.

- The Kansas Supreme Court held that a law requiring that an agreement to give a sperm donor parental rights must be in writing was constitutional—in other words, if there was no written agreement to the contrary, the donor was not a dad. The sperm donor in that case wanted parental rights, and the court denied the petition.

- In a Connecticut case, a trial court allowed a sperm donor to sue for custody and visitation based on the fact that both the donor and the lesbian mother signed written acknowledgments of the donor's paternity. This doesn't mean he'll actually get visitation, only that he gets his day in court.

- The New Mexico Court of Appeals ruled in 2008 that a written agreement between a lesbian and a sperm donor excusing the donor from child support obligations was unenforceable, and that the donor could be held responsible for supporting the children. A New York court reached the same conclusion with regard to a sperm donor even though 18 years had passed since he donated the sperm.

- A man donated sperm to a lesbian couple in Ohio and, despite their agreement that he would not be a parent, got a court order of paternity. The county child support agency immediately ordered him to pay child support, and although he objected to the support order, he didn't challenge the paternity determination, which he had wanted. The support order withstood the challenge, so he remained a legal father with an obligation to pay support.

- An Indiana man served as donor for a friend and her lesbian partner, and they signed a donor agreement in which the donor agreed not to seek paternity and the women agreed not to seek support. After the women's relationship ended, the biological mother sought support from the donor. The mother challenged the contract, but the court held that it was valid. In order to find otherwise, the judge said, the mother would have had to prove that the insemination occurred through intercourse so that the rule requiring a physician's involvement didn't apply. Because the mother hadn't proved that, the donor wasn't a legal father.

(!) CAUTION

Be careful about donor contact with the child at first. Even though these laws are clear about the donor not being a legal father, they are not completely foolproof. If the donor spends a lot of time with the child, tells others that the child is his, brings the child into his home, and otherwise treats the child as his own, some courts might consider him a legal father—especially if you have consented to all of this contact. If you use a known donor and you expect him to be involved in the child's life but want your partner to adopt the child, it's prudent to limit the donor's involvement with the child until the adoption is final. Even after the adoption is final, many states allow the donor to bring a parentage action within the first two years of the child's life. And if you have fostered a parent-child relationship between the donor and the child, an adoption may not be enough to prevent a court from granting the donor some rights.

Unfortunately, physicians in some parts of the country will not participate in donor insemination for an unmarried woman, so you may have to shop around. Another potential problem is that some doctors will not perform an insemination with fresh sperm, because of FDA regulations requiring that donations be frozen and quarantined for at least six months to make sure they are free from HIV, hepatitis, and other transmissible diseases (this period can be waived or reduced in some states). If you need referrals to a doctor who can help you with donor insemination, contact a local sperm bank, women's clinic, or Planned Parenthood office. If there's no such agency near you, it's now possible to have sperm shipped in special receptacles—so look around for a sperm bank that offers this service.

Donor Insemination Agreements

If you decide to use a known donor to conceive a child, it is of course important for you and the donor to discuss the practical, emotional, and legal issues that are likely to arise.

The problem with even the most honest and respectful discussions of this kind is that it is never possible to predict how any particular parent—mother, father, or donor—will feel once the child is born. And even if you've carefully put your agreements into writing, the documents won't be legally binding. In all states, judges make decisions about children on the basis of the child's best interests. This means that a written agreement between the child's parents—for example, one stating that the donor won't seek custody or visitation—is not controlling if the judge doesn't think it is in the child's best interests.

Still, donor insemination contracts have their place. They are most useful when you intend for the donor to have some contact with the child, but even if you don't, the best reason to have a donor contract is to make sure that everyone involved has a clear understanding of the agreement.

So if you think that you and your donor have agreed that he won't be a legal father, won't visit the child, won't claim any relationship with the child, and won't be responsible to support the child, put it in writing and show it to the donor. That is the only way you will know whether you truly have the same understanding about what his role will be. Likewise, if you and your donor have agreed that he will be treated as a beloved uncle but not a parent, will visit your family once a week but won't visit the child alone until the child is a certain age, or will put money into a trust fund for the child, write it down. Make sure that communication is clear and open and that everyone's expectations are on the table. While these agreements may not be enforceable in a courthouse, they will go a long way toward preventing problems in the first place and helping you resolve them together if they do arise.

A sample donor agreement is shown below. It's fairly short, and covers a situation where the parties used a doctor in order to guarantee the donor wouldn't be considered a legal parent. If you don't use a doctor, you can take out that paragraph and still use this agreement as a way to be clear that you don't want the donor to be a parent, but remember that legally, in most states the donor will be the child's father until a court terminates his rights. This agreement also states that the donor will have some contact with the child as a family friend. If you intend for the donor to have no contact with the child, you would change that paragraph.

Sample Donor Insemination Agreement

This agreement is made between Tom Duncan, ("Tom"), and Elaine Alvarez ("Elaine") and Susan Farmer ("Susan"), who agree as follows:

1. If a court refuses to enforce one or more clauses of this agreement, the others are still valid and in full force.

2. Tom agrees provide his sperm to Elaine for the purpose of donor insemination, at least once a month for at least 12 months for the purpose of conceiving a child. If Elaine doesn't conceive by then, they'll discuss whether to continue. Tom will provide sperm at the time during the month when Elaine requests it, according to her cycle. If Elaine wants to, she can ask Tom for sperm and freeze it to use later.

3. Elaine will pay Tom $1.00 every time he makes a sperm donation. Also, Elaine will pay any uninsured expenses for Tom to have a physical exam, blood screening, and semen analysis before the first insemination, and also for all office visits he makes for the purpose of making semen donations. If Tom asks her to, Elaine will also pay his transportation expenses for any of these medical appointments.

4. Tom has been tested for HIV and other STDs, and tested negative. He engaged in "safer sex" activities for six (6) months before the test, and he agrees to continue to do so while Elaine is trying to get pregnant using his sperm.

5. Tom is single. Elaine and Susan are registered domestic partners in California, where they live. Both of them intend to be legal parents of any child born as a result of these inseminations, and they will file a petition for Susan to adopt the child as soon as possible after its birth. Tom will cooperate in the adoption and will sign any papers needed to affirm Susan's coparental rights.

6. Tom agrees that he won't try to become a legal parent of any child born from these inseminations, or ask for custody or visitation rights at any time. Tom understands that he will have no paternal rights. Elaine and Susan won't ever ask Tom to pay child support for any child born from these inseminations. If any agency or entity ever requires Tom to pay child support, Elaine and Susan will indemnify him and pay him back any money that he's required to pay.

7. Tom will donate sperm to a licensed physician or a sperm bank. The purpose of this is to make sure California Family Code Section 7613(b), applies, which says that a sperm donor is not a legal father if the sperm was provided to a doctor.

8. Elaine and Susan will name any child born from these inseminations. Tom's name will not be put on the birth certificate, but Susan's will.

9. Elaine, and Susan when her parental rights are established, will be the only people with authority to name a guardian for their child. They are not required to name Tom as guardian.

10. Tom's relationship with any child born from these inseminations will be as a family friend. Tom agrees that if the child is curious about its parentage, Elaine and Susan may tell the child that Tom donated sperm and is a biological parent.

11. Tom will not pay support nor assist financially with the child's upbringing in any way. Should any agency or institution require Tom to pay child support in relation to the child, Elaine and Susan agree to be jointly and severally responsible for indemnifying Tom for any amounts he actually pays as child support.

12. Neither the fact that the child may know that Tom is his/her biological parent, nor any contact Tom has with the child, nor any gifts or financial support that Tom gives or provides, means that any provisions of this agreement are waived.

13. It's okay for Tom to tell his parents and siblings that he donated sperm and, if a child is conceived, that he is the biological parent of the child. But he promises not to help or support his family if they try to establish a family relationship with the child, and any visits or other contact between the child and Tom's family will happen only if Elaine and Susan agree.

14. Tom, Elaine, and Susan know that there are legal questions raised by the issues involved in this agreement that have not been settled by statute or by court decisions. They still choose to enter into this agreement to state their intentions at the time they signed it. If there's a court dispute between them, this agreement can be used as evidence of their intent.

15. If any dispute arises between Tom, Elaine, and Susan about this agreement, they will attend mediation sessions in good faith to resolve

the dispute. All three of them, or the two that are in conflict, will participate in at least four mediation sessions, to be held weekly, with the cost of the mediation to be shared equally by the participants. The parties will select the mediator together and if they can't agree, they will ask their friend, Sally Martin, to choose a mediator.

16. Tom, Elaine, and Susan all had the chance to talk to a lawyer about this agreement.

17. Tom, Elaine, and Susan agree that any changes in this agreement must be made in writing and signed by all of them.

_10/16/20xx_
Date

Tom Duncan
Tom Duncan

_10/16/20xx_
Date

Elaine Alvarez
Elaine Alvarez

_10/16/20xx_
Date

Susan Farmer
Susan Farmer

Donor Insemination and Public Benefits

If you have a child by donor insemination and apply for welfare, be aware of the following: If your state law doesn't automatically terminate the donor's parental rights and obligations, the welfare department might look for the donor, bring a paternity action to have him declared the father, and request that he support the child. Before applying for welfare, consult a legal aid attorney who can help you keep the donor's identity private.

Egg Donation/Ovum Sharing

Advances in medical technology have made it possible for both partners in a lesbian couple to have a biological relationship with a child. One partner provides an egg (ovum), which is fertilized outside her body and then implanted in the body of the other partner, who carries the child to term and gives birth. Relatively few couples opt for this expensive and invasive process, but its great advantage is that in most states, the legal result of the procedure is that both women are considered legal parents of the child. The first partner is the child's genetic mother by virtue of having contributed the genetic material, and the second partner is the child's gestational mother because she carried and gave birth to the child.

However, it is usually still necessary for the genetic mother to go to court and get a ruling under the Uniform Parentage Act establishing her parental relationship with the child. Numerous egg donor cases have been completed in California, and lesbian parents are attempting to get these judgments in some of the other states that have adopted the Uniform Parentage Act.

CAUTION

Read fertility clinic forms carefully. Standard documents signed by an egg donor (most of whom donate eggs to infertile couples and don't have any intention of parenting) include provisions under which the donor gives up all parental rights to children conceived using her eggs. If that's not what you want, don't sign the form as it's written. In Marin County, California, a genetic mother donated eggs for fertilization and implantation in her partner, resulting in the birth of twins that she and her partner raised until they separated when the twins were about six years old. The birth mother denied visitation to the genetic mother, and the genetic mother sued. The trial court ruled that the genetic mother had given up her parental rights when she signed the standard fertility clinic forms before her eggs were harvested, even though the women went through the fertility process together as a couple and with the intention of parenting together. The California Court of Appeal upheld the trial court (in other words, ruled in favor of the birth mother). Fortunately, the California Supreme Court ultimately held that both women were legal parents despite the forms, but the lesson is clear—read whatever you are signing.

Surrogacy

Obviously, for gay men, having a baby that is genetically related to one partner is more difficult than it is for lesbians. Some gay men opt for a surrogacy agreement, in which one or both of the men provide sperm that is used to fertilize an egg that the surrogate then carries to term.

The surrogate may be inseminated with the father's semen directly (called traditional surrogacy), or eggs may be harvested from an egg donor, fertilized *in vitro* (outside the body), and implanted in the surrogate's womb (called gestational surrogacy, and much more commonly used). The father(s) pay the surrogate's medical expenses, and sometimes a fee for "gestational services."

If you opt for surrogacy, then either just before or just after the child is born, you will need to take legal action to establish who the child's parents are (and aren't). In states that have adopted the Uniform Parentage Act, establishing the rights of the father who provided the sperm may be relatively simple. But you also have to establish the legal rights of the second parent, if there is one. What you have to do and when you can do it are very different in different states, and you'll need to consult a lawyer.

Surrogacy is not legal everywhere. Surrogacy contracts are illegal in some states; in others they are permitted only if no money is exchanged. Only Arkansas and West Virginia have laws explicitly allowing money to change hands under surrogacy contracts. Other states don't have specific laws on surrogacy, and you will have to check with a local lawyer about what's allowed.

Where surrogacy is allowed, it's very important that the payment to the surrogate is for her services in carrying the child, not for giving up the child. It is, of course, illegal to sell children.

> **SEE AN EXPERT**
>
> **Consult a lawyer before making a surrogacy agreement.** You need to make sure that surrogacy is legal where you live, and you will need help preparing a legal agreement, negotiating with a potential surrogate, terminating the surrogate's rights, and establishing both partners' parental rights. It's important to find a lawyer who has experience with surrogacy issues, especially if you are considering using an overseas surrogate. Chapter 11 has more information about finding a lawyer.

When You Have a Child

Many practical issues come up when you have a child as an unmarried parent through donor insemination, egg donation, or surrogacy.

Naming the Child

You can name your child anything you want. Some couples hyphenate the last name or give the child the last name of the nonbiological parent, whether or not that parent will be considered a legal parent. In fact, when the nonbiological parent won't be considered a legal parent, giving the child that parent's last name can provide additional evidence that the partners intended to be equal parents.

Completing the Birth Certificate

When a child is born, the hospital will present the parent or parents with a form to fill out to request a birth certificate for the child. If the baby isn't born in a medical facility, the mother or the physician, midwife, or other person assisting in the delivery must notify health officials of the birth.

If you are a lesbian who has given birth to a child conceived by donor insemination or ovum sharing, you should leave blank the space for "father's name" unless you:

- used a known donor,
- did not have a physician supervise the insemination, and
- intend for the donor to be the child's other legal parent.

In that case, see "Lesbians and Gay Men Parenting Together," below. If the hospital insists on putting something in the blank, ask them to put in "name withheld."

Surrogacy is a different story. In a few places, courts will grant prebirth judgments that order the hospital to leave the surrogate's name off the birth certificate and to include the name of the intended parent or parents instead. But in most places, the surrogate's name will go on the birth certificate as the mother. When the intended parents are two men, the partner who donated the sperm will be listed as father. The birth certificate will be altered to remove the surrogate's name (and add the partner's, if applicable) after a court declares that she is not a legal parent. However, in some places it's not possible to remove or change a mother's name after the birth certificate has been issued, so it's important to get a prebirth judgment that includes an order that requires the hospital to put the male parent's name in the "mother" spot or to use the term "parent" for both parents instead. If you're a male using a surrogate, make sure you talk to a knowledgeable lawyer about the birth certificate issues.

CAUTION

Don't list your partner as a parent unless she is one! If you are married or in a marriage-like relationship in one of the marriage or marriage-equality states, you should be able to list both partners' names on the birth certificate at birth. If you live in any other state, or if you haven't entered into a marriage or marriage-like relationship, then under no circumstances should you put the second parent's name on the birth certificate before finalizing an adoption. It's fraud, for one thing, and it could slow down the adoption process while you wait to have the original birth certificate corrected.

> ## Adding the Second Parent's Name to the Birth Certificate After Adoption
>
> If you live in a state that allows second-parent or stepparent adoptions, the name of the second parent will usually be added to the child's birth certificate after the adoption is final. Some state vital statistics departments, like California's, will issue a new birth certificate that lists each partner as "parent," instead of designating one "mother" and one "father." See "Protections for Second Parents," above, for more about getting a new birth certificate after a second-parent adoption.

Lesbians and Gay Men Parenting Together

Some lesbians and gay man opt to parent together. Usually, they are close and trusting friends who make a commitment to conceive and raise a child together. They don't have to get married, and most often they don't. If they are both acknowledged as the biological parents of the child, they will both have full legal rights and duties—regardless of their sexual orientation or marital status. But if either parent is married or legally partnered with a same-sex partner, legal parenting status can become confusing. For example, depending on how the insemination was performed (at home versus with a doctor) there may be competing presumptions about who is a legal parent—the donor or the registered partner or spouse of the biological parent. If you have concerns like these, be sure to consult a local attorney with experience in parentage issues.

In this situation, it's very important that the donor's parental rights be established immediately after the baby is born. This protects the mother, the baby, and the donor father—ensuring that he won't be denied any rights to visitation and that the child will receive all the benefits and support that this second parent is required to provide.

The best way to establish the donor's paternity is by naming him on the birth certificate as described in "Completing the Birth Certificate," above. Under federal regulations, all states must offer unmarried fathers an opportunity to establish paternity by voluntarily signing an

Sample Contract Regarding Child Support and Custody

This agreement is made between Julie Shatz and Victor Lawrence. Neither of us is married or legally partnered. The purpose of this agreement is to express our understanding of our rights and responsibilities to our child. We realize that our power to make this contract is limited by state law. With this knowledge, and in a spirit of cooperation and mutual respect, we state the following agreement:

1. Within ten days after the birth, Victor will sign a statement acknowledging that he's the father; his name will be on the birth certificate.

2. Our child will be given the last name Shatz.

3. Julie will have physical custody; Victor will have reasonable rights of visitation. Julie will be sensitive to Victor's needs and will cooperate in all practical ways to make visitation as easy as possible.

4. Both of us will do our best to see that our child has a close and loving relationship with each parent.

5. Victor will provide support in the amount of $500 a month for the first year after our child is born. Thereafter, we will arrive at a mutual agreement each year for the amount Victor will pay, taking into account:
   a. the needs of our child
   b. increases in the cost of living
   c. changes in Victor's income, and
   d. changes in Julie's income.

6. We will make a good-faith effort to work together and to agree on all major decisions affecting our child's health and welfare.

7. If either Julie or Victor dies, our child will be cared for and raised by the other.

8. If any dispute or problem arises between us regarding our child, we agree to seek counseling and professional help to try to reach a resolution.

_____   _____
Date   Julie Shatz

_____   _____
Date   Victor Lawrence

acknowledgment of paternity, either at the hospital or at a later time. In some states, in fact, the only way that an unmarried father's name can be placed on the child's birth certificate is if the father signs such a form—so if he's not present at the birth, he will have to come in later and submit the form in order to have his name on the birth certificate as father.

Some lesbians and gay men parenting together prepare a written agreement about their plans to coparent. Because the courts will generally recognize both parties as parents, such an agreement isn't really necessary, nor is it enforceable—remember, the courts have to go by what is in the child's best interests. But like a donor insemination agreement, it can help to defuse conflict if you have different memories of what you agreed to before. Above is a sample agreement.

Adopting a Child

Another parenting option for same-sex couples is for one or both partners to adopt a child who is not biologically related to either partner—a process that can be accomplished through a public agency, a private agency, or private contact with birth parents. This section discusses all of these options.

Adoption Is Not Available Everywhere

In a few states, openly gay people—whether single or coupled—are not allowed to adopt a child. In other states, the law doesn't prohibit such adoptions but in practice they are very difficult to obtain. Accordingly, each state requires a customized legal strategy. If you live in a state where it's difficult or impossible for LGBT couples to adopt together, consider having one partner adopt as a single person. Of course, if you do this, the parent who doesn't do the adoption is at a legal disadvantage in a breakup, as discussed above and in Chapter 10.

In most states, if you want to adopt you will probably want to hire an attorney. Most adoptions aren't that legally complicated, but a judge will be reassured by the presence of a lawyer and may be disturbed otherwise—and this is not the time to make a procedural error. Obviously, you want the judge to be as comfortable as possible. Also, a lawyer with good local connections who has handled gay and lesbian legal issues before will know how to get a favorable social worker or disqualify a hostile judge.

If you are seeking to adopt a child through a private agency or through private contacts, it may take quite some time—perhaps a longer-than-average time—because you will be looking for birth parents willing to place a child with a same-sex couple. Don't be discouraged, but be realistic—and be prepared to wait. Of course, you will have many more options if you are open to adopting a child of a different race, a child who is slightly older or disabled in some way, or a pair (or more) of siblings together.

To evaluate your options, start with a local lesbian or gay parents' organization. Its members will know what's been done and what's possible in your area.

Overview of Adoption

In order to adopt a child, you must meet certain legal requirements. The following information is, by necessity, general. State laws vary considerably—but this section will give you a sense of some of the issues, and you can treat what you read here as a starting place for your research.

Age limits. In some states, the adoptive parent must be older than the adopted child by a specific number of years. Other states only require the adopting parent be over 21, and some states allow any person older than the child to adopt.

Residence. You will file your adoption case in the county where you, and normally the child, live. If you are adopting a child from another state, you will have to comply with a special law called the interstate compact on adoption, and you will definitely need an attorney to help you.

Who may be adopted. Interreligious and interracial adoptions used to be, and sometimes still are, refused by adoption agencies and courts as not being in the "best interests of the child." Special laws apply to the adoption of Native American children, with preference being given to family members, other members of the child's tribe, and then other Native American families. The law also requires that the tribe be notified of most foster-adoption placements of Native American children and provides that some state adoptions can be set aside by tribal courts.

Name changes. All states permit the adoptive parent(s) to change the child's last name at the time of adoption.

Records and birth certificates. Nearly all states seal adoption records so that they can't be inspected without a court order except by the parties or the lawyer involved. Adoptive parents can usually obtain a new birth certificate showing the child's new name and listing the adoptive parents as the child's parents.

Consent of the child. Most state laws say that children over a certain age must consent to the adoption. The age varies from state to state, but is usually between ten and 14.

Termination of birth parents' rights. In all but second-parent and stepparent adoptions, the parental rights of both of the adopted child's birth parents are forever terminated when the adoption is finalized.

Social worker investigation. Every proposed adoption must be evaluated by a social worker or another qualified adoption worker, who submits a report to the court with a recommendation about whether the adoption should be granted.

Court hearing. Every adoption requires a court hearing. The adoptive parents and the child must attend, and the parents must sign consent forms in front of the judge. The hearing is private and is usually held in the chambers of the judge, who is generally friendly and quite pleased to be presiding over such a happy occasion.

Methods of Adoption

The most common methods of adoption are:
- through a public or private agency doing domestic adoptions
- through a private agency doing international adoptions, and
- through the birth parents or a private intermediary.

Second-parent and stepparent adoptions are quite different, and are addressed separately in "Protections for Second Parents," above.

"Open" and "Closed" Adoptions

Agency and private adoptions can be either open or closed. In an open adoption, the adopting parents and the birth parents meet to share information and get to know each other. Generally, even after the adoption is finalized, the birth parents (or, often, just the birth mother) continue to have some contact with the adoptive family—exactly how much contact is up to all the parties. Some adoptive parents prefer an open adoption because they want to have access to medical information and want their child to know the birth parents. Research shows that children benefit from open adoptions. Others prefer a closed adoption, where neither set of parents knows the other's identity, and the paperwork is sealed and becomes legally inaccessible. If you have a strong preference one way or the other, you may wait a bit longer, because birth parents who have a strong preference the other way won't consider you a match.

With both open and closed adoptions, the birth parents' rights are terminated when the adoption is finalized in court. Agreements for contact in an open adoption are not enforceable by a court, because the birth parents no longer have any rights in relation to the child they gave up for adoption. But because the two families generally communicate during the adoption process about what level of contact is appropriate, conflicts don't occur that often. Still, if you are concerned about making sure that you won't run into anything unexpected in connection with the birth parents, a closed adoption will probably be a better option for you.

Agency Adoptions

Many gay men and lesbians adopt through an agency—either a public agency, such as the county welfare department, or a private adoption agency. In agency adoptions, the agency locates children available for adoption and matches them with prospective adoptive parents—or, in the case of many private agency adoptions, the birth parents choose from a list of prospective adoptive parents supplied by the agency.

In the past, most private and public agencies favored married couples over single parents, and many still do. But so many children are waiting for adoption though public agencies that social workers in some areas are opening their minds to new possibilities. And some private agencies are simply willing to take on more diverse clients. At this point, some agencies treat LGBT singles like any other single people, and treat same-sex couples, married or not, like opposite-sex married couples. In some places, public agencies actively recruit lesbian and gay adoptive parents.

Unfortunately, however, many agencies still won't even accept LGBT singles or couples as prospective adoptive parents. That kind of discrimination against same-sex singles and couples in adoption is perfectly legal in most places. As a practical matter, if you encounter resistance in a private agency you probably want to look elsewhere—there's no point in pushing to have an agency accept you as a client when you can be pretty sure they won't work hard to find a child to place with you.

Before signing on with an adoption agency, you'll be subject to extensive interviews, questionnaires, and home visits to make sure that you are suitable parents. In a private agency adoption, the birth parents have relinquished a child for adoption, sometimes with specific requirements about the type of people they want to adopt their child. In public agency adoptions, the child has already been removed from the home and the parents' rights often have been terminated by court order. In that case, the agency will decide who are appropriate adoptive parents for the child. Many public agencies have fost-adopt programs. See "Foster Parenting," below.

Both types of agencies will work to find a match between the children waiting to be adopted and the parents waiting for a child. When a possible match has been identified, a social worker will again interview you to make sure that the match is appropriate, and will evaluate your home in order to make a formal report to the court. The agency will recommend to the judge whether or not the adoption should be granted. As a practical matter, once you have signed on with the agency you are unlikely to get an unfavorable recommendation, because the prescreening pretty much guarantees that they consider you suitable.

Assuming all goes well, you will attend a court hearing at which the judge will declare you the legal parents of your new child.

One advantage of adopting through a public agency is that these adoptions are very low-cost. Usually, the agency is responsible for children who are removed from their parents' custody because of abuse or neglect, and the social workers are eager to place the children in loving homes. In order to encourage prospective adoptive parents, the costs are kept extremely low, and there are no birth mother expenses to consider.

A private agency adoption can be much more expensive—anywhere between $5,000 and $25,000, depending on how many specific requirements you have about what type of child you will adopt (the more detailed your requirements, the more searching the agency will have to do), the financial needs of the birth mother, and the agency's fees. Shop around for a good private agency until you find one that has the right combination of experience, openness to LGBT families, and reasonable fees.

Fighting Discrimination by Adoption Agencies

In December 2003, a gay couple in California sued two online adoption agencies, Adoption.com and ParentProfiles.com, for refusing to allow the gay men to submit a paid posting to the site as prospective adoptive parents. The defendants' websites charge fees for posting profiles of potential adoptive parents. Using the websites, birth parents can search those profiles to choose potential adoptive parents for their children. The agencies challenged the lawsuit, but a federal district court judge allowed the case to go forward, and in May of 2007 the parties reached a settlement when the defendants agreed to stop discriminating in California and to allow all California residents to post profiles on the sites.

In New York, the Attorney General challenged two online adoption services that refused services to same-sex couples, arguing that the denial violates the state's Human Rights Law. The adoption services stopped doing business in New York rather than comply with the law.

TIP

Do your homework. Lots of adoption information is available over the Internet, and there are websites where you can register as a prospective adoptive family for review by birth mothers who are considering adoption or choosing adoptive parents for an unborn baby. (But check out the online agency's rules carefully—see "Fighting Discrimination by Adoption Agencies," above.)

Private Adoptions

In a private adoption, sometimes also called an independent adoption, you find the child yourself or with the aid of a private intermediary other than an agency. Sometimes a friend or relative knows someone who's planning to relinquish a child for adoption, or knows someone who knows someone. Private intermediaries, sometimes called adoption facilitators, are only legal in some states.

Private adoptions are legal in most states and are quite common for parents adopting infants. The adopting parents normally pay the birth mother's medical expenses and sometimes her living expenses, in addition to paying the legal fees. Paying any other fee, however, is illegal, and in most states you must sign an affidavit that you did not pay the birth mother for anything other than the expenses allowed by law.

In many states it's illegal for the prospective adoptive parents or the birth mother to advertise for an adoption, and using an intermediary to locate or place an adopted child is also questionable. Nonetheless, many lawyers help with placement, and if it is legal in your state, there is nothing wrong with asking an attorney to help you find a child to adopt and to do the legal paperwork for you—assuming you can afford it.

CAUTION

Beware of "black market" adoptions. The idea of people skulking down dark alleys to buy a baby from a mother or an intermediary isn't just unpleasant—it's illegal. One way this works is to have the biological mother register at a hospital in the name of the adoptive mother so that the birth certificate contains the "adopting" parent's name. However handled, it leaves the adoptive parent open to the risk of prosecution, as well as the risk of losing the child if the biological mother changes her mind.

Once you or your intermediary locate a baby, the biological parent(s) must sign a consent form, and you must file an adoption request with the court and submit to an investigation by a state or local agency appointed by the court to evaluate private adoptions. The social worker who investigates the adoption request will make a report and recommendation to the court, and a judge will approve your adoption at a court hearing that you, your partner, and the child all attend.

International Adoptions

Currently, no foreign country allows adoption by same-sex couples or openly gay singles. Some countries do allow adoption by single people, though many strongly prefer that the adopting parents be married, and some countries have recently established new policies against allowing any adoptions at all by single people. For example, China—which had been a popular adoption destination for same-sex couples for many years—has a set of policies that took effect on May 1, 2007, that include the rule that single people may no longer adopt children from China under any circumstances. If a country requires adoptive parents to be married, then obviously neither a same-sex couple nor a lesbian or gay individual can adopt there. And the ability to marry makes no difference, because no country will allow an openly gay or lesbian couple to adopt. In fact, you'll be required to disclose your marital status and getting married probably will preclude an international adoption.

If you are proceeding with a foreign adoption, you will need to keep your sexual orientation—and your relationship with your partner—hidden from the host country. It is a judgment call whether or not you tell the agency helping you with the adoption about your sexual orientation. Many agencies operate on a wink-and-nod basis—they are fully aware of the nature of your relationship with your partner, but refer to the partner as a "roommate" in their reports to the host country, and simply ignore the issue of sexual orientation.

The United States now participates in the Hague Adoption Convention, which has added some additional layers of rules onto the adoption process and made it even more difficult for LGBT would-be parents to adopt. The information in this section will give you an idea of what the process looks like generally, but you'll need to consult an attorney to find out where things stand in terms of your ability to actually proceed with an adoption.

Like domestic agency adoption, adopting a child who was born in another country takes patience and perseverance, as well as the ability to tolerate a lot of paperwork, bureaucracy, and foreign travel. Many children available for international adoption are living in orphanages. International adoptions are nearly always closed adoptions, and most of the time there will be little or no information available about the child's birth parents. International adoptions are expensive, costing no less than $10,000 and often up to $30,000.

⚠ **CAUTION**

International adoption can be risky for reasons unrelated to sexual orientation. Global politics and changing conditions, as well as problems with adoption fraud, lead to frequent shifts in the availability of children in different countries—shifts that can affect adoptions in process. For example, during the 2003 epidemic of Severe Acute Respiratory Syndrome (SARS) in China, all adoptions were suspended (the paperwork could go forward, but you couldn't pick up a child in China). Adoptions in Cambodia were discontinued for a period of time because of the difficulty there of ensuring that children available for adoption were actually orphans or were properly placed for adoption and that there was no fraud or child stealing involved. Similar problems have arisen recently in Costa Rica, where babies from Guatemala were smuggled in for adoption. Again, make sure you stay up to date through the Department of State website (http://travel.state.gov), and make sure you use a reputable adoption agency.

Most people adopting internationally use a United States agency to help them identify a child and navigate the international adoption procedures. It's very difficult, if not impossible, to do an international adoption on your own—there are simply too many hoops to jump through. But it's critically important that you find a reputable agency. Make sure that you check the agency's success rate, talk with a significant number of former clients, and find every piece of information you can before you sign up. Referrals from friends or others who have used an agency are your best source of information, but make sure you check out the objective facts as well. Stick with a licensed agency. Adoption "facilitators" often charge exorbitant sums and make extravagant claims about their connections in foreign countries, promising results that don't pan out.

If you do find an agency to work with and you get through the paperwork, you must next be prepared to become a world traveler. In most cases, adoptive parents travel to the host country to meet a child who has already been identified as a potential adoptive child. Often, you must make two trips—one to meet the child and agree to the adoption, and a second, a few months later, to attend a final adoption hearing and bring the child home.

Because only one partner in a lesbian and gay couple can be the adopting parent, the question often comes up whether the partner who is not adopting should travel with the adoptive parent. Doing so raises the possibility that the relationship may become an issue in the host country or among other couples traveling, since an agency usually arranges for numerous couples to travel together to pick up children. On the other hand, the second parent is likely to want to be involved in every aspect of the process, and the adopting parent will probably want support during the stressful trip. This is a judgment call that you can make based on the openness of your agency, the current climate at the time you are adopting, and the country to which you are traveling.

When you return home with your child, you may be required to file a petition for "readoption" in your home state. Not all states require this, but some do, and even if your state does not require it, it's a good idea. A readoption is a simple process through which an American court confirms that you are the legal parent of the child you have already adopted internationally. The primary benefit of the readoption is that you will receive a birth certificate from your home state listing you as the child's parent. This is a convenience that may save you hassles later, as the birth certificate and adoption order that you receive from the host country will not be in English, and the translation, if you get one, can be sketchy.

You can't use a readoption as a shortcut to getting parental rights for the second parent—you will still have to do a second-parent or stepparent adoption.

TIP

If you live in a state where second-parent adoption is available, you may not need to do a readoption. If the readoption is required by state law or by the host country, then you will have to do it no matter what. But if it's not, and you live in a state where second-parent or stepparent adoptions are allowed, then the adoption by the second parent will achieve the same result as a readoption—a birth certificate in English, showing both partners as legal parents.

Citizenship Issues

A child adopted from a foreign country automatically becomes a U.S. citizen upon arrival in the United States as long as the foreign adoption is final—as is the case in nearly all international adoptions. In the few cases where the adoption remains pending for a period of time after the child comes to live in the United States, citizenship is not final until the adoption is complete. Information about visa and citizenship issues in international adoption is available at the Department of State website at http://travel.state.gov (click the link for "children & family").

RESOURCE

For more information about adoption in your state, check with a local attorney, your local social services agency, and/or the website of the National Center for Lesbian Rights (www.nclrights.org) or Lambda Legal Defense and Education Fund (www.lambdalegal.org) to find out what is possible in your local area.

Foster Parenting

Growing numbers of foster care placement agencies are placing children with gay and lesbian foster parents. Children who need foster homes are those who have become wards of the state for one reason or another—most often, because they have suffered abuse or neglect by their birth parents or because they have gotten into trouble with the law.

Foster placements can last anywhere from days to years. A foster parent is only a temporary guardian of a child, and in most cases the state attempts to rehabilitate the neglectful or abusive parent with the goal of returning the child to them. If the reunification is unsuccessful, the foster parent may get the opportunity to adopt—and in many states, there is a growing acceptance of adoption by foster parents—but as a foster parent, you must face the fact that the child may be returned to his or her family of origin.

States pay foster parents a monthly amount for support of each foster child. The amount varies, but in many urban areas the allowance is several hundred dollars per month. Obviously, people don't become foster parents for the money. Still, the monthly stipend can help pay the bills.

Some kids in foster care may be gay teenagers who can't get along with their parents—often the underlying problem is the teen's emerging sexual identity. Others may be children of gay or lesbian parents removed from the parents' home because of neglect, substance abuse, or another problem. In both of these cases, placement with an LGBT family can provide the most supportive environment possible. In some cities, such as New York, San Francisco, Los Angeles, and Trenton, New Jersey, agencies have actively recruited gay foster parents for such placements.

On the other hand, in many places, an LGBT household has no chance of being approved as a foster home. Nebraska, for example, will not place foster children with lesbian or gay parents, and North Dakota allows only married couples to become foster parents.

A battle has been raging in Arkansas for a few years over whether the state must allow lesbians and gay men to serve as foster parents. The state Supreme Court ultimately struck down a ban on foster care by lesbians and gay men, and the legislature responded in March 2007 by introducing a bill that would ban gay people and most unmarried heterosexual couples who live together from adopting or serving as foster parents.

In November 2008, the voters passed the Unmarried Couple Adoption Ban, making it illegal for any couples or individuals cohabiting outside of a valid marriage to be foster parents or adopt children. Although the purpose of the measure was to prohibit same-sex couples from being adoptive or foster parents, it also has the effect of keeping all otherwise qualified couples who are not legally married from adopting or being foster parents. In 2011, the Arkansas Supreme Court unanimously struck down the ban as unconstitutional.

In West Virginia, the Supreme Court recently prevented the removal of a foster child from the lesbian family she was living with, rejecting a lower court's ruling that foster children should be placed with "traditional families."

Some states accept LGBT families but then give them low priority for placement. And it sometimes happens that children are placed for foster care with an LGBT couple or family, and then removed when a homophobic social worker or judge learns about the situation. Just such a case went all the way to the Illinois Supreme Court, where a lesbian fought and won a battle to keep custody of a young boy who lived with her for two years but was removed—and returned to his abusive grandparents—when a young social worker recommended against his continued placement. The court held that the child's best interests would be served by allowing his foster parent to adopt him.

Applying to Become a Foster Parent

If you want to become foster parents, how out can you be? Should one partner apply to the licensing agency as a single person, or should you apply as a couple? And what is involved in the process?

A single adult sharing space with another adult can become a licensed foster parent in most states. So if you want to keep your relationship private, have one person apply as a single individual. But foster care placement is always supervised by an agency and the court, so be prepared to have social workers march into your home to look about.

Generally, being closeted is risky. The agency may find out the truth, but more likely, the child will, and it's not appropriate to ask the child to lie.

Before you can become a foster parent, your home must be licensed by an agency (state operated or private) approved by the state. To get a list of agencies, call the foster-home division of the county welfare department. Finding an agency willing to place foster kids with lesbian and gay couples may take a little work. Ask a local LGBT organization which agencies are sympathetic. Agencies and social workers willing to make such placements often keep a low profile, believing they are more effective that way.

Because you can be licensed by only one agency at a time, investigate carefully before you choose to make sure you have found the most gay-friendly agency. Once you select an agency, you fill out an application and are interviewed by an employee of the agency. Some common requirements for foster parents are:

- you should be able to provide a separate room for the child
- you must undergo a medical exam to make sure you are in reasonably good health
- you must be fingerprinted—ex-felons and sex offenders aren't eligible, and
- if you're open to having a young child placed with you, you must demonstrate that you have time to care for the child or have arranged for child care.

Above all, you must demonstrate that you are stable and responsible and will provide a good temporary home for a child who has often already suffered trauma.

You may have a choice of getting a general foster-home license and having the agency place a child, or becoming licensed as a foster home for a particular child. When on the general list, you have the option of refusing a child if you and the child don't hit it off. Getting licensed to foster a specific child works differently, as described in this example.

EXAMPLE: Michael and Ron had befriended Scott, a gay boy of 14. Scott was living at an institution and on weekend days caught a bus to Michael and Ron's. They drove him back in the evenings. On Thanksgiving, Scott said to Ron, "Wouldn't it be great to live here all the time?" Ron sighed. "It'd be wonderful—but it's impossible. We all know that." Later, Michael and Ron wondered if it really was impossible. They contacted Scott's social worker, who agreed that placing Scott in Michael and Ron's home would be good for him. The social worker sent Michael and Ron the application forms, and a license was granted. Scott lived happily in Michael and Ron's home.

Getting licensed as a foster parent takes some paperwork. Usually the agency will assist you with it, so you shouldn't need an attorney. If, however, you want some help or you think you're being discriminated against, you may need to hire a lawyer.

It's often easier for a gay person or couple to become licensed foster parents than it is to actually have children placed in their home. And because foster placement is always considered temporary, the child can be removed at your request, the child's request, or the request of the agency or government probation officers. So there are uncertainties to being a foster parent, especially for an LGBT family.

Placing Gay Kids (and Kids of Gays) in Gay Homes

Placing gay kids, especially teens, in large group homes can be problematic because of homophobia and the special needs of LGBT (and questioning) youth. Some agencies will approve stable, caring, gay households for placement of LGBT teenagers or children of gay or lesbian parents who need foster care. If you have a particular interest in fostering a lesbian or gay teenager and you live in an area where the foster care agency is supportive, let your caseworker know.

TIP

In California, numerous agencies support placement of lesbian and gay youth with LGBT families. The Foster Licensing Division of the Department of Social Services in San Francisco licenses lesbian and gay foster homes. In Los Angeles, Gay and Lesbian Adolescent Social Services (GLASS) certifies gay and lesbian families to become licensed foster parents. GLASS also runs group homes to place gay, lesbian, and HIV-positive teens. A private agency called Alternative

Family Services of San Francisco and Sonoma counties licenses the homes of lesbians and gay men, single people, unmarried heterosexual couples, and groups; places gay teenagers in gay homes; and provides support to these families.

Becoming a Guardian

A guardian is an adult other than a legal parent who is legally responsible for taking care of a minor. Usually, the guardian takes physical custody of the child, and sometimes is also given authority to manage the minor's assets.

Some guardianships are informal; others are court appointed. In informal guardianships, the legal parents consent to the arrangement. Informal guardianships are temporary and can be changed at any time by whoever placed the child. Informal guardianships are most common when a parent becomes ill, is incarcerated, or travels extensively and asks a relative or friend to temporarily take over parenting. There is no legal process. The parent simply delivers the child to the guardian, usually with a simple document of authorization.

Formal guardianships involve court proceedings. The proposed guardian files a petition and the court decides whether the guardianship is in the best interests of the child. As long as everyone agrees, the judge usually grants the guardianship and issues an order establishing its terms.

A guardian generally isn't legally or financially responsible for a child's actions—if a child causes damage by vandalism, in most states a parent is liable but a guardian isn't. But a guardian can be liable if the guardian promises, on the child's driver's license application, to be responsible for damage the child causes while driving.

TIP

Welfare benefits usually follow the child. But be sure to check your state's laws. Normally, if the guardian is a close relative or meets the welfare department formalities (which are less rigid than with formal guardianships), the benefits will follow.

Informal Guardianships

Here's an example of a situation in which an informal guardianship worked well for a set of friends.

EXAMPLE: Ben, a gay man, and Paula were old friends. Paula's son Mark had confided in Ben the summer before coming out to his mother. Paula wasn't shocked to learn that Mark was gay, but was finding him hard to handle. Mark emailed Ben the following letter.

Dear Ben:

Remember how we talked last summer about my parents' divorce? Well, I find there's another reason I want to come to Boston to go to school. I just told my mother I'm gay and she said, "No 15-year-old can be gay!" Can you call her and ask if I can come stay with you for the school year? I can't even get any studying done around here! She respects you. Please!

Love,
Mark

Paula wrote to Ben at almost the same time. She had no intention of relinquishing custody or abandoning her duties as Mark's mother. She just knew they needed time apart. Her letter was a little different.

Dear Ben,

I need to talk to you. Mark has just been impossible lately, and nothing I can do or say seems to help. Of course I have known that he's gay for a long time, but he has come out to me very belligerently and accuses me of never understanding him. Frankly, right now, I don't. I wonder if some time living apart would help our relationship. He has been talking about writing you. I sure hope he does.

Love,
Paula

Paula reflected on the various possibilities and concluded that allowing Mark to live with Ben, a long-time friend and mature gay man, made sense. Fortunately, it made sense to Mark and Ben, too. And Mark's father readily agreed—he'd taken little interest in raising Mark for years and was for any solution that didn't involve work or money on his part. A court proceeding was unnecessary and undesirable. Paula's concern was with Mark's well-being. And going to court could produce a nasty reaction from a judge. So Mark lived with Ben during the school year, and returned to his mother during the summer.

Written documents aren't essential to establish an informal guardianship, but they're desirable. To continue our story, suppose Mark suffered a serious cut on his arm at school while staying at Ben's. The wound would be sewn up by a doctor, under laws authorizing doctors to do what's necessary in an emergency. But what if the doctor also recommended plastic surgery, surgery that had to be done (if at all) within 24 hours? As this surgery is elective, not emergency, the doctor would require Mark's parents' permission before operating. If Ben had no document authorizing him to make medical decisions for Mark, he'd have an obvious problem if he could not find Paula. Or, to switch to a more pleasant example, suppose Mark wanted to go on a school trip and needed written permission to attend. Ben would need Paula's written authorization in order to sign a permission slip.

And then there's the question of support. Who pays Mark's living expenses? Paula and Ben discussed it and then wrote down their agreement, shown below as a sample informal guardianship agreement. You can download this form (and all the other forms in this book) from nolo.com. See the Appendix for the link. Just following the Temporary Guardianship Agreement is a form of authorization to consent to medical treatment, which is useful for a shorter stay.

After you write your agreement, make at least four originals: one for the school, one for the hospital, and others for the unexpected. Have the forms notarized. In most situations, documents like these should suffice when a school official, doctor, or bank needs proof that the guardian can act for the child. If someone refuses to honor the agreement, point out that you have the legal authority to act. After all, that's what the agreement says. If that doesn't work, call the child's parents fast. And if a school or other public agency insists that you use its form, use it.

Sample Temporary Guardianship Agreement

We, Paula Ruiz of 1811 Main Street, Cleveland, Ohio, and John Ruiz of 493 Oak Street, Cincinnati, Ohio, are the parents of Mark Ruiz, born on August 18, 1997. We grant Ben Jacobs, of 44 Tea Road, Boston, Massachusetts, temporary guardianship of Mark Ruiz. We give Ben Jacobs the power to act in our place as parents of Mark Ruiz, to authorize any medical examination, tests, operations, or treatment that in Ben Jacobs's opinion are needed or useful to Mark Ruiz.

We also grant to Ben Jacobs the power to act in our place as parents of Mark Ruiz in connection with any school activities, including, but not limited to, enrollment and permission for trips and other activities.

While Ben Jacobs acts as guardian of Mark Ruiz, we agree to pay Ben $300 per month toward Mark's support, to provide Mark with an allowance of $50 per month, and to keep Mark on Paula's health insurance.

_____   _____
Date   Paula Ruiz

_____   _____
Date   John Ruiz

_____   _____
Date   Mark Ruiz

_____   _____
Date   Ben Jacobs

Notarization

Sample Authorization to Consent to Medical, Surgical, or Dental Examination or Treatment of a Minor

I, Paula Ruiz, being the parent with legal custody of Mark Ruiz, born August 18, 1997, hereby authorize Ben Jacobs, into whose care Mark Ruiz has been entrusted, to consent to any X-ray, examination, anesthetic, medical or surgical diagnosis, or treatment and hospital care to be rendered to Mark Ruiz under the general or special supervision and upon the advice of a physician or surgeon licensed to practice medicine in any state of the United States, or to consent to an X-ray, examination, anesthetic, dental, or surgical diagnosis, or treatment and hospital care to be rendered to Mark Ruiz by a dentist licensed to practice dentistry in any state of the United States.

This authorization is valid from September 1, 2011, to June 30, 2012.

_____   _____

Date   Paula Ruiz

_____   _____

Date   Ben Jacobs

Notarization

RESOURCE

For more information about guardianships in California, see *The Guardianship Book for California*, by David Brown and Emily Doskow (Nolo).

Court-Appointed Guardianships

A court-ordered guardianship makes sense if the parent is mentally ill or incarcerated or if a third party—usually a relative—may try to intervene and get custody.

The guardianship process differs from state to state, and you will probably need to consult an attorney to learn your local procedures. If relatives or others object to the guardianship, you'll definitely need an attorney's help. If you anticipate problems with the guardianship process, you should see an attorney before you begin.

Agreements With Teenagers

When a teen comes to live with gay or lesbian adults—through foster parenting or a guardianship—the teen and the adults can also consider making an agreement between them. The purpose isn't to sue each other if the garbage isn't taken out, but to discuss and write down understandings and expectations. Our sample agreement concerns Eric, a 16-year-old who has come to live with John and David. This form is just an example to provide food for thought should you find yourself taking care of a teenager.

Sample Contract Between a Teenager and the Adults He Will Live With

Eric is coming into John and David's home; we are making this agreement to help make our family life together as harmonious and enjoyable as possible. We realize that circumstances change and we agree to review this agreement every six months or when one of us requests a review.

All disputes will be carried out with words. This means no punching. It also means that we will do our best to communicate openly and not assume that the others should automatically know our concerns.

Eric's parents will be encouraged to visit if they wish to do so and will be made as welcome as possible.

John and David will receive $300 from the welfare department as a stipend for Eric's support. The money will be used as follows:

> $100 for rent
>
> $100 for food
>
> $50 for clothing
>
> $50 for Eric for spending money.

John and David will contribute more to Eric's support than they are compensated by welfare. Further, Eric's $50 per month spending money isn't conditioned upon his doing chores. John will be the banker.

Eric agrees to be home by 7 p.m. on school nights and by 1 a.m. on weekends. He agrees to let John and David know what he's doing. He also agrees to call home by 6:30 p.m. on school nights and by 9 p.m. on weekends to request any later hours.

John and David agree that at least one of them will be home by 6:30 pm on weeknights and by 1 a.m. on weekends, and agree to leave a note on the refrigerator or call if there's any change.

Dinner is considered a special time, and will be served around 7:30 pm. Everyone is expected to be present if at all possible.

Eric will not use drugs.

Eric will be enrolled in public school and agrees to attend regularly.

John and David will shop, do the general cleaning, cook, keep the household accounts, do the wash, and do the maintenance around the house.

Eric will clean up after dinner and wash dishes twice a week. He will also take out the garbage—without being asked—and pitch in on small chores and large cleaning jobs. We will divide the yard work.

John agrees to be home at least two nights a week and David agrees to be home two nights a week. Tuesday nights and Saturday afternoons are times together and no one can make plans unless they include everyone—except if we all agree otherwise.

The stereo equipment is David's. He admits he's a fanatic about it, but it was expensive. So everyone agrees only David will use it. He will attempt to either play music everyone enjoys or use earphones. He's willing to put albums, tapes, and CDs on for others. The radio and TV can be used by all, and the volume is to be kept at a moderate level.

Smoking is permitted only in the back room.

Eric has his room and is free to lock it if he chooses. John and David have their room, and they may lock it if they choose. Everyone's privacy is respected. Eric will keep his room neat—but it's his room and as long as he confines his mess to this area, there will be peace. Eric won't spread his belongings around the rest of the house. If he does, they will be placed in his room.

John and David aren't used to sharing their home with a lot of people so Eric is permitted only one guest at a time and only when someone else is home, unless other arrangements have been made; Eric is responsible for his guest's behavior.

We agree to meet with Jeff Lakely, the social worker, every other week and candidly discuss our joys and problems.

5/15/20xx	*Eric Farmer*
Date	Eric Farmer

5/15/20xx	*David Roberts*
Date	David Roberts

5/15/20xx	*John Torres*
Date	John Torres

Medical and Financial Matters: Delegating Authority

Health Care Decisions... 164

    Documents Protecting Choice About Medical Care... 165

    Differences Among Types of Medical Care Documents................................... 167

    Where to Get Medical Care Documents 168

    What to Include in a Medical Care Form.. 168

    Choosing Your Attorney-in-Fact 173

    Preparing Your Health Care Documents... 174

    What to Do With Your Completed Documents.. 175

Physician-Assisted Suicide 176

Burial and Body Disposition 177

    Written Instructions... 177

    Choices Regarding Disposition of the Body... 178

Estate Planning Note... 180

Durable Power of Attorney for Finances 181

All lesbians and gay men, coupled or not, should consider what will happen if they become seriously ill or suffer a medical emergency and can't make their own medical and financial decisions. Ask yourself several questions: What are your desires for health care if you are in a terminal condition or coma? Who do you want to authorize to enforce your desires if you're incapacitated? How much authority do you want the person to have? Who do you want to have legal authority to handle your finances if you can't? What rights are bestowed by marriage or registration?

You should prepare some simple legal forms that will ensure that your desires are carried out if you become incapacitated. Using these forms, discussed below, you can create binding documents governing your health care and management of your finances.

If you don't create these important documents, your wishes may not be respected. In a well-known case, Karen Thompson was denied contact with, and authority to act for, her incapacitated lover, Sharon Kowalski, after Sharon was seriously injured in a car accident. Sharon's mother and father removed her from Karen's care after learning that the women were lovers. Karen and her lawyer persisted, and after a seven-year battle, the Minnesota Court of Appeals finally named Karen as Sharon's legal guardian. By then, however, Sharon had lost years of Karen's aid.

In another, more recent case, Terri Schiavo lingered on life support for years while her husband and her parents argued about whether she would have wanted life support withdrawn when she was determined to be in a persistent vegetative state. Even with the protection of the marital relationship, Terri's husband was required to litigate for the right to carry out his wife's wishes. If she had prepared a medical directive stating her desires, everyone would have been spared years of heartache. Legally married or partnered same-sex couples could face the same problems—with homophobia often thrown in the mix—so these documents are a smart thing to have even if your state's marital laws allow for a spouse to make medical decisions.

Without legal documents, your lover and other people you may regard as "family" may be prevented from visiting you in the hospital. Also, because hospitals and doctors conventionally look to the immediate family for authority to act (if there is no document giving a partner that power), a partner is sometimes forced to look on in horror while the doctor is instructed to act in ways that are contrary to the patient's wishes.

Then there's the issue of money. When a person is incapacitated, someone must pay the bills, deposit checks, and take care of other financial matters. The authority to make financial decisions traditionally belongs to a spouse, not a lover or friend. But you can use a simple legal document called a "durable power of attorney for finances" to name and authorize another person to manage your money matters whether you have a partner or not.

This chapter explains how you can arrange for the handling of your medical and financial matters during a medical crisis or prolonged incapacity.

CAUTION

Make sure your documents are up to date. Even if you have already completed your health care documents, check your state's laws to be sure the documents have not expired. Older documents may be past the legal expiration date and should be reexecuted.

Domestic Partners' Authority to Make Health Care Decisions

A married or state-registered partner has the legal authority to make medical decisions for an incapacitated partner. However, even if you live in a marriage-equality or marriage-equivalent state, you should prepare medical care documents. First, if you go away for the weekend or are in another state that doesn't recognize your relationship, you may not have the rights you have at home if you don't have a written health care document. Just as important, through focusing on the issues raised, you and your partner will gain a better understanding of what's really involved, and (hopefully) clarify what you want. Further, it's best to have your medical wishes set out in writing, so hospitals and other medical personnel can have no doubt what you wanted, and do not have to rely on the word of your mate. Finally, these documents are not technically hard to prepare.

RELATED TOPIC

AIDS referral organizations. The AIDS epidemic has been responsible for the incapacity and deaths of thousands of people. AIDS has made people aware of their mortality and their need to be responsible to themselves and their loved ones. Chapter 11 provides information on organizations that provide legal assistance or referrals for people with HIV or AIDS.

Terminal Illnesses and Hospices

All over the country, hospice programs help terminally ill people maintain control over how they live and, ultimately, die. There are over 2,000 hospices in the United States Cancer patients make up the highest proportion of hospice patients. In addition, thousands of AIDS patients use hospices each year.

Typically, the terminally ill person stays at home, where care is provided by family, close friends, and medical professionals through the home hospice program. Some hospices provide housing for terminally ill patients just before death. Special counseling is given to the terminally ill person and those close to him. Hospice programs help ensure that a terminally ill person gets the type of medical care he wants. For example, if a patient is opposed to being connected to respirators or other life support systems, a hospice can provide alternatives, or just provide pain relief.

Information about hospices throughout the country can be obtained from the National Hospice and Palliative Care Help Line, 800-658-8898.

Health Care Decisions

The increasing use of life-sustaining medical technology has raised fears that our lives may be artificially prolonged against our wishes. But the right to die with dignity, in one's own time, has been addressed and confirmed by the U.S. Supreme Court, the federal government, and the legislatures in every state.

The United States Supreme Court has ruled that every individual has the constitutional right to make medical decisions without interference. The Court also has held that medical personnel must follow "clear and convincing evidence" of a person's wishes—even if the patient's family opposes those wishes.

The same right to choose or refuse medical treatment protects against the situation where doctors might wish to provide a patient with less care than the partner would like. For example, a doctor may be unwilling to try experimental treatments or maintain long-term treatments on a patient who the doctor feels has slim chances of recovering. And an insurer or HMO might not want to provide even minimal treatment to a patient who seems likely to die soon.

Below we explain the legal documents you can use to establish control over your health care if you become incapacitated. While these matters can seem dry or technical, the underlying reality is anything but. You are making choices that are profound and deeply personal, and may be wrenching at the time you make them. While it's vital to prepare these documents, it's equally vital to proceed carefully. Take time to understand your own desires and your options. And take time to discuss your decisions with whomever you appoint to act for you.

Documents Protecting Choice About Medical Care

Every state has laws authorizing individuals to create medical care documents that provide the "clear and convincing evidence" of that person's wishes concerning life-prolonging medical care. Validly prepared and executed, these documents are binding on medical personnel and institutions. There are two basic types of documents. You should prepare both:

- specific written directions—called a "living will," declaration, or health care directive—that describe the medical care you want (and don't want) if you can no longer express your wishes;
- written authorization—usually called a durable power of attorney for health care, or sometimes a health care proxy or patient advocate designation—that names a person you choose to supervise

implementation of your expressed wishes and to make other medical decisions for you, and describes the circumstances under which the person may act, such as if you are mentally incapacitated.

Some states combine the two types of documents into a single form. For instance, California's single form is called an "Advance Health Care Directive."

Most medical care documents are drafted to provide that the person creating them must be incapacitated and unable to make medical care decisions before the documents become effective. In legalese, this is called a "springing" document or power, because it only springs into effect if and when it's needed.

> CAUTION
>
> **Determination of incapacity.** Traditionally in our culture, mental incapacity must be determined by a doctor. So a durable power of attorney for health care generally states that a doctor must sign a written statement of a person's incapacity in order for the document to become effective. As anyone who has visited a doctor's office in the last few years has learned, a federal law (the "Health Insurance Portability and Accountability Act," commonly referred to as HIPAA) now imposes patient privacy rights on health care providers. HIPAA rules also govern the release of a patient's medical information, including a doctor's statement that a patient has become incapacitated. What this means, practically, is that every durable power of attorney for health care must contain a provision specifically authorizing doctors to make a determination of incapacity, and, if necessary, releasing any of the medical records needed or used in making that determination. The forms in this book include that provision.

You can impose further limits on when your health care documents become effective by restricting them, say, to when you are in a coma or have a terminal condition. But these limits may be overly restrictive. If you cannot or do not want to make your own medical decisions, even if you're not in a coma or in a terminal condition, you will want the person you've named to be able to make decisions for you.

Differences Among Types of Medical Care Documents

The difference between the two types of documents described in the previous section—a declaration and a durable power of attorney for health care—is simple. The declaration or living will is a statement you make directly to medical personnel that spells out the medical care you do or do not wish to receive if you become incapacitated. It functions as a contract with your treating doctors, who must either honor your wishes or transfer you to other doctors or a facility that will.

In a durable power of attorney, you appoint someone else (called your "attorney-in-fact" or "agent") to see that your doctors and health care providers give you the kind of medical care you want. You usually also give your attorney-in-fact the authority to make medical care decisions on your behalf when you can't make them yourself. In some states, you can give your agent broader authority to make decisions on your behalf, such as when to hire and fire doctors.

When Your State Form Is Not Enough

When it comes to medical care forms, there are many differences in the documents and formats used by different states. Some state laws require that a specific form must be used for a directive to be valid. Because the Supreme Court has ruled that every individual has a constitutional right to direct his or her own medical care, however, the most important thing for you to keep in mind is that your directions should be clear and in writing. If you feel strongly about a particular kind of care—even if your state law or the form you get does not address it—it is a good idea to include your specific thoughts in your written document. If you are using a state form that does not adequately address your concerns, write them in on the form with the additional request that your wishes be respected and followed.

CAUTION

It's best to use your state's forms. Each state has its own specific rules and requirements for making medical care forms. With a durable power of attorney for health care, you must use your state's forms. With a living will, you may have a constitutional right to create your own form, but there's no good reason to start from scratch. Begin with your state's form, which is fine for most people. If you want to be more specific than your state form provides for, you can insert additional provisions into that form.

Where to Get Medical Care Documents

You can obtain medical care documents free or for a nominal fee from a number of sources, including:

- local senior centers
- local hospitals (ask to speak to the patient representative; by law, any hospital that receives federal funds must provide patients with appropriate medical care forms)
- your regular physician,
- your state's medical association, and
- *Quicken WillMaker Plus* software from Nolo. Californians can also use *Living Wills & Powers of Attorney for California,* by Shae Irving (Nolo).

What to Include in a Medical Care Form

The problem many people have in filling out their state medical directive forms is that they are not sure how to fill in the blanks—and are not sure what much of the terminology means. Generally, in your directive, you can:

- specify whether or not you want your life prolonged with medical treatment and procedures, and
- identify specific medical treatments and procedures that you want provided or withheld.

In an Emergency: DNR Orders

In addition to your living will and durable power of attorney for health care, you may want to prepare a "do not resuscitate" order, or DNR order. A DNR order is used for the specific purpose of alerting medical personnel to the fact that you do not want to receive cardiopulmonary resuscitation (CPR) in the event of a medical emergency.

You may want to consider a DNR order if:

- you have a terminal illness
- you are at increased risk for cardiac or respiratory arrest and feel you wouldn't want CPR if you became ill, or
- you have strong feelings against the use of CPR under any circumstances.

In most states, any adult may secure a DNR order. But a few states allow you to create an order only if you have been diagnosed as having a terminal illness. If you want a DNR order, or you want more information about DNR orders, talk with a doctor. A doctor's signature is required to make the DNR valid—and in most states, the doctor will obtain and complete the necessary paperwork. If the doctor does not have the information you need, call the health department in your state and ask to speak with someone in the division of emergency medical services.

If you sign a DNR order, discuss your decision with your partner or other caretakers. They should know where your form is located—and who to call if you require emergency treatment. Even if you are wearing identification, such as a bracelet or necklace, keep your DNR order in an obvious place. Consider keeping it by your bedside, on the front of your refrigerator, in your wallet, or in your suitcase if you are traveling. If your DNR order is not apparent and immediately available, or if it has been altered in any way, medical personnel who attend you will most likely perform CPR and other life-prolonging techniques.

However straightforward this may seem initially, preparing a medical care form can be difficult. First, you need to understand some basics about what kind of care you can select or prohibit. Then comes the often more wrenching task of facing up to what some choices may involve. For instance, do you want to allow, prohibit, or require that water or food be artificially administered to you through tubes if you are near death? If you prohibit this, you may die from dehydration or starvation. All of the choices you make have consequences that are difficult to predict.

Below, we discuss the basic types of life-prolonging medical treatment.

To make an informed decision about which procedures you do and do not want, we suggest discussing your medical directive with your physician, who can explain the medical procedures more fully and discuss the options with you. You will also find out whether your doctor has any medical or moral objections to following your wishes. If the doctor will not agree to follow your wishes, you can choose to change doctors.

The following medical procedures and treatments are usually considered to be "life prolonging."

Blood and blood products. Partial or full blood transfusions may be recommended to combat diseases that impair the blood system, to foster healing after a blood loss, or to replenish blood lost through surgery, disease, or injury.

Cardiopulmonary resuscitation. CPR is used when a person's heart or breathing has stopped. CPR includes applying physical pressure, using mouth-to-mouth resuscitation, using electrical shocks, administering intravenous drugs to normalize body systems, and attaching you to a respirator.

Diagnostic tests. Diagnostic tests are commonly used to evaluate urine, blood, and other body fluids and to check on all bodily functions. Diagnostic tests can include X-rays and more sophisticated tests of brainwaves and/or other internal body systems.

Dialysis. A dialysis machine is used to clean and add essential substances to the blood—through tubes placed in blood vessels or into the abdomen—when kidneys do not function properly.

Drugs. The most common and most controversial drugs given to seriously ill or comatose patients are antibiotics—administered by mouth, through a feeding tube, or by injection. Antibiotics are used to arrest infectious diseases. Drugs may also be used to eliminate or alleviate pain. Because high doses of pain control drugs can impair respiration, such drugs sometimes hasten death in a seriously ill patient.

Respirator. A mechanical respirator or ventilator assists or takes over breathing for a patient by pumping air in and out of the lungs. These machines dispense a regulated amount of air into the lungs at a set rate—and periodically purge the lungs. Patients are connected to respirators by a tube that goes through the mouth and throat into the lung or is surgically attached to the lung.

Surgery. Surgical procedures are often performed, even on people who are terminally ill or comatose, to stem the spread of life-threatening infections or to keep vital organs functioning.

In addition to life-prolonging procedures, you may want to include in your directive your wishes about comfort care and artificially administered food and water.

Comfort care. The laws of many states exclude pain-relieving procedures from definitions of life-prolonging treatments that may be withheld through a health care directive. If that was all there was to it, most people would agree with this and welcome the relief. But the medical community disagrees over whether providing drugs to make a person comfortable or alleviate pain will also have the effect of prolonging the person's life.

Some people are so adamant about not having their lives prolonged when they are comatose or likely to die that they direct that all comfort care and pain relief be withheld even if a doctor thinks those procedures are beneficial. Other people are willing to have their lives prolonged so that discomfort or pain will be treated.

Artificially administered food and water. If you are close to death from a terminal condition or in a permanent coma and cannot communicate your preferences, it is possible that you will also not be able to voluntarily take in water or food through your mouth. The medical solution is to provide you with food and water—as a mix of nutrients and fluids—through tubes inserted in a vein, into your stomach through your nose, or into your stomach through a surgical incision.

Intravenous feeding, where fluids are introduced through a vein in an arm or a leg, is a short-term procedure. Tube feeding through the nose (nasogastric tube), through the stomach (gastrostomy tube), intestines (jejunostomy tube), or largest vein, the vena cava (total parenteral nutrition), can be carried on indefinitely.

Similar to the controversy over comfort care, medical experts are split over whether artificial food and water prolongs life or is medically necessary.

Other options to be considered. You may want to include one or more of the following:

- naming the primary physician you want responsible for your care, if you have an established relationship with a doctor you trust
- specifying whether you wish to donate organs, tissues, or other body parts after death, or
- authorizing your attorney in fact to decide where you should live, if you are incapacitated and can no longer live at home. You can also add more specific directions of where you would like to be moved to, or other housing desires.

Even when you have specified your wishes regarding life-prolonging medical treatment and comfort care in a living will, certain decisions may still be difficult. They may include:

- when, exactly, to administer or withhold certain medical treatments
- whether to provide, withhold, or continue antibiotic or pain medication, and
- whether to pursue complex, painful, and expensive surgeries that may serve to prolong life but cannot reverse the medical condition.

Moreover, despite your living will, some medical personnel may prove reluctant to comply with your wishes. Or they may want interpretation as to how to apply your wishes to a specific situation. For all these possible reasons, you want to appoint someone with legal authority to enforce your wishes and decide any newly arising medical issues for you. That person, appointed in your durable power of attorney for health care, is generally called your "attorney-in-fact."

To help the appointed person carry out your decisions, the power of attorney may include specific authorizations:

- to give, withhold, or withdraw consent to medical or surgical procedures
- to consent to care for the end of life, including pain relief
- to hire and fire medical personnel
- to visit you in the hospital or other facility even when other visiting is restricted
- to have access to medical records and other personal information, and
- to get any court authorization required to obtain or withhold medical treatment if a hospital or doctor does not honor the document.

Choosing Your Attorney-in-Fact

The most important factor in choosing your attorney-in-fact is to select a person you totally trust. Most readers will choose their partner, but are not required to do so, even if you are legally married or partnered. If your partner or spouse can't serve because of health reasons or because of reluctance or inability to be a strong advocate, be sure you pick a person who truly understands you and your life, and whom, of course, you can rely on totally.

You should also appoint an alternate attorney-in-fact, in case your original choice cannot serve or continue to serve. Make it clear that the second person is only a backup. It is not a wise choice to appoint two people to do the job together; that is likely to complicate the process.

CAUTION

Do not appoint your doctor or any medical personnel as attorney-in-fact. Although your doctor is an important person for your attorney-in-fact to consult concerning all health care decisions, you should not appoint your doctor to act as attorney-in-fact. The same holds for all medical personnel. The laws in most states forbid treating physicians and medical personnel from acting in this role—to avoid the appearance that they may have their own interests at heart and may not be able to act purely according to your wishes.

Important Terms

Principal: The person who creates and signs the power of attorney document, authorizing someone else to act for him or her. If you make a durable power of attorney for health care or finances, you are the principal.

Attorney-in-Fact: The person who is authorized to act for the principal. In many states, the attorney-in-fact is also referred to as an agent of the principal.

Alternate Attorney-in-Fact: The person who takes over as attorney-in-fact if your first choice cannot or will not serve. Also called successor attorney-in-fact.

Durable Power of Attorney: A power of attorney that will remain in effect even if the principal becomes incapacitated, or will take effect only if the principal becomes incapacitated.

Incapacitated: Unable to handle one's own financial matters or health care decisions. Also called disabled or incompetent in some states. Usually, a physician makes the determination.

Springing Durable Power of Attorney: A durable power of attorney that takes effect only if a physician determines that the principal cannot handle his or her own financial affairs. In some states, this document may be called a conditional power of attorney. The form included in this book gives you the option of making your power of attorney springing.

Preparing Your Health Care Documents

You do not need to consult a lawyer to prepare a living will, durable power of attorney for health care, or other medical care form. While you may have to make difficult decisions about what types of care you want or do not want, these are not legal issues. It is wise to discuss what you want in depth with your attorney-in-fact. In grim reality, making a medical decision for a loved one can be confusing, painful, and difficult. You want your attorney-in-fact to understand as much as possible what you want so that you both can be certain the decisions made are the right ones.

What to Do With Your Completed Documents

Once you have completed the documents directing your medical care, there are several steps you should take.

Signing, witnessing, and notarizing. Follow your state's requirements for making your documents valid. Every state requires that you sign your documents—or direct another person to sign them for you—as a way of verifying that you understand them and that they contain your true wishes.

Most state laws also require that you sign your documents in the presence of witnesses. The purpose of this additional formality is so that there is at least one other person who can attest that you were of sound mind and of legal age when you made the documents.

Some states also require that you and/or the witnesses appear before a notary public and swear that the circumstances of your signing, as described in the documents, are true. In some states, you have the option of having a notary sign your document instead of having it witnessed. Notarized health care documents are more likely to be honored in other states than documents that are merely signed and witnessed.

Making and distributing copies. Ideally, you should make your wishes for your future health care widely known. Keep a copy of your medical documents, and give other copies to:

- any physician with whom you now consult regularly
- any attorney-in-fact or health care proxy you have named, including any backup
- the hospital or other care facility in which you are most likely to receive treatment, and
- any other people or institutions you think it's wise to inform of your medical intentions, such as a hospice program.

Qualifications for Witnesses

Many states require that two witnesses watch you sign your health care documents and that they verify in writing that you appeared to be of sound mind and signed the documents without anyone else influencing your decision.

Each state's qualifications for these witnesses are slightly different. In many states, for example, a spouse, another close relative, or any person who would get property from you at your death (this includes anyone you name in your will) is not allowed to act as a witness for the document directing health care. And many states prohibit your attending physician from being a witness.

The purpose of the laws restricting who can witness your documents is to avoid any appearance or possibility that another person was acting against your wishes in encouraging specific medical care. States that prevent close relatives or potential inheritors from being witnesses, for example, justify their restrictions by noting that these people may have a conflict of interest.

Physician-Assisted Suicide

Behind closed doors, many doctors acknowledge that they have helped gravely ill patients end their own lives—many of them by writing large prescriptions for drugs, ostensibly to help patients with sleeping or pain problems.

Doctor-assisted suicide is currently a crime in almost all states. Oregon is the only state that allows doctor-assisted life ending. But legislation arises each year in other states proposing to allow voters to consider allowing doctor-assisted lethal injections for incurably ill patients. Some states have established commissions to study and make recommendations on the issue.

The Internet provides current information about the legalities and practicalities of physician-assisted suicide. One of the most complete websites is the Euthanasia World Directory, at www.finalexit.org.

Burial and Body Disposition

In marriage-equality and marriage-equivalent states, a surviving spouse or registered partner can make decisions about the other person's burial and disposition of the body. In all other states, the right to make decisions regarding burial and body disposition does not automatically belong to a surviving partner. In many cases, that can be a source of conflict between your partner and your family of origin. If you don't have written instructions, your biological family can overrule your partner and make whatever arrangements they think are appropriate. In the past few years, a number of states have passed laws making it illegal for family members to violate a deceased person's wishes as to burial services and body disposition. Whether or not you live in one of these states, however, many painful situations can be avoided by proper planning and advance discussions, so lovers, friends, and biological families know what you want. Advance Health Care Directives often confer the right to make decisions regarding autopsy, burial instructions, and disposition of remains.

Written Instructions

After death, a body must be disposed of quickly. If you haven't left written instructions, nearly every state gives control to your closest legal relatives—your partner can be excluded from these important decisions. If your partner has the resources to sue to gain control over your body, the case may succeed, but it will be messy and expensive. Worse, given the time a lawsuit takes, the issue will probably be moot because the relatives will have time to take action before a judge hears the matter. Of course, if you are married or legally partnered, you have the automatic right to make decisions about the disposition of your partner's remains— but if your partner dies when not in your home state, that right may not be recognized.

In most states, written body disposition instructions are legally binding. Written instructions let you state your wishes and name someone to carry them out. Contrary to what many believe, your will is not the best place to leave these instructions. A will is not likely to be found and acted upon right away after your death. If you anticipate objections from your family, make sure to write your instructions in a separate document—either your health care document or another, separate one—then sign and date it. Here are two examples:

I have made arrangements with the Tri-City Funeral Society regarding my funeral and burial. I appoint Alfred Gwynne to be responsible for implementing these arrangements regarding my death.

I have made the following arrangements regarding my death:
1. I have made an agreement with Hillman Hospital, San Francisco, California, to donate any of my organs or body parts needed by the hospital.
2. After any such donation, I direct that my remains be cremated, and my ashes scattered at sea. I have made written arrangements with the Nicean Society regarding my cremation.
3. I direct that Anna Rodriguez, my good friend and executor, be solely responsible for ensuring that these instructions are carried out.

Choices Regarding Disposition of the Body

In preparing for your death, you have a number of choices regarding disposition of your body, including esoteric ones like cryonics—body-freezing with the hope of being brought back to life sometime later. Among the most common are:

- a traditional funeral at a commercial mortuary or funeral home, which can include embalming; it may also include burial and religious or social ceremonies for the survivors
- a funeral you arrange with the help of a funeral society—in many states these organizations provide information about low-cost funerals and burials, and simple, dignified memorial services.

You can find the nearest organization by contacting the Funeral Consumers' Alliance, 800-765-0107

- cremation, either through a for-profit cremation company, mortuary, or funeral home
- donation of your body to a medical school, and
- donation of body parts and organs to hospitals or organ banks.

For decades, funerals and burials were controlled by commercial funeral parlors, which were both secretive and expensive. The business of funerals first came under attack in the 1960s, especially through Jessica Mitford's muckraking book *The American Way of Death.* Since then, reforms have been instituted in most states. Today it's usually possible to find good funeral services at a reasonable price if you ask knowledgeable friends for recommendations and monitor costs closely—and most importantly, plan in advance to target the services that fit your budget.

A few significant points are:

- Embalming is generally not necessary. It is usually required by law only when a body must be transported out of the state or country.
- Commercial funerals can cost many thousands of dollars. So shop around—compare services offered and check the prices charged by nonprofit funeral societies. Mortuaries are required by law to give you a list of their goods and services if you ask for one.
- Burial is expensive—especially given the high costs of "perpetual care" that many cemeteries charge for maintaining the gravesites.
- Donation of your body to a medical school requires specific arrangements in advance.
- Kidneys, corneas, pituitary glands, heart tissues, and even knee parts can be transplanted. Some states have adopted the Uniform Anatomical Gift Act, which lets you authorize the donation of body parts simply by carrying a short, signed donor card with you. It's useful, though, to arrange with a hospital or organ bank to receive, and use, your donation. Bodies from which organs have been transplanted may be returned for burial or may be cremated.
- Cremations have increased over the past few years. Cremation is the burning of the body, followed by the inurnment or scattering of the ashes. Some state laws allow ashes to be scattered over private land;

other states forbid it. Cremations are offered by most commercial funeral homes and by for-profit organizations such as the Neptune Society. Be careful how you specify the service you want. Some funeral homes provide—and charge for—the presence of a coffin at the memorial service, even if you have been cremated.

- Many funeral-burial businesses have couple rates, allowing a couple to pay for services in advance. It's legal for a business to refuse to give its couple rate to a gay couple in most states. However, it is illegal in most states for a mortuary to refuse to handle or to charge more for handling the remains of a person who died from AIDS.

Estate Planning Note

When you prepare for death or a possible medical crisis, consider what will happen to your property after you die. This is what lawyers call "estate planning," and it's particularly important for seriously ill people. After you die, your property will be transferred either by your estate planning documents, such as a will, living trust, or joint tenancy document, or by the default laws imposed by your state. No other method is possible. Oral statements you make before your death about who should get your property have no legal effect. A durable power of attorney for finances (discussed just below) expires when you die, so you can't use that document to transfer your property. Even while you are alive, an attorney-in-fact doesn't have the power to make a will or estate plan for you unless the document gives that power.

Every state has rules of "intestate succession" defining your "heirs at law"—the people who inherit if you die without a will. If you are married or legally registered, your partner will inherit your estate, or a portion of it, under those rules if you don't have a will. Everywhere else, though, if you don't have estate planning documents your partner has no rights over any aspect of what happens to you and your property after your death. Unless you've left written instructions, your partner can't receive any of your property, decide how to distribute or dispose of it, or arrange for your burial and body disposition.

These dire consequences can be avoided by proper estate planning, which we discuss in Chapter 7. If you do nothing else, at least prepare a will so that you, not your state's laws, determine who gets your property.

Durable Power of Attorney for Finances

During a medical crisis, you may be unable to manage your own financial affairs. Exhaustion, recurring dementia, long periods of treatment, or other hardships may leave you unable to tend to practical matters. If this happens, you'll need someone to take care of basic tasks such as paying bills, making bank deposits, watching over investments, or collecting insurance and government benefits. If you don't plan ahead and you become incapacitated, a court will decide who should handle your finances—and it might not appoint the person you would have chosen. Fortunately, there's a simple way to name a trusted person to handle your money matters: prepare a durable power of attorney for finances.

With a durable power of attorney for finances, you can:

- name the person who will handle your financial tasks (this person is called your attorney-in-fact)
- appoint an alternate person to replace your attorney-in-fact if your original choice cannot serve
- define precisely the authority you want your attorney-in-fact to have over your finances, and
- specify when the document should become effective (when the attorney-in-fact has authority to act for you).

Most durable powers of attorney for financial matters become effective if and only if the principal (that's you) has become mentally incapacitated to the degree the principal can't manage his or her own affairs. This is called a "springing" durable power of attorney. In some states you can set up equivalent protection with specific provisions in your revocable living trust.

You can use your document to place limits on the power of your attorney-in-fact. For example, you might want to forbid your attorney-in-fact from selling your home, or require that money from specified bank accounts be used to pay certain bills. You can include such restrictions in the "special instructions" section of the document.

The most important decision you'll make when you create a durable power of attorney for finances is choosing your attorney-in-fact. It's crucial to name someone you trust completely. In most situations, the attorney-in-fact does not need extensive experience in financial management: common sense, dependability, and complete honesty are enough. Your attorney-in-fact can get any reasonably necessary professional help—from an accountant, lawyer, or tax preparer, perhaps—and pay for it out of your assets.

Most people name the person they've appointed to make medical decisions as their attorney-in-fact for financial decisions. They understandably don't want to risk a possible conflict between one person handling medical matters and another handling finances. However, if the person you chose to handle medical matters is otherwise trustworthy but simply can't handle money reliably, you may feel you have to name another person as your financial attorney-in-fact but you are not required to do so. If you must do this, talk to both people involved, and do all you can to ensure that they will get along and can work together in harmony.

Again, you will probably want to name your partner as your financial attorney-in-fact. Keep in mind that it's best to appoint just one person to serve as your financial attorney-in-fact but you are not required to do so. Appointing more than one person opens the door to conflicts between them and may disrupt the handling of your finances. That said, however, it *is* important to name at least one trusted person as an alternate attorney-in-fact—someone to take over if your first choice can't serve.

All states permit some form of durable power of attorney for finances. At the end of this chapter we provide a sample durable power of attorney for finances, so you can get a general idea of what one looks like. This sample form has been filled out by the principal.

 CAUTION

Do not try to use or adapt this personal form for your own personal use. Get the form best suited for your state.

RESOURCE

Getting your state's durable power of attorney form. You can make a durable power of attorney for finances that's tailored to your state's laws by using *Quicken WillMaker Plus* software by Nolo. Californians can also use the Nolo book *Living Wills & Powers of Attorney for California*, by Shae Irving.

CAUTION

Your financial institutions may use different forms. Many banks and other financial institutions have their own durable power of attorney for finances forms. It's a good idea to use the financial institution's form in addition to your own form. Using the form that your financial institution is most familiar with will make it easier for your attorney-in-fact to get things done.

After you've prepared your durable power of attorney for finances, you must take just a few simple steps to make sure the document is legally valid.

Notarization. You must sign your power of attorney in the presence of a notary public for your state. In some states, notarization is required by law to make the power of attorney valid. But even where law doesn't require it, custom does. A power of attorney that isn't notarized may not be accepted by people or institutions with whom your attorney-in-fact must deal.

Obtaining the attorney-in-fact's signature. In the vast majority of states, the attorney-in-fact does not have to agree in writing to serve to make your financial DPA effective. However, the following states require the attorney-in-fact to sign the document: California, Georgia, New Hampshire, Pennsylvania, Vermont, and Wisconsin.

Witnesses. Most states don't require a power of attorney to be signed in front of witnesses. About a dozen states require either one or two witnesses. Witness requirements normally include:

- Witnesses must be present when you sign the document in front of the notary.
- Witnesses must be mentally competent adults.
- Your attorney-in-fact can't be a witness.

In case they're ever needed, it's a good idea to choose witnesses who live nearby and will be easy to contact.

Recording. You may need to put a copy of your durable power of attorney on file in the land records office of any counties where you own real estate. This office is called the county recorder's or land registry office in most states.

Montana, New York, and North and South Carolina require you to record a power of attorney for it to be durable—that is, for it to remain in effect if you become incapacitated. In other states, you must record the power of attorney only if it gives your attorney-in-fact authority over your real estate. If the document isn't in the public records, your attorney-in-fact won't be able to sell, mortgage, or transfer your property.

Sample Durable Power of Attorney for Finances

WARNING TO PERSON EXECUTING THIS DOCUMENT

THIS IS AN IMPORTANT LEGAL DOCUMENT. IT CREATES A POWER OF ATTORNEY FOR FINANCES. BEFORE EXECUTING THIS DOCUMENT, YOU SHOULD KNOW THESE IMPORTANT FACTS:

THIS DOCUMENT MAY PROVIDE THE PERSON YOU DESIGNATE AS YOUR ATTORNEY-IN-FACT WITH BROAD LEGAL POWERS, INCLUDING THE POWERS TO MANAGE, DISPOSE, SELL, AND CONVEY YOUR REAL AND PERSONAL PROPERTY AND TO BORROW MONEY USING YOUR PROPERTY AS SECURITY FOR THE LOAN. THESE POWERS WILL EXIST UNTIL YOU REVOKE OR TERMINATE THIS POWER OF ATTORNEY. IF YOU SO STATE, THESE POWERS WILL CONTINUE TO EXIST EVEN IF YOU BECOME DISABLED OR INCAPACITATED. YOU HAVE THE RIGHT TO REVOKE OR TERMINATE THIS POWER OF ATTORNEY AT ANY TIME.

THIS DOCUMENT DOES NOT AUTHORIZE ANYONE TO MAKE MEDICAL OR OTHER HEALTH CARE DECISIONS FOR YOU. IF THERE IS ANYTHING ABOUT THIS FORM THAT YOU DO NOT UNDERSTAND, YOU SHOULD ASK A LAWYER TO EXPLAIN IT TO YOU.

1. **Principal and Attorney-in-Fact**

   I, __Deborah Chen__, of __Lincoln, Nebraska__, appoint __Suzanne Hardy__ as my attorney-in-fact to act for me in any lawful way with respect to the powers delegated in Part 6 below. If that person (or all of those persons, if I name more than one) is unable or unwilling to serve as attorney-in-fact, I appoint the following alternates, to serve alone in the order named:

   First Alternate

   Edward Chen
   Name

   2461 Derby Street
   Address

   Lincoln, Nebraska 68501

Second Alternate

_____

Name

_____

Address

_____

2. **Authorization of Attorneys-in-Fact**

   If I have named more than one attorney-in-fact, they are authorized to act:

   ☐ jointly.

   ☐ independently.

3. **Delegation of Authority**

   ☒ My attorney-in-fact may delegate, in writing, any authority granted under this power of attorney to a person he or she selects. Any such delegation shall state the period during which it is valid and specify the extent of the delegation.

   ☐ My attorney-in-fact may not delegate any authority granted under this power of attorney.

4. **Effective Date**

   ☒ This power of attorney is durable. It is effective immediately, and shall continue in effect if I become incapacitated or disabled.

   ☐ This power of attorney is durable. It shall take effect only if I become incapacitated or disabled and unable to manage my financial affairs.

5. **Determination of Incapacity**

   If I am creating a springing durable power of attorney under Part 4 of this document, my incapacity or disability shall be determined by written declaration of ☐ one ☐ two licensed physician(s). Each declaration shall be made under penalty of perjury and shall state that in the physician's opinion I am substantially unable to manage my financial affairs. If possible, the declaration(s) shall be made by:

   _____ .

   _____ .

   _____ .

No licensed physician shall be liable to me for any actions taken under this part which are done in good faith.

6. **Powers of the Attorney-in-Fact**

   I grant my attorney-in-fact power to act on my behalf in the following matters, as indicated by my initials next to each granted power or on line (14), granting all the listed powers. Powers that are struck through are not granted.

   INITIALS

   _____ (1) Real estate transactions

   _____ (2) Tangible personal property transactions

   _____ (3) Stock and bond, commodity, and option transactions

   _____ (4) Banking and other financial institution transactions

   _____ (5) Business operating transactions

   _____ (6) Insurance and annuity transactions

   _____ (7) Estate, trust, and other beneficiary transactions

   _____ (8) Living trust transactions

   _____ (9) Legal actions

   _____ (10) Personal and family maintenance

   _____ (11) Government benefits

   _____ (12) Retirement plan transactions

   _____ (13) Tax matters

   ____*QC*____ (14) ALL POWERS (1 THROUGH 13) LISTED ABOVE.

   These powers are defined in Part 14, below.

7. **Special Instructions to the Attorney-in-Fact**

   _____ .

   _____ .

   _____ .

   _____ .

   _____ .

   _____ .

   _____ .

8. **Compensation and Reimbursement of the Attorney-in-Fact**

☒ My attorney-in-fact shall not be compensated for services, but shall be entitled to reimbursement, from my assets, for reasonable expenses. Reasonable expenses include but are not limited to reasonable fees for information or advice from accountants, lawyers, or investment experts relating to my attorney-in-fact's responsibilities under this power of attorney.

□ My attorney-in-fact shall be entitled to reimbursement for reasonable expenses and reasonable compensation for services. What constitutes reasonable compensation shall be determined exclusively by my attorney-in-fact. If more than one attorney-in-fact is named in this document, each shall have the exclusive right to determine what constitutes reasonable compensation for his or her own duties.

□ My attorney-in-fact shall be entitled to reimbursement for reasonable expenses and compensation for services in the amount of $_____ . If more than one attorney-in-fact is named in this document, each shall be entitled to receive this amount.

9. **Personal Benefit to the Attorney-in-Fact**

☒ My attorney-in-fact may buy any assets of mine or engage in any trans-action he or she deems in good faith to be in my interest, no matter what the interest or benefit to my attorney-in-fact.

□ My attorney-in-fact may not benefit personally from any transaction engaged in on my behalf.

□ Although my attorney-in-fact may receive gifts of my property as described in Part 7 of this document, my attorney-in-fact may not benefit personally from any other transaction he or she engages in on my behalf.

10. **Commingling by the Attorney-in-Fact**

□ My attorney-in-fact may commingle any of my funds with any funds of his or hers.

☒ My attorney-in-fact may not commingle any of my funds with any funds of his or hers.

11. **Liability of the Attorney-in-Fact**

My attorney-in-fact shall not incur any liability to me, my estate, my heirs, successors, or assigns for acting or refraining from acting under this document, except for willful misconduct or gross negligence. My attorney-in-fact is not required to make my assets produce income, increase the value of my estate, diversify my investments, or enter into transactions authorized by this document, as long as my attorney-in-fact believes his or her actions are in my best interests or in the interests of my estate and of those interested in my estate. A successor attorney-in-fact shall not be liable for acts of a prior attorney-in-fact.

12. Reliance on This Power of Attorney

Any third party who receives a copy of this document may rely on and act under it. Revocation of the power of attorney is not effective as to a third party until the third party has actual knowledge of the revocation. I agree to indemnify the third party for any claims that arise against the third party because of reliance on this power of attorney.

13. Severability

If any provision of this document is ruled unenforceable, the remaining provisions shall stay in effect.

14. Definition of Powers Granted to the Attorney-in-Fact

The powers granted in Part 6 of this document authorize my attorney-in-fact to do the following.

(1) Real estate transactions

Act for me in any manner to deal with all or any part of any interest in real property that I own at the time of execution of this document or later acquire, under such terms, conditions, and covenants as my attorney-in-fact deems proper. My attorney-in-fact's powers include but are not limited to the power to:

(a) Accept as a gift, or as security for a loan, reject, demand, buy, lease, receive, or otherwise acquire ownership or possession of any estate or interest in real property.

(b) Sell, exchange, convey with or without covenants, quitclaim, release, surrender, mortgage, encumber, partition or consent to the partitioning of, grant options concerning, lease, sublet, or otherwise dispose of any interest in real property.

(c) Maintain, repair, improve, insure, rent, lease, and pay or contest taxes or assessments on any estate or interest in real property I own or claim to own.

(d) Prosecute, defend, intervene in, submit to arbitration, settle, and propose or accept a compromise with respect to any claim in favor of or against me based on or involving any real estate transaction.

(2) **Tangible personal property transactions**

Act for me in any manner to deal with all or any part of any interest in personal property that I own at the time of execution of this document or later acquire, under such terms as my attorney-in-fact deems proper. My attorney-in-fact's powers include but are not limited to the power to lease, buy, exchange, accept as a gift or as security for a loan, acquire, possess, maintain, repair, improve, insure, rent, convey, mortgage, pledge, and pay or contest taxes and assessments on any tangible personal property.

(3) **Stock and bond, commodity, option, and other securities transactions**

Do any act which I can do through an agent, with respect to any interest in a bond, share, other instrument of similar character, or commodity. My attorney-in-fact's powers include but are not limited to the power to:

(a) Accept as a gift or as security for a loan, reject, demand, buy, receive, or otherwise acquire ownership or possession of any bond, share, instrument of similar character, commodity interest, or any investment with respect thereto, together with the interest, dividends, proceeds, or other distributions connected with it.

(b) Sell (including short sales), exchange, transfer, release, surrender, pledge, trade in, or otherwise dispose of any bond, share, instrument of similar character, or commodity interest.

(c) Demand, receive, and obtain any money or other thing of value to which I am or may become or may claim to be entitled as the proceeds of any interest in a bond, share, other instrument of similar character, or commodity interest.

(d) Agree and contract, in any manner, and with any broker or other person and on any terms, for the accomplishment of any purpose listed in this section.

(e) Execute, acknowledge, seal, and deliver any instrument my attorney-in-fact thinks useful to accomplish a purpose listed in this section, or any report or certificate required by law or regulation.

(4) Banking and other financial institution transactions

Do any act that I can do through an agent in connection with any banking transaction that might affect my financial or other interests. My attorney-in-fact's powers include but are not limited to the power to:

(a) Continue, modify, and terminate any deposit account or other banking arrangement, or open either in the name of the agent alone or my name alone or in both our names jointly, a deposit account of any type in any financial institution, rent a safe deposit box or vault space, have access to a safe deposit box or vault to which I would have access, and make other contracts with the institution.

(b) Make, sign, and deliver checks or drafts, and withdraw my funds or property from any financial institution by check, order, or otherwise.

(c) Prepare financial statements concerning my assets and liabilities or income and expenses and deliver them to any financial institution, and receive statements, notices or other documents from any financial institution.

(d) Borrow money from a financial institution on terms my attorney-in-fact deems acceptable, give security out of my assets, and pay, renew, or extend the time of payment of any note given by or on my behalf.

(5) Business operating transactions

Do any act that I can do through an agent in connection with any business operated by me that my attorney-in-fact deems desirable. My attorney-in-fact's powers include but are not limited to the power to:

(a) Perform any duty and exercise any right, privilege, or option which I have or claim to have under any contract of partnership, enforce the terms of any partnership agreement, and defend, submit to arbitration, or settle any legal proceeding to which I am a party because of membership in a partnership.

(b) Exercise in person or by proxy and enforce any right, privilege, or option which I have as the holder of any bond, share, or instrument of similar character and defend, submit to arbitration, or settle a legal proceeding to which I am a party because of any such bond, share, or instrument of similar character.

(c) With respect to a business owned solely by me, continue, modify, extend, or terminate any contract on my behalf, demand and receive all money that is due or claimed by me, and use such funds in the operation of the business, engage in banking transactions my attorney-in-fact deems desirable, determine the location of the operation, the nature of the business it undertakes, its name, methods of manufacturing, selling, marketing, financing, accounting, form of organization and insurance, and hiring and paying employees and independent contractors.

(d) Execute, acknowledge, seal, and deliver any instrument of any kind that my attorney-in-fact thinks useful to accomplish any purpose listed in this section.

(e) Pay, compromise, or contest business taxes or assessments.

(f) Demand and receive money or other things of value to which I am or claim to be entitled as the proceeds of any business operation, and conserve, invest, disburse, or use anything so received for purposes listed in this section.

(6) Insurance and annuity transactions

Do any act that I can do through an agent, in connection with any insurance or annuity policy, that my attorney-in-fact deems desirable. My attorney-in-fact's powers include but are not limited to the power to:

(a) Continue, pay the premium on, modify, rescind, or terminate any annuity or policy of life, accident, health, disability, or liability insurance procured by me or on my behalf before the execution of this power of attorney. My attorney-in-fact cannot name himself or herself as beneficiary of a renewal, extension, or substitute for such a policy unless he or she was already the beneficiary before I signed the power of attorney.

(b) Procure new, different, or additional contracts of health, disability, accident, or liability insurance on my life, modify, rescind, or terminate any such contract, and designate the beneficiary of any such contract.

(c) Sell, assign, borrow on, pledge, or surrender and receive the cash surrender value of any policy.

(7) Estate, trust, and other beneficiary transactions

Act for me in all matters that affect a trust, probate estate, guardianship, conservatorship, escrow, custodianship, or other fund from which I am, may become, or claim to be entitled, as a beneficiary, to a share or payment. My attorney-in-fact's authority includes the power to disclaim any assets from which I am, may become, or claim to be entitled, as a beneficiary, to a share or payment.

(8) Living trust transactions

Transfer ownership of any property over which he or she has authority under this document to the trustee of a revocable trust I have created as settlor. Such property may include real estate, stocks, bonds, accounts with financial institutions, insurance policies, or other property.

(9) Legal actions

Act for me in all matters that affect claims in favor of or against me and proceedings in any court or administrative body. My attorney-in-fact's powers include but are not limited to the power to:

(a) Hire an attorney to assert any claim or defense before any court, administrative board, or other tribunal.

(b) Submit to arbitration or mediation or settle any claim in favor of or against me or any litigation to which I am a party, pay any judgment or settlement, and receive any money or other things of value paid in settlement.

(10) Personal and family maintenance

Do all acts necessary to maintain my customary standard of living, and that of my partner and children and other persons customarily supported by or legally entitled to be supported by me. My attorney-in-fact's powers include but are not limited to the power to:

(a) Pay for medical, dental, and surgical care, living quarters, usual vacations and travel expenses, shelter, clothing, food, appropriate education, and other living costs.

(b) Continue arrangements with respect to automobiles or other means of transportation, charge accounts, discharge of any services or duties assumed by me to any parent, relative, or friend, contributions or payments incidental to membership or affiliation in any church, club, society, or other organization.

(11) Government benefits

Act for me in all matters that affect my right to government benefits, including Social Security, Medicare, Medicaid, or other governmental programs, or civil or military service. My attorney-in-fact's powers include but are not limited to the power to:

(a) Prepare, execute, file, prosecute, defend, submit to arbitration, or settle a claim on my behalf to benefits or assistance, financial or otherwise.

(b) Receive the proceeds of such a claim and conserve, invest, disburse, or use them on my behalf.

(12) Retirement plan transactions

Act for me in all matters that affect my retirement plans. My attorney-in-fact's powers include but are not limited to the power to select payment options under any retirement plan in which I participate, make contributions to those plans, exercise investment options, receive payment from a plan, roll over plan benefits into other retirement plans, designate beneficiaries under those plans, and change existing beneficiary designations.

(13) Tax matters

Act for me in all matters that affect my local, state, and federal taxes. My attorney-in-fact's powers include but are not limited to the power to:

(a) Prepare, sign, and file federal, state, local, and foreign income, gift, payroll, Federal Insurance Contributions Act returns, and other tax returns, claims for refunds, requests for extension of time, petitions, any power of attorney required by the Internal Revenue Service or other taxing authority, and other documents.

(b) Pay taxes due, collect refunds, post bonds, receive confidential information, exercise any election available to me, and contest deficiencies determined by a taxing authority.

I understand the importance of the powers I delegate to my attorney-in-fact in this document. I recognize that the document gives my attorney-in-fact broad powers over my assets.

Signed this ___*6th*___ day of ___*October*___, ___*20XX*___.

State of ___*Michigan*___, County of ___*Wayne*___.

___*Jonathan Chen*___   ___123-45-6788___
Signature   Social Security Number

WITNESSES

On the date written above, the principal declared to me that this instrument is his or her financial power of attorney, and that he or she willingly executed it as a free and voluntary act. The principal signed this instrument in my presence.

_____   _____
Name   Name

_____   _____
Address   Address

_____   _____

_____   _____
County   County

CERTIFICATE OF ACKNOWLEDGMENT OF NOTARY PUBLIC

State of _____ ⎫
County of _____ ⎬ ss
                                       ⎭

On _____, before me, _____

_____, a notary public in and for said

state, personally appeared _____, personally

known to me (or proved on the basis of satisfactory evidence) to be the person whose name is subscribed to the within instrument, and acknowledged to me that he or she executed the same in his or her authorized capacity and that by his or her signature on the instrument the person, or the entity upon behalf of which the person acted, executed the instrument.

WITNESS my hand and official seal.

_____

Notary Public for the State of

[notarial seal]

_____

My commission expires: _____

PREPARATION STATEMENT

This document was prepared by:

_Jonathan Chen_____
Name

_147 Iris Street, Detroit, Michigan 48231_____
Address

_____

Looking Ahead: Estate Planning

Death and Living Together Contracts.. 199

Wills 200

Who Can Make a Will?... 202

Providing for Your Children.. 203

Your Executor 206

Typical Will Provisions... 207

Technical Requirements in Preparing a Will..208

Handwritten Wills 210

Electronic Wills... 210

Video or Film Wills... 210

Are Joint Wills Valid?.. 211

Is My Will Valid If I Move to a New State? 211

A Sample Will... 211

Storing and Copying Your Will 223

Changing or Revoking Your Will 223

Estate Planning Beyond a Will..227

Estimate the Value of Your Property..228

Probate Avoidance 228

Estate Taxes... 234

Changes to the Federal Estate Tax Law... 237

Gifts and Gift Taxes 241

Retirement Plans 243

F ew people look forward to the day when they will die; making plans for that inevitable time can even seem macabre. But it's vitally important that lesbians and gay men—especially those who are coupled—plan what they want to happen to their property after they die. This is called estate planning. Generally, if you die without a will (or a living trust or other legal means for transferring your property), your property will be distributed under your state's "intestacy" laws. These laws require that all your property pass to certain specified relatives, namely a spouse, children, parents, and siblings. State inheritance laws don't recognize lesbian and gay relationships, except in the marriage-equality and marriage-equivalent states. In these states, domestic partners and partners in civil unions and marriages can inherit some or all of the property even if the deceased partner did not make a will.

CAUTION

Prepare a will even if you are legally registered or married. Even if you have registered as domestic partners, entered into a civil union, or legally married, you should still prepare a will. Decide for yourself how you want to leave your property—it's simply not wise to let the state do any of your estate planning for you. Also, be sure to learn whether or not your state's laws require you to make some provision in your will for your spouse.

It's not hard to do basic estate planning. It's foolish not to do at least the minimum, which is preparing a basic will. Some years ago, an article in a national gay and lesbian news magazine described the plight of one man whose lover died and left no will. The deceased's family quickly appeared and started removing property from the couple's apartment. "His mother took the pillows and pillowcases off the bed," the lover said. "I ended up having to fight for my own clothes. We wore the same size."

Deciding what you want done with your property after you die isn't the only benefit of estate planning. If you and your lover are raising a child together but only you are a recognized legal parent, you can nominate your lover as a personal guardian for your child. Further, you can appoint the person you want to be responsible for supervising the distribution of your property—called your executor.

This chapter covers wills, the most basic of all estate planning documents, and contains a sample completed will form. There is also a sample of a basic will later in this chapter. It also covers more extensive estate planning. Transferring all your property by a will can have drawbacks. The principal one is probate, a legal proceeding where your will is filed with a court, your assets identified, your debts paid, and your property distributed to your heirs. Probate is usually expensive and time-consuming. By planning ahead, you can eliminate or lessen the need for probate, and sometimes decrease estate taxes. "Estate Planning Beyond a Will," below, can help you to decide whether your estate planning needs will be taken care of through a will or whether something more is warranted.

Death and Living Together Contracts

In Chapter 8, we explain that most states will enforce written living together contracts that cover property. If you have a contract stating that you're the half-owner of specific property, your partner has no power to dispose of your share, either during your life or at your death. While a living together contract will establish who owns what, you cannot rely on a living together contract (even one that provides that the survivor inherits the deceased partner's property) as a valid means for transferring property held in one partner's name upon the death of that person.

> (!) CAUTION
>
> **A living together contract is not a will.** If you have a living together contract, you may think you've done enough. But that's definitely not the case. A living together contract defines how a couple owns property while both partners are alive. It's not a substitute for a will or living trust, documents that specify what happens to a person's property after he or she dies.

Still, a living together contract is important. If you and your lover have no written contract, you could have trouble proving your agreements about property ownership after your partner's death. If your lover dies without a will, you will face an uphill battle trying to convince any court you had an ownership interest in property held in his name. And even if you could prove it in the end, it would be a difficult, costly process. You'd have to persuade a judge or jury that you had an oral contract about property, or that you had contributed to the purchase or creation of the property—and in many states, oral contracts aren't a valid way to transfer or share ownership of real property no matter what the circumstances are. The best way to avoid this is to prepare both a will and a living together contract, and leave the lawsuits to others.

Wills

A will is a document in which you specify who gets your property when you die—your "beneficiaries." This is the heart of will writing. You decide how you want your property distributed. Often, partners want to leave much or even all of their property to their mate. Whatever the legal status of your relationship—whether legally acknowledged by your state law or not—you have an absolute right to leave your property to your partner. Frequently, each partner also leaves other gifts to friends, children, family members, charities, or causes. The vital matter is for you to reflect on how you want to leave your property and then make those desires legally binding.

The advantages of a will are:

- A will is relatively easy to create.
- You can leave your property to anyone you wish. No laws prohibit you from leaving your property to your partner (or anyone else, for that matter).
- A will is easy to change or revoke; you're not stuck with it once you make it.
- Your will is your own business. Discussing it with your lover is often a good idea, but generally you're not required to reveal its contents to anyone. (However, if you are a registered domestic partner in California, the community property rules of that state apply to all of your property, and you can bequeath no more than half of your community property to someone other than your partner. If that's

your situation, you should consult an attorney about the extent of your right to keep your will private.)

The drawback to using a will is probate. After reading "Estate Planning Beyond a Will," below, you may decide to take steps to avoid probate. Even if you do, you should still definitely make a will. First, you may have property at your death that you hadn't thought of or known of when planning your estate, such as a suddenly inherited house, a gift of an expensive stereo or computer, big winnings at the races, or a personal injury lawsuit recovery. If you have a will, you can simply pass the "residue of your estate" (any property not specifically left to beneficiaries in your will or by other methods) to your partner or whomever you choose. You can also name who will supervise distribution of your property (your executor), and nominate a guardian for your minor child—something you can't do in other estate planning devices, such as a living trust.

Once you decide what property you want to transfer by will, don't delay. There is no benefit to postponing the drafting of your will; delay only increases the risks of the consequences of an untimely death—that is, your parents or siblings inheriting all of your property, rather than having it distributed as you've chosen.

CAUTION

Providing for your domestic partner. If you are in a marriage, domestic partnership, or civil union in a marriage-equality or marriage-equivalent state, you should leave some portion of your property to your spouse, or see a lawyer if you are leaving less than half. Each of these state's laws grant a surviving spouse rights to a percentage of the deceased spouse's estate. This percentage generally varies from one-third to one-half, depending on the state. A surviving spouse who is left less than the statutory share can choose to take the higher share provided by law. It is not (yet) clear whether these laws apply to domestic partnerships or civil unions in every state, but you should act as if they do. If you leave your partner half or more of your estate, there should be no problem if these laws do apply. If you want to leave your partner less, talk with a knowledgeable lawyer and see if you're running any risks.

Challenges to Your Will

Some LGBT folks (coupled or not) worry that their will could be challenged in court, perhaps by a disgruntled relative who does not approve of the will writer's choice of beneficiaries. Even if such a lawsuit were filed, it would be highly unlikely to prevail. The legal grounds for invalidating a will are limited to extreme circumstances. It must be proved that the will was procured by fraud, duress (undue influence), or the legal incompetence of the will writer. Beyond these, the will writer's choice of beneficiaries is final, and not subject to court review.

If you think someone might contest your will, it's best to prepare in advance to defeat any lawsuit. Consult a lawyer, discuss your concerns, and decide on the steps you'll take to protect your will. For instance, you may decide to have the signing of your will videotaped, as proof (if needed) that you were competent and acting freely when you signed it. Also, the lawyer could serve as a witness to your competence and freedom from coercion.

Who Can Make a Will?

Anyone who's legally an adult and "of sound mind" can make a valid will. An adult is anyone 18 years or older. You have to be very far gone before your will can be invalidated on the grounds that you weren't "of sound mind." If you understand this book, you're competent to draft a will.

Will I Need a Lawyer to Prepare My Will?

Many people can safely prepare their will without hiring a lawyer. If you have a moderate estate (generally speaking, under $2 million including the value of your house) and envision a straightforward distribution of property, you should be able to prepare your own will. After all, your intent is simply to define who gets your property when you die. You can probably state that in two or three sentences.

If you have a large estate and want extensive estate planning (for example, reducing estate taxes through complicated trusts or "pour-over" wills), you'll need to have your will prepared by a lawyer. But many ordinary folks usually don't need such costly planning.

RELATED TOPIC

Preparing your own will. If you want to explore preparing your will on your own, check out Nolo's will books and software in the list of estate planning resources at the end of this chapter.

Providing for Your Children

Either member of a couple can leave property to their own or their lover's children. You simply name the children in your will and leave them whatever you want. Or, you and your lover can leave all property to each other, and then name the children as alternate beneficiaries.

Providing for your minor children, however, does inevitably raise concerns. If you die before they're grown, who will care for them and how can you leave property to them? Let's look at each of these concerns separately.

Custody and Care

The legal parents of a minor child are the people entitled to custody of that child. When there are two legal parents, each is entitled to custody. If one dies, the other automatically gets custody, unless a compelling reason—such as the incompetence of the surviving parent—dictates otherwise.

Some lesbian and gay couples share legal custody of a child. But others do not. In some cases, one member of the couple—the biological parent or sole adoptive parent—is the sole custodial parent. In such a situation, if the legal parent dies, another adult must take legal responsibility for the minor child. This adult is called the child's personal guardian. Only a legal parent can use a will to nominate a personal guardian for a minor child.

The nomination of a minor child's personal guardian in a will is not legally binding. Children are not property and cannot be transferred by will. The final decision is made by a judge, usually using the standard of the "best interest of the child." But in most cases, the personal guardian nominated by a parent is confirmed by the court. Only when someone contests the custody proceeding, or the guardian is obviously unfit to serve, will a court reject the guardian nominated by the parent.

If you and your partner are raising a child together but only one of you is the legal parent, the legal parent should nominate the other as the child's personal guardian. You can explain, in your will or in a separate document, why your partner would be the best guardian for your child. If he or she is not nominated as guardian, the surviving partner may have an uphill battle to gain custody. You should also name an alternate guardian, in case the first choice can't serve.

Gifts of Property

Either parent can leave property to the couple's minor child, regardless of who is the recognized legal parent.

> **TIP**
>
> **Of course, before you can make gifts to your child in your will, you must have something to leave.** If you have little beyond a big mortgage and car payments, consider buying a moderate amount of term life insurance to help provide for your child. Because term life insurance pays benefits only if you die during the covered period (often five or ten years), it's cheaper than other types of life insurance.

Assuming you have property to leave to your child, your first concern is who will manage it. Except for property of minimal value, the law requires that an adult manage property inherited by minors until they turn 18 (and you can delay this age for property you leave in a will). If you don't designate a manager in your estate plan, a court will appoint one for you. These court procedures are time-consuming, costly, and may produce a result you wouldn't approve of. Here are several ways to do it yourself:

- **Leave property directly to your children's other parent.** This makes the most sense if you and your partner are coraising a child and only you are the recognized legal parent. You can use the basic will at the end of this chapter for this purpose.
- **Use the provisions of the Uniform Transfers to Minors Act (UTMA).** In all states but South Carolina and Vermont, you can use the UTMA to name a custodian to manage property you leave to your minor children for their benefit until the children are 18 or 21 (up to 25 in California, Alaska, Nevada, Oregon, Pennsylvania, and Tennessee). The UTMA works particularly well if you leave your children $100,000 or less, because money or property in this range will likely be spent for the child's education and living expenses by age 21. To use the UTMA, you can use one of Nolo's specialized estate planning or will-drafting products. (See "Nolo's Estate Planning Resources" at the end of this chapter.)
- **Create a child's trust.** For large estates ($100,000 or more) and in the two states where the UTMA is not available, consider establishing a simple child's trust, in either your will or a living trust. The trustee of a child's trust manages the money for the child and doles it out for education, health care, and other needs under the terms of the trust. If you choose, the child's trust can end and any remaining money can be turned over to your child outright at whatever age you designate, or you can choose to have the trust last for the child's full life. Again, see "Nolo's Estate Planning Resources" at the end of the chapter.

TIP

Name the same person to care for your child and any property you leave that child. Usually, it's wise to nominate the same person you nominated as personal guardian to serve as custodian of your children's money and other property, unless that person doesn't have good financial sense. If you face this problem, you are better off naming two different people: one to care for your child and another to manage his or her finances. Make sure the two people you name get along, because they will have to work together.

Your Executor

Who should you choose to serve as your executor? The person you trust the most to handle your property—most often, your partner. You want someone reliable, with high ethical standards. The job doesn't demand a high level of technical competence or financial sophistication. Some states require out-of-state executors to post a bond (deposit money as a guarantee that they'll do their job properly), so it is a good idea to name an executor who lives in the same state you do.

What does an executor actually do? Simply put, the executor's job is to gather and take care of the deceased person's will assets, handle probate, pay any valid debts, and distribute what's left to the beneficiaries who inherit it. Sounds pretty straightforward, and in many instances it is. But, of course, complications can arise.

- **Gathering assets.** If you've discussed your assets with your executor and left a clear record of what you own, gathering your will assets shouldn't be hard. If you leave behind murky finances and jumbled records, however, your executor could run into problems.

- **Taking care of assets.** Your executor must safeguard your will property until it's time to hand it over to your beneficiaries. For most financial accounts, the executor won't have to do anything. But some assets may require action by your executor. For example, if a house or condo is empty, your executor will need to make sure that it's secure.

- **Handling probate.** Most wills must go through a court process called probate, for which the executor most often hires a probate lawyer. Once the probate process gets underway, the executor usually does little more than provide the lawyer with the will and basic property information, and sign occasional legal documents the lawyer presents.

In California, an executor can use *How to Probate an Estate in California*, by Julia Nissley (Nolo), to do a nonlawyer probate. Also, California law provides a simplified procedure for transferring all of a deceased spouse's property left to a surviving spouse (Probate Code Sec. 13500). Because domestic partners in California have the rights of married persons, a surviving domestic partner should be entitled to use this procedure. Wisconsin has a simplified probate system, open to nonlawyers. Court personnel will give you help completing the necessary forms.

- **Petitioning for family allowances.** All states have laws allowing the court to order that payment be made from an estate in probate to a surviving spouse or minor children when they are in need. Logically, these laws should apply to domestic partners/members of civil unions in those states making partners equal in legal rights to married persons. However, this has not (yet) been tested, so it would be risky to rely on it.
- **Paying debts and taxes.** Most people don't leave behind outsized debts or tax bills, so this isn't often a problem. Further, some major types of debts, such as a mortgage on a house, are not paid off on death. Whoever inherits the house also inherits the mortgage. Finally, few estates are large enough so that federal or state estate tax returns must be filed. (See "Estate Taxes," below.)
- **Distributing property to will beneficiaries.** If the will is clear, and the property situation isn't a mess, this final task shouldn't be hard. Also, many major items, such as a house or investments, are commonly transferred outside of probate. (See "Probate Avoidance," below.)

An executor is entitled to compensation, from the will estate. Many executors don't accept payment, unless their responsibilities become onerous or long-lasting, because they will inherit under the will (and because they were close to the deceased). If an executor chooses to be paid, the fee depends on the terms of the will and your state's law. A few states set fee rates. However, most state laws simply provide that the fee must be "reasonable."

Typical Will Provisions

You can use a will to do the following:
- Leave anything you own to anyone or any institution you choose.

EXAMPLE:

- To my friend Nancy Pikes, I leave my rights to my season tickets to the Washington Wizards. To my friend Dan Feldstein, I leave my two etchings by Thomas Hart Benton.
- To the Washington Humane Society, I leave $10,000.
- To my partner Miranda Cortez, I leave all my interest in the condominium at 77 Flane Street, Washington, D.C., my investment account with Charles Schwab & Co., and all other property subject to this will not left to other specifically named beneficiaries.

- Forgive debts owed to you.
- Nominate a personal guardian for your minor children.
- Name a property guardian to manage your minor children's property.
- Set up simple trusts for your children or leave UTMA gifts.
- Name your executor (sometimes called your personal representative).
- Disinherit people. You can't completely disinherit a spouse or, most likely, a spouse equivalent in a marriage-equivalent state, especially if you have community property—but this is a problem few of our readers will face.

Technical Requirements in Preparing a Will

For your will to be valid:
- It must be typed or computer printed.
- It must state that it's your will—"This is the will of (your name)" suffices.
- It must contain at least one substantive provision, such as leaving property to a beneficiary or naming a guardian for your child.
- It must be signed and dated by you after declaring to witnesses that it's your will. Some authorities recommend you say, "This is my will," and have the witnesses answer, "He says it's his will." It sounds

like Gilbert and Sullivan, but it can't hurt. Although the witnesses must know the document is your will, they aren't expected (or required) to read it.

- It must be signed and dated by three witnesses who are not beneficiaries under the will. They sign after you do. In most all states, only two witnesses are legally required. Using a third, however, can't hurt and means the will is valid in all states.

- Once you draft your will, you don't have to hold onto property just because it's left to someone in your will. If you left your Renoir painting to your friend Bob in your will, but sell the painting before you die, Bob's out of luck—your will is completely valid even though the provision is void.

Disinheriting

You can disinherit almost anyone other than your spouse, by simply not mentioning that person in your will. To disinherit your child (or the child of your deceased child), however, you must take explicit action. The traditional method is to state the disinheritance expressly in your will—"I disinherit my son William Jones and direct that he receive nothing from my estate."

The basic will in this chapter provides a general clause that will result in a child's or children's disinheritance if you don't leave property to them. Specifically, the will states: "If I do not leave property in this will to one or more of my children or my grandchildren named above, my failure to do so is intentional." If you want to use an express disinheritance clause, you'll find a sample in *Nolo's Simple Will Book*, by Denis Clifford.

Some states have laws, called "pretermitted heir" statutes, that are designed to prevent accidental disinheritance of children. These laws provide that if you fail to mention a child born after your will was made, that child receives a set percentage of your estate. So, if you have a child after writing your will, you should revise the will to leave something to that child or specify that the child is disinherited.

Handwritten Wills

Handwritten, unwitnessed wills, called "holographic" wills, are legal in about half of the states. To be valid, a holographic will must be written, dated, and signed entirely in the handwriting of the person making the will. (Sometimes, form wills that contain some machine-printed information are allowed, but all of the important provisions must be in the deceased person's handwriting.)

Regardless of your state's rule, you should type your will and have it witnessed. Courts treat holographic wills with some suspicion, because they are far easier to forge than are witnessed wills. And if they contain crossouts, additions, or machine-printed type (even a date or heading), they might be invalidated. So if you're trapped in the woods, the wolves are coming, and you don't have a will, write one out and say your prayers. Otherwise, type your will and have it witnessed.

Electronic Wills

Just one state, Nevada, authorizes what's called an "electronic will." An electronic will is an original will that is created and stored exclusively in an electronic format—usually, on a computer. The will must use sophisticated technology to create a distinctive electronic signature and at least one other way to identify the will maker, such as a fingerprint, retinal scan, or voice recognition system. Currently, there is no readily available and trustworthy technology that can accomplish this. If and when that technology arrives, other states will likely follow Nevada's lead.

Video or Film Wills

Video or film wills are not valid under any state's law. However, films or videos of a person reciting his or her will provisions, such as who their beneficiaries are, can be helpful evidence if a will is challenged—this evidence can demonstrate that the will maker was of sound mind and doesn't appear to have been coerced or defrauded.

Are Joint Wills Valid?

A joint will is one document through which two people leave their property. After the first person dies, the joint will specifies what happens to the property of the second person when she dies. We don't recommend joint wills because they limit the survivor's freedom to dispose of property. If you're thinking of using a joint will, see a lawyer.

Is My Will Valid If I Move to a New State?

If your will is valid in the state where you prepare it, it remains valid if you move to another state. However, if you move to Louisiana, you should prepare a new will because Louisiana's laws are based on a different legal system than those of all other states. Also, you might want to draft a new will after you move if your personal or financial situation has changed. To make simple changes, you can revoke your will and write a new one, or add a "codicil" changing your executor.

The statement of residency you make in the first line of your will may become important if you live in one of the relationship-recognition states. If you die in a state other than the one you lived in when you made your will, then unless there's convincing evidence that you were a resident of the new state, your will is likely to be administered under the laws of the state where you made it. This may be helpful if someone challenges your will or if the will is invalidated for some reason and intestacy rules apply.

A Sample Will

We show you a sample will below, so you can get an idea what a basic one looks like. In this will form, Samuel Troplon has handwritten the information that he wants in his final will, and crossed out the information he doesn't need. He must then type up the will, sign, and have it witnessed.

This sample is a bare-bones will. It's far better to have a basic will than none at all, but most people will want a more thorough will, which they can prepare using one of Nolo's will-writing resources listed at the end of the chapter.

Sample Will

Will of _____ Samuel Troplon _____

I, _____ Samuel Troplon _____
, a resident of
___ Queens _____
County, _____ New York _____ , declare that this is my will.

1. Revocation

I revoke all wills and codicils that I have previously made.

2. Marriages

I am currently unmarried, and have never been married.

~~I was married to _____ and am now divorced.~~

~~I am currently in a _____ with~~

~~_____ . We entered into our~~

~~_____ on _____ .~~

3. Children

~~I have no children, living or dead.~~

A. I have ___1___ children now living, whose names and dates of birth is:

Name ___ Nina Yanes _____

Date of Birth ___ June 5, 1996 _____

~~[Repeat as needed.]~~

The terms "my children" as used in this will shall include any other children hereafter born to or adopted by me.

B. ~~I have the following grandchildren who are the children of my deceased~~ child.

Name _____

Date of Birth _____

~~[Repeat as needed.]~~

C. If I do not leave property in this will to one or more of my children or my grandchildren named above, my failure to do so is intentional.

D. If at my death any of my children are minors, and a personal guardian is needed, I recommend that ___Michael Haight___ be appointed as personal guardian of my minor children. If ___Michael Haight___ cannot or refuses to serve, I nominate ___Elizabeth Troplon___ as personal guardian of my minor children.

E. If at my death any of my children are minors and a property guardian is needed, I name ___Michael Haight___ as property guardian for the property of my minor children. If ___ ___Michael Haight___ cannot or refuses to serve, I name ___Elizabeth Troplon___ to be appointed as property guardian for my minor children. Until each of my children is 25 years of age, any funds left to them can be used for their health, education, maintenance, and support.

4. Gifts

A. I leave $ ___20,000___ to ___Nina Yanes___ or, if he/she/it does not survive me by 30 days, to ___Michael Haight___. [Repeat as needed.]

B. I leave ___my car___ to ___Elizabeth Troplon___ or, if he/she/it does not survive me by 30 days, to ___Michael Haight___. [Repeat as needed.]

C. I forgive and cancel the debt of $ ___2,500___ owed to me by ___James Troplon___. [Repeat as needed.]

5. Residue

I give the residue of my property subject to this will as follows:

A. To ___Nina Yanes___ if he/she/it survives me by 30 days.

B. If not, to ___Michael Haight___ if he/she/it survives me by 30 days.

C. If neither ___Nina Yanes___ nor ___Michael Haight___ survives me by 30 days, then to ___Elizabeth Troplon___.

6. Executor

A. I nominate ___Michael Haight___ as executor of this will, to serve without bond. If ___Michael Haight___ shall for any reason fail to qualify or cease to act as executor, I nominate

___Elizabeth Troplon_____ to serve without bond.

    B. I grant to my executor the right to place my obituary of her/his choosing in the papers she/he thinks appropriate.

7. No Contest

If any person or persons named to receive any of my property under my will in any manner contests or attacks this will or any of its provisions, that person or persons shall be disinherited and shall receive none of my property, and my property shall be disposed of as if that contesting beneficiary had died before me, leaving no children.

8. Simultaneous Death

If ____Nina Yanes____ and I should die simultaneously, or under such circumstances as to render it difficult or impossible to determine who predeceased the other, I shall be conclusively presumed to have survived ____Nina Yanes____ for purposes of this will.

Signature and Witnessing

I subscribe my name to this will this ___7th___ day of ___March, 20XX___ , at ___Queens___ , State of ___New York___ . I declare that I sign it willingly, that I execute it as my free and voluntary act for the purposes expressed, and that I am of the age of majority or otherwise legally empowered to make a will and under no constraint or undue influence.

___Samuel Troplon_____

9. Witnesses

On this ___7th___ day of ___March, 20XX___ , ___Samuel Troplon___ declared to us, the undersigned, that this instrument was [his/~~she~~] will, and requested us to act as witnesses to it. [He/~~she~~] thereupon signed this will in our presence, all of us being present at the time. We now, at [his/~~her~~] request, in [his/~~her~~] presence, and in the presence of each other, subscribe our names as witnesses and declare we understand this to be [his/~~her~~] will, and that to the best of our knowledge the testator is competent to make a will, and under no constraint or undue influence.

We declare under penalty of perjury that the foregoing is true and correct.

_____

Witness's Signature

_____

Name

_____

Address

_____

_____

Witness's Signature

_____

Name

_____

Address

_____

_____

Witness's Signature

_____

Name

_____

Address

See the Appendix for the link. Instructions are set out in the next section.

CAUTION

This will won't work for Louisianans. If you live in Louisiana, you can't use any of the estate planning documents in this book. See a lawyer about how to make a will.

Preparing a Basic Will Using Our Form

You can use the will form on the companion page to prepare a basic will. While we urge you to go deeper into preparing a will, we include this form so you can at least prepare some kind of will promptly. Here are some guidelines for preparing a basic will using this form.

- **Do it in two steps.** After reading this chapter, prepare a rough draft of your will, using or adapting the form at the end of this chapter as a sample—remember, you must then prepare an entirely new document. Once you're satisfied you've covered everything, use the form included on the companion page to develop your own will. Make sure that you type in all necessary information—don't leave anything out that you'll need to handwrite later. Delete any language that you don't need, so that you don't have to cross anything out by hand.

- **Complete only the clauses that pertain to you.** In some clauses, alternatives are offered. Choose the one that applies to you and delete the rest.

- **Use plain language and common sense.** If you write, "I leave my car to my sister Sue," she will receive whatever car you own when you die. If you write, "I leave my Toyota to my sister Sue," and sell it before you die and buy a Porsche, Sue gets no car. Courts try to give effect to the "intent" of the will writer, but they can't contradict clear words.

- **Don't make additional changes before you sign your will.** If you want to change your will before it's signed and witnessed, don't just cross something out and initial the change. Instead, you'll need to make the corrections and then reprint the document. And after the will has been completed—signed, dated, and witnessed—you can make changes only by using a "codicil," or by revoking your will and preparing an entirely new one.

Completing the Will Form

Here we cover some basics of how to complete the clauses of the will in this chapter.

Your Name and Address

Use your full name and use it the same way throughout the will.

Your address is important because if at the time of your death you had connections with more than one state, each state may try to impose estate taxes. Giving your residence will help minimize this, and will help establish in which county your will is to be probated. (It's probated in the county where you made your home.) If you have real ties to more than one state, see a lawyer to figure out how to keep more than one state from trying to impose estate taxes.

Clause 1. Revocation

This clause covers all prior wills, including any handwritten document that could be construed as a will.

Clause 2. Marriages

In this clause, you will state your marital status at the time you are making the will. If you are legally married, state that you are married. Likewise if you are registered domestic partners, reciprocal beneficiaries, or participants in a civil union, specify the nature of your legal relationship with your partner.

If you were married or in a marriage-like relationship in the past, and it has been ended by legal proceedings, indicate that. That includes any heterosexual marriage that you were in at any time.

If you have an ex-spouse or partner to whom you are still legally married or bound by some type of legal relationship, you will probably want to see a lawyer to make sure that your will is drawn up properly. This might be a good time to tie up loose ends and terminate that relationship legally, as well.

If your marital status is uncertain because you live in a nonrecognition state, a visit to a lawyer is advisable.

The form on the companion page offers options for this clause, depending on your situation.

Clause 3. Children

If you have any children, list them all, and all children of any child of yours who has died. Your children are those for whom you are a legally recognized parent—that is, children you have given birth to, biologically fathered, or legally adopted. If you are coparenting, but are not legally recognized as a parent, you would not include the children here. Instead, you can provide for them in Clause 4.

As previously mentioned, if you wish to disinherit a child using this will, you can do so by leaving nothing to that child. The child will be disinherited under the terms of Clause 3.C.

If you have custody of minor children, you can nominate a personal guardian for those children in Clause 3.D. See the discussion in "Providing for Your Children," above.

You can also use Clause 3.E to name a property guardian for your minor children; this person will manage any property you leave to your children and can manage any other property they acquire before they become 18. Again, see the discussion in "Providing for Your Children," above.

Standby Guardian

In some states, when a child has only one legal parent, the child may be placed in foster care after the parent dies but before the judge appoints the guardian.

Illinois, New York, and a few other states get around this by letting the legal parent appoint a standby guardian—likely to be the same person nominated to be the legal guardian—to have custody immediately after the parent dies. The child avoids foster care and is placed with the adult most likely to be the permanent caregiver.

Clause 4.A. Gifts of Money or Personal Property

In Clause 4.A, you name beneficiaries for your money and personal property. Your personal property is everything but your real estate. Clause 4.A lets you make direct, unconditional gifts to a single beneficiary, either a person or an organization.

RESOURCE

If you want to leave a certain item of property to be shared by two or more people, see Nolo's will resources, like *Quicken WillMaker Plus* or *Nolo's Simple Will Book*.

SEE AN EXPERT

See a lawyer if you want to impose control over a gift. If you want to place conditions on something you leave in your will—for example, "I leave my boat to Ronald but only if he graduates from culinary school"—you'll need to see a lawyer.

If you leave someone money, specific amounts will be distributed first. You might want to add to the gift "but in no event more than [number] percent of my (net or probate) estate," just in case there's not as much there as you'd planned.

You can also name an alternate beneficiary if the beneficiary doesn't survive you. If you don't name such a person, and the beneficiary dies before you, your property becomes part of your "residue" in Clause 5, and goes to your residuary beneficiary.

Many people don't want to leave something to someone who will never benefit from it, and so they require the beneficiary to survive them by some specified period of time. The forms in this book require the beneficiary to survive you by 30 days in order to receive the property. You can specify any other reasonable period you want, such as 60 or 100 days (two years isn't reasonable).

If you plan to give specific items of property to a beneficiary, describe them with sufficient detail so there is no question as to what property you mean. If you want to leave many small items to someone, however, and you don't want to list them all, you can state that you give "all my furniture [or "my tools" or "my records"] to [name]." If you don't care who gets your minor pieces of personal property, you can add a clause stating that these items "are to be distributed as my executor deems proper."

In Clause 4.C, you can also forgive debts owed you. Forgiving a debt is in reality making a gift to the debtor, who would otherwise owe the money to your estate.

Clause 5. Residue

The "residue" in your will is exactly what it sounds like—all property subject to your will left over after the specific gifts in Clause 4 have been distributed. You can select any person or organization you want to receive the "residue" of your estate. It's prudent to name an alternate beneficiary for your residue. If you want to be really careful, you can name a second alternate beneficiary to receive your will residue if the first two don't survive within the 30 (or however many you choose) days. Many people simply leave the bulk of their estate to their residuary beneficiary, rather than list all their property in Clause 4.

Clause 6. Executor

Your executor should be someone you trust and can rely on, and who will be available and competent when you die. You should name at least one successor executor in case your first choice dies before you, declines to serve, or is incompetent when you die. If your will names no executor or no alternate when an alternate is needed, the probate court appoints one.

If you don't state that the executor is "to serve without bond," the probate court may require the executor to post a sum of money. This means either that a large amount of cash from the estate is tied up or that the estate must pay a bondsman's fee—usually 10% of the amount of the bond. If you name an out-of-state executor, the court may require a bond, even if you stated "to serve without bond."

Clause 7. No Contest

This clause is designed to discourage will contests. We have not included any general disinheritance clause, or a clause giving $1 to all nieces and nephews. As discussed, your children are a special case and can be disinherited specifically if you want, or you can do so under the terms of the will by not leaving them property.

If your relatives object to your sexual orientation, it's possible that they will challenge your will on grounds that you were incompetent, or under "undue influence," when you made your will, especially if you have considerable money. This may be even more likely if you leave your property to your lover, other gay or lesbian friends, or an LGBT organization. Although will contests are rare, they do happen, especially in cases of people with AIDS or any other potentially life-threatening illness. Anyone diagnosed with any life-threatening illness should prepare a will as soon after diagnosis as possible, to minimize the chance that the will might be successfully challenged.

If there's any real possibility that a relative will challenge your will, take action to establish that you are competent and not under undue influence when you sign it. One way to do this is to have your will prepared by and signed in front of a lawyer, who can testify that you were obviously competent. Consider videotaping your will, so when you sign your will, you can look into the camera and tell the world how sane you are. Or follow the approach of one lawyer, who advises her lesbian and gay clients to insert a clause like the following, which shows you considered leaving your property to your relatives:

> I make my gifts to Ben Tymons not out of any lack of love for my parents, sister, brother, Aunt Susan, Uncle Jonathan, Cousin Cynthia, Cousin Harold, or other relatives, but rather because my relatives are adequately cared for and I specifically wish to benefit my friend Ben who has been a source of great love and comfort to me over many years.

Many lawyers encourage their clients to sit down with their family members and speak directly about their intentions. This isn't easy, but it can have a very powerful emotional impact and can help avoid later conflicts.

Clause 8. Simultaneous Death

This clause covers the unusual situation in which you are a member of a couple and you die at the same time as your mate. Most states have adopted the Uniform Simultaneous Death Act. This law presumes that when two people die together, and it's impossible to know who died first, each person is presumed to have survived the other for purposes of their estates.

> **EXAMPLE:** Colleen and Brigitte have been a couple for over two decades. They die together in a plane crash. (Estate planning examples are rarely cheerful.) In their wills, each named the other to receive all her property. They named different alternate beneficiaries. Colleen named her brother Dan; Brigitte named her two closest friends, Rebecca and Amanda. Colleen is presumed to have survived Brigitte, for purposes of Colleen's will, so her property goes to her brother. Brigitte is presumed to have survived Colleen, for purposes of Brigitte's will, so her property goes to her two friends.

You may wonder: How this can work, logically? Well, as Oliver Wendell Holmes famously put it, "The life of the law has not been logic: it has been experience." This method achieves the sensible result of having each person's property go where, and to whom, they wanted it to go. It also eliminates possible fights about which member of the couple survived a few seconds longer than the other.

We include a simultaneous death clause in this book's will in case your state hasn't adopted the uniform law. Another way to handle the simultaneous death possibility is to define a beneficiary survivorship period. But even if you do this, it can't hurt to include the simultaneous death clause in your will.

If you own property in joint tenancy, and you and the other joint tenant died simultaneously, you're presumed to have died last. Thus your share passes through your will and the other joint tenant's share passes in her or his will. (See "Estate Planning Beyond a Will," below, for more information on joint tenancy.)

If you own insurance, and you and the beneficiary die simultaneously, the proceeds of the policy are distributed as if the beneficiary had died before you—that is, to any alternate beneficiary named in the policy or under the residuary clause of your will.

Clause 9. Signature and Witnessing

Sign and date your will in front of your three witnesses, who then sign the witness clause in front of each other. In many states, a will can be witnessed by what's called a "self-proving affidavit," a notarized sworn statement that can simplify or even eliminate witnesses' need to go to court after the will writer dies. Explanations of self-proving affidavits and sample forms are in Nolo's will-writing books and software.

Storing and Copying Your Will

Store your will in a safe place, one that your executor has ready access to. A safe deposit box is generally not a good idea because your executor probably won't have access to the box after you die.

You can make copies of your will for any person you want to have one. But do not sign any copies directly (photocopies of your signature on the original are okay). The reason for this is to prevent any possibility of duplicate wills, which can cause trouble later if you revoke or amend your will.

Changing or Revoking Your Will

Suppose you want to make a minor change in your will. For example, Mary died, and the library of lesbian fiction you were going to leave her you now want to leave to Martha. Or suppose you want to revoke your will entirely—perhaps because you and your lover just split up. What do you do?

CAUTION

State law may affect the validity of your will. If you go through a legal dissolution of your relationship, any bequests you made to your ex-spouse in a previous will are automatically revoked in most states. But this is not the case if you've been cohabiting and you end your relationship. In either case, make sure your will reflects your current wishes. If you want to provide for your ex after divorce, you'll need to restate these intentions in an updated will or trust.

Changing Your Will

When you should change your will is a matter of common sense. Don't make impromptu changes. You can't just ink out a provision in your will or handwrite a change in the margin. Changes must be made formally.

The form used to make legal changes to a will is called a codicil. You can use a codicil to make an addition, modification, or deletion after your will is drafted, signed, and witnessed. A codicil is a sort of legal P.S. to a will, and it must be executed with the same formalities as the will itself. If possible, it should be typed on the last page of the will itself, or on an additional page or pages. It must be dated and signed by the will writer and three witnesses. They don't have to be the same ones who witnessed the will, but try to use them if they're available.

Codicils are usually used for relatively minor matters, like the change of the beneficiary for the lesbian fiction library in the example above. If you want to make a major revision, don't use a codicil. A will that has been substantially rewritten by a codicil is confusing, awkward to read, and may not clearly show the relationship of the codicil to the original will. For major revisions, draft a new will; the first provision in our will— "I revoke all wills and codicils that I have previously made"—will revoke your earlier will and any codicils to it. (See "Revoking Your Will," below, for information on revoking a will.)

Below is a sample codicil shown in completed draft stage, like the sample will above. This is the codicil form we provide in this chapter. Follow the same instructions. When you're done, make several copies and attach the original codicil to your original will. Attach a copy of the codicil to each copy of your will.

Sample Codicil

_____First_____ **Codicil to the Will of** _____Samuel Troplon_____

I, _____Samuel Troplon_____, a resident of _____Queens_____ County, _____New York_____ ,
declare this to be the first codicil to my will dated _____March 7, 20XX_____ .

First. I revoke the provision of Clause _____4_____ of my will that provided:
I leave my car to Nina Yanes or, if she does not survive me by 30
days, to Michael Haight .

Second. I add the following Provision to Clause _____4_____ of my will:
I leave my car to James Troplon or, if he does not survive me by 30
days, to Michael Haight .

Third. In all other respects I confirm and republish my will dated _March 7, 20XX_
this _14th_ day of _May 20XX_ at _Queens, New York_ ,
and declare that I sign and execute this codicil willingly and as my free and
voluntary act and that I am under no constraint or undue influence.

On the date written below, _____Samuel Troplon_____ declared to us, the
undersigned, that this instrument, consisting of _____2_____ pages, including this
page signed by us as witnesses, was the _____first_____ codicil to [his/~~her~~] will and
requested us to act as witnesses to it. [He/~~she~~] thereupon signed this codicil
in our presence, all of us being present at the same time. We now, at [his/~~her~~]
request, in [his/~~her~~] presence, and in the presence of each other, subscribe our
names as witnesses, and declare we understand this to be [his/~~her~~] codicil, and
that to the best of our knowledge the testator is competent to make a will, and
under no constraint or undue influence.

Executed on _____ at _____ , _____ .

We declare under penalty of perjury that the foregoing is true and correct.

_____

Witness's Signature

_____

Name

_____

Address

_____

Witness's Signature

_____

Name

_____

Address

_____

Witness's Signature

_____

Name

_____

Address

Revoking Your Will

Wills are easy to revoke. A will writer who wants to revoke a will or codicil should do so by:

- writing a new will, expressly stating that the person is revoking all previous wills, or
- destroying the old will—burn, tear, conceal, deface, obliterate, or otherwise destroy it with the intent to revoke it. If you destroy your will, do it in front of witnesses. Otherwise, after you die, it may be difficult to determine whether you really intended to destroy it, or if in fact, you did. Someone may have a copy and claim the original will was unintentionally lost, and your would-be inheritors would have a real mess, and probably a lawsuit, on their hands.

Estate Planning Beyond a Will

Lesbians and gay men with substantial amounts of property may obtain significant benefits for their surviving beneficiaries by more extensive estate planning than simply writing a will. If you have little property, planning beyond a will is probably not necessary. Likewise, if you are young (under age 40) and healthy, you can probably wait until later in life to bother with further estate planning. Our rough rule is that anyone over 40 or ill (at any age), with more than $100,000 in assets, can probably benefit from some estate planning beyond a will, which means setting up the least expensive and most efficient methods of transferring your property after death.

Property that passes through your will must go through probate. Probate can be expensive. These fees are taken out of your property and reduce the amount your beneficiaries receive. If you transfer your property by an estate planning device that avoids probate, you can eliminate probate fees.

In this section, we provide you with an overview of the primary estate planning methods. People with moderate estates can normally do most of the planning themselves, if they have good information. Start with *Plan Your Estate*, by Denis Clifford (Nolo).

Estimate the Value of Your Property

The first step for many people is to take stock of their net worth. You can do this in any way that makes sense to you. If you have just a few major assets, make a rough estimate of the value of each. Or, prepare a thorough list of your property. If you have a substantial estate, this can help you determine whether your estate will be likely to owe federal estate taxes, which are assessed for a net estate worth more than $5 million in 2011. (Basic federal estate tax rules are set out in "Estate Taxes," below.)

A property list may also help your survivors identify and locate all of your property.

RESOURCE

A helpful resource here is *Get It Together: Organize Your Records So Your Family Won't Have To*, by Melanie Cullen with Shae Irving (Nolo).

An example of a net value list is shown below.

Probate Avoidance

Probate is a court proceeding where your will is filed—or your property transferred under intestate laws if you didn't write a will or transfer your property by other methods. Your assets are identified, your debts and taxes are paid, and any remaining property is distributed to your beneficiaries. Probate is expensive. Lawyers and executors receive fees, often substantial fees, for what's usually routine, albeit tedious, paperwork. Probate also takes considerable time, normally a minimum of several months and often more than a year. By contrast, beneficiaries can usually receive property transferred outside of probate within a few weeks or months of the deceased's death.

Probate has acquired a rather notorious aura. Most people may not know exactly what it involves, but they sense it's a rip-off. There's a lot of truth in that. Probate in many states is largely an institutionalized racket. No European country has the expensive, form-filled probate process America has. Even in England, where our probate system got its start in

Net Estate of Leslie Grayson

Personal Property	Value	Location or Description
Cash	$500	Safe Deposit Box
Savings accounts	$8,500	Tyson Bank
Checking accounts	$1,500	Tyson Bank
Listed (private corporation) stocks	$11,000	Matco Corporation
and bonds	$14,000	Break-Monopoly Company
Money owed me including promissory notes, mortgages, leases, and accounts receivable	$5,000	Jason Michaels (sold him my car)
Vested interest in profit-sharing plan, pension rights, stock options, etc.	$17,000	401(k) from Invento Corporation
Automobile and other vehicles	$6,000	Honda motorcycle
(include boats and recreation	$12,000	Toyota Camry
vehicles; deduct any amounts owed)		
Household goods, net total	$10,000	In my house
Artwork	$33,000	Various pieces around my home
Miscellaneous	$3,000	Silver set in my house
Real estate		
Current market value	$375,000	1807 Saturn Drive, Newark, Delaware
Mortgages and other liens	($125,000)	
Equity (current market value less money owed)	$250,000	
My share of equity (co-owned)	$125,000	
Business interest—33% interest in Invento Corporation, maker of small telephone-related inventions	$250,000	Acquired in 1999; estimate of present market value of interest
AETCO life insurance policy, No. 12345B	$50,000	Name of insured: Leslie Grayson Owner of policy: Leslie Grayson Beneficiary: Robin Anderson
Total value of assets	$546,500	
Debts (not already calculated such as real estate mortgage)	($3,000)	
Taxes (excluding estate taxes)	($12,000)	
Total (other) liabilities	($15,000)	
Total net worth	$531,500	

feudal times, probate was simplified in 1926 so that now the court and lawyers only get involved when there is a conflict.

Probate fees are usually set by state law. Computation methods vary from state to state. In many states, fees are based on the size of the estate.

The well-established methods of transferring property to avoid probate include:

- revocable living trusts
- pay-on-death bank or stock accounts
- joint tenancy, and
- life insurance.

Each has advantages and drawbacks, which we briefly discuss below.

Revocable Living Trusts

A revocable living or "inter vivos" (Latin for "among the living") trust is the most commonly used method of avoiding probate. A revocable living trust is created by establishing a trust document and giving the trust a name (such as "The R.P. Payne Living Trust"). Because the trust states that it is revocable, you have the right to revoke or change any portion (or all) of it at any time before you die, as long as you are still mentally competent.

While you are still alive, the trust is essentially a paper transaction, with no real-world effects. You maintain full control over the property in the trust—you can spend, sell, or give it away—and can end the trust whenever you want. Trust transactions are reported as part of your regular income tax return; no separate tax forms are required. The only real downside is that property with a documented legal title, such as real estate and stocks, must actually be transferred into the trustee's name.

In the trust document, you name yourself as both the grantor (the person setting up the trust) and the initial trustee (the person managing the trust property). You list the property owned by the trust. You name your beneficiary or beneficiaries—naming yourself as beneficiary during your lifetime and then naming the people you want to receive the trust property after you die. You also name a successor trustee to manage the trust after you die or become incapacitated. The successor trustee can be a beneficiary.

You must sign the trust document and have it notarized. It doesn't have to be witnessed or recorded. Finally, you must transfer all trust property with documents of title into the trustee's name. For example, if you place your house in the trust, you must execute and record a new deed transferring the house from you as an individual to yourself as trustee of the trust.

When you die, your successor trustee transfers your trust property to your death beneficiaries without any court proceeding.

> **EXAMPLE:** Wayne creates a living trust with himself as the initial trustee and his lover, Mark, as successor trustee. In the trust, Wayne makes several small gifts to friends, and names Mark as the beneficiary of Wayne's principal assets—a house and an apartment building. Wayne then executes and records deeds transferring title to the house and apartment house into the name of the trustee. When Wayne dies, Mark, acting as successor trustee, distributes the small gifts to Wayne's friends, and executes new deeds transferring the house and apartment house to the beneficiary—that is, himself.

For more information on living trusts, see "Nolo's Estate Planning Resources" at the end of this chapter.

Pay-on-Death Bank Accounts

A "pay-on-death" bank account, sometimes called a bank trust or Totten trust, allows you to name one or more beneficiaries to receive all money or property in the account when you die. The property goes directly to the beneficiary, avoiding probate. You manage the account as you would any other bank deposit account. The only difference is that you name someone on the account form—such as your lover—as beneficiary of the account, to receive the balance after you die. During your life, you retain full and exclusive control over the account—you can remove any funds in the account for any reason, make deposits, close the account, or whatever else you want.

There are no drawbacks to a pay-on-death bank account. Most banks have standard forms allowing you to create this type of trust—by signing a simple form, opening a new account, or transferring an existing account, depending on your bank's policies. Pay-on-death account fees are normally no higher than the fees for other types of bank accounts.

Pay-on-Death Securities Accounts

In all states but Texas, you can add a transfer-on-death designation to brokerage accounts, or to individual securities (stocks and bonds) under the Uniform Transfer-on-Death Securities Registration Act. In these states, if you register your stocks, bonds, securities accounts, or mutual funds in a transfer-on-death form, the beneficiary or beneficiaries you designate will receive these securities promptly after your death. No probate will be necessary. If you live in one of these states, your broker can provide the forms you'll need to name a beneficiary for your securities or security account.

Transfer-on-Death Vehicle Registration

Currently, only ten states allow you to register cars or trucks in a transfer-on-death form: Arizona, Arkansas, California, Connecticut, Indiana, Kansas, Missouri, Nebraska, Ohio, and Oklahoma. A few others (Hawaii, Illinois, North Dakota, and Oregon) have laws that are ambiguous. If you live in one of these states and want to use transfer-on-death registration, contact your state's motor vehicles agency for the appropriate form.

Transfer-on-Death Deeds for Real Estate

In a few states you can prepare and record a deed that will transfer your real estate outside of probate after you die, even if you don't share joint tenancy ownership with the person you want to get the property. These states are: Arizona, Arkansas, Colorado, Indiana, Kansas, Minnesota, Missouri, Montana, Nevada, New Mexico, Ohio, Oklahoma, and Wisconsin. The deed should expressly state that it does not take effect until your death, and name the person to receive title to the property after you die. A transfer-on-death deed must be signed, notarized, and recorded just like a regular deed. But unlike a typical deed, you can revoke a transfer-on-death deed at any time before your death.

Joint Tenancy

Joint tenancy is a form of shared property ownership. What makes it unique is the "right of survivorship." Right of survivorship means that when one joint tenant dies, that person's share in the joint property automatically passes to the surviving joint tenants. (See Chapter 9.) If there's more than one survivor, each gets an equal share of the deceased tenant's original interest. It's not possible to leave your share of joint tenancy property to someone other than the joint tenants when you die. If you attempt to leave joint tenancy property in a will, the will provision will be ignored. In order to avoid confusion, however, it's a good idea to mention in your will that certain property is held in joint tenancy and therefore not covered by the will.

Any property can be bought and owned in joint tenancy, although it's most commonly used with real estate. (We discuss that in "Taking Title to Your New Home," in Chapter 9.) Joint tenancy is a good probate avoidance device for property you acquire 50-50 with your partner— assuming each of you wants your share to pass to the other after death. You can also create joint tenancy ownership for property you own alone by transferring title of the property from yourself to yourself and someone else as joint tenants. You may owe gift taxes, however, if you give property worth more than $13,000 to the new joint tenant. Also, transferring the property into joint tenancy means you are irrevocably giving up ownership of half the property while you are still alive and that your partner would get half of the property if your relationship ends. Usually, a living trust is a better probate avoidance device than a transfer into joint tenancy for solely owned property.

Joint tenancy has drawbacks. Any joint tenant can sell his or her interest in the joint tenancy at any time, thereby destroying the joint tenancy. If a joint tenant makes a sale or gift, the new owner and the remaining owners are called "tenants in common." Tenants in common don't have rights of survivorship. If a tenant in common dies, that person's share passes by will, or by state law if there was no will. Another drawback of joint tenancy is that joint tenants must own equal shares of the property. If you own unequal shares, joint tenancy won't work.

In some cases, having joint tenancy property can also increase the estate taxes of the first co-owner who dies. In some states, married or legally registered partners also can own property "with right of survivorship."

Life Insurance

Normally, life insurance proceeds are paid directly to the beneficiary you've chosen, without going through probate. The proceeds of a life insurance policy are only subject to probate and included in the value of the probate estate if the beneficiary is the "estate" itself, not a specific person or organization. Only in the rare case of a large estate with no other assets to pay the death taxes and probate costs is there any reason to name the estate as the beneficiary. Life insurance proceeds are included for estate valuation purposes even if they pass outside probate.

Retirement Accounts

You can name a specific beneficiary for your pension or retirement accounts, and that designation will supersede your will. If you want to change a beneficiary designation, you must notify your account administrator in writing—don't rely on a conflicting provision in your will to establish the change, because your estate planning documents will be ignored if there's a valid beneficiary designation on file.

Estate Taxes

All property owned at the time of death is subject to federal estate taxes, including insurance, retirement accounts, real and personal property, and financial assets. Also, a few states impose state inheritance taxes as well. Estate taxes are imposed whether the property is transferred by will (through probate) or by another device (outside of probate). Estate taxes are harder to reduce or avoid than are probate fees, but there are some ways to achieve savings.

Federal Estate Taxes

Federal estate taxes are assessed against the net worth of the estate (called the "taxable estate") of a person who died. A set amount of property is exempt from tax, depending on the year of death.

Federal law authorizes a couple of additional important exemptions to estate tax:

- the marital deduction, exempting all property left to a surviving spouse. This is one reason lesbian and gay couples want to be allowed to marry. The IRS has not extended this benefit to same-sex marriages or domestic partnerships—and as long as the federal Defense of Marriage Act exists, the exemption is unlikely to apply to any same-sex couples, even if they are legally married.
- the charitable deduction, which exempts all property left to qualified tax-exempt charities.

Federal law also allows deductions for some lesser debts, including:

- costs of last illness, burial, and probate fees and expenses, and
- certain debts, including a portion of any state estate taxes assessed.

To estimate whether your estate will be likely to owe estate tax, keep in mind these rules:

- All property you legally own will be included in your federal taxable estate.
- The worth of a house, or any other property, is your equity in it, not the market value—unless you own it free and clear.
- Property that you have transferred but still control, such as property you placed in a living trust, will be included in your estate.
- The total value of *all* property held in joint tenancy will be included in your taxable estate, minus the portion the surviving joint tenant can prove he or she contributed. The government presumes that a deceased person contributed 100% of any joint tenancy property, and the survivor contributed nothing. If the survivor can prove he or she contributed all or some of the money for joint tenancy property, the taxable portion will be reduced accordingly.

EXAMPLE 1: Eighteen years ago, Joe and Ben bought a lemon-yellow Jaguar XKE together, and have preserved it in mint condition. It's always been owned in joint tenancy, but the records proving that each person contributed half the purchase price have long since been lost. Joe dies. The government will include the current market value of the entire car in Joe's taxable estate unless Ben can somehow prove that he contributed half the cost.

EXAMPLE 2: The same facts, except Ben contributed all the money used to buy the car and maintain it, and kept the records. Joe dies. Even though the car was owned in joint tenancy, none of its value is included in Joe's taxable estate because Ben can prove that Joe didn't contribute any money to buy or maintain it.

The tax rates on property that is not exempt from estate tax are stiff. The technical workings of estate tax calculations are complex; they require the services of an estate lawyer or other tax expert. But the basic rules are easy to grasp. If an estate is over the exempt amount, the tax rate on the nonexempt portion is the rate for the full value of the estate. Then the tax on the exempt portion is deducted. What this means is that the effective tax rate starts at 45% or more, depending on the year of death.

EXAMPLE: Pete dies in 2009 with a net estate worth $3,600,000. The exempt amount for this year is $3.5 million. So $100,000 of the estate is subject to tax. But the tax rate applied is not the tax rate for an estate of $100,000 but that for estates of $3.5 million, which is 45%. Then the tax due on the exempt portion of the estate is forgiven. So, the tax on the $100,000 is $45,000.

State Inheritance Taxes

Until recently, only a few states still imposed inheritance taxes. Most states had effectively eliminated them. However, several of the marriage/domestic partnership/civil union states, including New York, Iowa, and New Jersey, have a state inheritance tax. If you are married or registered in a state that recognizes your relationship, bequests to your spouse will be exempt from taxation.

There is a new type of state estate tax that can be a concern for prosperous people, even if they don't live in a state that imposes traditional inheritance taxes. Here's the story.

Before 2002, under federal law most states collected what was called a "pick-up" tax from an estate large enough to have to pay federal estate taxes. A "pick-up" tax didn't increase the overall tax paid by the estate, but the state was entitled to take a certain percentage from the total federal tax due.

Congress changed this system in 2002. Under current federal law, states' entitlement to "pick-up" taxes decreased each year until 2005, when the amount went to zero. To make up for this loss of revenue, many states have enacted a new estate tax of their own—a tax that is no longer connected to the federal system. The states that haven't done so yet are likely to adopt similar laws soon. The details of these new laws can vary between different states. The common factor is that estates may have to pay state inheritance tax even if they are not large enough to have to pay federal estate tax.

Generally, even for those estates that must pay this new tax, the amount involved will not be huge. But if you are concerned about this new state tax, see a lawyer who can bring you up to date on this rapidly changing area of the law. You may well learn that unless you want to move to a different state, there's nothing you can do to avoid this tax.

Changes to the Federal Estate Tax Law

In 2011, the estate tax exemption increased to $5 million (from $3.5 million). At the same time, the highest marginal tax rate applied to estates over the exemption amount has decreased.

The future of the estate tax is uncertain. Efforts to repeal the tax entirely have failed. The current law only goes through 2012. So, if you have a large estate that might be impacted by shifts in the estate tax law, be sure you keep current on what that law is.

This makes estate planning tricky for those with potentially taxable estates, because no one can be certain what the law will be when he or she dies. For purposes of this discussion, we take the safe approach, and assume that the estate tax will be around for some time.

CAUTION

Estate tax laws are subject to change. If you have a large estate, you should consult one of Nolo's more comprehensive estate planning products. (See "Nolo's Estate Planning Resources," below.) Also, be sure to keep up with estate tax changes by visiting Nolo's website at www.nolo.com.

Avoiding or Reducing Federal and State Estate Taxes

Estate tax planning is often thought to be a form of lawyer's magic, or chicanery, to escape estate taxes. Certainly there's some gimmickry in many schemes used by the rich to escape or reduce estate taxes, although not as much as there used to be. The truth, however, is that for folks rich enough to be subject to them, estate taxes aren't easy to escape.

Here are some ways you may be able to reduce estate taxes.

Make tax-free gifts. (See "Gifts and Gift Taxes," below.)

Establish trusts. Tax-saving trusts are desirable only for net estates over the federal estate tax threshold. Because of the complex nature of tax-saving trusts, a serious discussion is beyond the scope of this book. Briefly, though, if you have a substantial estate, you may save considerably on estate taxes by using trusts, particularly if:

- the bulk of your estate will be left to a person who's not a spouse for federal purposes (which means all same-sex partners), or who's old or ill and likely to die soon. When that person dies, the property will be taxed again. If you set up a trust in your will leaving the beneficiary only the income from the trust and the right to use the principal for an IRS-approved reasons (including medical costs) during life, with the principal going to someone else, this "second tax" can be avoided. This is called an "AB" trust.
- you leave all your property to your children. It will be taxed when you die and then taxed again when the children die. For years, one of the death tax dodges of the very rich was to leave their wealth in trust for their grandchildren, escaping taxation on the middle generation. Tax law changes curtailed this by introducing a "generation-skipping transfer tax." Currently you can leave up

to $2 million in a trust for your grandchildren and escape estate taxes on the middle generation. Any amount over this exemption is subject to federal estate taxes in each generation. So if you have children, grandchildren, and a hunk of money, consider establishing a generation-skipping trust. You'll definitely need to see a good estate planning lawyer to do this.

Using a Charitable Trust

An irrevocable charitable remainder trust allows you to make a gift to charity, such as an LGBT or AIDS organization, and also name someone to receive income from the donated property. You donate property while you are alive to a charitable trust you have created. Then the trust sells the assets and reinvests them without paying capital gains on the sale—this is particularly useful for property that has appreciated in value. The trust then makes set payments, as defined by you in the trust document, to a beneficiary you've named—called the "income beneficiary." This beneficiary can be you, another person, or both, such as you and your partner. The payment can be either a fixed sum or a set percentage of the value of the trust assets, and can be made for a set number of years or for the life of the income beneficiary. After this period expires, all remaining trust income is turned over to the charity.

You have to want to make a gift to a charity to bother with a charitable trust. But if you do want to make a charitable gift, this type of trust offers other benefits. First, the person who creates the trust receives an income tax deduction for the worth of the donated property.

Second, a charitable trust can be particularly desirable if property has appreciated. The charity can sell it for its current market value without having to pay capital gains tax. The money the charity receives from the sale becomes part of the trust property. Third, for someone whose estate will be liable for federal estate taxes, all the donated property is removed from the estate, thereby lowering or eliminating those taxes.

This type of trust is called, in legalese, a "charitable remainder trust." For more information, see *Plan Your Estate*, by Denis Clifford (Nolo).

Transfer ownership of certain property, particularly life insurance, before death. Life insurance proceeds are not part of a deceased's federal taxable estate if the person did not own the policy for at least three years before death. If you did, the proceeds are included in your taxable estate. The IRS presumes you're trying to avoid taxes if you give the gift within three years of your death, and assesses taxes anyway. The IRS is strict in determining ownership. If you retained any significant power over an insurance policy within three years of your death, you will be held to be the owner. Significant powers include the rights to:

- make payments on the policy
- borrow against the policy, pledge any cash reserve it has, or cash it in
- surrender, convert, or cancel the policy
- select a payment option, such as lump sum or in installments, and
- change or name the beneficiaries of the policy.

There are two basic ways an insurance policy can be owned by someone other than the insured. First, a person having what's called an "insurable interest" can take out, and pay for, a policy on the insured's life. Historically, insurance companies have not allowed same sex couples to purchase policies on each other, because the companies have limited "insurable interest" to marriage or a business relationship. However, in states that recognize domestic partners, civil unions, or same sex marriage, partners may be able to purchase policies on each other. By doing so, then for estate tax purposes the insurance proceeds are not included in the property of the partner who died.

Second, you can buy a policy and transfer ownership to another, even if that person doesn't have an "insurable interest" in the insured. Of course, anyone has an "insurable interest" in his or her own life. So, you can buy a policy and assign it to your partner. Life insurance policies are usually transferred by making a gift to the new owner. Transfer forms should be available from your insurance company. The new owner is responsible for paying the premiums after the transfer. Gifts over $13,000 per year may be subject to gift tax.

Once you give a gift of a life insurance policy, that's it. Gifts are final. If you break up, your ex-lover has the right to continue to own the policy.

Thus, you can retain control over your life insurance policy, or reduce your taxable estate. But you can't do both.

Gifts and Gift Taxes

At first hearing, the concept of gift taxes may not sound fair. (You mean the feds even tax generosity?) But think of it this way. If a rich person could "give" away all his or her property tax free just before death, there wouldn't be any point to death taxes. So Congress has defined the point at which giving gifts becomes a matter for the tax collector. The current rule, stated simply, is that no tax is due until a taxpayer's lifetime gifts to others exceed $5 million, and gifts of up to $13,000 per person per year are exempt from reporting. If Adrian gives $14,000 to Justin, Adrian must report $1,000; if Adrian gives $13,000 to Justin and $13,000 to Jack, no gift taxes are assessed. Also, if Adrian gives $13,000 to Justin each year for three years, no reporting is required.

Because federal estate and gift taxes are connected, taxable gifts made during life have an effect on estate tax owed at death.

> **EXAMPLE:** Kelly gives Irene $63,000. The first $13,000 is exempt from gift tax but the remaining $50,000 is subject to it. This means $50,000 of Kelly's personal estate tax credit has been used up. If Kelly dies in 2011, when the exemption is $5 million, her (remaining) exemption will be $4,950,000, assuming Congress reinstates the tax.

The $13,000 annual gift tax exemption can be used to lower the eventual value of your estate.

> **EXAMPLE:** Sarah, who is in her late 60s, has an estate of over $5 million. She wants to help a couple she's close to, Marcy and Louise. She gives each $13,000 a year. In five years she has removed $130,000 from her estate, tax free.

If you have excess wealth (a self-defined term, of course), other options exist for making charitable gifts during your life or at your death. Many people with average incomes and wealth during life find it easier to make charitable contributions part of their estate planning. Anyone making, or contemplating making, a really substantial charitable gift should check it out with a tax attorney or an accountant.

Document Any Large Gifts to Your Partner

Any noncommercial transfer of property between unmarried couples is a legal gift. If the value of the gift is over $13,000, the person making the gift is legally required to file a gift tax return. No gift taxes must actually be paid, however, until the giver uses up his or her $5 million lifetime exemption from gift taxes.

Why bother with the hassle of filing a gift tax return if you won't even have to pay a tax? Because without documenting the gift, you could encounter income tax problems down the line. If you two decide to sell a property after you've made a gift of a portion of it to your partner, how do you establish to the IRS that each of you is a co-owner? You might have to file a retroactive gift tax return and be hit with fines and penalties.

EXAMPLE: Annie moves in with Candace, who owns her house. After five years together, they have a formal commitment ceremony. As one part of that ceremony, Candace announces that she's giving Annie one-half interest in the house. But they do not record a new deed, nor does Candace file a gift return. Three years later, the couple sells the house. When Annie claims half the profits on her income tax, the IRS disallows it, asserting that legally, Candace remains the sole owner.

Some attorneys are concerned that transfers between registered domestic partners and same-sex married couples could be construed as taxable gifts, even though federally recognized (in other words, opposite-sex) spouses are exempt from gift tax rules. If you are married or registered and have significant assets, talk to an accountant who is up to date on these subjects.

Retirement Plans

Upon retirement, the bulk of many people's assets is sitting in retirement plans. These valuable assets provide security to the retiring worker, of course, and may also provide for a surviving mate if the worker dies prematurely.

Same-sex unmarried couples can use retirement plans in much the same way—to provide for a surviving partner. But unmarried couples need to jump through a few more hoops to accomplish the same thing.

Naming a Beneficiary

Whether you have an IRA, a 401(k), or another type of individual retirement plan, you may name any beneficiary you want. You must name the beneficiary by filling out a beneficiary designation form provided by the plan administrator that states your wishes. Generally, the plan administrator will require you to complete a beneficiary designation form when you first open an IRA or a 401(k).

Many employer plans name a surviving spouse as a default beneficiary in the event a worker fails to designate a beneficiary in writing. However, as most of these plans are governed by federal law, unmarried partners are not default beneficiaries—most likely, even if you are married, registered, or partners in a civil union—so it is important that you complete a beneficiary form and then keep a copy in your files and give one to the plan administrator. Most forms allow you to name a primary and contingent beneficiary. It's prudent to name both. (The only exception to this is a state-governed retirement plan, which may be governed by state, rather than federal law, so that your partner would be a default beneficiary. For example, in California the partners of members of CalPERS, the state retirement program, are considered the default beneficiaries—and if members want to designate someone other than their partners they must fill out a beneficiary form.) Most forms allow for a primary and contingent beneficiary designation, and it may be prudent to designate a contingent beneficiary in case you and your partner should die at the same time.

Naming a beneficiary of your retirement plan accomplishes several things. First, it ensures that the assets are distributed to the people you intend. Second, designating a beneficiary avoids probate. (Retirement plan assets go directly to the named beneficiary without probate court proceedings.) Third, when you name a beneficiary of your retirement plan, the individual or individuals who inherit the money will have more control over how quickly or slowly the assets are distributed, potentially saving your beneficiary a bundle in taxes.

Bear in mind that naming a beneficiary is not an irrevocable action. You may change your beneficiary at any time by completing a new beneficiary designation form. (It's also important to update your beneficiary designations if you get married or divorced.)

CAUTION

An individual retirement account is a "wasting asset." Once you reach age 70½, you must withdraw a certain percentage of your account each year. The withdrawal percentage is calculated on the basis of the combination of your life expectancy and that of your (oldest) beneficiary. So, if you live a long life, the bulk of the funds in your account will have been withdrawn.

Wills and Retirement Plans

Some people make the mistake of failing to name a beneficiary or simply naming "my estate," believing their will should take care of everything. But in the case of a retirement plan or an IRA, it is the beneficiary designation form, not the will, that governs what happens to the assets. For example, if your beneficiary designation names your brother as beneficiary of your IRA, but your will says that you want your IRA assets to go to your partner, the assets will go to your brother. There's one exception to this general rule: Washington's "superwill" statute allows people to use their wills to override beneficiary designations. Basically, the latest designation is the one that's followed. (Wash. Rev. Code § 11.11.020.)

How Inheritors Must Withdraw Funds

Federal law provides benefits to a spouse inheriting an individual retirement account that may not be granted to a survivor of a same-sex couple, even if they have been registered domestic partners. Specifically, a spouse can roll over an inherited retirement account into a retirement account of his or her own, and is not compelled to take immediate distribution. But in most cases, a lesbian or gay partner inheriting an individual retirement account must start taking distributions within a year after the partner's death, and the funds count as income to the recipient. At the same time, the funds are also included as part of the taxable estate of the deceased partner.

Under the Pension Protection Act of 2006, "nonspousal beneficiaries," including same-sex partners, will be able to defer paying taxes on inherited 401(k) plans in some circumstances by rolling them over into an "inherited retirement account" if the plan allows it. Generally, they must start taking distribution right away but they can avoid a lump-sum distribution and instead spread distributions over life expectancy, thereby reducing the tax burden.

Another option that some companies have come up with is a compromise that the IRS seems to accept: The company can arrange for your inherited retirement assets to be used to purchase an annuity. If everything is done by the book, you would only have to pay taxes on the annuity payments as you receive them. For this option to work, the company's plan documents must clearly state that such a transaction is permitted under the terms of the plan.

RESOURCE

For more information about inheriting money from retirement plans and IRAs, see *IRAs, 401(k)s & Other Retirement Plans: Taking Your Money Out*, by Twila Slesnick and John C. Suttle (Nolo).

RESOURCE

Nolo's Estate Planning Resources. Nolo publishes the following estate planning books and software:

- *Quicken WillMaker Plus* software, by Nolo, is a complete estate planning tool. You can use the software to prepare a customized will, living trust, health care directive, and durable power of attorney for finances.
- *Nolo's Simple Will Book*, by Denis Clifford, gives all the instructions necessary for drafting and updating a will.
- *The Executor's Guide: Settling a Loved One's Estate or Trust*, by Mary Randolph, is a complete plain-English guide to being an executor, covering every task and issue you may encounter.
- *Plan Your Estate*, by Denis Clifford, covers every significant aspect of estate planning. It is especially valuable for people with larger estates (over $2 million).
- *Make Your Own Living Trust*, by Denis Clifford, provides a thorough explanation of this most popular probate avoidance device, including forms and explanation for an AB trust.
- *8 Ways to Avoid Probate*, by Mary Randolph, offers a thorough discussion of all the major ways to transfer property at death outside of a will.
- *Estate Planning Basics*, by Denis Clifford, provides concise and easy-to-read explanations of the major components of estate planning.
- *Living Wills & Powers of Attorney for California*, by Shae Irving, helps Californians avoid legal hassles and personal disputes if they ever become unable to make financial or health care decisions for themselves.
- *Quick & Legal Will Book*, by Denis Clifford, contains thorough forms and instructions for preparing a basic will.

Living Together Contracts for Lesbian and Gay Couples

Living Together Contracts Are Legal 250

When You Need a Living Together Contract 252

What to Include in a Living Together Contract 253

    Property and Finances Clauses 254

    Cooling Off Clause 256

    Arbitration and Mediation Clause 257

Sample Living Together Contracts 260

    Short and Simple Living Together Contracts 262

Contracts for Jointly Acquired Items 265

    Contracts for Long-Term Couples 267

    Contracts for Sharing Household Expenses and Chores 274

    Contracts for Joint Projects 274

    Contracts to Give a Partner "Time Off" 278

    Contracts for People in School 281

    Contracts for Work Done Around the House 282

Modifying Your Agreement 285

Beware the Tax Man! 285

A contract is an agreement to do (or not do) something. Promises made by one person in exchange for another's actions or promises form a contract. Marriage is essentially a government-arranged contractual relationship, even though the terms of the contract are rarely stated explicitly, or even known, by the marrying couple. Saying "I do" commits a couple to a well-established set of state laws and rules governing, among other things, the couple's property rights. While it might be upsetting to some people that they weren't informed of all of the rules before they reached the altar, the rules are binding if disagreements arise during the relationship—or if one spouse dies or the couple splits up.

Unlike married couples, until recently most gay and lesbian couples generally did not automatically take on any contractual agreements when they started a committed relationship. Gay and lesbian partners may have an obligation to a landlord or mortgage company if they rent or buy a place together, but that obligation would be no different if they were roommates. Getting together, in and of itself, or forming a personal opinion about what is fair or what should happen, does not create a contractual relationship. If the couple chooses to make an agreement, however, or in some states if they act as though an agreement exists, that agreement will sometimes be considered an enforceable contract—a "nonmarital agreement," in legal terms.

SPECIAL ISSUES

If you marry or register as domestic partners, you will be entering into a marriage-based contract with your partner. The state sets the terms of that contract; if you want to opt out of any of its provisions, you must prepare a separate written agreement, often called a premarital, prenuptial, or in your case, prepartnership agreement.

Many unmarried couples buy property, mix assets, and invest together—often without writing down or talking about their intentions. Then, if problems around money and property come up, they try to work out an understanding or reach a compromise. Sometimes they visit a therapist or ask their friends to help. If they split up, they quietly divide their accumulations and go their separate ways, and are not required to go through a court process or follow the legal rules of marriage and divorce.

Unfortunately, some couples don't quietly divide the property and move apart. They battle in a courtroom, forcing the courts to deal with their claims. The first unmarried couples to bring their disputes to court were heterosexual couples, and most courts responded to these claims by trying to figure out what the couple had agreed to and dividing their property accordingly. By doing so, the courts ruled that unmarried couples have the right to create whatever kind of living together contracts they want to when it comes to financial and property concerns, and that courts should enforce these contracts whenever there's a dispute. In most states this goes for same-sex unmarried couples too.

A chapter that tells you how to create contracts so you can break up amicably might seem pretty depressing—few people starting a relationship or working to protect the relationship they've built plan on splitting up. Instead, this chapter discusses living together contracts so the two of you can figure out what you intend while you're together. This should lessen disagreements and misunderstandings even when things are going well. Talking out your intentions should bring you closer, and can actually help you overcome fears about money, property, and your future.

Nag, Nag, Nag

One thing that has not changed from the first edition of the *Legal Guide for Lesbian and Gay Couples* to this one is our emphasis on making legal contracts. Nor have the reasons changed—as we said in the first edition, "If you do not reach an understanding and write a contract, there is a good chance that an unsympathetic judge will end up writing one for you." In every edition for 30 years, an entire chapter has been devoted to the details of discussing and drafting these contracts—and even though the marriage contract, or something similar, is available in some states these days, written contracts are no less important now than they were in 1980.

And if you do in fact split up, having an agreement helps you avoid taking your troubles to court. The risks, trauma, and expense of litigation are far less likely to be visited on those who have taken the time to define their understanding in an agreement.

Living Together Contracts Are Legal

The legal rules governing nonmarital cohabitation contracts have mostly been made by courts and judges, not by legislatures. The leading court case is *Marvin v. Marvin* (557 P.2d 106 (1976)). The case involved the late actor Lee Marvin and the woman he lived with, Michele Triola Marvin. (She used his last name even though they were not legally married.) In the *Marvin* case, the California Supreme Court announced new legal principles involving the right of unmarried couples to make contracts. First, the court ruled that marital property laws do not apply to couples who are not legally married. Then, the court recognized that unmarried couples are here to stay, saying:

The fact that a man and a woman live together without marriage, and engage in a sexual relationship, doesn't in itself invalidate agreements between them relating to their earnings, property, or expenses. Neither is such an agreement invalid merely because the parties may have contemplated the creation and continuation of a non-marital relationship when they entered into it.

The court concluded by stating that agreements between nonmarried partners are valid unless they are based on an exchange of sex for money. The court in *Marvin* declared four principles of contract formation:

- Unmarried couples may make written contracts.
- Unmarried couples may make oral contracts.
- If a couple hasn't made a written or an oral contract, the court may examine the couple's actions to decide whether an "implied" contract exists.
- If a judge can't find an implied contract, the court may still presume that the parties intend to deal fairly with each other, and may find one indebted to the other by invoking well-established legal doctrines of equity and fairness.

Since the *Marvin* decision, several cases in different states have applied these principles to contracts made by gay and lesbian partners. Most states enforce contracts between gay and lesbian partners, but in some states only written contracts will be enforced. A small number of states prohibit contracts between unmarried couples on the basis that they foster immorality, and a few haven't considered the question. Most distressingly, some recent laws relating to gay marriage purport to ban private contracts between same-sex partners. It's uncertain whether these laws will be validated by the courts, but at the very least they will be a nuisance to anyone trying to enforce a living together contract in states that have them.

Any contract that even hints that sex is the basis for the deal will be thrown out of court. A California appellate court refused to uphold a gay living together contract, declaring that it explicitly referred to rendering sexual "services" as a lover in exchange for assets, and was therefore, in effect, an agreement for prostitution. So don't make any reference to sex in your contract. Identify yourselves as "partners," not "lovers."

Of course, you can feel free to discuss your sexual relationship with each other when preparing your contract (or any other time). But discussing with each other what's sexually expected, permitted, condoned, or forbidden isn't the same as mentioning sexuality in a property contract. It is especially important that you not make monogamy a condition for any financial provision, however important fidelity may be for you.

Most courts faced with enforcing a living together contract uphold written ones, reject implied ones unless there is very clear evidence supporting the claims, and fall somewhere in the middle with oral ones. When one partner says there was an oral contract while the other emphatically denies it, a judge is unlikely to find that the contract existed unless other evidence (such as a witness to a discussion about the contract or subsequent action) substantiates it. General vows, such as those uttered in a commitment ceremony, usually aren't considered to be legally binding. Paradoxically, when one partner dies and the other claims there was an oral contract entitling him to property, a judge is more likely to sympathize with the survivor and find in favor of a contract, especially if no one refutes it.

Thus, the purpose of this chapter is to encourage you and help you write down your understanding about your life as a couple. This chapter doesn't contain strategies on legally enforcing your living together contract in a courtroom. If it ever comes to that, you will need to read Chapters 10 and 11 and possibly seek help beyond this book.

Keep in mind that although you have the right to rely on the rules of contract law—meaning that written, oral, and even implied contracts should be enforceable and a court can invoke the doctrine of fair dealings in your favor—this doesn't mean that you should put all your faith in legal protections. Going to court to prove your contract will be time-consuming, expensive, and emotionally draining. In other words, it's better to truly trust your partner before you take a precipitous financial step together than to rely on the notion that your contract will bail you out.

> **EXAMPLE:** Patti and Katherine move in together. After graduating from college, Patti enters dental school. Katherine, too, intended to finish school, but postpones her plans and supports them both until Patti is finished. They had many conversations about their long-term plans, but wrote nothing down about sharing the benefits of Patti's new career. After four years, Patti passed her dental boards. Katherine was ready to resume her education, but Patti fell in love with a classmate and moved out. Katherine was left with the flea market furniture, the flea-ridden dog, and a feeling she was ripped off—and Patti went on to enjoy a flourishing new career and luxurious life with her new partner.
>
> Remember—they had no contract. Assuming that Patti and Katherine intended to treat each other fairly, we can reasonably assume that because Katherine put Patti through dental school, Patti would reciprocate and pay Katherine's school expenses. Would a court find an implied agreement? Could Katherine prove an oral one? Maybe, but maybe not, even though Katherine has a sympathetic case.

When You Need a Living Together Contract

Obviously, you don't need a contract if you have no assets or are in a brief relationship. But in a long-term and serious relationship, whether you're basking in the glow of just having joined forces or you've been together 20 years, you should consider the legal consequences of how you live. If you mix assets or share expenses, please do everyone a big favor and put your agreement in writing, especially if significant money or property is involved.

> **TIP**
>
> **If you have decided to marry, enter into a civil union, or register as domestic partners, you may want to sign the equivalent of a prenuptial agreement.** By doing so, you can opt out of some of the rules of the marriage or marriage-like relationship you are entering. Each state has very detailed rules for prenuptial contracts, and making an agreement can be rather complicated. You will need a lawyer's help to draft an agreement, and in many states, each of you will have to retain your own independent attorney, or the agreement will be presumed to be invalid. Also, if you register or marry, chances are your old agreements—even the written ones—will be superseded by the marriage "contract," unless you sign a new agreement that deals with any discrepancies between the old agreement and the marital rules that now apply to you. Better still, draft an entirely new one. Use *Prenuptial Agreements: How to Write a Fair & Lasting Contract*, by Katherine E. Stoner and Shae Irving (Nolo).

What to Include in a Living Together Contract

A living together contract can be comprehensive, covering every aspect of your relationship, or it can be specific, covering only your new house purchase. (We provide sample contracts specifically for purchasing a house together in Chapter 9.) These contracts need not be like the fine-print monsters foisted on you when you buy insurance or a car. You can, and should, design your contract to say exactly what you both want, in words you both understand. A simple, comprehensible, and functional document using common English is much better than one loaded with "heretofores" and "pursuants." And it's better to make a simple agreement that covers the basics than to ponder endlessly over a complex one that you never sign.

If you want your living together contract to include the day-to-day details of your relationship, write up two agreements. The first one should be only about property and finances. Then, if one of you ever sues the other in court, the property and finance terms should be the only ones a judge ever sees. Write up a second agreement if you wish about who will do the dishes, who will walk the dog, how many overnight guests you'll allow, and whose art goes in the living room. A court probably won't— and shouldn't be asked to—enforce this kind of agreement. As a result, if you do just one agreement that includes the personal as well as financial clauses, a court might get distracted by the personal clauses, declare the contract illegal or frivolous, and refuse to enforce the more important financial clauses.

The following sections discuss some of the types of clauses you may want in an agreement.

Property and Finances Clauses

Your living together agreement should cover all of your property— including the property you had before you began the relationship and the property either or both of you accumulate during it.

Property owned before living together. You probably each had some property before you met. Just because you move in together doesn't mean you can't continue to solely own your TV, oriental tapestry, and floppy-eared cocker spaniel, while your lover holds onto his or her car and collected works of Virginia Woolf. But just as with property you want to own together, you should have a written agreement. Making an agreement about the property you bring into the relationship may seem unnecessary, but it's not. Think about trying to separate it all ten years from now, when you've both been referring to everything around the house as "ours."

You can deal with the use of valuable items as well as ownership. Who gets to use the property? Who pays for upkeep? For instance, Alan owns a boat that he'll want to keep if he and Fred ever split up. Fred agrees to help with upkeep in exchange for using it, without acquiring any ownership interest.

Property inherited or received by gift during the relationship. Many people want to keep separate any property they inherit or receive by gift. Others want to "donate" the property to the relationship. Again, it's up to you. If you plan to keep inherited or gift property separate, don't forget to cover questions of use and control. Remember, though, any property given to *both* of you is legally owned by both—this includes gifts you receive at your wedding, commitment ceremony, or anniversary party, even if the gift is given by a relative or friend of just one of you.

Property bought during the relationship. Many people make purchases item by item, understanding that whoever makes the purchase owns the property. George buys the kitchen table and chairs, and Ham buys the lamp and stereo. If they split up, each keeps the property he bought.

Purchases also can be pooled. Ham and George can jointly own everything bought during the relationship, and divide it all 50-50 if they separate. A consistent approach to property ownership may simplify things, but is required by neither law nor logic. Ham and George could choose a combination of the two methods. Some items may be separately owned, some pooled 50-50, and some shared in proportion to how much money each contributed toward the purchase price or how much labor each put into upkeep.

Expenses during the relationship. How will you divide the day-to-day costs for food, utilities, laundry, housing, and the like, especially if expenses go up or incomes go down? Here are some suggestions of ways you can share expenses.

- **Share and share alike.** The couple has only one checking account. They both deposit their paychecks into it and pay all household bills out of it. Over the course of the relationship, incomes shift and who earns more varies year to year. They figure it all evens out in the end, and whatever savings or debts accumulate are viewed as equally shared regardless of who had the higher income.

- **Split 50-50.** Any time one person buys something for the house or pays a bill, that person initials the receipt and throws it into a jar. Every few months, they empty out the receipt jar and total up how much each has spent. One then writes the other a check to even things up.

- **Each contributes in proportion to income.** This works especially well for people with large income discrepancies. If one partner earns $100,000 a year and the other gets Social Security, the partner with less income will never keep up. Under this plan all expenses are divided in proportion to earnings.

> **CAUTION**
>
> **Watch out for gift tax issues.** Income pooling can trigger gift tax problems for high-earning partners, so if there's a big discrepancy, talk to an accountant before making decisions about how you will deal with sharing your money.

Cooling Off Clause

Consider including a clause to remind yourselves of your commitment should the stress of a moment threaten to drive you apart. We call this a "cooling off" clause. Although it's not always enforceable in court, it's an excellent expression of intention. It can simply state that if one person wants to leave the relationship, he or she will take some time to cool off before grabbing the cat and the good wine glasses and heading for the hills. Imperfect souls that we are, we make a lot of hasty, irrational decisions when we're hurt or angry that we later come to regret. A cooling off provision can give you time to try to work things out.

Noel Coward understood the value— and the limits—of this kind of agreement in *Private Lives*. If either spouse called "Solomon Isaacs" during a fight, a truce would immediately begin. It worked well until one day, when the husband cried "Solomon Isaacs" and his wife broke a record over his head, shouting "Solomon Isaacs, yourself." Cooling off clauses don't always cool people off, but you can try.

Here are a few sample cooling off clauses:

Option 1

> In the event either person is seriously considering ending the relationship, that person will take a vacation, finding another place to stay, whether with a friend or at a hotel, for at least one week before making a final decision. At least two more weeks will pass before we divide the property. In addition, we agree to attend at least one counseling or mediation session if either one of us wants it.

Option 2

> Either of us can request a cooling off period for any reason, including that we are fighting. We will spend one week separately. At the end of the week, we will meet and try to discuss our difficulties rationally, and with affection for each other.

Option 3

> At the request of either one of us, we agree to attend a minimum of four counseling sessions with a friend or professional before making any irrevocable decisions concerning our relationship.

If you wish, you can specify who you will meet with for counseling. Your choices are a professional mediator, an attorney-mediator, your therapist, a trusted friend, a group of three colleagues, the minister of the local gay church, or anyone else you know. Be creative to get the best person for the two of you. For example, many years ago, a New York couple split up. They needed help resolving a few issues and wanted someone who shared their experiences as African American lesbians. They called the late poet/writer Audre Lorde, who met with and assisted them. You might also look to see if a local gay and lesbian group or counseling center has any organized mediation or arbitration services.

Arbitration and Mediation Clause

If you split up and disagree over a provision in your contract, you have several ways to resolve the conflict. Mediation is an increasingly popular option, and for good reason. It keeps the parties involved in the resolution process, is cheaper and faster than court, and can help to preserve or even improve communication. If mediation isn't successful, binding arbitration can also be less expensive and time-consuming than litigation. You can include a mediation-arbitration clause in your contract and spell out exactly how you want to proceed.

Mediation is an informal process where you, your lover, and a mediator work together to reach a mutually satisfactory compromise. You then write out your agreement, agree to be bound by it, and sign it. No decision is imposed on you. Many attorneys and therapists serve as mediators for couples splitting up.

> **TIP**
>
> **If you want the mediation to focus on practical resolutions, rather than emotional undercurrents, an attorney-mediator might make the most sense for you.** An attorney-mediator also will likely be able to help you draft an agreement setting out the resolution. However, if emotional dynamics are keeping you polarized, a therapist-mediator might be a better option. Sometimes, lawyers and mediators work in teams as comediators. For some couples this is a perfect combination.

Arbitration is quite a bit different. It, too, can be informal, but you and your partner each present your version of the dispute to a person or persons you've designated and empowered to make a decision. Unlike mediation, the decision is made by the arbitrator, not by the two of you. The parties usually agree in advance to be bound by the arbitrator's decision—otherwise, there's little point to the process. This means that if one of you sues in court, the court will merely enforce the arbitrator's decision. Business and labor disputes have been resolved through arbitration for years, partly because having a dispute settled quickly can be as important as who wins and who loses.

Below are two sample mediation-arbitration provisions you can add to any agreement. For example, the first sample agreement doesn't allow lawyers to be present at the arbitration. If you have significant assets at stake, you might prefer to delete this provision. If you don't like these, take a look at other mediation and arbitration provisions in contract forms books available at local law libraries.

Sample Mediation-Arbitration Clause #1

Any dispute arising out of this agreement will be mediated by a third person mutually acceptable to both of us. If we can't agree on a mediator, we will each appoint a representative and the two of them will choose the mediator. The mediator's role will be to help us arrive at our solution, not to impose one on us. If good-faith efforts to arrive at our own solution with the help of a mediator prove to be fruitless after a minimum of four sessions, either of us may make a written request to the other that our dispute be arbitrated. This will be done as follows:

1. Either of us may initiate arbitration by making a written demand for arbitration, defining the dispute, and nominating one arbitrator.
2. Within five days from receipt of the demand, the other will either accept the proposed arbitrator or nominate a second arbitrator.
3. If a second arbitrator is nominated, the two nominated arbitrators will within ten days nominate a third person, who will serve as the sole arbitrator.
4. Within 30 days, an arbitration meeting will be held. Neither of us may have a lawyer present, but we may consult with an attorney beforehand and we may present evidence and bring relevant witnesses. The arbitration will be conducted according to the procedures of the American Arbitration Association.
5. The arbitrator will make a decision within 15 days after the hearing. The decision will be in writing, will be binding upon us, and will be enforceable by a local court.
6. If the person to whom the demand for arbitration is directed fails to respond within five days, the other must give an additional five days' written notice of his or her intent to proceed. If there is no response, the person initiating the arbitration may proceed with the arbitration before the arbitrator designated, and any award will have the same force as if it had been settled by the mutually selected arbitrator.

Sample Mediation-Arbitration Clause #2

> Any dispute arising under this agreement will be mediated by a third person mutually acceptable to both parties. The mediator's role will be to help us arrive at an agreement, not to impose one on us. If good-faith efforts to arrive at our own solution to all issues in dispute with the help of a mediator aren't successful, either of us may make a written request to the other that the dispute be arbitrated. If such a request is made, the dispute will be submitted to arbitration under the rules of the American Arbitration Association, and one arbitrator will hear our dispute. The decision of the arbitrator will be binding on us and will be enforceable in any court that has jurisdiction over the dispute. We each agree to give up the right to a jury trial.

RELATED TOPIC

There's more about mediation and arbitration in Chapter 10. A useful resource if you're considering mediation is *Divorce Without Court: A Guide to Mediation and Collaborative Divorce*, by Katherine E. Stoner (Nolo).

Sample Living Together Contracts

Read this section carefully and look over the sample contracts shown below. When you are ready to make your agreement, use the blank forms on the book's companion page to type up your own contract using the sample agreement that most closely matches your situation and your goals. The contracts in this section are designed to cover the major areas of concern to most unmarried, unregistered lesbian and gay couples.

By the time you finish modifying one of our agreements, your changes may pretty much replace the original. You've created your own contract. If you're at all nervous about the legality of the new document, especially if it refers to significant amounts of money or if real estate is involved, have a lawyer look at it. But be careful when choosing an attorney. Many charge high prices and have little experience with lesbian and gay couples. See Chapter 11 for more about how to find a lawyer. Call to ask about the fee before scheduling a meeting. Remember—you've already done most of the work; you're just asking the lawyer to check it over. You shouldn't be charged much more than $1,000 for such a review. If you have substantial assets, you may want to also consult with a tax expert to avoid any potential IRS problems.

> ⚠ CAUTION
>
> **Don't use these agreements if you are in or intend to enter into a marriage or marriage-like relationship!** If you are planning to get married, register as domestic partners, or enter into a civil union, consult a lawyer before preparing a premarital or prepartnership agreement. Some of these states have very specific requirements for such an agreement, including the requirement that both parties to the agreement have their own attorney. It's fine to use these agreements to get a sense of what you might want to include in your own contract, but make sure you see a lawyer before you finalize a draft or sign anything.

> ⚠ CAUTION
>
> **Signing the contract.** Whether you use one of our living together contracts or design your own, photocopy the final version so you each have a duplicate original. You and your partner should each initial every page and then sign and date both originals. It makes no difference who keeps which—both are "originals." Having it notarized isn't necessary unless, in some states, it covers real estate. If that is required in your state, you must notarize your signatures and then, if you wish, you can record the agreement at your county records office. Notarization doesn't make the contract legal or enforceable. It simply proves that your signatures aren't forged, which can never hurt.

Creating a contract is hard work. If either of you begins to feel overwhelmed, stop and regroup. Some couples will design a good agreement in an hour; other couples will take a month.

It's probable that one or both of you will engage in the dangerous practice of "strategic ambiguity" as to one or another of the issues that should be included in your living together contract. What is "strategic ambiguity"? It is when you deliberately work to keep things vague in your relationship so you can avoid facing a difficult issue. For example, if you are paying most of the rent each month because you make more money, you may not want to confront the question of whether this is a gift or a loan to your partner—and your partner may be equally uncomfortable talking about it. You may hope that your relationship will last forever and you'll never need to discuss the question. But it's better to face things openly—even if you have to hear or say something that makes you uncomfortable—than to pretend that these financial realities do not matter. This is not easy work, but unless you deal directly with these questions, you won't be able to create the agreements you need to have if your relationship is going to flourish in the long term. And if there are some issues you really can't agree on, it's still better to acknowledge that reality and have an agreement on the other issues.

Short and Simple Living Together Contracts

The sample living together agreements presented later in this chapter are quite thorough. For those of you who don't want such detailed agreements, here are two simple, one-page living together agreements.

Agreement to Keep Income and Accumulations Separate

Roosevelt Jackson and Alan Stein make the following agreement:

1. They are living together now and plan to continue doing so, and do not intend to marry or legally register.

2. All property owned by either Roosevelt or Alan as of the date of this agreement (listed here or documented by a purchase receipt) remains the separate property of the original owner and cannot be transferred to the other unless the transfer is done in writing.

3. The income of each person, as well as any accumulations of property from that income, belongs absolutely to the person who earns the money. Joint purchases are covered under Clause 7.

4. If Roosevelt and Alan separate, neither has a claim against the other for any money or property, for any reason, with the exception of property covered under Clause 7, or unless a subsequent written agreement specifically changes this contract.

5. Roosevelt and Alan will keep separate bank and credit accounts, and neither will be responsible for the debts of the other.

6. Living expenses, which include groceries, utilities, rent, and day-to-day household upkeep, will be shared equally. Roosevelt and Alan agree to open a joint bank account into which each agrees to contribute $1,100 per month to pay for living expenses.

7. If Roosevelt and Alan make any joint purchases, ownership of each specific item will be reflected on any title to the property. If the property has no title or deed, or if the title document is insufficient to record all details of their agreement, Alan and Roosevelt will prepare a separate, written, joint ownership agreement. Any such agreement will apply to the specific jointly owned property only, and won't create an implication that any other property is jointly owned.

8. This agreement sets forth Roosevelt and Alan's complete understanding concerning real and personal property ownership except ownership agreements made pursuant to clause 7, and takes the place of any and all prior contracts or understanding, whether written or oral.

9. This agreement can be added to or changed only by a subsequent written agreement.

10. Any provision in this agreement found to be invalid shall have no effect on the validity of the remaining provisions.

[optional: add mediation-arbitration provision]

_____   _____
Date   Roosevelt Jackson

_____   _____
Date   Alan Stein

Agreement to Combine Income and Accumulations

Aline Jones and Mary Wiebel agree that:

1. We live together now and plan to continue doing so, and we do not intend to marry or legally register.

2. All property earned or accumulated prior to our living together (which began on September 12, 2009) belongs absolutely to the person earning or accumulating it, and cannot be transferred to the other unless it's done in writing.

3. All income earned by either of us while we live together and all property accumulated from that income belongs equally to both of us, and should we separate, all accumulated property will be divided equally, regardless of whose name is listed on the asset or account.

4. Should either of us receive real or personal property by gift or inheritance, the property belongs absolutely to the person receiving the inheritance or gift and it cannot be transferred to the other unless it's done in writing.

5. In the event that either of us wishes to separate, we will divide equally all jointly owned property under Clause 3 and honor the separate property provisions of Clauses 2 and 4.

6. Once we divide the jointly owned property, neither of us will have any claim to any money or property from the other for any reason.

7. This agreement is our complete understanding regarding our living together, replaces any and all prior agreements, whether written or oral, and can be added to or changed only by a subsequent written agreement.

8. Any provision in this agreement found to be invalid shall have no effect on the validity of the remaining provisions.

[optional: add mediation-arbitration provision]

_____   _____
Date   Aline Jones

_____   _____
Date   Mary Wiebel

Contracts for Jointly Acquired Items

Many couples adopt the basic keep-things-separate approach. Often, however, they want to own some major items together. The keep-things-separate contract in the previous section provides a structure for joint ownership of some property, where you prepare a separate written contract covering each jointly owned item. The following contracts accomplish this task. Modify one or the other to meet your needs, sign it, and staple or clip it to your keep-things-separate contract.

If you completed a combine-income-and-accumulations contract, you don't need this joint-ownership agreement. You already provide for equal ownership.

Agreement for Joint Outright Purchase

Carol Takahashi and Louise Orlean agree as follows:

1. We will jointly purchase and own a carved oak table costing $1,000.
2. If we separate and both want to keep the table, we will agree on its fair market price and flip a coin. [For a very expensive item, you may want to add a mediation-arbitration clause.] The winner keeps the table after paying the loser one-half of the agreed-upon price. If we can't agree on a price, we will abide by the decision of a neutral appraiser.
3. If we decide to separate and neither wants the table, or if we both want it but can't arrive at a price we agree is fair, we will sell the table at the best available price and divide the proceeds equally.
4. Any provision in this agreement found to be invalid will have no effect on the validity of the remaining provisions.

_____   _____
Date   Carol Takahashi

_____   _____
Date   Louise Orlean

Sometimes, only one partner is able to make a purchase. This commonly occurs when the purchase is made with a credit card in only one person's name. Here's a contract to make sure that the item bought on credit is jointly owned.

Agreement Regarding Jointly Owned Item
Purchased on Credit in One Partner's Name

James O'Brien and Brian Joyce make the following agreement:

1. James has a credit card with Sears. James and Brian purchased a washer-dryer for $1,000 from Sears using James's credit card.

2. James and Brian intend that the washer-dryer be owned equally and that each will pay one-half of the $1,000, plus interest accrued on the credit card bill.

3. Neither James nor Brian wants to incur a lot of interest on the purchase. Therefore, they agree to jointly pay $250 per month for four months to pay it off. They acknowledge that the final payment will be more than $250, as it will include interest accumulated on the bill for the previous three months.

4. Each month, Brian will give James $125. James will then pay Sears the entire $250 on or before the date it's due.

5. If one person fails to pay his share, the other has the right to make the entire payment and will proportionally own more of the washer-dryer. Thus, if James ends up paying $750 and Brian $250, Brian will own it three-fourths and James, one-fourth.

6. If James or Brian dies, the financial interest in the washer-dryer belonging to the deceased person will go to the survivor, who will be obligated to pay the entire amount still due. [For an expensive item, such as a car, consider adding: "This provision shall be incorporated into James's will and Brian's will."]

7. If James and Brian separate, either may buy out the other's interest in the washer-dryer by paying one-half the fair market value, less any money still owing.

8. If James or Brian can't agree on who will buy the other out or the amount to be paid, the washer-dryer will be sold. Each will receive one-half of the net proceeds from the sale, unless one has paid more than the other, as provided in Clause 5. In that case, each will receive the percentage of the net proceeds corresponding to the percentage of the payments he's made.

9. Any provision in this agreement found to be invalid shall have no effect on the validity of the remaining provisions.

Date	James O'Brien
Date	Brian Joyce

> **CAUTION**
>
> **Only the partner whose name is on the credit card is legally obligated to pay, even if you have an agreement splitting the cost.** Thus, if Brian and James buy an expensive item on James's credit card with the understanding both will be responsible, Brian still doesn't have to pay Sears if James stops paying the bill. Brian has a legal contract with James, but not with Sears. Of course, the store doesn't care who pays the bill. Brian can send the money and the store will credit James's account.

Contracts for Long-Term Couples

Long-term couples who want to draw up a contract must decide one important issue: Do we keep things as is or start all over? In either case, you must acknowledge how it's been—that is, what you've orally or implicitly agreed to over the years—and how you want it to be in the future.

There are two situations that cry out for a written agreement. The first is where one of you is making significant contributions to a property that is titled in the name of the other alone—for example, where your partner owns the house, but you pay for remodeling the kitchen and other repairs, in addition to paying half of the mortgage. The other is where your contributions to a joint purchase are dramatically unequal.

No matter what else you do, be sure to draw up an agreement that describes your understanding about the specific item or expense that falls into one of these categories. Do it not because you are preparing for the relationship to end, but to make sure that you share the same understanding about what you are doing, and to be clear and open about financial matters.

A Simple Contract for Long-Term Couples

Ralph Palme and Hinton Wayne agree as follows:

1. We have been living together for 20 years and are neither married nor legally partnered; we are not planning to marry or legally partner. We moved in together in 1992, and have been in a continuous relationship since then.

2. We each had very little money and property when we first got together. Ralph moved here from Sweden and left his belongings behind. He had his clothes and some Swedish albums and books. Hinton furnished the apartment with hand-me-down furniture from his parents. The art that decorated our apartment was movie posters from our friend Cynthia, who worked at a retro movie house.

3. Since we have been together, we have pooled all our money and jointly paid all our expenses. Over the years, one of us may have been out of work or in school while the other worked full time. When we've both been working, our salaries have varied a lot. Sometimes Ralph earns more; sometimes Hinton does.

4. We agree that our financial life is so intertwined that as of this date, everything we have will be considered jointly owned, and all debts will be treated as joint obligations. We agree to review all title documents (for the two cars and deposit accounts) and change all title slips to include both names.

5. We recognize that one or the other of us may have a preference for certain things we own. Therefore, we attach three lists to this agreement. List 1 is the property we agree Ralph gets if we split up. List 2 is the same for Hinton. List 3 is the rest of our property.

6. We agree to continue living as we have. Once a year, during the week of our anniversary, we will pull out our lists and add purchases made during the past year to List 1, 2, or 3.

7. We each agree to make a valid will, revocable upon the termination of this agreement, leaving all property to the other upon death.

8. If we separate, Ralph gets the items on List 1 and Hinton the items on List 2. We will equally divide the items on List 3 by each taking one item in turn, with the first chooser to be selected by flipping a coin.

9. Any provision in this agreement found to be invalid shall have no effect on the validity of the remaining provisions.

[optional: add mediation-arbitration provision]

_____   _____
Date   Ralph Palme

_____   _____
Date   Hinton Wayne

For couples with greater assets and those wanting more formal agreements, here are two longer contracts.

Living Together Agreement—Keeping Things Separate

We, ____Susana Lopez____ and ____Anne Murphy____ , agree as follows:

1. This contract sets forth our rights and obligations toward each other, which we intend to abide by in the spirit of joy, cooperation, and good faith.

2. We agree that any and all property (real, personal, and otherwise) owned by either one of us as of the date of this agreement shall remain that person's separate property and cannot be transferred to the other unless done by writing. We have attached a list of our major items of separate property.

3. The income of each person, as well as any accumulations of property from that income, belongs absolutely to the person who earns the money.

4. We shall each keep our own bank accounts, credit accounts, etc., and neither is in any way responsible for the debts of the other.

5. Living expenses, which include groceries, utilities, rent, and day-to-day expenses, shall be shared equally.

6. We may from time to time decide to keep a joint checking or savings account for some specific purpose, or to own some property jointly. Any joint ownership shall be reflected in writing or shall be reflected

on the ownership document of the property. If we fail to otherwise provide in writing for the disposition of our jointly owned property should we separate, we agree to divide the jointly held property equally. Such agreements aren't to be interpreted as creating an implication that any other property is jointly owned.

7. If either of us receives real or personal property by gift or inheritance, the property belongs absolutely to the person receiving the gift or inheritance and cannot be transferred to the other except by writing.

8. We agree that neither of us will have any rights to, or financial interest in, any separate real property of the other, whether obtained before or after the date of this contract, unless that right or interest is in writing.

9. Either one of us may terminate this contract by giving the other a one-week written notice. In the event either of us is seriously considering leaving or ending the relationship, that person shall take at least a three-day vacation from the relationship. We also agree to at least one counseling session if either one of us requests it.

10. In the event that we separate, all jointly owned property shall be divided equally, and neither of us shall have any claim for postseparation support or for any other money or property from the other.

11. We agree that any dispute arising out of this contract will be mediated by a third person mutually acceptable to both of us. The mediator's role will be to help us arrive at our solution, not to impose one on us. If good-faith efforts to arrive at our own solution to all issues in dispute with the help of a mediation prove to be fruitless, either of us may:

    (a) Initiate arbitration by making a written demand for arbitration, defining the dispute, and nominating one arbitrator;

    (b) Within five days from receipt of this notice, the other shall either agree to the person nominated, or nominate a second arbitrator;

    (c) If a second arbitrator is named, the two nominated arbitrators shall within ten days name a third arbitrator, who shall be the arbitrator;

    (d) Within 30 days an arbitration meeting will be held. Each of us may have counsel present at the arbitration if we choose, and may present pertinent evidence and witnesses;

    (e) The arbitrator will make a decision within five days after the hearing. The decision will be in writing and will be binding upon us;

    (f) If the person to whom the demand for arbitration is directed fails to respond within five days, the other must give an additional five days' written notice of intent to proceed. If there's no response, the person initiating the arbitration may proceed with the arbitration before the arbitrator designated, and the award shall have the same force as if it had been settled by the mutually selected arbitrator.

12. This agreement represents our complete understanding regarding our living together and replaces any and all prior agreements, written or oral. It can be amended, but only in writing, and any written amendment must be signed by both of us.

13. We agree that if a court finds any portion of this contract to be illegal or otherwise unenforceable, the remainder of the contract is still in full force and effect.

Signed this _____14th_____ day of _____April, 20XX_____

Susana Lopez
Signature

Anne Murphy
Signature

[Attach lists of separate property.]

Living Together Agreement—Sharing Most Property

We, _____Daniel Huang_____ and _____Peter Ross_____ , agree as follows:

1. This contract sets forth our rights and obligations toward each other, which we intend to abide by in a spirit of joy, cooperation, and good faith.

2. All property (real, personal, or otherwise) earned or accumulated before this date belongs absolutely to the person who earned or accumulated it and cannot be transferred to the other except in writing. Attached is a list of the major items of property we own separately.

3. All income earned by either of us while we are living together and all property (real, personal, or otherwise) accumulated from that income belongs in equal shares to both of us, and should we separate, all accumulated property shall be divided equally, regardless of who is the legal owner or whose name is on the asset's title.

4. Should either of us receive real or personal property by gift or inheritance, the property belongs absolutely to the person receiving the gift or inheritance and cannot be transferred to the other except by writing.

5. We agree that neither of us has any rights to, or financial interest in, any separate real property of the other, whether obtained before or after the date of this contract, unless that right or interest is in writing.

6. Either one of us may terminate this contract by giving the other a one-week written notice. In the event either of us is seriously considering leaving or ending the relationship, that person shall take at least a three-day vacation from the relationship. We also agree to at least one counseling session if either one of us requests it.

7. In the event we separate, all assets or property other than the listed separate property shall be divided equally, and neither of us shall have any claim for support or for any other money or property from the other.

8. We agree that any dispute arising out of this contract will be mediated by a third person mutually acceptable to both of us. The mediator's role will be to help us arrive at our solution, not to impose one on us. If good faith efforts to arrive at our own solution to all issues in dispute with the help of a mediation prove to be fruitless, either of us may:

    (a) Initiate arbitration by making a written demand for arbitration, defining the dispute, and nominating one arbitrator;

(b) Within five days from receipt of this notice, the other will either agree to the person nominated, or nominate a second arbitrator;

(c) If a second arbitrator is named, the two nominated arbitrators will within ten days name a third arbitrator, who will be the arbitrator;

(d) Within 30 days an arbitration meeting will be held. Each of us may have counsel present if we choose, and may present pertinent evidence and witnesses;

(e) The arbitrator will make a decision within five days after the hearing. The decision will be in writing and will be binding upon us;

(f) If the person to whom the demand for arbitration is directed fails to respond within five days, the other must give an additional five days' written notice of intent to proceed. If there's no response, the person initiating the arbitration may proceed with the arbitration before the arbitrator designated, and the award will have the same force as if it had been settled by the mutually selected arbitrator.

9. This agreement represents our complete understanding regarding our living together and replaces any and all prior agreements, written or oral. It can be amended, but only in writing, and any written amendment must be signed by both of us.

10. We agree that if the court finds any portion of this contract to be illegal or otherwise unenforceable, the remainder of the contract is still in full force and effect.

Signed this _____3rd_____ day of _____October, 20XX_____

Daniel Huang   _Peter Ross_
Signature   Signature

[Attach lists of separate property.]

Contracts for Sharing Household Expenses and Chores

Thousands of gay and lesbian couples find themselves in the same situation as Lynne and Sarah. They are both professionals—Lynne's an ad executive and Sarah works as a designer—who make about the same amount of money. They want to keep their property separate, but want to share household expenses.

Contracts for Joint Projects

A joint project agreement can cover building a cabin, refurbishing a boat, or any other major project. Below are two sample contracts, although, of course, they don't cover every contingency.

> **EXAMPLE:** Tony and Ray live together. Both are landscape gardeners and share a dream of building a greenhouse and raising orchids on a piece of land they jointly own. They know it's a big job and want to anchor their dream on a strong foundation of good business practice, so they make an agreement reflecting that.

Because this contract is so specific, it's not included on the companion page, but you can use it as a sample to create your own, or use the online version of the Sample Joint Project Agreement #2, below.

Tony and Ray's joint project was personal and augmented their home. Other couples use a joint project agreement to cover professional endeavors.

> **EXAMPLE:** Patti and Maria's shared dream is to own and run a bakery—supporting themselves through their mutual love of scones and croissants. They know the odds are against any small business succeeding and that they'll have to work extremely hard to make their dream a reality. They want to protect their enterprise if they separate, or if one loses interest but the other wants to continue. They face another challenge—Patti has more cash to invest initially, but they eventually want to own the business equally.

Sample Agreement for Sharing Household Expenses

Lynne Jacobs and Sarah Elderberry agree as follows:

1. We plan to live together indefinitely, but do not currently intend to marry or legally partner.
2. We will each maintain our own separate bank and credit accounts.
3. Our earnings and the property we each accumulate will be kept separate, unless we agree in writing to share something jointly.
4. Any item of separate property can become joint property or the separate property of the other only by a written agreement signed by the person whose property is to be reclassified or by putting both names on a title document.
5. We will each be responsible for our own personal expenses. This includes clothing, medical/dental bills, and long-distance telephone calls. We will pay household expenses, including rent, food, utilities, and cleaning, jointly. We agree to keep receipts for all expenses, and to do an accounting every six months. The person who spends less will pay the other whatever sum is necessary to arrive at a 50-50 split.
6. Lynne generally will food shop and cook. Sarah generally will wash dishes and do general cleaning. We will both maintain the plants and pets.
7. We each agree to make a valid will, revocable upon the termination of this agreement, leaving all property to the other upon death.
8. Either of us can end this agreement at any time. If we separate, we will equally divide jointly purchased property, and each retain our separate assets. Neither, however, will be obligated to support the other.
9. Any provision in this agreement found to be invalid shall have no effect on the validity of the remaining provisions.

[optional: add mediation-arbitration provision]

_____   _____
Date   Lynne Jacobs

_____   _____
Date   Sarah Elderberry

Sample Joint Project Agreement #1

Tony Freeling and Ray Vivaldi agree as follows:

1. We both want to build a glass and wood greenhouse to house tropical orchids on our property at 25 Woodland Lane.

2. We each will contribute $9,000 toward the purchase of construction materials. The money will be kept in a joint bank account and both of our signatures will be required on checks.

3. We each will work at least 40 hours per month on building the greenhouse.

4. We will keep records of all hours worked and money spent for materials.

5. If we separate, Ray will have the opportunity to buy Tony's share for an amount equal to Tony's actual cash investment plus $20 per hour for the time he has worked on building the greenhouse. [If Tony was a professional carpenter and Ray was not, it may be fairer for Ray to contribute more money (Clause 2) or for Tony's hourly salary to be greater.]

6. At separation, if Ray decides not to buy Tony's share under the terms of Clause 5, Tony will have the opportunity to buy Ray's share on the same terms.

7. If neither of us elect to purchase the other's share of the greenhouse, we will sell it and equally divide the proceeds.

8. If either of us fails to work on the greenhouse 40 hours per month for three consecutive months, the other may buy out his share under the terms set out in Clauses 5 and 6.

9. If either of us dies, the other becomes sole owner of the greenhouse. If either of us makes a will, this provision will be incorporated into that will.

10. Any provision in this agreement found to be invalid shall have no effect on the validity of the remaining provisions.

[optional: add mediation-arbitration provision]

_____   _____
Date   Tony Freeling

_____   _____
Date   Ray Vivaldi

Sample Joint Project Agreement #2

Patti Valdez and Maria Ness agree as follows:

1. We desire and intend to jointly own and operate a bakery in San Francisco, California (at a rented location not yet ascertained).

2. Patti will contribute $75,000 and Maria $25,000 toward the working capital of the business.

3. We both will work diligently in our bakery business, and it will be the principal business endeavor of each.

4. Initially, Patti will own three quarters of the business and Maria one quarter. Each of us will receive pay of $700 a week for her work in the bakery. Any profits beyond salaries and operating expenses will be paid to Patti, until she receives $50,000 plus interest at 10% per year on her excess contribution of $50,000. Once Patti receives the $50,000 plus interest, we will co-own the business equally, and divide all profits equally beyond salaries and operating expenses. If we break up prior to full repayment of Patti's excess contribution, the ownership shares will be adjusted pro rata.

5. If either of us decides she no longer wants to operate the bakery, the person wishing to continue may purchase the other's interest in the bakery as set out under Paragraph 7.

6. If we separate and are unable to work together, but both want to continue the bakery under sole ownership, we will ask someone to flip a coin; the winner will have the right to purchase the loser's interest as provided in Paragraph 7. Likewise, if we separate and only one of us wishes to maintain the bakery, that person has the right to purchase the other's interest as provided in Paragraph 7.

7. If for any reason one of us wants to purchase the other's interest in the business, she will pay the fair market value of the other's share. If we cannot agree on the fair market value, we agree to accept the fair market value as determined by Bill's Commercial Real Estate Appraisers.

8. If either of us dies, the other will become the sole owner of the bakery. We agree to each make a will containing this provision.

9. Any provision in this agreement found to be invalid shall have no effect on the validity of the remaining provisions.

[optional: add mediation-arbitration provision]

Date	Patti Valdez
Date	Maria Ness

RESOURCE

Help with starting a small business. If you and your lover are opening a business together, you will be investing a great deal of time —and money. *The Small Business Start-Up Kit*, by Peri Pakroo, gives you the information you need to get your small business off the ground. If you want to organize your business as a partnership, check out *Form a Partnership: The Complete Legal Guide*, by Denis Clifford and Ralph Warner. Both books are published by Nolo. You can also look for small business information at www.nolo.com.

Contracts to Give a Partner "Time Off"

Often, when both partners work outside the home, one wants to take time off to study, travel, have a child, or just stay home. If the person taking time off will be raising a child, clearly both partners are contributing to the relationship. Otherwise, the challenge is working out the details so that the person who continues to earn a living doesn't get resentful and the person taking time off doesn't start feeling guilty. One option is to alternate earning an income and taking time off; that way, each partner takes time to financially support the couple. Another possibility is for the person working to lend money to the one taking time off. No matter what you arrange, you must specify how much time equals how much money, and, if appropriate, set a method of repayment.

If you are married or legally partnered, marital rules will impose some sort of financial safety net, usually in the form of rules about alimony that will reimburse a spouse who supports a partner for a significant period of time. If you want to opt out of alimony and reimbursement rules, you'll need to use a prenuptial or postnuptial agreement rather than these cohabitation contracts, which don't meet the standard for marital contracts.

Below is a "time-off" agreement for a couple who are both artists, but need to hold regular jobs to pay the bills.

> **EXAMPLE:** Martha and Lianne have lived together on and off for three years. Martha is a poet and Lianne an illustrator, but both have other part-time jobs to make ends meet. They recently moved in together, and decided to "trade" working. Each will work full time at her art, as they take turns supporting each other. This way, they can be creative while also paying their rent and groceries.

Sample Agreement Allowing Alternating Time Off

Martha Rutherford and Lianne Wu agree as follows:

1. Each of us will keep as our separate property all property (and any income generated by that property) each of us owns as of the date of this agreement. We have each attached a list of our major items of separate property to this contract. (See Attachment A, Separately Owned Property.)

2. Starting as of the date this agreement is signed and continuing for as long as we live together, any property or income, including salaries or financial returns from artistic pursuits, earned by either of us (except for inheritances and gifts—see Paragraph 3) belongs equally to both of us. All joint funds will be kept in joint bank or securities accounts.

3. Money or property inherited by either of us or gifts given to either of us during the time we live together will be and remain the separate property of the person inheriting it. Separate property belonging to one of us cannot become the separate property of the other or the joint property of both without a written agreement signed by the person whose separate property is to be reclassified.

4. We agree to take turns working at regular full-time jobs in order to earn enough money for the two of us to live on. While one person

works, the other will be free to pursue creative endeavors. Martha will work for the first six months, Lianne the next six months, and so on, alternating six-month periods of work and creative time for the duration of this agreement.

5. All our household expenses and personal expenses will be paid by the one of us who's employed at the time the expense is incurred.

6. Should our living together relationship end at a point when one partner has been employed for a longer period of time than the other, the partner employed for less time will reimburse the other partner for one-half of the living expenses incurred during the extra months that the other partner has worked.

7. Should our living together relationship end, each of us will keep our separate property (property we owned prior to living together, income from that property, and any property inherited or received as a gift while we are together). All property, other than intellectual property, that was acquired or created while we lived together will be considered to be jointly owned and will be evenly divided.

8. All works created by either partner during our living together relationship that can be protected by copyright, patent, trade secret, or trademark laws (intellectual property), will be owned by the creating partner. All income from the sale, license, or exploitation of any of this intellectual property will also be owned by the creating partner.

9. This agreement represents our complete understanding regarding our living together and replaces any and all prior agreements, written or oral. It can be changed, but only in writing, and any change must be signed by both of us.

10. If a court finds any portion of this contract to be illegal or otherwise unenforceable, the remainder of the contract is still in full force and effect.

[optional: add mediation-arbitration provision]

_____   _____
Date   Martha Rutherford

_____   _____
Date   Lianne Wu

Contracts for People in School

It's common for one partner to help the other with educational expenses or support while in school. This is a situation for a written agreement.

EXAMPLE: George supports Sam while he's in plumber's school. George expects their financial lives to improve once Sam graduates. If Sam leaves George just after graduating, George is likely to feel that Sam owes him something. A court might agree, but the couple doesn't want to leave it to a court to decide. So they define their expectations in a written agreement.

Sample Agreement for Educational Support

Sam Adaba and George Fujimoto make the following agreement:

1. Each wants to further his education, and so they will take turns going to school. Sam has already started school to learn plumbing, and his schooling is shorter than George's, so he will go first. George will pay Sam's educational expenses and pay their joint living expenses for the next 18 months. After 18 months, Sam will assume these responsibilities for two years while George finishes his accountant's training. If their relationship dissolves during the first three and one-half years, the financial responsibilities still apply.

   Specifically, if Sam and George separate during the first 18 months, George will continue to pay Sam's tuition and will pay Sam $5,000 per year for living expenses. At the end of the 18 months, Sam will pay George's tuition, and his living expenses at $5,000 per year, for two years. If they separate after George starts school, Sam will pay George's remaining tuition up to two full years in accounting school and pay him $5,000 a year for living expenses. Expenses will be paid in 12 equal monthly installments on the first day of each month.

2. All property owned by Sam or George before the date of this contract remains the owner's separate property and can't be transferred to the other except by a written agreement.

3. During the first three and one-half years of this agreement, all income and property accumulated with that income, except gifts and inheritances, will be jointly owned. When both Sam and George finish school, they will make a list of all jointly accumulated property. That property will be divided equally if they separate. Thereafter, each person's earnings will be his separate property and neither will have any right in the property of the other. If they separate before the end of three and one-half years, all property accumulated since the beginning of this agreement will be divided according to the fraction of the time each provided support. (For example, if Sam supports George for 18 months and George supports Sam for 12, Sam is entitled to three-fifths of the property.)

4. If any tax obligations arise as a result of these agreements, each party will bear half of the tax liabilities.

5. Any provision in this agreement found to be invalid shall have no effect on the validity of the remaining provisions.

_____   _____
Date   Sam Adaba

_____   _____
Date   George Fujimoto

Contracts for Work Done Around the House

In some relationships, one person works outside the home while the other cooks, cleans, shops, and otherwise takes care of the place. This sort of labor division can raise questions, such as whether the homemaker should be compensated, especially if there are major tasks or renovation work to be done. It can become even more significant if there are kids in the household.

Sometimes, both partners work outside the home, but one also makes significant improvements to the home while the other idles in the sauna. Is it fair that the person who does the extra work should receive nothing for his or her labor? For you, it may be—only you can answer these questions. But these situations are likely to lead to misunderstandings unless you discuss them openly, and write down your agreement.

The worst thing you can do if one person contributes all the money or does all the work around the house is ignore it. First, a person with money also has power and may be the only legal owner of the property, and relationships rarely prosper when one person has too much of anything. Second, a person who does all the work around the house tends to feel resentful toward the other, especially if the working partner is not a full legal owner.

Here are some suggestions. A person who spends all weekend fixing up a jointly owned house or a home solely owned by the other partner can be paid an agreed-upon hourly rate, with the compensation either paid in cash by the other or added to the carpenter's equity in the house. A stay-at-home mate can be given a weekly salary or can trade services (you fix the car while your lover does the laundry). You should also think about the homemaker's future if you split up. You can agree on a period of support payments for the homemaker, thereby creating your own alimony-like arrangement by contract, and such an agreement generally will be legally valid.

Make sure you give some thought to the tax implications of your arrangements, however. Giving your partner more than $13,000 per year can trigger a gift tax obligation (see Chapter 7), and paying "wages" to a partner for domestic services can trigger Social Security and income tax withholding obligations. There may be some alternatives that reduce the tax risks, so if a lot of money is involved, consult with a tax expert.

Sample Agreement for Compensating a Homemaker

Sandi Potter and Carole Samworthe agree that as long as they live together:

1. Sandi will work full-time (at least 40 hours a week).
2. Carole will work in the home, taking care of her daughter, Judy, and performing household chores, including cleaning, laundry, cooking, and yard work. Sandi will contribute $200 a week to Carole's personal expenses [or will pay Carole $200 per week for her services]. This payment will be adjusted from time to time to reflect changes in the cost of living.
3. Sandi will also provide reasonable amounts of money each month for food, clothing, shelter, and recreation for the entire family as long as they live together. This payment will be adjusted from time to time to reflect changes in the cost of living. Sandi, however, assumes no obligation to support Carole or Judy upon termination of this agreement.
4. [If Carole is treated as Sandi's employee] Sandi, as Carole's "employer," will make Social Security payments for her and will obtain medical insurance for her and Judy.
5. All property purchased or accumulated by either Carole or Sandi will be owned by the person purchasing or accumulating it. The property cannot be transferred from one person to the other except by a written agreement. The house will be provided by Sandi and will be owned solely by her.
6. Either Sandi or Carole can end this agreement by giving the other two months' written notice. If Sandi and Carole separate, Sandi will pay Carole severance pay at the rate of two months for every year the agreement has been in effect. Sandi's agreement to pay this money is part of the consideration necessary to get Carole to agree to this contract. This money will be paid in a lump sum at the time of separation. Neither Carole nor Sandi will have any other financial obligation to the other upon separation.
7. Any provision in this agreement found to be invalid shall have no effect on the validity of the remaining provisions.

[optional: add mediation-arbitration provision]

_____   _____
Date   Sandi Potter

_____   _____
Date   Carole Samworthe

Modifying Your Agreement

Modifications of a written living together contract should always be in writing. This is because ancient, but still applicable, legal doctrines usually make oral modifications of a written contract invalid. In addition, these contracts expressly state that any modifications must be in writing. A modification can simply state that you agree to change your contract, and then set out the change. Date and sign all modifications. But if you're making really major changes, tear up the old agreement and start over.

Beware the Tax Man!

The government's rules about money often create serious problems for same-sex couples, and constitute some of the worst examples of antigay government bias. Transfers of property or debt can be construed as taxable income or as legal gifts, and if the amount is sufficiently high, this can trigger a serious gift tax liability. If one of you is receiving government benefits or alimony from a prior marriage, the legal implications can be even more complicated. If you are contemplating a transfer of more than $13,000 per year in assets (for example, where you put your partner's name on a property title without requiring payment for the ownership interest) or debts (for example, when you "lend" your partner $15,000 but don't ever collect on the debt), it's crucial that you speak with an accountant who knows the rules for unmarried couples.

One of the trickier ramifications of the new relationship laws in marriage-equality and marriage-equivalent states is dealing with tax issues. Your state law may treat your assets as jointly owned and not tax you because your relationship is legally recognized, while the IRS may consider the merging of assets a taxable transfer. It is likely to be quite a few years before these confusing issues are ironed out; in the meantime, try to stay up to date on current developments (Chapter 11 tells you how), and consult a lawyer or tax accountant if you have questions.

Buying a Home Together
(and Other Real Estate Ventures)

Finding a House...289

How Much House Can You Afford?...292

    Prepare a Financial Statement 294

    How Much Down Payment Will You Make?..................................295

    Estimate the Mortgage Interest Rate You'll Likely Pay..................296

    Calculate How Much House You Can Afford.................................296

Proceeding With Your Purchase 300

    Inspections 300

    Financing That White Picket Fence..301

    Escrow and Closing Costs..303

Taking Title to Your New Home...305

    Title in One Person's Name 305

    Joint Tenancy...306

    Tenancy-in-Common...308

    Changing Title...308

Contracts for Home Purchase and Ownership 309

    Agreement for Equal Ownership...310

    Owning a House in Unequal Shares...313

    When Not All Owners Live in the House..323

    When You Move Into a Home Owned by Your Lover....................330

    Moving On...334

For LGBT couples, buying and fixing up a home with a lover can be a symbol of commitment and a wonderful foundation for a relationship, both spiritually and economically. Of course, it can be scary too. Owning property can raise all sorts of thorny issues of money, class, status, and the sharing of responsibility.

Beyond the symbolic and emotional value and the issues it may raise in a relationship, there are many practical reasons to own a home—as a hedge against rent increases and an unstable economy, to avoid the powerlessness of being a tenant, and to gain the tax advantages of paying mortgage interest.

At the same time, home ownership has some very real drawbacks. When the boiler explodes, you may pine for the days when you could just call your landlord. And if the property declines in value you can lose all or part of your down payment. Still, despite the drawbacks, it is your home. It can be fun to tear down walls, plant trees, paint an ivy decoration across the dining room walls, or even fix the boiler. Most Americans agree with Mark Twain, who advised, "Buy land. They aren't making any more of it."

Your Home as Investment and Tax Shelter

There are many financial benefits to owning a home, especially in times of rapid appreciation. With any luck your investment will go up in value—but remember, as so many homeowners have learned in recent years prices can also go down, and selling a home can be expensive, too. You can deduct from your taxable income all interest you pay on your mortgage, and all your property taxes. Renters get no such deductions and never acquire any equity in their residence.

Homeowners qualify for another tax advantage. If you sell your home and have lived there two of the prior five years, you are allowed to reap any profits (up to $250,000 per owner) without paying federal taxes on the sale, ever—and most states offer a parallel exemption from state taxes. This means you can keep buying up more expensive properties and avoid paying taxes on your accumulated profits while you're doing it. Gay and straight couples alike can take advantage of this exemption, regardless of their marital status, as long as both partners have been on title for the requisite number of years.

This chapter suggests ways to handle the practical aspects of buying a home. Even if you skipped Chapter 8 on living together contracts, you definitely will need a contract regarding ownership of a house (unless you are married or legally partnered and you are content to accept marital rules). Because it's so common in the LGBT community to own property with friends or with other couples, some of these contracts are designed for situations other than one couple buying a single-family home.

Of course, before you can pin down your agreement, you have to find the house, arrange for financing, and understand the ways in which you can hold title to the property. These steps are discussed just below.

Property Through the Years

Owning property is another area where not that much has changed—well, outside of the fact that marital rules now apply to many same-sex couples owning property in certain states. While that is a big deal, the basic principles of homebuying and home ownership have stayed the same from the first edition to this one—both books have sections on figuring out how much house you can afford, and both offer sample contracts for owning a home together. These agreements are crucial for same-sex couples, and even those who live in a marriage-equality or marriage-equivalent state may choose to use prenuptial or prepartnership agreements to serve the same purposes that these agreements do.

Finding a House

Given your needs, tastes, and finances, you probably already have a good idea of the type of house you want to buy. Indeed, if you sit quietly for a few moments, shut your eyes, and let your imagination do the walking, you can probably conjure up an image of the house, or perhaps if you're a flexible sort, several houses that you would dearly love to call home.

Some folks love living on a dusty road in outer suburbia; others want the convenience of living in a townhouse in a major city. Many people enjoy fixing a place up, while others insist that it be in move-in condition. Some have to have a big kitchen with lots of cupboards, and for others the back yard is the most important feature.

Whatever your preferences, you will need an organized house-buying method to translate your dream into reality. This is particularly true in high-priced markets where most buyers face an affordability gap between the house they'd like to buy and the one they can afford. Without an organized approach, there is a good chance you'll be talked into compromising on the wrong house by friends, relatives, a real estate agent, or even yourself or your partner.

Here is our method to all but ensure that you will buy a house you'll enjoy living in, even if it's substantially more modest than your dream house:

- Firmly establish your priorities before you look at a house—and that means your shared priorities as a couple.
- Insist that any house you offer to buy meets at least your most important priorities.
- Insist on your most important priorities even if, in buying the house that meets those priorities, you must compromise in other areas and purchase a house that is less desirable than you really want.

The reason this method works well should be obvious. If your priorities are clearly set in advance, you're likely to compromise on less important features, and not on those that are most important. Otherwise, it's possible to become so disoriented by the house purchase process that you buy a house that lacks the basic features that motivated you to buy in the first place.

Lesbian and gay couples usually have no special problems in finding a house to buy. Be aware, however, that some communities (or neighborhoods) have zoning ordinances prohibiting groups of unrelated people from living together. Most of these laws are aimed at barring groups, foster families, shelters, or boarding houses. Very few prohibit two unrelated adults from living together. But some of these laws have been used to harass lesbians and gays who lived together, just as they have been used to discriminate against unmarried heterosexual couples. Before you buy, make sure the town—or neighborhood—isn't zoned only for people related by "blood, marriage, or adoption."

In some locations a seller may hesitate to sell to you because of a belief that your relationship is immoral or even criminal, or an agent may try to steer you into certain "gay-friendly" neighborhoods. But generally, most sellers feel that lesbian and gay money is as green as all other money. Still, be sensible and strategic if your preferred neighborhood has been hostile to gay buyers.

The most common way to find a home is to use an agent, broker, or realtor. (We use the term agent for simplicity.) Again, you may encounter an agent who refuses to work with a lesbian or gay couple. But it's a rare location that doesn't have more than one real estate agent, so your best bet is just to look for another agent who is gay or gay friendly. (Ask your gay homeowning friends who they used.) Because the home buying process is a very intense, personal experience, you must feel comfortable being open with your agent.

You can also buy on your own, without an agent. Indeed, you may well be tempted to proceed on your own. But bear in mind that buying real estate takes a lot of work and patience, and involves a lot of strange jargon. In some places, where the market is competitive, using an agent is virtually a necessity. And remember, you rarely save much money by not using your own agent, as you are essentially using the seller's agent, and sellers rarely adjust the price to reflect that, but instead will pocket most of the savings. Given all this, it's often easier to let someone knowledgeable do the work. If you decide to use an agent, initially you are not obligated to work with just one. Shop around until you find the agent you are most comfortable with.

Just as you (the buyers) don't have to use an agent, neither does the seller. A small but significant number of people sell their homes without an agent. You can find homes sold by owners by checking newspaper ads or driving around and looking for "for sale by owner" or "FSBO" (pronounced fizzbo) signs. You can also check out websites like www. forsalebyowner.com.

RESOURCE

There are several books that explain the ins and outs of buying or selling a home yourself, including *Nolo's Essential Guide to Buying Your First Home,* by Ilona Bray, Alayna Schroeder, and Marcia Stewart (Nolo). For California residents, there's also *How to Buy a House in California,* by Ralph Warner, Ira Serkes, and George Devine, and *For Sale by Owner in California,* by George Devine (both by Nolo).

How Much House Can You Afford?

Notwithstanding the recent drop in home values, many prospective homebuyers face an affordability problem when it comes to buying the house they'd really like to live in, even when interest rates are at a fairly low level. In that type of market, it's essential to determine how much you can afford to pay before you start looking. Many people don't understand how institutional lenders (banks, savings and loans, and credit unions) determine how much money they'll lend to you. If you don't do the calculations or talk to a loan broker ahead of time, you may enter into a home purchase contract and then not qualify for the necessary loan.

As part of this initial evaluation, you must also decide whether both of you or just one of you will own the property. Deciding to buy jointly is primarily a relationship issue, but knowing your financial limitations is an important part of the discussion about how you will take title.

As a broad generalization, most people can afford to purchase a house worth about three times their total (gross) annual income, assuming a 20% down payment and a moderate amount of other long-term debts. With no other debts, most people can afford a house worth up to four times their annual income.

A more specific way to determine how much house you can afford is to compare your monthly carrying costs (monthly payments of mortgage principal and interest, insurance, and property taxes) plus your monthly payments on other long-term debts, to your gross (total) monthly income. This is called the "debt-to-income ratio." Lenders normally want you to make all monthly payments with 28%–38% of your monthly income. You can qualify near the bottom or the top of this range depending

Your Credit Score Is Important When Applying for a Home Loan

When deciding whether to approve your home loan application, most lenders will consider your credit score. Credit scores are numerical calculations that are supposed to indicate the risk that you will default on your payments. High credit scores indicate less risk and low scores indicate potential problems.

Factors that credit bureaus use when generating credit scores include:

- your payment history
- amounts you owe on credit accounts
- length of your credit history—in general, a longer credit history increases the score
- your new credit. It helps to have an established credit history without too many new accounts. Opening several accounts in a short period of time can represent greater risk.
- types of credit—credit scorers look for a "healthy mix" of different types of credit.

You can get your credit score from the nation's biggest credit scoring company, Fair, Isaac, and Company, for a fee of $12.95. Visit www.equifax.com, www.myfico.com, or www.scorepower.com for a report. And if you live in California, you're in luck. A new California law requires that mortgage lenders disclose a consumer's credit scores when the consumer is shopping for a mortgage.

If you do get your credit score and it seems lower than it should be, there may be a mistake on your credit report. (See Chapter 3 for information on how to get a free copy of your credit report and correct errors, if necessary.)

To keep up on credit scoring developments, visit www.creditscoring.com, a private website devoted to credit scoring.

on the amount of your down payment, the interest rate on the type of mortgage you want, your credit history, the amount of your other long-term debts, your employment stability and prospects, the lender's philosophy, and the money supply in the general economy. In some cities, there are special subsidies to help first-time homebuyers, often with the down payment or mortgage.

Generally, the greater your other debts, the lower the percentage of your income lenders will assume you have available to spend each month on housing. Conversely, if you have no long-term debts, a great credit history, and will make a larger than normal down payment, a lender may approve carrying costs that exceed 38% of your monthly income— sometimes as high as 40% or 42%. In any case, these rules aren't absolute. And bear in mind that getting a loan isn't as easy as it once was.

Prepare a Financial Statement

The first step in determining the purchase price you can afford is to prepare a thorough list of your monthly income and your monthly expenses.

Total monthly gross income. List your combined gross monthly income from all sources. Gross income is total income before withholdings are deducted. Include income from:

- employment—your base salary or wages plus any bonuses, tips, commissions, or overtime you regularly receive
- public benefits
- dividends from stocks, bonds, and similar investments
- freelance income, self-employment, and hobbies, and
- royalties and rents.

Total monthly deductions. Total up all required monthly deductions from your income (such as taxes and Social Security deducted from your paycheck). Don't include money deducted to pay credit unions, child support, or other debts. If you deliberately have more money than necessary subtracted from federal or state income tax by underclaiming deductions, ask your employer what amount you are obligated to pay.

Total monthly net income. Subtract your total monthly deductions from your total monthly gross income to arrive at your net income.

Total monthly expenses. List and total up what you spend each month on the following:

- child care
- clothing
- current educational costs
- food—include eating at restaurants, as well as at home
- insurance—auto, life, medical, disability
- medical expenses not covered by insurance
- personal expenses—include costs for personal care (haircuts, shoe repairs, and toiletries) and fun (attending movies and theater, renting DVDs and videos, buying CDs, books, and lottery tickets, subscribing to newspapers and magazines)
- installment payments—student loans, car payments, child support, alimony, personal loans, credit cards, and any others
- taxes
- transportation
- utilities, and
- other—such as regular charitable or community donations and savings deposits.

How Much Down Payment Will You Make?

Unless you're eligible for a government-subsidized mortgage that has a low (or even no) down payment, you'll probably need to put down 5%–10% of the cost of the house to qualify for a loan. Also, you'll have to pay the closing costs, which will be an additional 2%–5% of the cost of the home. Some banks still will make mortgage loans with less than 5% down, although the monthly interest rate may be higher than if you put down more.

Generally speaking, the larger the percentage of the total price of a house you can put down, the easier it will be for you to qualify for a mortgage. This is because larger down payments mean less money due each month to pay off your mortgage. The monthly mortgage payment (plus taxes and insurance) is the major factor in determining the purchase price of the house you can afford.

Total up the money you have for a down payment and then multiply this number first by five and then by ten. These figures represent the very broad price range of house prices you can likely afford, based on your ability to make a down payment. Of course, you must be able to afford the monthly mortgage, interest, and property tax payments too. If your income is relatively low, you'll have to increase your down payment to 25%–30% or even more to bring down the monthly payments.

Estimate the Mortgage Interest Rate You'll Likely Pay

Because different mortgage types carry different interest rates, start by deciding the type of mortgage you want. For a reading of the market's direction, check the mortgage interest rate roundup published in the real estate sections of many Sunday newspapers.

In general, adjustable rate mortgages (ARMs) have slightly lower initial interest rates and payment requirements than do fixed rate loans, and are therefore more affordable than fixed rate loans. This isn't saying they're better, however. Before selecting an ARM, compare interest rates by looking at the ARM's annual percentage rate (APR), not just its introductory rate. (APR is an estimate of the credit cost over the entire life of the loan.)

Calculate How Much House You Can Afford

Now that you have a pretty good idea of the size of your down payment and the interest rate you expect to pay, you can calculate how much house you can afford.

Step 1. Estimate how much you think a house that has the features you consider your highest priorities will cost.

Step 2. Estimate the likely mortgage interest rate you'll end up paying. If you're eligible for a government-subsidized mortgage, be sure to use those rates.

Step 3. Find your mortgage interest and principal payment factors per $1,000 over the length of the loan (30 years is most common) on the mortgate payment chart.

Mortgage Principal and Interest Payment Factors (Per $1,000)

Interest rate	15-year mortgage	20-year mortgage	25-year mortgage	30-year mortgage
2.00	6.44	5.06	4.24	3.70
2.25	6.55	5.18	4.36	3.82
2.50	6.67	5.30	4.49	3.95
2.75	6.79	5.42	4.61	4.08
3.00	6.91	5.55	4.74	4.22
3.25	7.03	5.67	4.87	4.35
3.50	7.15	5.80	5.01	4.49
3.75	7.27	5.93	5.14	4.63
4.00	7.40	6.06	5.28	4.77
4.25	7.52	6.19	5.42	4.92
4.50	7.65	6.33	5.56	5.07
4.75	7.78	6.46	5.70	5.22
5.00	7.91	6.60	5.85	5.37
5.25	8.04	6.74	5.99	5.52
5.50	8.17	6.88	6.14	5.68
5.75	8.30	7.02	6.29	5.84
6.00	8.44	7.16	6.44	6.00
6.25	8.57	7.31	6.60	6.16
6.50	8.71	7.46	6.75	6.32
6.75	8.85	7.60	6.91	6.49
7.00	8.99	7.75	7.07	6.65
7.25	9.13	7.90	7.23	6.82
7.50	9.27	8.06	7.39	6.99
7.75	9.41	8.21	7.55	7.16
8.00	9.56	8.36	7.72	7.34
8.25	9.70	8.52	7.88	7.51
8.50	9.85	8.68	8.05	7.69
8.75	9.99	8.84	8.22	7.87
9.00	10.14	9.00	8.39	8.05
9.25	10.29	9.16	8.56	8.23
9.50	10.44	9.32	8.74	8.41

Step 4. Subtract the down payment you want to make from your estimated purchase price. The result is the amount you'll need to borrow.

Step 5. Multiply the factor from the mortgage principle and interest chart by the number of thousands you'll need to borrow. The result is your monthly principal and interest payment.

Here's an example of how to put the first five steps together.

> **EXAMPLE:** Bill and Mark estimate the house they want to buy will cost $200,000. A 20% down payment of $40,000 leaves them with a $160,000 mortgage loan. They plan to finance with an adjustable rate mortgage (ARM), which they believe they can get at an interest rate of 6%. The monthly factor per $1,000 for a 30-year loan at 6% rate is 6. So their monthly payments will begin at 160 x 6, or $960.

Step 6. To get the total carrying costs for the mortgage loan, add the estimated monthly costs of homeowners' insurance and property taxes. Very roughly, homeowners' insurance costs about $400 per $100,000 of house value. On a $200,000 house, expect to pay $800 per year, or $67 per month.

Step 7. Property taxes are initially based on the new assessed value (market price) of the house as of the date of transfer of title. They vary from state to state and even county to county, so use 1% of the market value as an estimated annual tax. (For an exact number, call the tax assessor in the county in which you're looking to buy.) On a $200,000 house, taxes would be about $2,000 per year, or $167 per month.

Step 8. Now total up your mortgage/interest payment, insurance, and taxes. These are your monthly carrying costs.

Step 9. Total up the monthly payments on your long-term debts and add this number to the monthly carrying costs you arrived at in Step 8. Then, divide that total by a number between .28 and .38, depending on your debt level (the fewer your debts, the higher number to divide by), to determine the monthly income needed to qualify.

If You Are Married or State Registered

The rules for buying and owning a home if you are legally married or state registered in a jurisdiction that recognizes your relationship as "marriage-like" can be very different than the rules for unmarried buyers. The rules differ during the purchasing and financing phase, the ownership phase, and the "exit" phase. While the specific rules differ from state to state, and while federal rules won't apply to you, here's a summary of what's at stake for you and what you need to pay attention to:

1. **Purchase and Financing.** In most states, a married couple is considered a single economic unit. That means that you have one credit rating, and you are evaluated as a unified borrower for loan qualification purposes. If these same rules are applied to you, your partner's bad credit or bankruptcy could jeopardize your loan approval—in ways that unmarried and unregistered couples don't encounter. While the rules are changing so quickly, it's quite possible that your mortgage broker or title officer won't know about the new rules, so your application may be mishandled at first.

2. **Owning the House.** Whether only one partner is an owner or you are both legally on title, the rules about financial obligations may differ dramatically if you are registered or married. You may be jointly liable for each other's debts, so one partner's creditor may be able to put a "lien" on the house even if it's owned by the other partner. Allocating the tax benefits under state tax law may be different than if you were unregistered, though the IRS is not likely to honor your partnership as a legal marriage. If you decide to refinance your house, your spouse or partner may need to "sign off" the loan, even if the partner isn't on title. Remember, if you are married or registered you may be treated as a single economic unit, with all these delightful consequences.

   Being married or registered also changes the way you can take title. In some states you can take title as community property or tenant by the entireties, and the rights of survivorship (i.e., who gets the house if one owner dies) may be different. If you have any questions about these rules, you may need to check with an attorney, as your real estate agent may not be aware of the new rules for your particular state.

If You Are Married or State Registered (continued)

3. **Exiting the Home Ownership.** Whether you are exiting through death, dissolution, or merely the sale of the house, the legal, tax, and financial rules may be different if you are married or registered. If the house is one of your assets and you are breaking up, the Family Court probably will have jurisdiction over the house, even if only one partner is on the title. Any claims of excess monetary or labor contribution will be resolved according to marital law, not property law. If one of you dies while you are co-owners, the rules for who gets the house may be different if you are married or registered. And finally, because the IRS doesn't recognize our partnerships as legal marriages, none of the favorable tax treatments for selling your house will apply. Yes, you can each take the residential exemption, but probably only if you are both on the title. And you won't be able to postpone the sale on the grounds that your divorce decree forced you to wait a while longer to sell it. Once again, these rules are changing quickly, and your real estate agent or accountant may not be aware of the new rules, so you may need to consult a knowledgeable attorney in your area.

Proceeding With Your Purchase

Once you find the house you want to buy that is in your price range, you will need to take care of a few details before you actually buy it.

Inspections

Any contract to purchase a home should allow you a few weeks to make all necessary inspections. A buyer usually pays for inspections, but it may be possible to negotiate to have the seller pay a portion. Inspections routinely include termite, electrical and plumbing, and a roof inspection. In addition, you may want a soil engineer to check the foundation or a general contractor to do a full inspection of the house. Your purchase contract should be contingent upon these experts reporting that the house either is in good condition or can be repaired for a reasonable price, and you may want to negotiate for a price reduction if the repairs will be extensive (or expensive).

Financing That White Picket Fence

After you've conducted the inspections and reached a firm agreement on price and terms, you will have to come up with the money. Usually, your obligation to buy is contingent on your finding financing for a specific amount at a specific interest rate. Obviously, you don't want to sign a contract to purchase a home and then not be able to find a loan you can afford.

> **TIP**
>
> **In really competitive real estate markets, it's best to have a firm commitment.** Ask your lender to give you a letter committing to lend you a specific amount at a specific rate, so that you can make a bid without the financing contingency. When sellers receive multiple bids for their property, the most attractive will be the bid with the fewest contingencies.

Few of us can pay all cash for a house. We borrow money from a lending institution, family member, the seller, or a loan shark, and accept whatever conditions the lenders impose. Most often you'll borrow from a bank. In exchange, the bank will require you to sign a note promising to repay the money plus a healthy interest. Your promise to pay, standing alone, however, won't be sufficient security for the bank; it will also require you to sign a document giving it the power to foreclose on the house if you default on your payments. This document is normally called a mortgage or a deed of trust.

A few lenders admit that they view lesbian and gay relationships as inherently unstable and therefore consider it too risky to lend to lesbian and gay couples. Unfortunately, this kind of discrimination is legal in most places. To avoid it, you will need to present yourselves as sophisticated buyers. Do your homework. Know the interest rates from several other lenders before you walk in the door. Get familiar with fixed rate loans, adjustable rate mortgages, special 15-year mortgages, points, closing costs, and the rest. Provide information showing that you're both on your jobs for the long haul (get letters from your supervisors) and are up for a promotion or a raise. And then be persistent. Having a hard-working loan broker on your side might be very helpful.

To the extent it's possible, try to be creative in your financing. You may be able to "assume" a seller's loan, or the seller may be willing to finance some portion of the purchase. If the seller doesn't need all the money at once, you might get a second mortgage.

> **EXAMPLE:** Wendy and Alice love a home that is on the market for $180,000. Their savings, plus borrowing from parents and friends, total $36,000. They need $144,000 more (plus $9,000 for closing costs). The seller has owned the home for a few years and has a $90,000 mortgage at 6% interest. Here are several possible methods of financing their purchase:
>
> - Plan A
> $36,000 down payment
> $144,000 at current bank interest rates.
> - Plan B
> $36,000 down payment
> $90,000 by assuming the seller's old mortgage at 6%
> $54,000 loan from the seller including interest at 7%, with a final (balloon) payment for whatever balance is due in seven years. (The monthly interest payment rate and the time of the balloon payment will be negotiable.)
> - Plan C
>   To make it more attractive to the seller, an offer of $2,000 above the sales price
> $36,000 cash down
> $90,000 by assuming the seller's old mortgage at 6%
> $56,000 loan from seller including interest at 7%, with a final (balloon) payment for whatever balance is due in seven years.

Escrow and Closing Costs

In a house purchase, paperwork and money must eventually change hands. The common practice is for parties to open an "escrow," which means that an escrow holder, usually a title company, will hold the buyers' money and the sellers' deed to the property until the time comes for the property to change hands—after all inspections are complete, the papers are signed, and financing is arranged. Then, escrow closes, the deed is recorded with the county, the buyers receive the deed establishing that they now own the house, and the seller gets the money.

Closing Costs and Loan Fees

Closing costs and loan fees can add up to 5% to your mortgage. Some fees are paid to the bank when you apply for the loan, but most are paid the day you close escrow. Not all lenders and escrow holders require the same fees (some are waived as part of special offers). When escrow closes, you'll receive a statement with an itemized list of the closing costs.

Typical closing costs and loan fees are:

Application fee: Loan application fees (typically $200–$350) cover the lender's cost of processing your loan.

Appraisal fees: Most lenders hire an appraiser to be sure the property is worth the sales price. Appraisals usually cost $250 to $500 for a regular single-family home, and somewhat more for a very large or multiple-unit building.

Assumption fee: Typically 1% of the loan balance to assume the seller's existing ARM; to assume an FHA or VA loan, the fee will range from $50 to $100.

Credit report: It can cost up to $75 to check each partner's credit. While standard credit checks with scores cost $8–$15, for home loans, lenders check two credit reporting agencies' files and the county records for judgment and tax liens.

Escrow company fees: An escrow company that is not a title insurance company may charge a nominal fee for doing the escrow work.

Garbage fees: Real estate business slang for a number of small fees, including notary, courier, and filing fees, which typically run from $150 to $250.

Loan fees: This includes points (one point is 1% of the loan principal), a fee the bank charges you for the privilege of making a loan, and an additional

Closing Costs and Loan Fees (continued)

fee, usually between $100 and $450. Lenders also often charge $150 to $250 to complete the loan paperwork.

Physical inspection reports: Inspection reports may add several hundred dollars or more, depending on how many are requested.

Prepaid homeowners' insurance: This varies depending on what the lender requires and on the house's value, coverage, and location.

Prepaid interest on the loan: You'll be asked to pay per diem interest in advance, from the date your loan is funded to the end of that month. The maximum you'll be charged is 30 days of interest.

Prepaid property taxes: You'll be asked to pay property taxes for the period between the closing date and your first monthly mortgage payment.

Private mortgage insurance (PMI): This insurance protects the lender in the event of a foreclosure, in case the property is worth less than what you paid for it. For a loan with less than 10% down, the total PMI you will pay is about 1.6%–2% of the loan. In the first year, you'll pay approximately 0.5% of the total loan. For each year you renew your PMI policy, you'll pay about 0.35% of the outstanding loan. PMI on FHA loans costs 3.8% of the loan. Most lenders require the first few payments to be made up front.

Recording and filing fees: The escrow holder will charge about $100 for drawing up, reviewing, and recording the deed of trust and other legal documents. The total escrow and title fees can amount to 0.5% of the loan.

Survey fee: If the house has easements or is in a rural location, a survey may be needed to establish the precise measurements of the lot. A survey will run as much as $400 or more.

Tax service fee: This fee is for a service that will notify the lender if you default on your property taxes; it usually costs about $60 to $100.

Title search and title insurance: Not all buyers have to pay all of the title costs. Most lenders require title insurance for the face amount of their mortgage or for the value of the loan. Title insurance is a one-time premium that costs about 0.075% of the cost of your house. The title search confirms that the seller of the property is really the legal owner.

Transfer tax: Tax assessed by the county when the property changes hands. This tax may be split with the seller if you negotiate an agreement, and costs about 55 cents per $1,000 of value transferred. Many cities also charge transfer tax; it varies city to city, but can be as much as 1.5% of the purchase price.

In some states, a lawyer is required to handle the real estate closing. Title companies and real estate agents cannot conduct closings, or even give their clients advice about them, as that would be practicing law without a license. In many other states, attorneys are not usually involved in residential property sales, and a title or escrow company handles the entire closing process.

Taking Title to Your New Home

When you buy your home with your partner, you must decide how you will own the property, or in real estate talk, how you "take title." This decision has important consequences, especially for estate planning. You have four choices:

- Only one person holds title.
- Both of you hold title as "joint tenants."
- Both of you hold title as "tenants-in-common."
- If you are married or legally partnered, both of you hold title as "married persons" "community property," or "tenancy by the entirety."

Title in One Person's Name

As we've mentioned earlier, sometimes a couple is tempted to put only one name on the deed to save on taxes or avoid one partner's creditors. The tax savings are attractive if one of you has a lot of income and the other makes very little money; the high-income person takes all the house tax deductions. But in general, this is a bad strategy. If only one person's name is on the title, that person is the sole owner unless you make a separate contract that says otherwise. And if the person whose name is on the deed (and who is therefore the presumed sole owner) sells the house and pockets the money or dies without making provisions for the other partner, that partner may be out of luck.

> ! CAUTION
>
> **Do not let a mortgage broker persuade you that a second owner can be easily added to the title later on.** It is possible, but in many states it can be difficult and expensive, and can sometimes involve paying transfer or gift taxes.

If you do have compelling reasons to keep one partner's name off the deed, but want to protect that partner's share of the house ownership, have a lawyer draft a contract that spells out the rights of both owners—after you make sure that such a contract is valid in your state. If it isn't, the partner who is not on the title may be considered a creditor rather than a co-owner.

Joint Tenancy

Joint tenancy means you share property ownership equally, and that each of you owns and has the right to use the entire property. Joint tenancy also comes with something called a "right of survivorship." In fact, the deed sometimes reads "joint tenancy with right of survivorship." This means that if one joint tenant dies, the other one automatically receives the deceased person's share, even if there's a will to the contrary. And when joint tenancy property passes to the other joint tenant at death, there's no need for any probate proceedings.

> ! CAUTION
>
> **Each joint tenant has the right to sell his or her interest, regardless of whether the other joint tenant agrees—or is even aware of the sale.** If one joint tenant sells his or her share or transfers it to a living trust, the sale or transfer ends the joint tenancy, and a tenancy-in-common is created between the new owner (or the trust) and the other original owner. (See below for the definition of tenants-in-common.)

If you and your partner own unequal shares in the house, joint tenancy isn't the appropriate way to hold title—it's only for when each joint tenant owns the same portion. This means that you and your partner could put a house you owned 50-50 in joint tenancy or that three people could have joint tenancy with each owning one-third of a property. If you own 65% of a house, however, and your lover owns 35%, joint tenancy won't work. Joint tenancy can also create some serious adverse tax consequences for high-asset couples. If that's a concern for you, see a tax specialist before making a final decision.

If one of you contributed more to the down payment, you can equalize things even if you hold title as joint tenants and own the property equally. You would do this by establishing a dollar amount that the higher contributor would receive as reimbursement, instead of by giving that person a greater ownership interest. (You could do this through a promissory note, through the other partner paying more than half of the expenses, or, in some states, simply by signing a written agreement setting forth the reimbursement details.) But again, if you want to own the property in other than equal shares, use tenancy-in-common.

> **EXAMPLE:** Tom and Liam decide to buy a house together; they want to own it equally as joint tenants and pay the monthly expenses equally, but they've kept their savings separate so far and they've each saved different amounts. Tom is going to contribute $10,000 toward the $40,000 down payment, and Liam is going to contribute $30,000. They've decided to honor their unequal contributions by Tom committing to pay Liam $10,000 (so that they each will have contributed an equal $20,000), either over time as Tom can afford it, or out of Tom's share of the proceeds of the sale if and when they sell the house.
>
> Tom and Liam should put this commitment in writing as part of their co-ownership agreement. They will own the property equally as joint tenants, but Tom will have a debt to Liam.

We discourage partners from using a recorded mortgage to secure a loan between partners, primarily because we think that partners shouldn't act like bankers. But if this is something you really want to do, check with a real estate lawyer about how to do it in your particular state.

> **TIP**
> **Tenancy by the entireties is available to married couples.** In some states, married couples, including same-sex couples and registered partners in marriage-equivalent states, can take title as tenancy by the entireties. Both spouses have the right to enjoy the entire property. Neither one can unilaterally end the tenancy, and creditors of one spouse cannot force a sale of the property to collect on a debt. When one dies, the survivor automatically gets title to the entire property without a probate court proceeding.

Tenancy-in-Common

Tenancy-in-common is the other way to hold title when there's more than one owner. The major difference between joint tenancy and tenancy-in-common is that tenancy-in-common has no right of survivorship. This means that when a tenant-in-common dies, that person's share of property is left to whomever is specified in a will, or if there's no will, by the process of "intestate succession."

Of particular importance in many lesbian or gay real estate ventures, tenants-in-common can own property in unequal shares—one person can own 80% of the property, another 15% and a third 5%. All are listed on the deed as tenants-in-common. You can specify the precise percentages on the deed if you wish—for example, "The owners named are tenants-in-common; Sophie has a one-third interest and Janet has a two-thirds interest." More commonly, you can simply list all owners' names on the deed and set out the shares in a separate written agreement. Especially if shares are unequal, it's essential that you prepare a contract.

Changing Title

If you take title in one format and later agree you want to change it, you can do so; you need only record a new deed. For instance, if you want to start as tenants-in-common and later change to joint tenants, make and record a deed granting the property "from Sophie and Janet as Tenants-in-Common, to Sophie and Janet as Joint Tenants, with right of survivorship."

CAUTION

If you add another owner to the deed when you are changing the form of title, the IRS will call it either a sale or a gift. You will be taxed accordingly, which can be expensive.

Contracts for Home Purchase and Ownership

A house is a major economic asset. It's foolish to avoid or postpone making an agreement clearly defining your mutual expectations and obligations, especially if your contributions are unequal. This section discusses ways to handle joint ownership issues and gives sample contracts to cover the most common situations.

Not having an agreement can lead to all kinds of unpleasant conflicts if your relationship ends. You may disagree about percentages of co-ownership, or simply about the process of selling the house. Lawyers already have made far too much money trying to help couples sort out such messes, so please, don't ignore these issues when setting up your household.

If you've entered into a marriage or a marriage-like relationship, such as a civil union or domestic partnership, the need for a private contract is slightly less pressing. These legal relationships will usually provide a framework for dividing property equally if you split up. But if your contributions are unequal, it's still best to make a simple written agreement even if you are in a marriage-equivalent relationship. If you do live in a marriage-equivalent state, your written agreement must comply with your state's rules of prenuptial agreements, and you will need help from attorneys in preparing it. And if one of you bought the property before you entered into the relationship, you will need to take steps to put it in joint ownership for it to be considered shared property.

TIP

Often, the couples that resist making contracts are those who don't have a solid agreement between them in the first place. If this is true for you, sit down immediately and have a long, honest talk. It may be the conversation that keeps you out of court if you and your partner or co-owner part ways later.

Although the simple contracts shown here suffice for many situations, some home ownership arrangements will require more complicated written agreements. If this is your situation, have your agreement checked by a lawyer. This doesn't mean you have to pay a fortune or turn over control of the whole process. Do as much work as possible yourself and then ask the lawyer to help you with particular problem areas or check the entire agreement when you're finished.

RELATED TOPIC

Chapter 11 has information on how to find a gay-friendly lawyer and how to get the most out of working with a lawyer.

Agreement for Equal Ownership

The first sample contract is an agreement between two people who contribute equal amounts of money for the down payment and intend to share all costs and eventual profits equally.

In this contract, Michael and Hadrian take title as joint tenants. As discussed above, this means that if either of them dies, the survivor would automatically get the other's share.

Michael and Hadrian also want to make sure Michael's mother would receive credit for the $20,000 she gave him for the down payment if he died while she was still alive. This clause is an example of how you can tailor these samples to your own specific needs and circumstances.

Sample Contract for Equal Ownership of Real Property

Michael Angelo and Hadrian Rifkin make the following agreement to jointly purchase a house that they will live in. They agree that:

1. They will buy a house at 423 Bliss Street, Chicago, Illinois, for $180,000.

2. They will take title as joint tenants with right of survivorship, and they both agree not to modify this form of co-ownership unless both of them agree to do so.

3. They will each contribute $20,000 to the down payment and closing costs and will each pay one-half of the monthly mortgage and insurance costs, as well as one-half of the property taxes and costs for repairs that both agree are needed.

4. If either Michael or Hadrian wants to end the relationship and living arrangement, and if both men want to keep the house, they will ask a friend to flip a coin within 60 days of the decision to separate. [For information on mediation as an alternative method of resolving this dispute, see Chapter 10.] The winner of the coin toss will be entitled to purchase the house from the loser, provided that the winner pays the loser the fair market value (see Clause 5) of his 50% share and refinances the property in his name alone within 90 days. When payment is made, Michael and Hadrian will deed the house to the person retaining it in his name alone. If payment isn't made within 90 days, the other owner will have a similar 90-day period to buy the house. If neither makes the purchase or if neither person wants to buy the house, it will be sold and the proceeds divided equally after payment of all encumbrances. During the buyout periods, both parties remain jointly responsible for the mortgage and other expenses.

5. If Michael and Hadrian cannot agree on the fair market value of the house, the value will be determined by an appraisal conducted by Sheila Lim, the real estate agent they used when they bought the house, or an appraiser appointed by her successor.

6. Michael and Hadrian each agree to maintain life insurance policies for at least $100,000, naming the other as beneficiary. If Michael dies while his mother is alive, Hadrian agrees to pay her $20,000 out of the proceeds of Michael's life insurance policy.

7. If either Michael or Hadrian must make a payment of mortgage, taxes, or insurance for the other because the other is either unable or unwilling to make the payment, that payment will be treated as a loan to be paid back within six months, including 10% interest per year.

8. This contract is binding on our heirs and our estates.

9. Any dispute arising under this agreement will be mediated by a third person mutually acceptable to both parties. The mediator's role will be to help us arrive at an agreement, not to impose one on us. If good-faith efforts to arrive at our own solution to all issues in dispute with the help of a mediator aren't successful, either of us may make a written request to the other that the dispute be arbitrated. If such a request is made, the dispute will be submitted to arbitration under the rules of the American Arbitration Association, and one arbitrator will hear our dispute. The decision of the arbitrator will be binding on us and will be enforceable in any court that has jurisdiction over the dispute. We each agree to give up the right to a jury trial.

_____   _____
Date   Michael Angelo

_____   _____
Date   Hadrian Rifkin

Owning a House in Unequal Shares

If each person puts up the same amount for the down payment, pays equal shares of the mortgage and other expenses, and contributes equally to fix-up fees, each will have an equal share of the ownership. It's common, however, for joint purchasers to contribute unequally. One person may have more money for the down payment. Another person may be able to afford larger monthly payments than the other, or may have skills (such as carpentry) to renovate the house while the other sits by and kibbitzes.

In such situations, you have two options. You can agree on equal co-ownership but provide for reimbursement for one party's excess contributions. You would use the equal co-ownership contract, but add a clause stating the amount of reimbursement for the excess contributions and how and when it will be paid. Alternatively, you can make an agreement to own the property in unequal shares according to the sample contracts shown below. Depending on whether or not the house goes up a lot in value, your choice of options could have significant financial consequences for both of you.

Some things are easier to value in money than others. For example, work done on the house can be given a cash value by establishing an hourly wage and multiplying it by the number of hours worked. But what value do you assign to someone's ability to borrow the down payment from his parents, which may be the difference between being able to buy the house and not? These agreements suggest that it's enough to decide on rough values that satisfy you both; if you come up with more precise criteria, modify the agreement accordingly.

Two-Thirds/One-Third Ownership

Tina and Barb purchased a home. Tina had more capital, so she made two-thirds of the down payment and owns two-thirds of the house. To keep things simple, Tina will pay two-thirds of the mortgage, taxes, and insurance.

Their contract is below (the form contract on the companion page allows you to use whatever ownership percentages you agree on).

Sample Contract for Ownership of Real Property and Payments Split Unequally

We, Tina Foote and Barb Bibbige, enter into this contract and agree as follows:

1. Property: We will purchase the house at 451 Morton Street, in Upper Montclair, New Jersey.

2. Contributions: We will contribute the following money to the down payment:

    Tina $20,000

    Barb $10,000

3. Ownership: We will own the property as tenants-in-common with the following shares:

    Tina 2/3

    Barb 1/3

4. Expenses and Mortgage: Even though we will share equally in living in the house, all expenses, including mortgage, taxes, insurance, and major repairs on the house, will be paid as follows:

    Tina 2/3

    Barb 1/3

    Utilities and minor repairs (under $500) will be split equally, reflecting the fact that we equally occupy the property.

5. Division Upon Sale: In the event the house is sold or one of us buys the other out, the initial contributions ($20,000 to Tina and $10,000 to Barb) will be paid back first, and the remainder of the proceeds will be divided two-thirds to Tina and one-third to Barb. If the property's value has decreased, the loss will be distributed two-thirds to Tina and one-third to Barb.

6. Contingencies:

    a. We agree to hold the house for three years unless we mutually agree otherwise. After three years, either person may request the house be sold. The person who doesn't want to sell has the right to purchase the house at the agreed-upon price, and must state in writing that she will exercise this right within two weeks of the setting of the price. She has 60 days to complete the purchase, or the right lapses. If we can't agree on a price, we will jointly select an appraiser to set the price.

    b. If one owner moves out of the house before it's sold, she will remain responsible for her share of the mortgage, taxes, insurance, and repairs. She may rent her quarters with the approval (which won't be unreasonably withheld) of the other. The person who stays in the house has the right to rent the quarters herself or assume the cost if she so chooses.

c. If Tina and Barb decide to separate and both want to keep the house, they will try to reach a satisfactory arrangement. If by the end of two weeks they can't, they will ask a friend to flip a coin. The winner has the right to purchase the loser's share provided the winner pays the loser her share of the fair market value within 90 days of the toss. We will use an appraiser to set the value.

d. If either Tina or Barb dies, the other, if she hasn't been left the deceased person's share, has the right to purchase that share from the deceased's estate within six months. The value of the share will be determined as set out above.

7. Binding: This agreement is binding on us and our heirs, executors, administrators, successors, and assigns.

8. Mediation: Any dispute arising under this agreement will be mediated by a third person mutually acceptable to both parties. The mediator's role will be to help us arrive at an agreement, not to impose one on us. If good-faith efforts to arrive at our own solution to all issues in dispute with the help of a mediator aren't successful, either of us may make a written request to the other that the dispute be arbitrated. If such a request is made, the dispute will be submitted to arbitration under the rules of the American Arbitration Association, and one arbitrator will hear our dispute. The decision of the arbitrator will be binding on us and will be enforceable in any court that has jurisdiction over the dispute. We each agree to give up the right to a jury trial.

_____   _____
Date   Tina Foote

_____   _____
Date   Barb Bibbige

Unequal Ownership Turns Into Equal Ownership

The next example is a contract for Gertrude and Alice. Gertrude can sell some valuable antiques and come up with the full $50,000 down payment for a little cottage with a mansard roof. Alice can pay one-half the monthly mortgage, insurance, and maintenance costs, but has no money for the down payment. They eventually want to equally own the home, but also want to fairly account for Gertrude's down payment.

Gertrude could make a gift of one-half of the down payment to Alice, but she'd have to file a gift tax return, and she doesn't feel quite that generous. We suggest that Gertrude call one-half of the down payment a loan to Alice that can either be paid back in monthly installments or deferred until the house is sold. She can always forgive all or part of the loan, as a gift, but she's not obligated to do so. To do this, they should write a contract similar to Michael and Hadrian's, indicating a 50-50 ownership. They should also prepare a promissory note providing a record of the loan. And it's good news for Gertrude. If she records the note, turning it into a secured mortgage, she can deduct the loan interest on her tax return—though there are many couples who prefer to keep loans private, especially if they plan to refinance in the not-too-distant future.

Sample Promissory Note for Down Payment Money

I, Alice B. Toklas, acknowledge receipt of a loan of $25,000 from Gertrude Stein, to be used as my 50% share of the down payment for our house located at 10 Rue de There, Oakland, California. I agree to pay this sum back, plus interest, at the rate of 6% per year, by making monthly payments of $_____ , in seven years. [*Or:* I agree to pay the entire loan and interest at 6% per year when and if the house is sold.]

I agree that if the loan and all interest due haven't been repaid when the house is sold, the remaining balance owed will be paid to Gertrude out of my share of the proceeds from that sale.

_____   _____
Date   Alice B. Toklas

One Person Buys the House and the Other Fixes It Up

Sometimes, one or more owners contribute a greater portion, or even all, of the down payment, and another contributes labor or materials to fix a place up. For this situation, a simple contract should be enough. (As with all the contracts, if special circumstances require more complex details, have a lawyer review your agreement.)

Stephan, Bob, and Lyn decide to purchase a graceful but dilapidated Victorian. Stephan and Bob can put up the cash for the down payment and Lyn the expertise and time to make the necessary repairs. They can each afford to pay one-third of the monthly expenses. Like Gertrude and Alice, they want to own the place in equal shares. Because Stephan and Bob are each going to contribute $17,000 to the down payment, they agree that Lyn should contribute $17,000 worth of materials and labor (at $20 an hour) to fix up the house.

Because this contract is so specific, it's not included on the book's companion page, but you can use it as a sample to create your own.

Sample Agreement to Contribute Cash and Labor

We, Stephan, Bob, and Lyn, agree as follows:

1. We will purchase the house at 225 Peaches Street, Atlanta, Georgia, for $200,000, and we will own the house equally in thirds as tenants-in-common. All of us will live there.

2. Stephan and Bob will each contribute $17,000 to be used as the down payment.

3. Over the next seven months, Lyn will contribute $11,000 for materials and 300 hours of labor (valued at $20 per hour), making a total contribution of $17,000, toward fixing up the house.

4. If we all agree that more labor or materials are needed to fix up the house, the materials will be paid for equally by Lyn, Bob, and Stephan, and Lyn (or Bob or Stephan if they work) will be credited $20 an hour unless all three work an equal number of hours.

5. All monthly expenses will be shared equally among the parties.

6. This contract may be amended in writing at any time by unanimous consent.

7. If any of the parties wants to end the ownership and living arrangement, and if all three, or two of the three, want to keep the house, a friend will be asked to flip a coin (once between two competing parties; twice between three competing parties) within 60 days of the decision to stop owning the house together. [For information on mediation as an alternative method of resolving this dispute, see Chapter 10.] The winner of the coin tosses will be entitled to purchase the house from the losers, provided that the winner pays each of the losers the fair market value (see Clause 5) of their one-third shares and refinances the property in his name alone within 90 days. When payment is made, the three parties will deed the house to the person retaining it in that person's name alone. If payment for the buyout isn't made within 90 days, the other owners will have a similar 90-day period to buy the house (the person who won the first coin toss, but lost the second, will have the first right to buy, under the same terms set out in this paragraph). If no party succeeds in buying out the others or if none of the parties wants to buy the house, it will be sold and the profits will be divided equally among the parties.

8. If the parties cannot agree on the fair market value of the house, the value will be determined by an appraisal conducted by Kathy Campbell, the real estate agent they used when they bought the house, or an appraiser appointed by her successor.

9. Any dispute arising under this agreement will be mediated by a third person mutually acceptable to all parties. The mediator's role will be to help us arrive at an agreement, not to impose one on us. If good-faith efforts to arrive at our own solution to all issues in dispute with the help of a mediator aren't successful, any of us may make a written request to the others that the dispute be arbitrated. If such a request is made, the dispute will be submitted to arbitration under the rules of the American Arbitration Association, and one arbitrator will hear our dispute. The decision of the arbitrator will be binding on us and will be enforceable in any court that has jurisdiction over the dispute. We all agree to give up the right to a jury trial.

_____   _____
Date   Stephan Valery

_____   _____
Date   Bob Bisell

_____   _____
Date   Lyn Rosenthal

It's easy to determine ownership interests based on the contributions made (or promised) at the time the contact is drafted. It's also possible, however, to provide for ownership shares that will fluctuate over time. Obviously, doing this can get complicated. If Stephan, Bob, and Lyn want to vary their shares, with Stephan and Bob owning the place to start with and Lyn's share growing as he contributes labor and materials, they could attach to their contract a sheet showing all contributions. Such a sheet might look like this when Lyn finished his work:

Sheet 1—Capital Contributions

Nature of Contribution	Date	Value	Contributed by:		
			Stephan	Bob	Lyn
Cash	1/29	$34,000	$17,000	$17,000	
Paint, Roof Supplies	3/10	4,000			$4,000
Wood	3/12	3,500			3,500
Floor Supplies	3/12	3,500			3,500
Labor	3/13–6/15	6,000			6,000
Cash: Hot Tub	7/20	1,500	500	500	500
Totals		$52,500	$17,500	$17,500	$17,500

Complicated Contribution Contracts

Sometimes it does make sense to make a more complicated contract. For example, Rosemary is a carpenter by trade, and she and Glenna agreed that her carpentry work should be valued at a higher hourly rate than the ordinary labor of either. Here's the contract they drew up. It's probably more cumbersome than most people need, but for those of you with very tidy minds, it can work well. Because this contract is so specific, you won't find a form on the book's companion page, but you can use it as a sample to create your own.

Sample Detailed Property Agreement

Glenna O'Brien and Rosemary Avila agree as follows:

1. They will buy the house at 15 Snake Hill Road, Cold Springs Harbor, New York, for a total price of $300,000. The initial investment (down payment and closing costs) of $24,988 will be contributed by Rosemary. The title to the house will be recorded as Rosemary Avila and Glenna O'Brien as tenants-in-common.

2. Glenna and Rosemary will each pay one-half of the monthly mortgage, tax, and homeowners' insurance payments, and will each be responsible for one-half of any costs necessary for maintenance and repairs.

3. They will contribute labor and materials to improve the house. Rosemary's labor—doing skilled carpentry—will be valued at $24 per hour, and both Glenna and Rosemary's labor making other house repairs will be valued at $10 per hour. These rates may be raised in the future if both agree in writing. Materials will be valued at their actual cost.

4. They will maintain a ledger marked "Exhibit I—15 Snake Hill Road Homeowners' Record." This ledger is considered a part of this contract. They will record the following information in the Homeowners' Record:

   a. The $24,988 initial contribution made to purchase the house by Rosemary

   b. Their monthly payments for the mortgage, property taxes, and homeowners' insurance

   c. Rosemary's labor as a carpenter on home improvements valued as stated in Clause 3

   d. Their labor on noncarpentry home improvements valued as stated in Clause 3

   e. All money that they pay for supplies and materials necessary for home improvements, and

   f. Any other money that either spends for improvements as long as the expenditure has been approved in advance by the other.

5. Their ownership shares of the house are determined as follows:

   a. The dollar value of all contributions made by either will be separately totaled, using the figures set out in the 15 Snake Hill Road Homeowners' Record.

   b. The owners will add interest to their investment totals in any amount with the value of those additional contributions increased by 5% per year simple interest. Simple interest will be calculated twice a year (January 1 and July 1), with the interest being added to each person's total investment as of that date.

c. The total equity interest in the house will be computed by subtracting all mortgages and encumbrances outstanding from the fair market value as of the date of the computation. If the owners can't agree on the fair market value, each will have the house appraised by choosing a licensed real estate agent familiar with their neighborhood to estimate the market value. The average of the two estimates will be deemed the fair market value of the house.

d. Each owner will be entitled to that percentage of the equity that equals the ratio of that owner's total contributions (4a–f, above) to the parties' total joint contributions. In other words, if one owner contributes 40% of the total contributions, she will get 40% of the equity.

6. If either owner does not pay her equal share of the mortgage, taxes, or insurance in a timely manner, the other person may make the payment, and that payment will be treated as a loan to be paid back as soon as possible, but not later than six months, plus interest at the rate of 5% per annum.

7. Either person can terminate this agreement at any time. If this occurs, and both women want to remain in the house and can afford to buy the other out in 90 days, a third party will flip a coin to determine who keeps the house. If only one person wants the house, she will pay the other her share within 90 days. If the person who wants to keep the house is unable to pay the other within 90 days, the other owner will have a similar 90-day opportunity. If neither elects to or is able to purchase the house, the house will be sold and the proceeds divided according to the shares established under Clause 5d.

8. Any dispute arising under this agreement will be mediated by a third person mutually acceptable to both parties. The mediator's role will be to help us arrive at an agreement, not to impose one on us. If good-faith efforts to arrive at our own solution to all issues in dispute with the help of a mediator aren't successful, either of us may make a written request to the other that the dispute be arbitrated. If such a request is made, the dispute will be submitted to arbitration under the rules of the American

Arbitration Association, and one arbitrator will hear our dispute. The decision of the arbitrator will be binding on us and will be enforceable in any court that has jurisdiction over the dispute. We each agree to give up the right to a jury trial.

Date	Glenna O'Brien

Date	Rosemary Avila

Strive for Simplicity

The best contracts are simple contracts. For example, round off ownership interests (e.g., 25% and 75%, not 26.328% and 73.672%). Why? Because trying to achieve absolute accuracy—even if such a thing were possible—is usually more trouble than it's worth. If one person puts up a little extra cash or labor, or forks out more money in an emergency, consider the extra contribution a loan to be paid back, either when the house is sold or by the other owner making a similar extra contribution, rather than redrafting the basic agreement. As long as any promissory notes are paid off before the house is sold, this approach is safe and simple.

When Not All Owners Live in the House

If a group of friends, or a couple and a friend, invest in property and not all the owners live there, those who live in the house usually contribute more to the property than the nonresident owners. The excess contributions reflect a kind of fair rental value or occupancy payment to the group of owners. If these payments don't cover the monthly expenses, then each owner (including those living in the house) must pay a share of the difference. If the payment exceeds the monthly expenses, the extra payments should be deposited into a bank account and divided among the owners once a year, in proportion to ownership shares after all repairs are made and bills paid. The amount paid as fair rental value should be adjusted every year or two.

The resident owners will want low rent-based costs and will resist sale of the house. It is their home, not just an investment. The outside investors might want high rent-based payments, low maintenance, and sale for peak profit. Expectations can differ considerably concerning the quality of maintenance and improvements. What happens, for example, when the occupants want to put in a hot tub costing $1,500, of no immediate benefit (but perhaps an expense) to the investors? These problems can be intensified when the occupants are a couple, while the outside investors are friends or relatives.

Potential conflicts should be addressed in advance in a written contract. Some issues to address in the contract include:

- the set period of time after the purchase when the house will be sold or the nonoccupant investors may withdraw their money and profit
- the fair rent-based payments to be paid by the occupants; rental value should be based on a comparable rental market analysis, reduced by the on-site management services provided by the occupants, and not simply on the total of all ordinary monthly payments for mortgages, insurance, and taxes, plus something extra to cover minor repairs; the rental value ought to be adjusted every year or two
- an understanding that the occupants may be reimbursed if they improve the premises, but that purely decorative improvements are at their own expense; necessary improvements and major repairs are usually charged to the entire ownership group, and
- the right of the occupant-owners to buy out the nonoccupant-owners at a specific time for the net fair market value.

The contract below assumes that Violet Clarke and Teresa Conroy are lovers who want to buy a little island of peace. Their friend Melanie Stuart has some money, is looking for an investment, and wants to help. Their contract is simple and to the point. If Melanie's lover, Janet, wants to help out too, this contract can easily be modified to provide for four owners.

Sample Contract When One Owner Does Not Live on the Premises #1

We, Violet Clarke, Teresa Conroy, and Melanie Stuart, agree as follows:

1. We agree to purchase the home known as 21 Island Retreat, Wilton Manors, Florida.

2. We will contribute the following money for the down payment:

   Melanie: $10,000

   Violet: $5,000

   Teresa: $5,000

3. We will own the property in the following proportions: Melanie—50%, Violet—25%, and Teresa—25%. If we sell the house, each person will be repaid her initial contribution or a pro rata share if the property has declined in value; then the remaining profit or loss will be divided: Melanie—50%, Violet—25%, and Teresa—25%.

4. Violet and Teresa will live on the property and will contribute a total of $750 per month for the first two years. At the end of two years, we will decide what is a fair rent-based contribution, taking into consideration the fair market rent, adjusted to reflect that Violet and Teresa do all the work necessary to maintain and manage the property.

5. Mortgage payments, insurance, and taxes total $695 per month. These expenses will be paid from Violet and Teresa's contribution. Violet and Teresa will be responsible for all maintenance and repair costs. Any excess or shortfall will be allocated pro rata according to ownership shares. If there's a shortfall, each of us must contribute pro rata to make it up. If there's an overage, it will be retained in the house account until we all agree to disburse it or until the property is sold as described in this agreement.

6. We will sell the house within five years unless we unanimously agree in writing to keep it longer. If at any time after two years and before five years Violet and Teresa desire to purchase Melanie's share, they may do so at the fair market value of Melanie's interest.

7. Any dispute arising under this agreement will be mediated by a third person mutually acceptable to all parties. The mediator's role will be to help us arrive at an agreement, not to impose one on us. If good-faith efforts to arrive at our own solution to all issues in dispute with the help

of a mediator aren't successful, any of us may make a written request to the others that the dispute be arbitrated. If such a request is made, the dispute will be submitted to arbitration under the rules of the American Arbitration Association, and one arbitrator will hear our dispute. The decision of the arbitrator will be binding on us and will be enforceable in any court that has jurisdiction over the dispute. We all agree to give up the right to a jury trial.

8. Moving-on clause. [See "Moving On," below.]

9. If one of us isn't able to make a timely payment, then either one or both of the other women may make the payment, and the payment will be considered a loan at 5% interest to be paid back within six months.

10. If any one of us dies and doesn't leave her share to the other owners, the survivors have the right to purchase that share from her estate. The value of that share will be the initial down payment plus an increase of 3% per year (simple interest). The surviving owners may buy this share with no down payment and pay the estate over a ten-year period, including interest of 5% per year on the share.

11. This agreement is binding on our heirs, executors, administrators, successors, and assigns.

_____   _____
Date   Violet Clarke

_____   _____
Date   Teresa Conroy

_____   _____
Date   Melanie Stuart

Another example of group ownership is provided by Sarah, Guy, and Millet. They bought a duplex together with the understanding that Sarah and her children would live in one half and Guy would live in the other half. Millet joined the venture to invest some money and aid her friends. Here's their contract.

Sample Contract When One Owner Does
Not Live on the Premises #2

We, Sarah Wren, Guy Wright, and Millet Victor, on December 9, 20xx, agree to co-own the property described below as follows:

1. Purpose: The purpose of the joint venture is to purchase the property known as 1 Lake Front, Jefferson, Iowa.

2. Duration: The co-ownership will commence the date this agreement is signed and will continue until dissolved by mutual agreement or sale of the property.

3. Contributions: The parties will make the following contributions, which will be known as their Capital Contribution:

    Guy Wright $20,000

    Sarah Wren $12,000

    Millet Victor $8,000

4. Responsibility for Loans: In addition to the Capital Contribution, the parties agree to be responsible for the loans and mortgages as follows:

    a. Sarah will be responsible for 50% of all payments due to The Jean Mortgage Company.

    b. Guy will be responsible for 50% of all mortgage payments due to The Jean Mortgage Company.

    c. Millet will have no additional responsibility beyond her initial capital contribution.

5. Mortgages: If at any time Sarah or Guy cannot pay the required share of the mortgage payment in a timely manner, one or both of the other parties, at their option, may make the payment in order to keep the property from being foreclosed. The person(s) making the payment will be repaid within six months, with 5% annual interest.

6. Rights and Duties of the Parties: Guy has the right to live in the upper unit of the building or to rent it out at whatever rate he may choose. If he rents it out, he remains responsible for 50% of The Jean Mortgage Company payment, and, in either case, he's responsible for all repairs and maintenance of the upper unit.

    Sarah has the right to live in the lower unit of the building or to rent it out in whole or part at whatever rate she may choose. If she rents it out, she remains responsible for 50% of The Jean Mortgage

Company payment, and, in either case, she's responsible for all repairs and maintenance of the lower unit.

Millet will not occupy either unit, and she isn't responsible for any payments beyond her initial Capital Contribution.

7. Repairs: Either Guy or Sarah may need to make repairs to the building. The cost of major repairs (like the roof or boiler) will be divided evenly between the two of them. If either wants to improve her or his unit, either may do so under the following rules:

   - Any repairs or additions costing more than one thousand dollars ($1,000) will be considered a capital investment, credited to the party's Capital Account and paid back upon sale of the building.
   - Repairs or additions above $1,000 must be approved by Sarah, Guy, and Millet in writing if the person paying is to be paid back.

8. Shares: Sarah will own 30% of the property, Guy will own 50%, and Millet will own 20%.

9. Profit and Loss: Upon the sale of the building, the respective capital investments, reflected by the Capital Account, will first be returned to the parties. The remaining profit or loss will be distributed as follows: Sarah 30%; Guy 50%; Millet 20%.

10. Regular books will be kept that are open to inspection by all parties upon reasonable notice.

11. Time: Sarah, Guy, and Millet agree to hold the property for five years; no sale or encumbrance will be made during that time without unanimous consent. At the end of five years, any one of the parties may request a sale of her or his share by giving four months' written notice.

12. Election to Keep Building or Sell: If the co-ownership is dissolved due to the death, withdrawal, or other act of any party before the expiration of the five years, the remaining parties may continue to own the building. If the remaining owners so elect, they will have the right to purchase the interest of the other person in the building by paying to such person, or the legal representatives of such person, the pro rata value of such interest as follows:

    Appointment of Appraisers. The parties desiring to continue ownership will appoint one appraiser; the withdrawing person or the legal representative of a deceased or incapacitated person may appoint a second appraiser. The appraisers will determine the value of the assets and liabilities of the co-ownership, and the parties desiring to continue ownership will pay to the other, or the representative, the departing partner's capital investment plus the share (as set out in Clause 9 above) of the gain or loss of the venture. The withdrawing person or the legal representative will execute the documents necessary to convey such person's interest in the venture to the other parties.

　　Additional Appraiser in Event of Disagreement. In the event the appraisers cannot agree on the value of the property within 15 days after their appointment, they will designate an additional appraiser whose appraisal will be binding on all parties. If any selected appraiser becomes unable or unwilling to serve, the person(s) originally selecting him or her shall appoint a substitute. In the event the two appraisers first appointed cannot agree on a third appraiser, such appraiser will be appointed by the director of the _____ [for instance, a local gay rights organization].

　　Rights and Obligations of Continuing Parties. The parties continuing the co-ownership will assume all of the existing obligations and will indemnify the withdrawing party against all liability.

13. Dissolution: In the event that all parties agree to dissolve the venture, the building will be sold, the debts paid, and the surplus divided among the parties in accordance with their interests as set out in Clause 9.

14. Amendments: This agreement may be amended at any time in writing by unanimous agreement.

_____　　_____
Date　　　　　　　　　　　　Sarah Wren

_____　　_____
Date　　　　　　　　　　　　Guy Wright

_____　　_____
Date　　　　　　　　　　　　Millet Victor

In the last two contracts, the owners agreed that the persons not living in the house shouldn't be responsible for maintenance and repairs. Often, the nonoccupant wants to limit her or his liability. A simple method for this is Clause 4c, above, in Sarah, Guy, and Millet's contract, where Millet isn't obligated to make any payments beyond her initial capital contribution.

Although the agreement is binding between the three partners, if a new roof is added and Sarah and Guy fail to pay the roofer, the roofer could sue Millet. To ensure that Millet wouldn't have to pay the roofer, or face any other liability on the basis of another partner's acts, they could form a limited partnership.

A limited partnership is a special type of legal entity. You must follow specific state laws and registration procedures to create a valid limited partnership. Each investor is called a "partner." The ones with limited liability are called "limited partners." The partners fully liable are called "general partners." A disadvantage is that a limited partnership is a legal entity of its own, and requires a tax ID number and a tax accounting each year. Another disadvantage is that limited partners cannot claim some of the tax deductions general partners can claim, and may not be able to get the lowest loan rates. These may be reasons enough not to form a limited partnership. But a limited partnership is an excellent idea if one investor (who cannot have a management role) wants to be protected. The limited partner is liable only for the money he or she has invested; he or she is not liable for anything beyond that.

 RESOURCE
To learn more about limited partnerships, see *Form a Partnership: The Complete Legal Guide,* by Denis Clifford and Ralph Warner (Nolo).

When You Move Into a Home Owned by Your Lover

Nate fell in love with Alan and wanted to move in with him. Alan agreed, asking Nate to share the monthly house payments, property taxes, homeowner's insurance, and utilities. Nate agreed, "But only if I somehow get to own part of the house." Alan, in the rush of first love, murmured he'd be willing to give Nate half of everything. But he later had some second thoughts and realized he wanted to take things a little slower.

Should You Just Add Your Lover's Name to the Deed?

Like Alan, some lesbians and gay men who own their own houses are tempted to put the deed into joint tenancy with their lovers when their lovers move in. This assures that the lover will get the house if the original owner dies.

But it's not always wise. By putting the house in joint tenancy, you are making a gift of one-half of it to your lover. Not only might you owe gift taxes or reduce your exemption from inheritance taxes, but if you later split up, you will have no right to have the house deeded back to you. It makes more sense for you to keep the house in your name and make a will or living trust leaving the house to your lover. Then, if you split up, you will retain ownership and can change the will or trust.

The other option is for the lover to buy into the house by paying a share of the mortgage payments. The agreement below is an example of that.

Alan's house is worth $220,000; his existing mortgage is $120,000, so his equity is $100,000. After careful thought, Alan tells Nate that if he pays one-half of all the monthly payments and contributes to the ongoing repair costs, it would be fair to turn over some of the equity in the house to him. But Alan still wonders how Nate will ever manage to accumulate a significant share, and doesn't know how to work out the details of their arrangement.

Nate and Alan have a few different options. The simplest is for Nate to forget buying part of the house and instead pay Alan monthly rent. With this alternative, Nate's rent should be considerably less than one-half the mortgage, taxes, and insurance, because Nate would be getting no equity. A fair rent could be determined by checking the rents for sharing a similar home in the neighborhood. Alan might also agree that if the relationship falters, he'll pay Nate's relocation costs.

Another easy solution would be for Nate to take out a loan or dip into savings to pay Alan $50,000. This is one-half of Alan's equity in the house and Alan could then deed the house to himself and Nate as either joint tenants or tenants-in-common.

A more intricate solution is that the two men could sign a contract where Nate agrees to pay one-half (or all, or any other fraction) of the monthly mortgage, taxes, and insurance in exchange for a share of the equity in the house equal to the percentage that his total principal payments plus capital investment bear to the total amount of money invested in the house by both men, with Alan starting out with credit for the $100,000 in equity to date. Sound complicated? Here's what it would look like: After one year in which each partner put in principal payments and improvements totaling $7,000, Alan would own ($107,000/$114,000) x 100 or 94% and Nate would own ($7,000/$114,000) x 100 or 6%.

A final possibility is that Alan could sell Nate one-half of the house— or some other specified percentage—either at the fair market value or at some discounted amount, and take a promissory note for the payment with a favorable interest rate (the note would be paid over time or when the house is sold). Remember that there is no law against being generous to your partner when setting the buy-in price and interest rate, although the IRS can treat your generosity as a taxable gift if you set the price and interest rate extremely low. You must be certain to learn the applicable rules regarding transfer taxes, possible property tax increases, and capital gains consequences. This method is generous to Nate because he'd be getting the advantage of ownership (tax advantages and market-caused value increases) with no money down. But the simplicity appealed to both, and that's what they did. Here's the agreement they prepared.

Sample Contract for Sale of a Share of House

We, Alan Zoloff and Nate Nichols, agree as follows:

1. Alan now owns the house at 1919 Church Street, Seattle, Washington, subject to a mortgage for $120,000.
2. The present value of the home is $220,000.
3. Alan hereby sells one-half of the home to Nate for $110,000 and retains a one-half interest in the house, also valued at $110,000, and agrees to sign the deed within ten days of the signing of this agreement.
4. The $110,000 will be paid by Nate as follows:
   - $60,000: Nate agrees to assume responsibility for one-half of the $120,000 mortgage and to pay one-half of the monthly mortgage payments.
   - $50,000: Nate will sign a note to Alan for $50,000 plus 5% (simple) interest per year to be paid in full when the house is sold. If Nate so chooses, he can pay any amount in principal or interest at any time, thereby reducing the amount of his debt.
5. All other costs for the home, including taxes, insurance, utilities, repairs, and maintenance will be divided evenly.
6. When the house is sold, after all other costs are paid, the remaining proceeds will be divided evenly between Nate and Alan. Nate will pay Alan all sums due to Alan out of Nate's share. If Nate's share is less than what he owes Alan, Nate will sign a promissory note providing for full payment of the balance due within a period of time agreed to by the parties but in no event longer than five years.

[Other clauses, such as separation provisions, mediation clauses, and the like should be included.]

_____   _____
Date   Alan Zoloff

_____   _____
Date   Nate Nichols

Moving On

Relationships can end, and planning for this possibility in advance is always wise. If you don't plan, and one person wants to move or sell, the entire household could be forced to move out. Problems can also develop for the person wanting to move. If the agreement requires the leaver to continue to pay some expenses after moving out because there's no buyer, the leaver may become a prisoner in the house and quite bitter. More details about separating are included in Chapter 10, and below is a clause to cover the contingency of one person wanting to move on. Include it in the original contract, as an amendment to the original contract, or as its own "moving on" contract.

Sample Moving-On Clause

If one owner moves out of the house, that owner remains responsible for the existing share of the mortgage, taxes, and insurance. He may rent his quarters with the approval of the rest of the household (which won't be unreasonably withheld). The remaining owners have the first right to rent the quarters themselves or assume the cost if they so choose at a fair market value. The remainder of the house owners must rent the quarters themselves or assume the cost if they reject at least three people the owner moving out proposes as renters.

At the end of two years following the owner's moving out, that owner will have the right to sell his share to the remaining owners or to a new person completely, subject to the approval (which won't be unreasonably withheld) of the remaining owners.

Going Separate Ways:
Issues at the End of a Relationship

Breaking Up: An Overview 336

The Separation Process: What to Do 338

    Advance Planning 338

    Practical Aspects of Separating 339

Getting to Yes: How to Work Toward Resolution 343

    Methods of Resolving Disputes 344

    Preparing a Settlement Agreement 350

    Litigation 352

Ideas for Solving Some Common Problems 353

    What to Do With a Rented Home 354

    What to Do With a Home You Own 354

    Dividing Other Assets and Debts 359

    Working Out Child Custody and Support 360

Breaking Up When There's No Legal Relationship 371

Dissolving a Same-Sex Marriage 373

    Getting a Divorce 375

    Dividing Your Property and Debts 376

    Alimony 379

    The New Tax Headaches for Same-Sex Couples 379

    Cooperating in Your Divorce 380

    Child Custody 381

    Child Support 386

Dissolving a Straight Marriage 387

    Issues of Money and Property 388

    Sexual Orientation and Custody 388

Domestic Violence in Same-Sex Relationships 392

What if the romance begins to fade or the relationship begins to disintegrate? It happens all too often, to gay and straight couples alike. This chapter addresses the end of relationships—both straight marriages where one partner comes out as lesbian or gay, and same-sex relationships—whether or not they involve marriage or a marriage-like relationship.

The anger and sense of loss that so often accompany a separation cannot be overcome by any legal counsel. Emotional crises are best addressed through the help of friends, family, and maybe a good therapist. And even though the breakup may, in time, emerge as the best thing that ever happened to you, along the way you will surely have to wade through a morass of emotional and practical obstacles.

On the legal front, a dissolution (the common legal term for the end of a marriage, which we use for married and unmarried relationships) does not have to be a complete disaster. If you and your ex can work together rationally to divide up your property and sort through your financial affairs, it's possible to avoid the costs and heartache of an ugly breakup.

This chapter deals with three different breakup scenarios: those where same-sex partners aren't in any kind of formal legal relationship such as marriage, domestic partnership, or civil union; those where same-sex partners are legally married or registered in one of the states that allows for such legal relationships; and those in which a lesbian or gay individual is coming out and leaving a heterosexual marriage.

Many issues are the same for all three scenarios, so the bulk of the chapter discusses matters that are common to all three. Later, there are sections that deal with the specific issues, concerns, and legal rules involved in each different scenario.

Breaking Up: An Overview

American legal rules on divorce are an odd amalgam of anthropology, social history, economics, and law, and are continually evolving. In one sense, marriage is a "contract" between two consenting adults—except that unlike most other contracts, neither party ever reads or approves of the contract provisions. These provisions are established by the state, and

Divorce Then and Now

The first edition of this book had a chapter titled "Marriage, Children, and Divorce." It began like this: "Many lesbians and gay men have been involved in a heterosexual marriage and become parents." The assumption was that the only way an LGBT person would need a divorce was if they had been in a straight marriage—and that it was also the most likely way that they would have come to be parents.

These days, innumerable lesbians and gay men have children without ever having been involved in a heterosexual marriage. And these days, in 16 states and in Canada, same-sex partners can marry or enter a marriage-equivalent relationship. Although these are the only places where a same-sex couple can legally partner, they are not the only places that a same-sex couple can divorce. For example, even though California and New Jersey explicitly prohibit same-sex marriage, they're just fine with same-sex divorce. In fact, most couples who enter into domestic partnerships or civil unions in these states are legally required to end their relationships using the same legal system that denies them the right to marry.

On the other hand, much of the content of this chapter is unchanged from 1980. We still encourage you to avoid a custody fight whenever possible—whether with your spouse from a straight marriage, or with the same-sex partner with whom you share parenting responsibilities. And we still believe that a good divorce can be as precious as a good marriage.

once the couple says "I do" all the laws of marriage apply automatically. So do the laws of divorce.

The most important differences between being married and unmarried when you're breaking up are that unmarried couples are not required to take court action to end their relationships, and marital property rules generally don't apply. If you go to court because you can't work out a custody arrangement for your children, you'll find that issues involving children will be heard in family court exactly as they are with married folks. But in most instances, property and financial disputes will be judged by contract and business principles, with few accommodations made to account for the fact that your financial connections arose out of a committed personal relationship.

In general, the laws governing married couples do not apply to same-sex couples outside of the marriage-equality and marriage-equivalent states.

The Separation Process: What to Do

Married or not, breaking up is hard to do. Here are some suggestions that may help to make a painful process as good as it can get. This section describes a typical separation process, in basically chronological order.

Advance Planning

If you are the one initiating the dissolution or you sense that the sky is growing cloudy, you might consider taking some precautionary steps. Which of these steps you decide to take will depend on how amicable you think the breakup might be. If you think things will be difficult, you will need to take more precautions than if you think the trust between you will support a calmer process.

Here are some tasks you can consider attending to, depending on your assessment of the risks:

- Locate the critical documents of your joint financial lives; make copies and store them in a safe place. These documents include bank records, property deeds, business records, insurance policies, and credit card account information. It's important that you have a complete picture of your financial situation, no matter how confident you feel about your ability to reach a cooperative resolution.
- Think about securing particularly valuable items of personal property. If you own precious art or irreplaceable family heirlooms that are yours alone, store them with a friend or be prepared to remove them quickly.
- Start considering who is going to live where. Some couples continue living in the same house even after officially breaking up; for many,

though, living apart will be important. If you have a friend or close relative you can stay with for a while, make some preliminary arrangements.

- Learn about the laws that might be relevant to your situation, particularly if you have children or if your legal partnership must be dissolved through filing termination documents or through formal court proceedings. (Chapter 11 has information on researching the law, and Chapter 5 has information on legal rules relating to parenting.) If you're having trouble understanding your state's rules or how they apply to your situation, talk with a qualified attorney who can explain the dissolution process.

- For those who are married or in marriage-like legal relationships and live in a state that recognizes their relationship, get some more legal information and advice before doing anything that affects your jointly owned property. For others, avoid putting large sums of money into joint accounts. Consider closing joint credit card accounts. But unless your partner is irresponsible with credit, it's probably best to discuss this before doing it—taking unilateral action on a jointly owned account can escalate conflict. Whatever you do, don't empty joint accounts into your own pocket.

- If you are concerned about domestic violence or other abuse, set up a support system for yourself. You may want to talk with a therapist, trusted friend, or family member, or seek assistance at a gay community center or domestic violence agency. (There's more about this in "Domestic Violence in Same-Sex Relationships," below.)

Your goal is to minimize conflict and confusion, understanding that you can't avoid them altogether. If your relationship is characterized by high-pitched emotions and strong, impulsive actions, you may need to act very quickly if the conflicts suddenly explode.

Practical Aspects of Separating

Once the split is agreed on or inevitable, or even if you choose a "trial" separation, each of you will face a few immediate tasks. While every breakup presents its own particular challenges, here are a few simple guidelines that should help keep things under control.

If you have children, work on making cooperative and realistic decisions about their custody. Your children's needs should come first. If you've been denied access to your kids or you urgently need child support payments that your ex is refusing to make, consult an attorney right away. But try as hard as you can to work it out between the two of you, possibly with the help of a custody mediator or therapist. Keep in mind that from your kids' point of view, harmony and predictability are more important than you getting your way on every issue.

Close joint accounts and credit cards, and if you leave any accounts open in order to pay joint obligations, make sure that joint authority is needed to withdraw any joint funds. This may limit your access to some of your own money, but that is far better than having your ex simply take everything.

Figure out which bills are essential to pay, such as home insurance or the mortgage payment, and make arrangements to keep these bills current. If necessary, ask a trusted friend or an accountant to make these payments for you, so you don't lose your house or find yourself uninsured in the midst of a relationship crisis. Next, make arrangements for paying the less urgent bills.

Make some practical decisions about furniture and personal possessions, but don't feel compelled to sort everything out the moment you break up. Valuable items should be handled with some thought, and it may be necessary to put them into storage for a few months. Spending a few hundred dollars to store disputed valuables safely is wiser than letting them be destroyed or stolen, or giving up on them and handing them over because it's easier than trying to work it out right away.

Assess what the longer-range issues may be, and agree to disagree if necessary. If you can both acknowledge that certain conflicts remain unresolved, and can agree on a method of resolving them, you will both feel far more at ease—and less compelled to sort everything out the day you leave.

Figure out who is going to live where and try to put together a simple written agreement on how you are going to handle the costs and legal implications of your short-term housing decisions. If you own a home together, you will need to decide whether the person who moves out should pay any portion of the mortgage or insurance costs, and you'll want to make it clear that a temporary departure is not a permanent abandonment of the residence, which might give the partner who stays an advantage if you litigate ownership shares later. If you are renters, you may need to decide who is going to stay on the lease and who is entitled to the return of the security deposit. There's a sample agreement below that you can use when you first separate, to memorialize your agreements about housing.

Sample Postseparation Agreement Regarding Housing

Adrian Wallace and Chris Urban hereby agree as follows:

1. We will live apart, effective March 1, 20xx.
2. Chris will remain in our apartment, and Adrian will move out no later than March 1, 20xx. If Adrian leaves any of his personal belongings behind, he will remove them no later than April 1, 20xx at his expense, with three days' prior notice to Chris. Any of Adrian's personal belongings that he does not remove by April 1 may be kept or disposed of by Chris, unless we agree otherwise in writing.
3. Any household-related expenses incurred before March 1, 20xx will be split between Adrian and Chris, following the allocation generally followed by us before that date. Any household expenses incurred after March 1, 20xx, will be Chris's sole responsibility.
4. [If you are renters] Chris will be solely responsible for all rent due after March 1, 20xx. Chris will retain the right to claim the existing security deposit of $1,000, in exchange for his agreeing to pay the utility bills, telephone bills, and insurance after March 1, 20xx.

---

5. [If you are homeowners] Effective March 1, 20xx, Chris will pay all monthly bills for the residence, including the mortgage, insurance, all utilities, and related expenses. The property taxes and all necessary repairs will be split equally between Adrian and Chris. However, as long as Adrian continues to pay his share of these expenses, Adrian shall be entitled to half of any increase in the property's value between March 1, 20xx, and the time the house is sold. Adrian and Chris agree to make a good-faith effort to promptly resolve the issue of long-term ownership of the residence. Unless an agreement is reached by December 31, 20xx, or we agree in writing to extend this agreement, the property will be listed for sale in January 20xx and the proceeds of sale will be split equally. Adrian's agreement to leave the residence now is not a waiver of his claim to an equal share of the equity, either through a buyout or a sale.

6. Any dispute arising under this agreement will be mediated by a third person mutually acceptable to both parties. The mediator's role will be to help us arrive at an agreement, not to impose one on us. If good-faith efforts to arrive at our own solution to all issues in dispute with the help of a mediator aren't successful, either of us may make a written request to the other that the dispute be arbitrated. If such a request is made, the dispute will be submitted to arbitration under the rules of the American Arbitration Association, and one arbitrator will hear our dispute. The decision of the arbitrator will be binding on us and will be enforceable in any court that has jurisdiction over the dispute. We each agree to give up the right to a jury trial.

Date   Adrian Wallace

Date   Chris Urban

Getting to Yes: How to Work Toward Resolution

At this point, you probably don't even know what all the issues are that need to be resolved—getting through all the questions and disputes that arise during a breakup can seem daunting. Figuring out how to make decisions together with the person you're separating from may also seem nearly impossible. But there are a lot of ways to do that without escalating conflict.

Breaking the decision-making process down into a series of tasks may help you feel less overwhelmed. Here are some of the things you'll need to do in order to get things underway.

Make a list of what needs to be resolved. Anything that is on either partner's list is by definition a problem needing to be resolved. Don't argue over what is appropriate to argue over.

Make a realistic timetable. Don't feel compelled to resolve everything in a day, but don't let the process drag on for years. Commit to a schedule of meetings or phone calls, and then make a conscious effort to keep the ball rolling. If you will have to go through a legal divorce process, learn what is required and how long it will take.

Pick a process. You may have several options depending on which laws apply to your relationship. (These are covered in "Methods of Resolving Disputes," below.)

Gather the facts you need. For example, you may need to get your house or car appraised, or learn the basics about your financial situation. If you have major investments or you are in a marriage or marriage-like relationship, a visit to a tax consultant may be necessary.

Take stock of the emotional barriers that may prevent resolution, and work on trying to overcome them. You may need to get counseling or enlist a mutual friend who can work with one or both of you to calm your anger.

Start the process. Begin working together toward resolution.

Put your agreements in writing. A simple exchange of letters or a basic settlement agreement will be sufficient, as long as it's clear. If a few issues remain unresolved, you can write up what you've agreed to thus far, but make it clear that you're not completely done yet.

Implement your agreement. For items such as furniture and art objects, it may simply be a matter of hiring a mover. For financial accounts, a joint letter to the bank or the stockbroker will usually be enough. For real estate, a more formal set of tasks await you. You may need to work with a broker or an attorney to be sure you fill out the transfer forms correctly. In some places, real estate transfers involve paying taxes or other fees, so be sure you allocate who is going to pay any such costs. And in those states where your breakup must follow the marital rules, you will need to obtain a court judgment of dissolution.

Methods of Resolving Disputes

There are several ways that you can work together (or, in the case of litigation, against each other) to make decisions about the dissolution of your relationship.

Direct Discussions

Obviously, one way to resolve your conflicts is to talk them out with each other. Whether you do this face-to-face, by phone, or in writing or by email, it is likely to be the cheapest and the quickest approach, if you can manage it—but not everyone can, when feelings are running high. If you want to give it a try, here are a few simple tips to help it go more smoothly.

- Schedule your discussions ahead of time, and pick a location and method that ensures privacy and supports concentration and a calm interchange. Don't talk about heavy topics in the middle of the workday, if at all possible.
- Do your homework, and don't be afraid to postpone a discussion a few days if you aren't ready.
- Keep good notes of your discussions, and make a record of any agreements you reach and of what additional information you need to gather.
- Focus on finding solutions, not allocating blame. Don't view your disputes as opportunities for resolving the emotional rifts of your dissolution or assigning blame for the breakup.

- Be careful about email habits—sometimes a well-considered handwritten letter invokes a more thoughtful response than a rapid-fire email sent to your ex while she is at work. On the other hand, email can enable you to track the exchanges carefully and can enable you to compose your thoughts in an organized manner.

If you can't resolve things by communicating directly, or if you resolve most issues but have a few lingering conflicts, you probably will need to ask a third party—or more than one—to facilitate your conversation. This can be done in several different ways.

Mediation

In mediation, you and your partner meet face-to-face to talk about the things you haven't yet resolved, together with a neutral mediator who works with you to help you find realistic solutions. You can come to mediation solo or you can each bring an advocate along—either a friend or an attorney, depending on how complex your disagreements are. Mediation can produce great results, and it is more efficient than a long exchange of letters or back-and-forth between negotiators. The keys to success are having a good mediator and allowing enough time to air the conflicts and find solutions. Most people find that a series of short sessions works best, although sessions as long as four to six hours can be useful if you have the time and can handle the emotional strain.

The biggest advantage of mediation is that you keep control of the decision-making process. Unlike arbitration or litigation, where an arbitrator or judge will make the decision for you, no resolution will be reached in mediation until both of you agree. Some mediators will suggest solutions, and others prefer to let you generate all the ideas, but in either case, the decisions are in your hands. The other advantage is that mediation might actually improve communication between you and your ex, because the process is designed to promote greater understanding.

Many mediators are attorneys or therapists, and many cities also have volunteer community mediation services, which can be a great option. The charges are usually nominal, and most community mediation services use panels, so you get the benefits of two or three mediators working together. However, community mediators usually won't be able to give you information about the legal issues that can come up when you are resolving financial or property conflicts (one of the advantages of a lawyer-mediator). Still, you could try reaching a decision in principle and then meet with a lawyer to reality-test the agreement and make sure it is legally feasible.

While it isn't necessary to have a lawyer with you in a mediation session or to use a lawyer as your negotiator, it is often useful to meet with a lawyer for an hour or so before you start the mediation or negotiation. The lawyer can explain the basic law that affects you and advise you about the best course of action based on your needs and wishes. Choose an attorney who has worked with unmarried couples— gay or straight—so you don't have to pay to educate the lawyer, and come prepared with a detailed outline of the facts and issues.

RESOURCE

Finding a mediator. If you have any friends who've been through a breakup and used a mediator, find out if they were happy with that person. You can also call an LGBT organization for referrals to mediators. Some areas even have lesbian/gay mediation services. And the same resources that are useful for finding a lawyer, like Nolo's lawyer directory at www.nolo.com, will help you find a mediator. See Chapter 11 for more about finding a lawyer.

Collaborative Practice

There's a relatively new way of settling family cases, called "collaborative practice" or "collaborative divorce." In a collaborative arrangement, you and your partner each hire an attorney who is trained in collaborative practice. All four of you sign an agreement saying that you will negotiate a settlement and will not go to court. If anyone decides to take the case to court despite the agreement, then the original collaborative attorneys must withdraw from the case and the parties must find new lawyers. During the collaborative process, you and your lawyer will meet with your partner and your partner's lawyer in four-way meetings to hammer out a solution. You may also jointly hire experts, like appraisers or accountants or, if you have kids, custody experts, to help you sort things out, in a multidisciplinary approach that's designed to have a positive impact on the family.

Collaboration can be expensive, but it is a great way to go for people who want the assistance of experts, and may want the protection and distance that having an attorney can provide, but still are committed to a negotiated solution rather than a court battle.

> **RESOURCE**
> **To learn more about collaborative law and mediation,** see *Divorce Without Court: A Guide to Mediation and Collaborative Divorce,* by Katherine E. Stoner (Nolo).

Arbitration

Arbitration is sometimes called a private trial. The procedure is like a court trial, but less formal, and it doesn't take place in a courtroom. There is no jury. Instead, you and your partner each present your case to a neutral decision maker that you select—typically either a retired judge or an experienced attorney—who acts much like a judge. In most cases, you agree to be bound by the decision and give up the right to go to court if you don't like it.

In some cases, especially where the issue in dispute is the value of property or the share to which each person is entitled, arbitration can be a good option—but it can be expensive, so it's not necessarily the right choice where the amount in dispute is small. If you are in one of those jurisdictions where a formal dissolution is required for married or registered couples, you may not be able to use private arbitration to resolve all of your disputes—some jurisdictions don't allow it. Consult an attorney to learn what rules apply.

Here are the steps you will need to take to set up and go through an arbitration.

1. Decide whether you will have the right to bring attorneys or advocates with you to the arbitration hearing. If you do want to

have that right, decide whether the arbitrator has the authority to order the loser to pay the winner's attorneys' fees and arbitration costs (which could get expensive).

2. Decide how many witnesses, if any, will be allowed for each side.

3. Decide whether you will be able to ask the other person for documents, or do any investigation on your own, before the arbitration. If only one of you has access to the real estate or the financial documents, you may need to agree to exchange documents as part of your agreement to arbitrate.

4. Agree on a rough timetable for the arbitration. Even though the precise date of the hearing can't be set until you select your arbitrator, try to get a sense of how long you will need to prepare. And ask the arbitrator to agree to give you a decision within a certain time period after the arbitration.

5. If at all possible, make a list of the issues that need to be resolved. Acknowledge that some new issues may arise later on, but try to be as thorough and specific as you can.

6. Choose an arbitrator. You can delegate the choice to a friend or an attorney, use a local arbitration service that provides a list of arbitrators, or jointly pick someone whom you know or who has been referred to you. The arbitrator doesn't have to be gay, but should be comfortable with your family structure. If you don't know much about a proposed arbitrator, try to get some references.

7. Sign a written agreement stating that you will be bound by the arbitrator's decision, agreeing to waive any rights of appeal, and setting out the other agreements you made from the list above. In most states, arbitration agreements are enforceable in court if your ex doesn't comply with the arbitrator's order. Include in the agreement how you will pay for the arbitration—usually the arbitrator's fee is split equally.

Below is a sample agreement to mediate and arbitrate.

Sample Agreement Regarding Mediation and Arbitration

Sandy Stone and Erika Chavez hereby agree as follows:

1. We will submit the following disputes to mediation, and if mediation is unsuccessful, to arbitration:

   a. Ownership of our residence in Akron, Ohio, including the disposition of the residence and both our claims for reimbursement for contributions made to the purchase and upkeep of the residence.

   b. Ownership of our two automobiles, including disposition of the automobiles and both our claims for reimbursement for contributions made to the purchase and upkeep of the automobiles.

   c. Erika's claim for reimbursement of amounts paid to Oberlin College in connection with Sandy's education there.

   d. Erika's claim for a partial ownership in Sandy's accounting business.

2. We agree to submit these disputes to mediation with a mediator jointly selected by the two of us. However, if we haven't been able to select a mediator by April 1, 20xx, each of us will nominate one friend, and the two of them will choose the mediator.

3. We will meet no fewer than three times for two-hour mediation sessions, within one month of the appointment of the mediator, with all costs of mediation split equally between us. The mediator will determine the time and place of the mediation.

4. Until an agreement is reached, proposals made by us are nonbinding and confidential. Any evidence or materials prepared specifically for the mediation are confidential, and can't be brought up in a subsequent arbitration unless we agree to the use of the material. If we reach an agreement, we will write it down and both of us will sign it.

5. If we don't reach a settlement in mediation and we choose not to schedule any more mediation sessions, either of us may demand arbitration. We will jointly select an arbitrator, and if we cannot agree on an arbitrator within one month of a written demand for arbitration, Judge Strauss will select the arbitrator.

6. The costs of the arbitration will be split equally between the two of us. Either of us may bring an attorney to the hearing; however, each of us will be solely responsible for any attorneys' fees she incurs. Each of us will provide the other with copies of all documents relevant to this dispute

and a list of witnesses, no later than one week prior to the arbitration hearing.

7. The decision of the arbitrator will be binding on both of us, and either of us may enforce the decision through the local superior court if necessary. If an attorney is needed to enforce the decision, the prevailing party will have the right to seek reimbursement of the attorneys' fees incurred specifically for the enforcement of the arbitrator's decision.

Date   Sandy Stone

Date   Erika Chavez

Preparing a Settlement Agreement

However you arrive at a solution, you will need to prepare a written agreement setting down what you decided. This agreement will be legally binding. If you use a mediator to come to an agreement, the mediator most likely will prepare your settlement agreement. But if you decide on a settlement yourselves, or if you want to save the fees and prepare the settlement agreement yourselves, here's a sample agreement for a couple who owned a house together. Note that instead of the mediation-arbitration clause that is in many of the agreements in this book, these parties agreed to go directly to arbitration if there is a dispute over enforcement of the agreement.

CAUTION

If you are married or state registered, your state may have specific requirements for a settlement agreement that's part of your divorce. Go ahead and use this form as a sample or a starting point, but have your agreement reviewed by a lawyer before you sign it, to make sure it's valid in your state.

Sample Settlement Agreement

Arnie Cott and Stefan Catahoula agree as follows:

1. Arnie will purchase Stefan's interest in their house in Orlando, Florida, for a payment of $40,000, which will be paid by cashier's check no later than May 15, 20xx. Arnie will be responsible for all payments on the existing mortgage of approximately $150,000 after the buyout payment is made. Within three days of the payment, Stefan will sign a quitclaim deed for the property, which he will deliver to Arnie. Arnie will pay all costs of the deed transfer and recording. Arnie will be solely responsible for any future payments under the existing mortgage, but he will have no duty to refinance or formally assume the existing mortgage. All costs relating to the house incurred after April 1, 20xx, will be Arnie's sole responsibility.

2. Stefan will keep the Audi automobile currently registered in his name, and Arnie will keep the Jeep Cherokee that is currently in both parties' names. Stefan will sign the required transfer document for the Jeep, which Arnie will prepare. Any transfer costs will be split equally.

3. All items of shared or co-owned personal property have been distributed by the parties, and any items left remaining in the residence as of the date of this agreement belong to Arnie.

4. If at any time before December 31, 20xx, Stefan is able to sell the parties' antique music box collection that is currently in his possession, he will give one-half of the proceeds of sale to Arnie. However, if Stefan is unable to sell the collection by that date despite his best efforts to do so, he will pay $2,500 to Arnie and will be entitled to keep the collection, without any further liability to Arnie.

5. Any disputes arising out of this agreement will be resolved by binding arbitration, on the written demand of either party. The parties will jointly select an arbitrator, and if they cannot agree on an arbitrator within one month of a written demand for arbitration, Judge William Bennett of the superior court will select the arbitrator.

6. The costs of the arbitration will be split equally between the parties. Either party may bring an attorney to the hearing, but each party will be solely responsible for any attorneys' fees he incurs. Each party will give the other copies of all documents relevant to this dispute and a list of any and all witnesses, no later than one week prior to the arbitration hearing.

7. The decision of the arbitrator will be binding on both parties, and either party may enforce the decision through the local superior court if necessary. If an attorney is reasonably needed to enforce the decision, the prevailing party will have the right to seek reimbursement of the attorneys' fees incurred specifically for the enforcement of the arbitrator's decision.

_____   _____

Date   Arnie Cott

_____   _____

Date   Stefan Catahoula

Litigation

If all else fails and you aren't able to come to a settlement, taking your case to court is your last resort. If you aren't able to settle on your own, your first decision will be whether you can handle the case yourself or will need an attorney. Some attorneys will help pro per (self-represented) clients on an hourly basis, and others will help you only if they take on the entire case. If you need an attorney, make sure you go with someone whom you can afford and who has experience in this area of law. The sexual orientation of your attorney is far less important than experience and competence. Chapter 11 has more about finding a lawyer.

Bear in mind that by taking your dispute to court you are not only outing yourself and your ex, but you may also expose a lot of private information. You're also going to be spending a lot of your own time and energy on the litigation process. In other words, a lawsuit is going to be expensive, time-consuming, stressful, depressing, and often ugly, so use the courts only when nothing else will work.

Even if you handle your case by yourself, we recommend that you consult for at least an hour with an attorney who has handled same-sex dissolutions. Learn whether you need to file any papers immediately, which may be important, especially if your name isn't on title to property that you claim is part yours. Learn whether there are any legal deadlines that apply to your case, and learn how litigation works for your particular problems, such as dividing up real estate, allocating joint bank accounts, or deciding claims for postseparation support. Try to evaluate how litigation will actually proceed for your particular case: How much pretrial sharing of information will be required; how will the trial be handled; will there be a jury? The more you know ahead of time the better your decision making will be.

Finally, evaluate the strengths and weaknesses of your position and your partner's. And try to get a handle on whether you can afford the time and the likely costs of litigation.

> ⓘ CAUTION
>
> **Try, try again.** Make it clear to your lawyer—and acknowledge to yourself if you are acting on your own—that while you are initiating litigation out of desperation, you remain open to compromise. It is never too late to schedule a mediation session, and you should always remain open to settlement. In fact, more than 90% of lawsuits never get to trial. A breakup should never become a battle of principles; rather, always look for the opportunity to make a deal and move on. If you are using an attorney who doesn't share this philosophy, we recommend that you find one who has a more conciliatory approach. And after you've talked to a lawyer about your situation, consider approaching your ex about trying again to resolve your disputes another way. The mere mention of litigation will bring some people to the bargaining table—though it may make others more explosive. Also, keep in mind that the initial anger over a breakup often dissipates over time, and so a compromise that was rejected at the early stages might be better received a few months later.

Ideas for Solving Some Common Problems

The issues that most often arise in same-sex dissolutions (whether you were cohabitants, married spouses, or domestic partners) are the same as the issues in most straight divorces—the division of assets and debts, and, for some couples, the care and support of children. In many instances, the issue of housing tops the list.

What to Do With a Rented Home

Unless you are both leaving your rented home, you must decide who is staying and who is moving on, how to deal with your landlord, who gets the security deposit, and who will pay bills and debts in the process. There is no rule about which tenant gets to keep a rental apartment. If you agreed in advance, or only one of you is on the lease, the decision is easier. Otherwise, you'll need to decide what seems fair to both of you. If one of you lived in the place first or has a practical need for this particular apartment, that person should get the right to stay. But the person who moves out should probably receive some compensation to cover moving costs and perhaps some portion of increased rent in a new location. Also, if the person who's moving out paid some or all of the security deposit, that person should be reimbursed. If you're the one who stays, have the lease rewritten in your name alone.

What to Do With a Home You Own

Life is significantly more complex if you own your home and don't have a written agreement (like those shown in Chapter 9) that defines your respective rights and responsibilities. Your options if you own your home jointly are to have one person buy out the other's interest, to sell the house and split the proceeds, or to continue owning it jointly with only one person living there (or, sometimes, with the partners continuing to live together for a time). If you both want to stay and you don't have an agreement giving one of you the first right to buy out the other, you'll have to address that issue first.

Buyout

If both of you want to keep the house, you can flip a coin to see who gets first dibs, mediate the dispute, conduct an informal "auction" in which the high bidder gets the house, or submit the dispute to binding arbitration or to a judge. If your incomes are very different, obviously the person with more money will have an unfair advantage in an auction. Sometimes, even though it may seem silly, a coin flip can be the fairest way to decide.

If you agree on who will buy out whom but can't agree on a price, your first step is to get an appraisal. If you can't agree on an appraiser, you can each get an appraisal and then average them. Opinions by real estate brokers are cheaper than appraisals, but oftentimes less accurate. Loan appraisals often aren't very reliable, because they are done quickly and usually solely for the purpose of helping the lender decide whether to make the loan. A private appraiser is best when you are planning a buyout.

Keep in mind that an appraised price, like most estimates of fair market value, will probably assume there will be a broker's fee for selling the property. If you won't use a broker in the buyout, as most people don't, it may be fair to reduce the appraised value by the amount of the standard commission. Some people think it is still fair to keep the broker's fee in the buyout amount, because the buyer will incur a broker's fee if the property is sold at a later time. This is a point of negotiation between you.

To arrive at the buyout price, subtract the mortgage balance and any other joint debts on the house, such as an equity loan, from the amount you've agreed on as the fair market value. This will give you the equity in the house. Usually, a buyout means that the partner keeping the house (the buyer) pays the other partner (the seller) the seller's percentage of the equity—but there may be other negotiations involved in setting a final buyout price. For example, the person who is keeping the house may want to reduce the buyout amount to account for deferred maintenance that may be needed to make the place marketable later (but if your estimate of fair market value has already taken these repairs into account, you shouldn't deduct them again). Also, one party may have a claim for excess contributions—for example, a greater contribution to the down payment or a greater share of money paid for repairs or improvements.

Negotiations over the buyout amount can be difficult. Each party is taking a risk: the buyer will lose out if the property value goes down, but if it goes up soon after the buyout, the seller will have given up a share of that appreciation. And issues like the ones discussed above (commissions, repairs, etc.) can be serious points of contention. Mediation is a good option for trying to work out issues like these, but if you are still unable to agree, binding arbitration may be your best bet. If you have a house that is worth less than the mortgage, or if your house is already in foreclosure, you should consult an attorney to work out a strategy. Be sure to find out whether you will be personally liable for the mortgage loan, as that can have a long-term financial impact.

> CAUTION
>
> **Make sure you're aware of all local procedures.** Find out from a local broker or title company the procedures and costs for doing a buyout between owners. Some states and counties impose transfer taxes or recording fees, and if that's the case, you'll need to figure out how to allocate these expenses between you. In California, your property taxes can soar as a result of a buyout. But if you are married or in a marriage-like relationship, many of those expenses won't apply, so make sure you check with your local county recorder as well as a lawyer or an accountant familiar with real estate transfers between same-sex couples.

As part of any buyout agreement, you will have to resolve any disagreements you might have about whether one partner is entitled to reimbursement or to a greater share of the equity, based on having contributed more to the down payment or the mortgage loan.

Once you have arrived at a price, you will need to look at your options regarding the mortgage. In some states and with some banks, the buyer can retain the existing loan even after a buyout, while the seller's name is removed and the seller is relieved of any liability for the debt. In other situations, the buyer must get a new loan unless the selling partner agrees to stay on the loan—with the buyer giving written assurance that the mortgage will get paid each month so that the seller doesn't get a tarnished credit rating. (However, this also means that the selling partner's credit record will show the debt load of the mortgage, possibly impeding that person's ability to obtain credit for a new car or home.)

Sometimes only one person's name was on the deed, but the other partner has contributed labor or money beyond what might be considered "rent" for shared occupancy. If this describes you, you may need to check with a local attorney to learn what the legal rules are in your state for this sort of claim, and you certainly should consider mediating with your partner to come to an agreement about reimbursement.

Sale on the Open Market

If you agree to sell your house, choose a qualified broker to help you, and let the broker know that you are splitting up. The broker can then handle the delicate arrangements of fixing up and showing the home, knowing that things may be tense at times. Selling a house is stressful under the best of circumstances, and when it is the house that you lived in together while your relationship was intact, the process can be really painful. But you both want to get the best price for the house, so try to work cooperatively with each other and with the broker. We discourage the use of two agents, as having a single agent can help resolve marketing disputes between the feuding co-owners.

Once you've sold the house, you will have to divide the proceeds according to your ownership percentages, contributions, rights to reimbursement, and the like. Many of the same issues discussed above in the buyout section can also come up in a negotiation about dividing the proceeds of sale. If one of you put in more money up front or during the course of your relationship, or one of you has spent a lot of time renovating your home, you may feel you are entitled to a greater share of the proceeds or some amount of reimbursement. On the other hand, your partner might not agree, perhaps feeling that things were equalized by the partner's payment of other expenses or equally valuable contributions to the partnership. And again, if you are in a negative equity situation, a meeting with an experienced real estate lawyer would be a good idea.

> **TIP**
>
> **Put the house on the market even if you disagree about how the proceeds will be divided.** You can put the property on the market and sell it, and put the proceeds into an escrow account that won't be distributed until you agree (or an arbitrator makes an agreement for you) on how it will be divided. In fact, it's often easier to resolve the dispute over the proceeds once you know exactly how much money there is to divide.

The general rule for jointly titled property is that if there is no written agreement, it's presumed that the property is owned equally, and the person seeking a greater share of the proceeds must prove an agreement to the contrary. In most states, contributions to a down payment and to improvements that raise the value of the property are more frequently reimbursed than are greater-than-equal contributions to ongoing expenses such as mortgage interest or utilities. The rules can be very different, however, if you are married or registered as domestic partners or civil union partners.

If your house is worth less than the debt on it, you might be able to do a short sale—but that will require cooperation and joint strategizing with your partner.

Continue owning the house together

You and your partner can continue owning the house jointly while one (or both) of you lives there, or while you rent it out. You might choose to do this, for example, if you believe the real estate market is soft at the time you're separating, but is going to get better in the foreseeable future. You might also decide to keep the house in joint ownership until your kids are older and you are ready to make a decision about who keeps it permanently. There are pros and cons to continuing to own the house jointly—on the positive side, it can allow one person to stay there when otherwise they might not be able to afford it, can provide an income tax deduction for a party who needs it, and if you have kids, may be a good way to maintain some stability in their lives. On the other hand, it means that you and your partner continue to be financially enmeshed, and must continue making decisions together about things like repairs and improvements. You also have to figure out how you will deal with finances like paying the mortgage, insurance, and property taxes. If you're considering this option, make sure you go over all these questions, and the potential tax consequences, with a real estate lawyer and a tax expert before you make any final decisions.

Dividing Other Assets and Debts

If you own other real estate, such as investment property or a vacation home, you'll need to go through the same resolution process as with your primary residence. Decide whether one of you will buy out the other or whether you will sell the place, then figure out the fair market value and account for claims of reimbursement. You can continue owning the property jointly as an investment, and if it's in your mutual best interest and you can agree on its management, by all means do so. But be sure to have a written management agreement for the property—you are business partners now, not lovers.

You must also divide up bank, stock, and savings accounts. Remember —both names on an account means there's a legal presumption that it's owned 50-50, and the person claiming a greater percentage has to prove there was an enforceable agreement for other than equal ownership. Try to reach a compromise, and if you can't, consider submitting the dispute to binding arbitration if the amount is large enough to justify the expense. In the meantime, make sure all joint accounts require the approval of both owners for withdrawals. And, as with all assets, remember that the rules for married or state-registered partners may be quite different than those for people who simply own property together without any legal relationship surrounding the ownership.

If you have joint debts, try to pay them off sooner rather than later. If there are debts that were incurred by only one of you but were for joint expenses, you will need to figure out who really is responsible for what portion of the debt. If one person is willing to take full responsibility for the debts, then the debtor will need to pay them off or try to have the debt shifted away from the couple and to the debtor alone. Most banks and credit card companies will not remove one person's name just because you are breaking up. The creditor wants as many people as possible on the hook for the debt.

> **TIP**
>
> **When you close a credit account, ask the card issuer to put a "hard close" on the account.** It's a good idea to close all of your joint credit accounts to new activity when you separate, and have each person get new, separate cards. A hard close means that either person would have to submit a new application to reopen the account. If the card issuer doesn't put a hard close on the account, either of you could reopen it without applying.

Working Out Child Custody and Support

If you have children, you are likely to face some very difficult challenges. The law can be very unfair to same-sex parents—both as it is written and as it is practiced. Making matters even messier, the law changes constantly. Lesbian and gay parents are truly forging new territory—which is fine when you are in the mood to be a revolutionary, but not necessarily so when all you want to do is spend the day with your child.

Because of all these pressures and uncertainties, it is vital that you do everything you can to reach a compromise on all child-related issues. Try to reach a resolution through talking together, in therapy or with the help of a custody mediator—and remember that if you take your custody dispute to court, you're likely to be ordered to mediation anyway. Whatever you do, try to avoid a parentage or custody battle in court. You will only harm your child in the process, as well as bring on mountains of agony for yourselves. If you can agree on the issues of legal custody (who makes decisions about the child), physical custody (where the child lives), visitation (how often and under what conditions the noncustodial parent spends time with the child), and child support (the noncustodial parent's contribution to the costs of raising the child), you will save yourselves—and your kids—a great deal of pain.

And if you can't reach a resolution yourselves? Then you will have to submit your disputes to the legal system. The specific rules for child custody and visitation differ from state to state and are in tremendous flux with regard to gay parents these days. This section provides a summary of the basic rules.

Current Developments in LGBT Parentage Law

Here are some of the important cases that have been decided in recent years:

Arkansas. The state supreme court held that a mother's former lesbian partner was "in loco parentis" to their child (meaning she was in the same relation to the child as a parent) and it was in the child's best interest that she have visitation.

California: Three important cases were decided by the California Supreme Court in late 2005. In the first, *K.M. v. E.G.*, a lesbian couple used ovum donation to conceive twins, and coparented the kids for six years. After they separated, the gestational parent refused visitation to the ovum donor parent. A trial court held that the ovum donor was not a parent because she signed a standard release of her rights when she donated the eggs. The appellate court affirmed the ruling, but the Supreme Court reversed and held that the ovum donor mom was a legal parent with a right to have contact with her children.

In the second California case, *Elisa B. v. Superior Court*, a lesbian parent sought child support from her former partner after they separated and the partner stopped providing care or support for the twin daughters born during the relationship. The Supreme Court held that because the two women had intended to conceive and raise the children together, and had done so for a period of time before separating, the nonbiological mom was a legal parent with an obligation of support.

In the third case, *Kristine H. v. Lisa R.*, the parties obtained a judgment of parentage for the second parent under the Uniform Parentage Act. When the parties later separated, the biological parent asked the court to vacate its earlier judgment and hold that the second parent was not a legal parent.

The Supreme Court ruled that the biological mom couldn't challenge the judgment because she had consented to it and had relied on it herself while the couple was still together.

Current Developments in LGBT Parentage Law (continued)

Based on the *Elisa B.* case, appellate courts in California have gone on to rule in favor of nonbiological moms in other custody cases. It's no longer possible for a biological parent in a same-sex relationship in California to deny a partner the right to coparent, as long as the parties planned for the child together and acted jointly as parents, even for a short period of time, after the child's birth.

In a 2009 case, the Court of Appeals ordered visitation for a nonbiological second parent, Charisma, despite the fact she actively parented the child for only a few months and then had no contact with the child for some years, as a result of the biological mom's denial of visitation. The court found that Charisma was a presumed parent under the domestic partnership laws and California's parentage rules, and ordered a process of supervised reunification. The court found the duration of the contact between parent and child to be irrelevant—if a person is a presumed parent under the law, then they're a presumed parent regardless of the amount of time they've spent with the child.

Colorado/Florida: Two women had a child together in Colorado; after they separated, a court there ordered that the nonbiological mom should have visitation. The bio mom moved to Florida and filed an action there, seeking an order that her ex-partner had no parental rights. The nonbiological parent successfully argued that Colorado, not Florida, had jurisdiction over the case.

Delaware: The state Supreme Court ruled that a lesbian parent who had accepted support payments from her former partner after they broke up could not challenge the partner's status as a de facto parent. But without the support payments, coparenting alone was not enough to give a lesbian second parent standing to seek custody or visitation after a breakup in another case.

Florida: A court of appeal rejected a claim for visitation by a lesbian second parent, despite the fact that while together, she and her partner had planned carefully to protect their family, including filing a domestic partnership declaration and signing a coparenting agreement. (Florida does not permit same-sex adoption of any kind.)

Current Developments in LGBT Parentage Law (continued)

Indiana: A woman who adopted her partner's children during their relationship could not terminate the relationship upon separation, and continued to have a duty to support the children.

In another Indiana case, the Court of Appeals ruled that a joint parenting order entered by a court was invalid, because the women should have used the state's adoption laws instead.

Kentucky: One partner in a lesbian couple adopted a child, and the couple raised him together for six years. After they separated, the only legal parent cut off contact between the second parent and the child. The Kentucky Supreme Court held the second parent was not a de facto parent and refused her claim for visitation. A nearly identical case a few years later had the same result.

Louisiana: A lesbian coparent was denied custody of her partner's biological child, with the court ignoring the fact that the child was the half-sibling of the coparent's biological child.

Maryland: A Maryland court lifted a previous order and allowed a gay man to live with his same-sex partner while having custody of his son. Another Maryland court held that a lesbian second parent was a de facto parent entitled to visitation, but not custody, with the child her former partner adopted during their relationship.

Massachusetts: In the absence of an adoption, a nonbiological parent could not get visitation rights over her ex-partner's objection, because she couldn't prove that she was the child's "primary caretaker" as required for a finding of de facto parentage.

Michigan: The Court of Appeals ruled that the state's constitutional amendment banning same-sex marriage was irrelevant to the question of whether a court could decide custody and visitation issues between a lesbian couple who had jointly adopted children in Illinois. Because their adoptions were valid where entered into, Michigan must respect them, and the relationship between the parent and child is the basis for the court's deciding the custody matters, regardless of the relationship between the parents.

Current Developments in LGBT Parentage Law (continued)

Minnesota: The state Supreme Court ruled in favor of a lesbian coparent seeking visitation with the children her partner adopted during their 22-year relationship, under a law that allows any nonparent to petition for visitation with a child the nonparent has lived with for more than two years and with whom the nonparent has a parent-child relationship, as long as the visitation would be in the child's best interest and would not interfere with the child's relationship with the custodial parent.

Montana: A judge ruled that a lesbian coparent could have continuing contact with the children adopted by her former partner during their relationship, basing the decision on the children's right to continuing contact with their second parent.

New Mexico. A lesbian parent was denied standing to seek custody, because the law in New Mexico requires that a parent must be unfit in order for a so-called third party to have standing in court. However, she might have standing to ask for visitation, which didn't have the same requirement.

New York: An appellate court upheld a trial court's decision that the partner of a lesbian who adopted a child from China was a legal stranger to the child she helped raise for five years, and could not seek custody or visitation because the women never formalized the second parent's relationship through an adoption. And a lesbian mother was prohibited from seeking child support from her former partner for the same reasons.

North Carolina: Because the biological parent hadn't engaged in "conduct inconsistent with her fundamental right to the custody, care, and control" of their two children, one lesbian second parent wasn't entitled to joint custody, despite her substantial bond with the children. But in another case, a mother who executed a parenting agreement with her partner and "voluntarily invested her same-sex partner with parent-like rights," was ordered to share custody.

Just last year, the North Carolina Supreme Court ruled that the second-parent adoption process is invalid, though limited visitation rights can be granted to second parents. The decision had the effect of invalidating even adoptions that were already completed in the state.

Ohio: A court upheld a cocustody agreement that a biological mom entered into with her lesbian partner, but returned the case to a lower court

Current Developments in LGBT Parentage Law (continued)

for findings about the suitability of the partner, a finding required in a case where a parent shares custody with a nonparent.

A lesbian was denied shared custody of her five-year-old daughter after the Ohio Supreme Court found there was no agreement between the parties under which the biological mother made a permanent commitment to share custody. The shared parenting for the first five years of the child's life were voluntary on the part of the biological mother, and she wasn't required to continue allowing the other mother a parental role.

Pennsylvania: The state Supreme Court ruled that a nonbiological mother in a lesbian couple could be awarded primary custody, holding that the best interests of the children, rather than biology, must be the primary focus in a custody decision.

Texas: While finding that same-sex adoptions are not permissible in Texas, the Texas Court of Appeals nonetheless upheld an adoption by a same-sex partner because the original legal parent did not object in time. The court also held that the second parent could be granted primary custody.

Utah: The Utah Supreme Court held that a nonbiological lesbian parent does not qualify for in loco parentis status (someone who's a parental figure), and upheld lower court decisions denying her the right to even seek visitation—despite the fact that when they were together, the parents went to Vermont to enter into a civil union, sought and received court approval for shared parenting, and gave the child both of their last names.

Vermont: Two lesbians entered into a civil union and had a child by donor insemination while their civil union was intact. After they separated, the biological mother moved to Virginia, where she sought and received a court order that her ex-partner was not a legal parent of their daughter. The nonbiological mother countered with a petition to the Vermont court, which ruled that she was in fact the child's legal parent by virtue of the civil union relationship. The biological mom challenged this order but lost when the Vermont Supreme Court held that the civil union conferred parentage on the nonbiological parent.

Virginia: The Court of Appeals ruled against a lesbian mom, finding she had no status to pursue visitation with her children, and in the process held

Current Developments in LGBT Parentage Law (continued)

that nonlegal parents in Virginia aren't entitled to "de facto" parental status.

Washington: A state court of appeals ruled that a lesbian second parent could seek parental rights to the child born to her former partner during their relationship. The court found that the second parent was a "de facto or psychological parent" and that the biological mother had encouraged her partner's relationship with the child.

West Virginia: A lesbian couple each bore a child through donor insemination. One partner died, and her partner sought custody of her biological child—a request that was opposed by the parents of the birth mother. The Supreme Court upheld the original trial court award of custody to the second parent.

Wisconsin. The Wisconsin Court of Appeals refused to broaden the state's definition of "parent" to include the same-sex partner of an adoptive mother, who had helped to raise the children for five years while the women were together.

For more information and the current status of all of these pending cases, visit the National Center for Lesbian Rights website at www.nclrights.org and click "NCLR cases."

If Both of You Are Legal Parents

Both partners may be legal parents of the child for any of the following reasons:

- The child was born into a marriage, registered domestic partnership, or civil union in a state where that confers parental rights on a non-biological parents.
- The nonbiological or nonadoptive parent adopted the child through a second-parent or stepparent adoption, or established a parent-child relationship through a parentage action.
- The two of you jointly adopted the child.

Where both parents have equal legal rights, child-related disputes should be handled just as they are for a straight divorce. See below for more on child custody cases where parentage rights aren't at issue.

If Only One of You Is the Legal Parent

If only one of you is the child's legal parent, things will be different. Generally speaking, it doesn't matter why the second parent isn't a legal parent (whether it's because you live in a state where there's no relationship recognition and second-parent adoption isn't available, or because the legal parent wouldn't agree). In many states, second parents have no rights whatsoever, and cannot seek either legal or physical custody. Often, there is no way to seek visitation either. These parents also rarely have any financial obligations to their partners' children, although in most contested situations the second parent would be glad to help out financially.

However, in some states courts have recognized second parents on the basis of their intent to conceive and raise children, or their established relationships with those children.

Here more than any other area of same-sex family law, it's critically important that before making decisions or taking action relating to your kids, you get advice from a skilled and knowledgeable attorney who knows the law and is familiar with your local judges. Not only does the law change rapidly, but the outcome of any particular dispute can depend on which judge hears the case.

It's hard to find a consistent thread in the parentage cases, but there are some things that seem only right when you are facing a breakup that involves kids. For example, put your child's needs first! Whether you are the legal parent and believe that your ex-partner should not visit your child, or the second parent seeking to maintain a relationship, make your child's emotional needs—not yours—your highest priority.

If you are the sole legal parent, and you truly believe that visitation with your ex-partner would be harmful to your child, then don't allow it. But if the only reason your partner doesn't have parental rights is because the two of you couldn't get married, and you would have married if you could have, then it is wrong—morally if not legally—to deny your partner access to a child you have raised together. The fact that your ex might be a flawed person doesn't justify it. Conflicts in your relationship aren't grounds to cut off your ex's contact with your child, either.

If you are denying visitation because you are trying to avoid ongoing contact with an ex you can't stand anymore, think about whether your child considers your ex a parent, and about how your child will feel about a sudden break in the relationship with an important caretaker. Make an effort to acknowledge honestly what agreements you and your partner made about parenting and about sharing custody. Don't use your power just because you have it—try to do the right thing. It will benefit you, your ex, your entire community, and, most importantly, your child.

If you are a second parent and your partner is denying you visitation with the child you have helped raise, you will want to ask some questions:

- Does your state allow you to present a claim for visitation or partial custody if you are not a legal parent? If so, what procedures must you follow?

- If no procedures have been established in your state, are you willing to be a "test case" and try to forge new law? Doing so will expose your most personal characteristics—positive and negative—to the scrutiny of lawyers, judges, and the public. Make sure you are ready to take this on before you begin.

- If the law is definitively against you, consider whether you want to try to change the law by pursuing your case up to the appellate court level. If not, you will have to explore more personal approaches, such as mediation or counseling with your former partner

Below is a sample parenting agreement for partners who have separated but intend to continue parenting together.

RESOURCE

For more on parenting agreements, check out: *Building a Parenting Agreement That Works*, by Mimi Lyster (Nolo). Another useful resource is *Divorce Without Court: A Guide to Mediation and Collaborative Divorce*, by Katherine E. Stoner (Nolo).

For more about child custody and support generally, see *Nolo's Essential Guide to Child Custody and Support*, by Emily Doskow (Nolo).

Sample Postseparation Parenting Agreement

This agreement is made on January 1, 20xx, between Ellen Donato ("Ellen") and Charlotte Frieden ("Charlie") of Cincinnati, Ohio, regarding the parenting of the minor child Brenda Sue Donato (referred to herein as "Brenda").

The parties agree as follows:

1. This agreement concerns the parenting of Brenda, who was adopted legally by Ellen on July 15, 2004. Brenda has been raised in the home of Ellen and Charlie since her adoption and is equally bonded to both women in mother-child relationships. Even though Ellen is the sole legal parent of Brenda, the parties intend that Brenda will continue to be raised by both Ellen and Charlie.

2. The parties agree that it's in Brenda's best interest for them to continue to share physical custody equally. The parties will work cooperatively to make reasonable arrangements for the physical custody of Brenda.

3. Each party will contribute equally to the financial costs of raising Brenda.

4. Each party will either maintain her current residence or will live within twenty (20) miles of the other's current home until Brenda reaches the age of 18. If either party changes her residence outside of this distance without the other party's written consent, she will lose the right to share equal physical custody of Brenda.

5. Charlie will have the same rights and obligations to Brenda as if she were her legal parent. Should any dispute arise between the parties, Ellen agrees that she will not at any time assert that Charlie is not Brenda's parent or that she has a lesser parental status by virtue of the lack of legal parentage. Moreover, the parties affirm that it is in Brenda's best interests to maintain a parent-child relationship with both of the parties.

6. In the event of any dispute between the parties regarding Brenda's custody, care, financial support, or upbringing, the parties agree to attend mediation sessions in good faith to resolve the dispute. Each party will participate in at least four mediation sessions, with the cost of the mediation to be shared equally.

7. The District Court of the State of Ohio will have jurisdiction to resolve all matters regarding custody, visitation, and support, and the enforcement of this agreement. Each party agrees to allow the participation of the other in any proceeding to determine parentage, custody, visitation, and/

or support, without any jurisdictional objection. Neither party will assert as a defense to a court action the lack of a legal parental status or rights of the other party.

8. If any attorneys' fees or costs are incurred by either party in a court proceeding regarding custody, visitation, or support, the court will have jurisdiction to award fees and costs as provided by the relevant sections of this state's family code, even though the proceedings may be in a parentage or other action rather than in a dissolution or separation proceeding.

9. Ellen nominates Charlie as the personal and property guardian of Brenda, in the event that Ellen becomes unable to care for Brenda, to serve without bond. If Charlie cannot serve as Brenda's guardian, then Ellen's mother Elaine Merritt is nominated to serve as guardian.

10. This agreement is the only agreement between the parties with respect to Brenda. It may be waived, altered, or modified only with the written consent of both parties. In the event that any part of this agreement is held to be invalid, the remainder of the agreement shall be in full force and effect.

_____   _____
Date   Ellen Donato

_____   _____
Date   Charlotte Frieden

Breaking Up When There's No Legal Relationship

If you and your partner have never married, registered as domestic partners, or entered into a civil union, then you can end your relationship without having any contact with a court—assuming you're able to agree on how to divide your assets. (The only exception to this rule is if you have children, in which case you may want to have the court enter an order relating to custody and visitation of your kids, even if you're in agreement about how to share time. There's more on that below.)

For some people, there's a downside to not having to involve a court in your breakup—the usual marital rules about sharing money and property don't apply, and that can cause a hardship in some circumstances. For example, unless one partner can prove a clear agreement that the other promised to provide postseparation support, neither partner is entitled to alimony—even if one partner gave up a lucrative career to run the household for the other partner. If you do have a written agreement, the court will probably enforce it. But if you don't, it will be very difficult to prove you had an oral agreement. The fact that one of you supported the other one during your relationship or that you signed wills to provide for each other upon death is almost always irrelevant.

Likewise, if there is no written agreement or clear history of actions showing that your intention was to merge your assets and debts (such as opening joint accounts or putting both names on the deed to your home), each partner will likely be found to solely own the assets and debts that partner has accumulated. Your salary, credit card accounts, and savings account are yours alone. In most states, this presumption of sole ownership can be overcome only by a written agreement. In others, a court may find and enforce an oral or implied agreement to share assets. But proving that such an agreement existed can be very difficult if you don't have written proof. Chapters 3, 4, 8, and 9 all address these issues in detail.

SEE AN EXPERT

You'll probably need legal help with a claim for an implied or oral contract. Oral or implied agreements may be enforceable in your state, but proving them is not easy. Having the right to launch a claim doesn't mean that you will win. Before you stake out your claim, get a realistic evaluation of its strength from a legal expert. It may not be easy to find an experienced local attorney who knows how to handle your case. Many family law attorneys only know marital rules, not nonmarital rules, and they may be uncomfortable working on a gay breakup. Most real estate attorneys are used to dealing with business partnership breakups, so they probably aren't accustomed to dealing with intense emotional conflicts. Chapter 11 has information about finding and working with an attorney.

On the other side of things, joint accounts and assets held in both names are generally presumed to be owned 50-50. The presumption can also be overcome by a written document, signed by both of you, saying that your shares are not equal, but in some states it also can be overcome if one party can prove that an oral or implied agreement supersedes the written document.

If you split up and you're able to agree how to divide your property, you can just do it and move on. If you can't, however, in most states your legal disputes about property will be handled by the general civil courts, not a special family court as in divorce cases. You are likely to be assigned to a regular judge and required to follow regular litigation procedures, as though you were dissolving a business partnership. The major exception to this is if you have children. In that case the issues of custody, visitation, and child support should be handled just as they are for straight couples—though if only one of you is the legal parent, the issues are more complex. There's more on this below and in Chapter 5.

CAUTION

Try to be fair. Remember that the person you are now fighting is someone you once loved. If you treated your relationship like a marriage, give some consideration to what the law would require if you were married, be honest about the agreements you had (and didn't have) with each other, and make every possible effort to compromise. Fighting for every last dollar will only cost both of you money and create more pain.

Real life rarely fits snugly into the legal rules for nonmarital dissolutions, and because you don't have to take your case to court, resolving the dispute through mediation or binding arbitration is very often the safest, sanest road to travel. Find out the legal rules in your jurisdiction, evaluate what really is most important for you to fight over, and approach the mediation and negotiation process with an understanding that compromise is going to be necessary. Make sure you get your final agreement in writing, and do whatever you can to avoid having to submit your lives to the court's jurisdiction.

Dissolving a Same-Sex Marriage

This section discusses what happens legally when a marriage or state-registered domestic partnership or civil union breaks up. It's not simple, because all of the standard divorce laws apply to same-sex couples in the marriage-equality and marriage-equivalent states.

Remember, even if you are living in one of those states that requires a court dissolution for registered or married couples, you still can agree on the substantive issues and simply file an "uncontested" divorce. This way, even though you have to file the paperwork in court, you won't have to go through an ugly and expensive court trial.

RESOURCE

If you're headed for a court dissolution in one of the states that recognizes legal same-sex relationships, you can use the same resources that heterosexual married couples do—but make sure you also consult a lawyer familiar with same-sex breakups. In the meantime, check out Nolo's *Essential Guide to Divorce* and Nolo's *Essential Guide to Child Custody and Support*, both by Emily Doskow, *Divorce Without Court: A Guide to Mediation and Collaborative Divorce*, by Katherine E. Stoner, and *A Judge's Guide to Divorce*, by Roderic Duncan (all from Nolo). There are many good divorce-related websites, too—www. divorceinfo.com and www.divorcenet.com are two of them.

A Good Divorce—As Precious as a Good Marriage

Divorce is a painful process. When you married or registered you probably felt you were taking part in a fabulously liberating opportunity—and now you are forced to spend money on lawyers and possibly participate in a grueling court drama. But you can avoid it. Whenever possible, try to keep your disputes out of court. Even if it seems impossible, take a deep breath and try again to work out a solution. Fighting about money and property in court only decreases what's left to divide and increases animosity and conflict. Seeing a therapist, engaging in mediation or arbitration, or even moving ten miles away can be more effective ways of handling serious disputes than battling them out in court. A court fight is emotionally draining, costly, and unpredictable, even if you're lucky enough to appear before a non-homophobic judge and can avoid being a "test case" for gay divorce law!

Compromise does not mean capitulation. The joy of moving on, the fear of public disclosure of your most private marital disputes, or the desire to be rid of the past are not reasons to stop parenting your children or to give up your share of the property you accumulated while married. You don't want to later spend months or years trying to obtain custody, support, or property that you impulsively abandoned. Instead, try to stay the course and work hard to reach fair agreements with your partner.

The rules governing divorce, child support, alimony, custody, and property division are officially the same whether both parties are straight, the couple is opposite-sex but one partner has come out as gay, or both people are the same sex. But applying existing divorce rules to these couples is not always going to be a simple process, and the first generation of couples to seek divorces may encounter complications.

The most basic legal rules for married couples (and those in marriage-like relationships that bring with them the rights and duties of marriage) can be summarized as follows:

- A spouse who wants to end a relationship must apply to the local family court for a divorce decree. If the spouses agree on how to divide their property and debts and share parenting, the judge will grant the request for a divorce and will approve the agreement unless the terms are substantially unfair. If the spouses cannot agree on distribution of their property, the court will divide the couple's property and debt in accordance with the state's particular rules— either 50-50 or in a way the court determines is equitable.

- A judge can order the higher earner in a marriage to pay alimony (also called spousal support or maintenance) to the other partner— sometimes just until the dependent partner can get a job, or in other instances, for as long as the recipient is alive and unmarried.
- If you have children and can't agree on custody or visitation, the judge will decide on a custody arrangement, how visits by the noncustodial parent will be arranged, who will pay child support, and how much will be paid. The courts make these decisions based upon what is in the best interest of the child. You will almost always have to go to mediation with your ex-partner before you can go to court about a custody dispute.

More detail about all of these rules, and how they may apply to same-sex couples, is set out below. This chapter provides a rough outline of the key issues, but each particular divorce can present new and complicated legal problems. Even though it's expensive, you may need to hire a lawyer to help sort out these issues and others. Most lawyers won't have represented same-sex couples in legal divorces before, but it's important that you choose a lawyer who is comfortable with your family and with working in an area of law that is not yet settled.

Getting a Divorce

In nearly all states, it's possible to end a marriage based on either separation or "no-fault" divorce. A separation-based divorce requires that the spouses live apart for a period of time—from six months to a few years—before divorcing (state rules vary on the length of time required). In a no-fault divorce, a spouse simply alleges "an irretrievable breakdown of the marriage," "incompatibility," or "irreconcilable differences."

States adopted separation-based and no-fault divorces in recognition of the fact that a courtroom is not the place to review what happened in a marriage, and that it is wasteful and degrading for spouses to allege and prove petty wrongs, unfulfilled expectations, and betrayals. All that is legally important is that the marriage no longer works and at least one partner wants out. In a separation-based divorce, even if one spouse is determined to stay married, that spouse can't force it. The same is true in a no-fault divorce. And so, who had the first affair really won't matter at all to the judge, however important it may seem to you!

Although every state now allows separation-based or no-fault divorce, a few states still permit divorces based on traditional fault grounds as well—grounds that include adultery, mental cruelty, and abandonment. If you live in one of these states and either of you is so inclined, you or your spouse could request a fault divorce—most likely asserting that the other person is guilty of mental cruelty or has committed adultery with a new lover. Some states don't allow you to allege fault as the basis for the divorce, but in many of those states it can be raised in a child custody or alimony dispute and in some states it can affect property division as well. (See below.) But our advice, in general, is to let go of this strategy, as it will only cost everyone more money and more aggravation.

Dividing Your Property and Debts

If you and your spouse have significant assets, how a court will divide them and allocate the debts incurred during your marriage depends on where you live. California, Nevada, Oregon, and Washington are all community property states that recognize same-sex marriages. Community property means that spouses own most or all of their property equally, and that the property is likely to be divided equally at divorce. All other states follow a system called "equitable distribution." Under both systems, property acquired during marriage (except gifts and inheritances) is generally divided "equitably," which might or might not mean the division is equal.

One of the key problems that will arise in many gay divorces is how to deal with assets or debts accumulated before you registered or married.

Many couples have been cohabiting for many years—years that generally aren't governed by marital rules. The legal rules for premarital assets or debts when the relationship changes into a marriage or registration are not at all simple, and if this is one of your issues, you probably will need to consult with an attorney who is familiar with both marital and nonmarital rules. Another point to keep in mind (as discussed more fully below) is that so long as DOMA is in effect, you are not federally recognized spouses, and so the tax protections bestowed on divorcing straight couples most likely won't apply to your divorce.

Regardless of your state's laws, you and your spouse may agree to whatever division of your property seems fair to both of you, settle your divorce yourselves, and ask a court to approve your settlement in the process of an uncontested divorce.

Where Are We Married? And Where Can We Get Divorced?

If you registered or married in a state other than the one you live in, will other states honor your out-of-state marriage or legal union and allow you to get a formal divorce? One of the biggest problems arising out of all the recent legal changes is what happens to couples who live in one state, but registered or married in another state or country?

As discussed in Chapter 1, all U.S. states are supposed to honor marriages from other states (and countries), and should treat you just as if you'd gotten married in the state where you're living. But Defense of Marriage (DOMA) laws and generalized homophobia are likely to get in the way. Further, many of the specifics of divorce, such as allocating pension benefits and tax burdens, are based on federal law. If the federal DOMA says those laws don't apply, it may be difficult to apply state laws that incorporate these federal rules.

All of the states that allow same-sex marriage or offer a marriage equivalent like domestic partnership or civil unions will recognize legal same-sex relationships from each of the other states that do. In addition, a few other states recognize same-sex marriages, at least for purposes of divorce. However, some states, including Texas, have refused to allow same-

Where Are We Married? And Where Can We Get Divorced? (continued)

sex divorces to go forward there on the basis that the marriage itself is not recognized, so no divorce can be granted.

People who married or registered in one place but live somewhere that the relationship isn't recognized are in a bind. If their home state won't allow the divorce, they may be required to establish residency in a state that will—and residency requirements can be as long as a year. However, at least two judges in New Jersey have waived the residency requirement for couples who were registered New Jersey domestic partners but no longer lived there, simply because the judges considered it unfair that the couple couldn't divorce elsewhere. However, these couples had resolved all of the issues in their divorce, and the courts indicated that only an uncontested divorce would be eligible for a waiver of the residency requirement—a couple with disputes over custody or property would have to establish residency.

In some states, you can dissolve a registration from another state right in your home town, but in other instances you may need to move to the state of registration or another recognition state and qualify for residency there, and then file your legal action there. And if you haven't taken the trouble to get a formal dissolution from your former partnership, your new partnership may be bigamous and therefore completely invalid. If you are facing such a situation, we urge you to consult with a local attorney who can help you sort through the options.

RESOURCE

Work on your settlement yourselves first. For help in dividing your property fairly and without incurring substantial professional fees—lawyers, accountants, appraisers, and the like—see *Divorce & Money: How to Make the Best Financial Decisions During Divorce*, by Violet Woodhouse, with Dale Fetherling (Nolo). Also take a look at *Nolo's Essential Guide to Divorce*, by Emily Doskow (Nolo).

Alimony

Alimony is the money paid by one ex-spouse to the other for support following a divorce. Some states call it "spousal support" or "maintenance."

In quite a few divorces, no alimony is awarded because both partners work. However, this doesn't mean that alimony is dead. Where one spouse earned the money while the other raised the children, alimony is probably still appropriate—at least until the children enter school full-time or the non–wage-earner develops skills necessary to enter (or reenter) the work force.

In a few remaining states, a court can find you at fault in ending the marriage and award you less than an equal share of the marital property or order you to pay more alimony. Divorce laws generally give courts discretion to consider "all factors," and as a practical matter, fault issues may influence judges' decisions.

If alimony is granted, it usually lasts until a specified period of time passes, the recipient dies, or the recipient remarries. Some states consider cohabitation to be the same as remarriage for purposes of ending alimony payments, and a growing number of states have applied these cohabiting laws to same-sex relationships.

One thing that is certainly going to be new is having judges consider alimony claims by gay and lesbian "wives" or "husbands." Even though the rules are supposed to be administered in a gender-neutral way, we wonder how open traditional judges will be to such claims. Again, remember that you may be the first such claimant who has appeared in the judge's courtroom, so don't be surprised if your case generates some confusion.

The New Tax Headaches for Same-Sex Couples

Along with all the other challenges gay and lesbian couples are now facing, the uncertainties regarding the federal tax code may well be the most significant. Here's the problem: If you live in a state that recognizes your union—either as a marriage, civil union, or domestic partnership—and your relationship ends, the settlement you make with your partner may involve paying your ex money, either as a property settlement or as alimony or spousal support. If you were heterosexual and married, those financial transactions related to your divorce would be tax-free events. But until DOMA is repealed, your relationship is not a federally recognized marriage, so you aren't eligible for the broad exemptions from taxation that are bestowed on straight spouses who divorce. This means the payments could be considered a gift from you to your ex, or could be classified as income on your partner's taxes. It's not even clear that same-sex couples can avoid taxes on child support, which is neither taxable nor deductible in a heterosexual divorce, because the technical rule only exempts payments to a former "spouse."

We are absolutely sure that this is an unfair situation, but we are less sure about what you can do about it. You certainly don't consider the payment to be a gift if you are being ordered to pay spousal support to an unfaithful ex. And as much as your ex may believe she has "earned" the payment, the idea of paying income tax won't be a pleasant one, especially where the earner has already paid tax on this same money.

It is going to take several years to sort out these questions, with possible audits of taxpayers, appeals from IRS and tax court rulings, and likely changes in court and government codes. In the meantime, we encourage you to talk with a local tax attorney or accountant who is familiar with the rules for same-sex couples in your particular state.

Cooperating in Your Divorce

Many divorcing couples make decisions about children, support, and property in a spirit of common sense and compromise, and we encourage you to follow this path. If the issues are complicated and you feel that you need an attorney to represent you, try to find one who will not engage in all-out warfare with your ex. In some areas, lawyers and clients are engaging in a process called "collaborative practice," in which all parties agree that they will not take the divorce dispute to court, but will negotiate a settlement together. (For more about mediation and collaboration, see "Methods of Resolving Disputes," above.)

RESOURCE

For more information about divorce mediation, see *Divorce Without Court: A Guide to Mediation and Collaborative Divorce*, by Katherine E. Stoner (Nolo), or *A Guide to Divorce Mediation*, by Gary Friedman (Workman Publishers).

Child Custody

Child custody is the issue that potentially can present the biggest problem for a lesbian or gay person going through a divorce. The best advice we can offer is to try as hard as you possibly can to work out a solution with your spouse or partner. Don't leave these intensely personal decisions up to a judge. If either parent is contesting legal parentage, you most likely will need the assistance of an experienced local attorney.

Transgender Parents and Child Custody

Transgender parents often have extra layers of legal complications to deal with. In a case in Florida, for example, a female-to-male transsexual, Michael Kantaras, married a woman and adopted his wife's infant son. Michael and his wife then had a child together through artificial insemination. At the time they married, Michael's wife knew that he was a transgender man. After they divorced nine years later, however, she claimed that the marriage was invalid, and that Michael was not entitled to custody of or visitation with the children. The first court to review the case found that the marriage was valid, and awarded primary custody of the two children to Michael. An appeals court in 2004 reversed the lower court's ruling that the marriage was valid—holding that a person's sex is immutably fixed at birth—but refused to strip Michael of his parental rights, sending the case back to the trial court to determine parental rights. In 2005, after television personality Dr. Phil got involved and urged the parties to mediate, they reached a settlement under which Michael retains all of his parental rights, and shares legal custody with the children's mother.

In Illinois, a court held that a marriage between a transgender man and a woman was void because the man had not yet undergone sex change surgery at the time of the marriage and thus was legally considered a

Transgender Parents and Child Custody

woman. Because the marriage was void, the court reasoned, the man also was not a legal parent of the child born to his wife during the relationship, and was not entitled to custody. The court did rule that the man should have visitation with the child, who was 11.

In a 2007 Washington State case, the Court of Appeals upheld a trial court's decision giving primary custody to Tracey Magnusen, the ex-wife of Robbie Magnusen, who was planning to have male-to-female gender reassignment surgery. The trial court's decision was made despite the findings of a guardian ad litem for the children, who conducted an extensive investigation and concluded that Robbie should be the primary custodial parent (the report noted that Robbie was the "more nurturing and engaged parent" and that Tracey had always been a "secondary parent"). The judge felt that the impact of Robbie's transition on the children was "unknown," and used that as the basis of the custody decision. The only upside is that the decision is the first to state explicitly that gender identity should not by itself be seen as a disqualifying factor for determining custody.

In Kentucky, a court allowed a woman's husband to complete a stepparent adoption of her daughter, in the process terminating the rights of the ex-husband, a male-to-female transsexual. The court held that the gender reassignment surgery, alone, did not cause the termination, but that the "entire series of events," including the parent's failure to inform the children about changes in appearance before a visit, had caused serious emotional harm that justified the termination of rights.

In a New York case, a transgender man won custody of his child even after his marriage to the child's mother was declared void. The court found that the child was conceived by donor insemination during the relationship, had bonded with the man as a parent, with the support of the mother, and that the man was the only father that child had known. The mother had also filed a birth certificate that named the man as the child's father. The court stopped short of finding the man a legal father, but did give him standing to seek custody and visitation. (*K.B. v. J.R.*, 887 N.Y.S.2d 516, New York 2009.)

Transgender parents will need the assistance of a knowledgeable attorney. See Chapter 11 for resource information.

Kinds of Custody

There are two types of child custody: physical and legal. Physical custody is the right to have your child live with you. Legal custody is the right to make important decisions about things such as the child's education, medical care, and activities.

Custody may be sole or joint. Joint legal custody means that parents continue to make decisions together about important issues even after the divorce. Courts order joint legal custody in most cases, regardless of how much time the child spends with each parent. Joint physical custody means that the parents share time with the child—it doesn't necessarily mean that time is split equally, only that both parents spend a significant amount of time parenting. Joint physical custody isn't for everyone, but it works well when the parents get along relatively well and live relatively close to each other.

Usually, a parent who doesn't have primary physical custody will be granted liberal parenting time. If incomes are unequal or if one parent is shouldering most of the costs of taking care of the child, the noncustodial parent will be ordered to pay child support. In most states, the family law court keeps the authority to resolve future disputes about custody or parenting time, and any orders or rulings can be revisited if circumstances change.

The local family court judge has the power to make all decisions about who will have legal or physical custody—and is required to consider the "best interest of the child" in all disputes.

 TIP

When you first separate, stay with your children if at all possible. If you leave your family home without the kids, even for the most logical and important reasons, you give away an advantage by allowing the other parent to become the primary caretaker of the kids. Courts don't like to disrupt the status quo and often put a high value on keeping kids with whomever they've been living with. If you have to get away for a period of time, try to first reach an understanding with your spouse that when you return, the two of you will share custody—and put your agreement in writing.

Avoiding a Custody Battle

If you and your spouse agree on custody, the court will almost certainly accept your arrangement with no questions asked. On the other hand, if you can't agree and you leave the question to the court, anything relating to your life and behavior can be raised in court if it is relevant, and sometimes even when it is not.

In most states, courts can and do order parents to attend mediation sessions any time they can't agree on custody or visitation. But even if a court doesn't order it, mediation is an excellent idea. Mediators work with parents to help them come to a mutually agreeable solution. Mediators, unlike judges, don't impose decisions on parents.

RESOURCE

Get more information. To learn more about child custody mediation and negotiating parenting issues, see *Building a Parenting Agreement That Works: Putting Your Kids First When Your Marriage Doesn't Last*, by Mimi Lyster (Nolo). Also see *Divorce Without Court: A Guide to Mediation and Collaborative Divorce*, by Katherine E. Stoner (Nolo), which has useful worksheets and advice about mediating custody issues.

If You End Up in Court

To decide a contested custody case, the judge will look at "the best interest of the child," sometimes using a report from the custody mediator as a guide. Once the case gets to a judge, any issue that is related to a child's best interest can come up, and your spouse may try to raise all kinds of things—your conviction for possession of hashish in college, your religious preferences, your sloppy housekeeping, and practically anything else that might garner an advantage.

CAUTION

Occasionally, the fact that you are living with a new lover can work against you. Especially if you live in a conservative area, consider carefully before moving in with a new partner while you are in a custody battle.

It's great to do your own legal work whenever possible, but a custody battle is not the time. It's important to work with someone who knows custody laws and has the respect of the local judges and attorneys. See Chapter 11 for advice on finding the right lawyer. Once you pick a lawyer, work with that person to figure out exactly what you want, and then to decide what compromises you're willing to make. In court, you'll have to be prepared to persuade a judge why your "wants" are in your children's best interests.

Visitation (Parenting Time)

If one parent gets sole physical custody, the other parent generally gets visitation rights. "Visitation" is the term that's been used for many years, but recently noncustodial parents have begun lobbying to replace it with "parenting time," a term that is in fact more accurate. Noncustodial parents are not visitors with their children, but parents. We'll use the terms interchangeably here, with a preference for the newer turn of phrase.

Again, you and your ex can make an agreement about visitation without fighting in court. But if you don't, then a judge will decide this issue too. In general, decisions about parenting time involve many of the same issues that come up with a custody case. The significant difference is that the court can deny parenting time only if it finds that the visitation would actually be detrimental to the child.

Before denying (or greatly restricting) a parent's time with the children, the court must find extreme behavior—for example, child abuse, violence, or substance abuse. There is no legal basis for one spouse to ask a court to deny shared parenting to a reasonably responsible parent.

If spouses agree that one parent should have some visitation, the court will probably say that parent should have "reasonable visitation rights" and leave them to work out the details. If, however, they cannot agree, a judge will spell out the parenting schedule, specifying the time, place, and duration of the visits. A judge can impose very specific rules on visitation. For example, a noncustodial parent may be required to give the custodial parent 48 hours' notice before coming to visit. Or a court may prohibit the noncustodial parent from removing the child from the county or the state or, in rare situations, from the child's own home or the home of a third party. It's common for courts to require that parents with histories of drinking not use alcohol while with the children.

But can the court restrain a gay or lesbian parent from visiting with children in the presence of a same-sex partner, or say that the child can't spend the night when the same-sex partner is also in the house? Some courts have said yes, others no. Can a court prohibit a gay father with AIDS from visiting with his children? In most cases, parenting time has been permitted. (Because the children are not at risk of contracting AIDS from their father, there's no medical ground for a prohibition.) But some judges prohibit visitation, supposedly to "protect" the children. If you challenge a judge's ruling in court, you will want an expert to testify on your behalf. If the court rules against you, consider appealing—but don't violate the court order.

Once an order relating to parenting time is entered, it's enforceable just like any other court order. Parents with custody have been known to refuse to comply with visitation orders to spite an ex-spouse. Whatever the motive, it's not in the best interests of the children, and it's illegal. A parent violating a court order can be held in contempt of court, fined, and even jailed. And remember, custody cases don't end until the child reaches age 18. Until that time, the court can change custody or the parenting schedule if the person seeking a change can show that circumstances have changed.

Child Support

In every state, parents are required to support their children. All states now have mathematical formulas to establish support based on each parent's income and how much time each spends with the kids. You can certainly agree to a higher amount, but to go below the guideline you will have to convince the judge that your child will be adequately supported and that there are good reasons for the deviation.

Only legal parents are obligated to support children. If you have a new partner, that person isn't a parent. Your new lover is welcome to pay the bills, but is not required to. However, if the new partner does contribute to your expenses, a court may decide that you need less child support. Or, if you're the person who pays support, the court might decide that your partner's generosity means you have more money to pay child support.

⊘ CAUTION
Failure to support your children is a crime. In all states, whether you were ever married or not, you can be prosecuted criminally for failing to pay child support. It also doesn't matter whether you've separated or actually divorced.

Must You Pay Child Support If Your Ex Prevents You From Visiting Your Kids?

Suppose your ex-spouse refuses to let you have the court-ordered parenting time you're entitled to. Can you retaliate by refusing to pay child support? No. The children have a right to support no matter what. A court may grant a reduction, but don't count on it. However, you probably can seek reimbursement from the custodial parent for costs incurred in trying to exercise your parenting rights.

Dissolving a Straight Marriage

If you are going through a divorce from a straight marriage, all of the basic rules about money, property, debts, and kids described in "Dissolving a Gay Marriage," above, will apply to your breakup—except that you won't have the worry about federal tax issues, because your monetary transfers will be nontaxable. "Officially" your sexual orientation should not matter—any more than having an opposite-sex affair should matter. But, life isn't that simple, and depending on how your spouse reacts to your coming out and depending on where you live, your sexual orientation may well matter a great deal.

Here are our suggestions on how to handle a divorce when you're coming out. As you will see, most of our suggestions aren't technically "legal," because most of the problems are not really legal ones. Rather, they are strategic suggestions on dealing with the very real human emotions of anger, bigotry, and irrationality that formerly married lesbians and gay men often face.

Issues of Money and Property

Your sexual orientation really shouldn't matter when it comes to dividing up the house or paying the debts, but it may well come up. Mostly it's a matter of the straight spouse playing on the guilt of the formerly closeted spouse, or banking on the bias of the judge in staking out an unfair claim on money or property. If this is happening in your divorce, think through whether the claims have any likelihood of succeeding, and also what it could cost you to fight these claims. When figuring out the cost of the fight, don't ignore the risks to your job, or your extended family's treatment of you, nor the impact such a fight can have on a new romantic relationship.

You also will need to get educated about what the legal process will involve, and what discretion the judge actually has in your case. We always urge our readers to fight hard to avoid the negative effects of homophobia, but we are also mindful of how costly these fights can be to the individual warrior! We also encourage you to slow down in your decision-making process, as we've seen many of our gay friends "throw in the towel" way too early out of a sense of guilt for having gotten married in the first place, and then regret those decisions later on. Counseling—for both you and your ex, and possibly jointly—can be extremely valuable in these struggles.

Sexual Orientation and Custody

An increasing number of courts—and even a few state legislatures—have held that a parent's sexual orientation cannot, in and of itself, be grounds for automatic denial of custody. Today, most states require that the person opposing custody by the gay or lesbian parent show an "adverse effect" before a parent's sexual orientation or relationship can be used to restrict custody (or visitation, discussed below).

But it is still fair to say that many judges are ignorant about, prejudiced against, or suspicious of gay and lesbian parents. In 1998, for example, the supreme courts of both Alabama and North Carolina denied custody to parents for the sole reason that the parents were gay. Similarly, the Missouri Supreme Court ruled that a homosexual parent is not automatically unfit to have custody, but denied a lesbian mother custody on the ground of "misconduct"—living with another woman. (*J.A.D. v. F.J.D.*, 978 S.W.2d 336 (1998).) And in Idaho a few years ago, a trial judge awarded sole custody to the former wife of a gay man. During the parties' marriage the husband was the primary caretaker of the children, and after the divorce the parties shared custody cooperatively until the father became involved with another man. The trial court also held that the father may have visitation with the children only if he does not live with his male partner. The case is currently on appeal to the Idaho Supreme Court.

On the other hand, a gay father in Louisiana was recently awarded primary custody of his children over the mother's objections that his "homosexual lifestyle" was detrimental to the kids, and a Michigan court refused to allow evidence of a lesbian mother's purported imposition of her lesbian lifestyle on her daughter, and left custody with the mom.

A Georgia appeals court reversed a decision by a trial court changing custody from a lesbian mother to the father based solely on the fact that the mother was living with another woman. The appeals court held there was no evidence of a change in circumstances or of any adverse affects on the child, and that the change in custody was not warranted.

In a mixed ruling in Virginia, an appeals court ruled that a gay father couldn't be denied joint custody or have his visitation limited because of his sexual orientation, but also upheld the lower court's requirement that the father's partner not spend the night when the children visited.

It's possible that a custody issue can be brought to court by someone other than a parent, and against both parents' wishes. Consider the case of Sharon Bottoms, the lesbian mother from Virginia who lives with her lover. Sharon's mother sued for custody of Sharon's son Tyler, even though Sharon wanted custody and her ex-husband agreed that she should have custody and even testified on her behalf. Nevertheless, the trial court granted custody of Tyler to his grandmother, holding that a lesbian is presumed to be unfit to have custody of her child if she lives with her lover.

National lesbian and gay organizations helped prepare Sharon's appeal, and she briefly regained custody of her son. Sadly, the Virginia Supreme Court ruled that "active lesbianism practiced in the home" could stigmatize the child, and returned Sharon's son to the custody of Sharon's mother. (*Bottoms v. Bottoms*, 457 S.E.2d 102 (1995).)

Some Tips on Custody Cases

If you are involved in a contested custody case because of your sexual orientation, you're in for an expensive process. If you can do some legwork, you'll be more connected to the case and will save some lawyer's fees. For example, don't pay your lawyer $300 an hour to do background preparation you can do yourself. It's often helpful if you give your attorney a list of friends, relatives, children's teachers or day care workers, neighbors, clergy, and anyone else willing to speak on your behalf. Outline what each person is prepared to say and who is likely to impress the judge. That will help your attorney decide whom to call to court. You can also help by gathering records—like school or medical records—that your lawyer needs.

In some custody cases, expert witness testimony is necessary. Expert witnesses are psychiatrists, caseworkers, psychologists, and other professionals who testify in order to educate judges and juries about issues that require specialized knowledge to decide. Experts are particularly important for a gay parent. An expert can evaluate your home environment and testify about your fitness as a parent, your child's health, welfare, relationship to you, and relationship to the home environment.

But most important, an expert can educate the judge about lesbian and gay parents in general. Attorneys who regularly handle custody cases for lesbian and gay parents say that overcoming myths and misconceptions about homosexuality—particularly that gay people are ill, perverted, abnormal, and child molesters, and that their children will be harassed at best and become gay at worst—is the biggest obstacle to winning.

You will need a great deal of support if you are going to engage in a court struggle, and no one can give it to you better than folks who have been there. Use the resources discussed in Chapter 11 to find a local support group for lesbian and gay parents and meet people who have dealt with custody issues.

In most custody cases, judges try to cut through accusations and arguments to learn the facts and decide what's in the child's best interest— and most judges at least try to be objective. While convincing a judge that your sexual orientation is irrelevant may be an uphill battle, it's possible.

Parents caught in custody battles often think about moving to a part of the country where judges are likely to have liberal views. San Francisco can seem like paradise to someone in Oklahoma. Although you may take your child to a new state unless a court order says otherwise, a law called the Uniform Child Custody Jurisdiction Enforcement Act (UCCJEA) may limit a judge's power to make a custody decision in the state to which you move. For instance, if you moved to San Francisco from Oklahoma, the San Francisco judge wouldn't have the authority (called "jurisdiction") to hear your custody request and would send you back to an Oklahoma court.

One purpose of the UCCJEA is to stop parents from moving about in a search for a friendly court. So a court that is asked to decide a custody issue must look at certain specific factors under the UCCJEA to see whether it has jurisdiction, and the judge will be reluctant to take the case if it looks like the parent relocated just to find a sympathetic court. If you've moved, you'd better be able to convince the judge it was for a better job and a better life for your kids, not to find a more enlightened court.

If you and your spouse each begin custody proceedings in different states, the UCCJEA determines which state has jurisdiction. This will probably be the state that you moved from. If your spouse can show that you moved just to find a friendly court, you might even get fined or have to pay the other parent's attorney fees and travel expenses.

If a court in one state has already issued a child custody order, your chance of persuading a court in another state to modify that order is extremely slim. And if you take the child out of state in violation of the order, you may be guilty of kidnapping.

The UCCJEA can work for both parents. Although it greatly limits a gay or lesbian parent's power to move to a more favorable state, it also limits the nongay parent's power to take a child to a conservative jurisdiction, hoping to get a custody change because the other parent is gay.

Domestic Violence in Same-Sex Relationships

Domestic violence and abuse do exist in the LGBT community. While there is still some denial about this, the community has become more responsive in recent years, and there are many more resources now available to those in crisis.

If you are the victim of domestic violence, your number one concern is your own safety. You may be ashamed, embarrassed, or feeling guilty, but it's most important that you get out of your living arrangement and into a safe environment. If you are a lesbian, contact a battered women's shelter. If you're concerned about encountering homophobia—or if you're a gay man with no shelter to turn to—then go to a friend or supportive relative.

A few states, including California, Massachusetts, and Ohio, cover same-sex relationships in their domestic violence statutes. This means that you can get a restraining order to keep the abuser away from you. You may need the help of a lawyer or women's clinic, but many counties now offer self-help information for restraining orders, either online or at the courthouse.

 RESOURCE

Learn more about dealing with domestic violence. Go to www. rainbowdomesticviolence.itgo.com, for research and links on domestic violence in the gay and lesbian community.

The National Domestic Violence Hotline, at 800-799-SAFE, is a toll-free number that provides information to callers (gay and straight) about shelters and assistance programs in their area. You can also check out the hotline's website at www.ndvh.org.

The New York City Gay & Lesbian Anti-Violence Project maintains a website at www.avp.org, and a 24-hour hotline number, 212-714-1141.

San Francisco's Community United Against Violence has a hotline at 415-333-HELP, and a website at www.cuav.org.

Gay Massachusetts residents can contact the Gay Men's Domestic Violence Project at 800-832-1901. Their website is at www.gmdvp.org.

Help Beyond the Book

Hiring a Lawyer 394

    Know What You Want Your Lawyer to Do 395

    Finding a Lawyer 395

    Working With a Lawyer 396

    How Much Lawyers Charge 397

Doing Your Own Legal Research 398

    Library Research 398

    Doing Research Online 402

Legal Organizations 403

    National Lesbian and Gay Legal Organizations 403

    Legal Referrals for People With HIV 405

While many relationship matters can be dealt with using the information and forms in this book, it's not unlikely that there will come a time when you need to get advice or help from a lawyer. Other times, you won't need a lawyer, but you may want to look up a law yourself. This chapter offers information on how to find and negotiate with a lawyer, how to do legal research yourself, and resources you can consult if you need more information or advice.

Hiring a Lawyer

Legal issues have become increasingly complex for same-sex couples in recent years, especially for those who are married or registered as domestic partners or civil union partners—or are considering entering into any of those legal relationships. For many same-sex couples considering a legal commitment, the cost of a consultation with a lawyer is money well spent. A knowledgeable attorney can advise you about the legal and financial consequences of entering into a legal relationship in your state. And if you do decide to marry or register, you may want a premarital or prepartnership agreement. In that case, it's always advisable to have a lawyer work with you on the agreement.

For same-sex partners in states that don't offer any kind of relationship recognition, many of the forms in this book will be adequate. But if you have a situation that isn't covered here or that seems outside the scope of these forms, by all means take your questions to a lawyer in your area. And if the situation is very complicated, there's a lot of money at stake, or children are involved, talk to a lawyer before making any big decisions.

You can ask a lawyer to help you in any of the following ways:
- review documents you've prepared using this book
- advise you about your best course of action in a given situation
- generate more complex forms than those that this book provides
- check your state's laws on a particular subject
- assist you with an adoption, or
- represent you in a breakup or help you get parental rights, custody, or visitation with a child.

Know What You Want Your Lawyer to Do

Before you contact a lawyer, it's important to consider what you want the lawyer to do. Do you want to hand the entire case over to the lawyer? Or do you want the lawyer to do only a part of the case, such as representing you at a court hearing or doing some legal research for you?

There are three primary ways a lawyer can help you.

Consultation and advice. A lawyer can analyze your situation and advise you on your best plan of action. Ideally, the lawyer will explain all of your options so you can make the choice. But keep on your toes. Some lawyers will subtly steer you in the direction they want you to go—and sometimes that will be the one that nets them the largest fee. (On the other hand, sometimes the plan that costs the most really is the best plan. If you feel confused, it may be worth your while to get a second opinion.)

Negotiation. The lawyer can help you negotiate—for example, if you and your ex are in the midst of a nasty breakup.

Representation. For almost any situation involving children—adoption or a fight to see a child you've been coparenting—you may need a lawyer to represent you in court. You might also need representation in a property dispute if you've unsuccessfully tried every possibility to settle your breakup issues.

Try to figure out what you are looking for before shopping for a lawyer, if possible. If you want to start out negotiating but fear you might end up in court, make sure you find a lawyer who is comfortable in both roles, as negotiator and litigator.

Finding a Lawyer

Finding a lawyer isn't a problem; the surplus is huge. But finding the right lawyer can be difficult. Make sure any lawyer you hire is familiar with the issues that are affecting you—don't hire a bankruptcy lawyer to review your contract to buy a house. Obviously, any lawyer you hire should have some knowledge of LGBT issues, but that doesn't mean they need be lesbian or gay themselves. Still, a lawyer-client relationship should be one of trust and confidence; you should feel very comfortable coming out to your lawyer, and should do so at the outset. Also, if your attorney doesn't meet your initial expectations, you have the absolute right to fire the first one and hire another lawyer.

A good way to find an attorney is through a referral from a satisfied and knowledgeable customer. People who have asked a lawyer to help them draw up prepartnership agreements or wills, or have been represented in a custody dispute, may be able to give you the name of a good lawyer for those tasks.

If that doesn't work, try a lawyer referral service, which can give you the names of lawyers in your area who handle the type of issue you have. Most county bar associations, which you can find listed in the phone book, operate these services. If you are lucky, you will get a referral to a competent, experienced person. Unfortunately, many lawyer referral services don't do much screening, so some of the lawyers who participate may not be the most experienced or competent available. This can be a problem when you are dealing with cutting-edge legal issues like same-sex marriages or custody cases, so be sure to check out the credentials and experience of any lawyer to whom you are referred.

You can try using a lawyer directory, too, including Nolo's directory at lawyers.nolo.com. Other legal websites, like findlaw.com, also have lawyer directories.

Another option is to call one of the organizations listed in "Legal Organizations," below. In some areas, lesbian and gay bar associations, like Bay Area Lawyers for Individual Freedom (BALIF) in San Francisco (www.balif.org), can provide referrals to local lawyers. LGBT websites often have referral links, too.

Working With a Lawyer

No matter what approach you take to finding a lawyer, here are some suggestions for making sure you have a good working relationship.

First, fight the urge to wholly surrender your problems to the "expert." You should be the one who decides what you feel comfortable doing about your legal affairs. Keep in mind that you're hiring the lawyer to perform legal services, not make decisions about what you should do.

When you talk with the lawyer, ask some specific questions. Do you get clear, concise answers? If not, try someone else. If the lawyer says little except to agree to take over your problem—with a substantial fee—watch out. You're probably talking with someone who doesn't know the answer and won't admit it, or someone who is likely to be paternalistic or pushy with you. If the lawyer admits lack of knowledge about some particular issue, that isn't necessarily bad. In most cases, the lawyer must do some research to find out how best to handle your specific situation.

Once you find a lawyer you like, make an appointment to discuss your situation fully. Most will agree to do this for a nominal cost. Your goal at this initial meeting is to find out what the lawyer recommends and how much it will cost. Go home and think about the lawyer's suggestions. If they don't make complete sense or if you have reservations, call another lawyer and continue the search.

How Much Lawyers Charge

Misunderstandings often arise between lawyers and clients over fees. You can help reduce the likelihood of a fee dispute if you have a clear agreement in writing, signed by both of you. If the lawyer doesn't mention a written fee agreement, ask about one.

If all you want is a consultation with an attorney to find out your options, in most cases the lawyer should not charge much more than $300 to $400 per hour. Some charge as little as $200 an hour, while others charge $350 or more. If the lawyer is a recognized expert in the field, or if you are in a major urban area, the fees are likely to be higher.

If you want the lawyer to do some negotiating on your behalf, the fees could be substantial. A letter doesn't take that long to write, however, and as long as you are clear about what you want the lawyer to do and not do, you can keep the bill on the low end.

If you hire a lawyer to represent you, the lawyer's fee will probably add up fast. Some lawyers might represent you for a flat fee, for example $1,000 to $2,000 for a routine adoption, but most charge by the hour. If you enter into an hourly arrangement, it's best to write into the agreement a cap on the amount of time or fees that the lawyer can charge without your permission.

Hiring a lawyer just to review your legal documents sounds like a good idea. It shouldn't cost much, and seems to offer a comforting security. But it may be difficult, or even impossible in some cases, to find a lawyer who will accept the job. From the lawyer's point of view, he or she is being asked to accept what might turn into a significant responsibility for not much compensation. Any prudent lawyer sees every client as a potential occasion for a malpractice claim, or at least, serious later hassles—a phone call four years down the line that begins, "We talked to you about our living together contract and now…." Many experienced lawyers want to avoid this kind of exposure.

Also, many lawyers feel they simply can't get deeply enough into a situation to be sure of their opinions if they're only reviewing someone else's work. All you can do here is keep trying to find a sympathetic lawyer—or be prepared to pay more, enough so the lawyer can feel secure in having had enough time to review your documents thoroughly.

Doing Your Own Legal Research

If you are not involved in contested litigation, you have an alternative to hiring a lawyer: Learn to do your own legal research, and learn about the law yourself. All you need is a little bit of patience and a good road map.

Library Research

Many courts all over the country maintain law libraries that are open to the public, not just to lawyers and judges. Public law libraries are often housed in county courthouses, state-funded law schools, and state capitals. If you can't find one, ask a reference librarian in the public library, a court clerk, or a lawyer.

Some larger public libraries also have extensive collections of law and legal research books, so before making a special trip to the law library, you may first want to check with your main branch public library.

If you conclude that you need to visit a law library to answer your question, a law librarian will be your most valuable guide. Most law librarians in public libraries are very helpful—as long as you don't expect them to do the research for you, they will be happy to help you locate the materials you need.

Here's what you should find in an average law library:

- the text of your state's laws (statutes and regulations)
- published court opinions interpreting your state's laws, and
- legal articles containing explanations of laws.

RESOURCE

For more on legal research: *Legal Research: How to Find & Understand the Law,* by Stephen Elias and Susan Levinkind (Nolo), can help you find your way around the law library.

Statutes and Regulations

Once you get to the library, ask a librarian to help locate your state's statutes—called "codes," "laws," or "statutes," depending on the state. These are the laws made for your state by the state legislature. You'll want the annotated version, which contains the statutes, excerpts from relevant cases, and cross-references to related articles.

Once you find the statutes, check the index for the subject you need to learn about. State statutes are often divided into sections. The major section often is the Civil Code, which usually contains laws relating to contracts, living together, divorce, custody, adoption, and credit. (Sometimes divorce and other family issues are broken out into a separate Family Code.) The Probate Code contains laws relating to wills and living trusts. There are other codes as well—insurance codes, real property codes, criminal codes, welfare codes, and more. The codes are each numbered sequentially, and once you get the code number from the index, it's easy to find the law you need. If you have trouble, ask the law librarian for help. Sample statute citations are shown below.

Once you look at the statute in the hardcover volume, check the paperback pocket part at the back of the book for any amendments. Then skim the summaries of recent court decisions contained in the "Annotation" section immediately following the statute itself. If a particular summary looks helpful, you can read the entire case from which the summary was taken.

Sample State Statute Citations

23   Vt. Stat. Ann.   § 1185

title (volume   Vermont Statutes   section
number)   Annotated   number

N.J. Stat. Ann.   2A: 170-90.1

New Jersey Statutes   volume   section
Annotated   number   number

Mich. Comp. Laws Ann.   421.27   (c)(2)(ii)

Michigan Compiled Laws   section   subsection
Annotated   number   letter

Some states' laws are divided up into several different topical sections. In states such as New York and California, citations look like those shown below.

Sample California and New York Citations

P.C.   § 518

Penal   section
Code   number

Penal Law   § 14025

Collection   section
of Penal   number
Statutes

Case Decisions

In addition to the laws made by the legislature, judges also make law when they decide cases. Judicial cases are printed in books called reporters. Interpreting a case citation is fairly simple once you learn the abbreviations. For example, the citation to the Hawaii marriage case is *Baehr v. Miike*, 852 P.2d 44 (Hawaii 1993). What does this mean?

Baehr is the plaintiff—the person bringing the lawsuit—and Miike is the defendant—the person who is sued. The "P" in P.2d stands for Pacific Reporter—and 2d means the case appears in the second series of these reporter volumes. The volume in which the case appears is the number before the name of the series; here you want Volume 852. The number after the reporter name is the page on which the case starts: Here it's page 44. The parentheses contain the jurisdiction that decided the case and the year of the decision.

You can also find cases from your state and all the others online—see "Doing Research Online," below.

Other Resources

Another important library tool may be a legal encyclopedia, such as the ALR and Am.Jur. series. These are indexed by subject (such as custody, insurance, homosexuality, guardianship) and provide a synopsis of your state's law on the subject.

Also, ask the law librarian to show you form books. These are collections of sample legal forms that lawyers use in dealing with common legal tasks. Finally, ask if your state has any books designed to keep lawyers up to date. Most larger states have practice manuals, which are fairly easy to use.

Unfortunately, the law for gay and lesbian couples is quite volatile and often hard to place into standard legal categories. For these reasons, doing legal research in this area can be particularly daunting.

Doing Research Online

Because the law dealing with gay and lesbian issues is changing fast, this area is especially well suited to online research. In looking for information on your issue, you can check general interest legal websites as well as sites that gather legal information of specific interest to gays and lesbians.

Below is a selection of general legal websites that can assist you in doing research.

- www.nolo.com. Nolo's website has a wide array of free legal information for consumers. You can also find links to state and federal statutes from the site.
- www.law.cornell.edu. The Legal Information Institute at Cornell Law School is a well-organized and easy to use general legal website.
- www.findlaw.com. FindLaw's extensive database allows you to search for state and federal statutes and cases, and provides links to many courts around the country.

"Legal Organizations," below, lists contact information—including website addresses—for several national gay and lesbian organizations. The websites of these organizations often contain legal updates on issues covered in this book. In addition, here is a list of other websites that can guide you in your research.

- www.hrc.org. This is the website of the Human Rights Campaign, a legislative advocacy group. The site contains news about legislation and court battles on the topics covered in this book.
- www.qrd.org. The family and parenting section of the *Queer Resources Directory* contains downloadable files and links on issues like same-sex marriage, domestic partnerships, and gay and lesbian adoption and parenting. This site isn't updated regularly but can be a useful archive. Just be aware the information isn't current.
- www.buddybuddy.com. This is the site sponsored by the Partners Task Force for Gay & Lesbian Couples. The site contains information and links of interest to gay and lesbians partners, covering topics such as marriage, immigration, and parenting.

New York's LGBT Community Center has an "Equality Map" on its website at www.gaycenter.org; you can learn about LGBT issues in your state.

Legal Organizations

Many national lesbian and gay legal organizations, local LGBT bar associations, and local LGBT community centers make lawyer referrals. If there's no referral organization near you and you can't find a lawyer to help you with your problem, try calling one of the national organizations, a local chapter of the American Civil Liberties Union (ACLU), or the National Lawyers Guild.

Someone on the other end of the phone may be able to give you the name of a local lawyer, or just offer a sympathetic ear. And if you have a lawyer, your lawyer may want to contact one of the national lesbian and gay legal groups to get some support. Many of the legal problems lesbians and gay men encounter have been faced before—a lawyer who works full time in the struggle for gay and lesbian rights probably has helpful materials or suggestions.

National Lesbian and Gay Legal Organizations

Lambda Legal Defense and Education Fund
National Office
120 Wall Street, Suite 1500
New York, NY 10005-3904
212-809-8585 (voice)
212-809-0055 (fax)
www.lambdalegal.org

Midwestern Regional Office
11 East Adams Street, Suite 1008
Chicago, IL 60603-6303
312-663-4413 (voice)
312-663-4307 (fax)

Southern Regional Office
730 Peachtree Street, NE, Suite 1070
Atlanta, GA 30309-3027
404-897-1880 (voice)
404-897-1884 (fax)

South Central Regional Office
3500 Oak Lawn Avenue, Suite 500
Dallas, TX 75219-6722
214-219-8585 (voice)
214-219-4455 (fax)
www.lambdalegal.org/scro

Western Regional Office
3325 Wilshire Blvd., Suite 1800
Los Angeles, CA 90036-3617
213-382-7600 (voice)
213-351-6050 (fax)

National Center for Lesbian Rights
870 Market Street, Suite 370
San Francisco, CA 94102
415-392-6257 (voice)
415-392-8442 (fax)
www.nclrights.org

Human Rights Campaign
1640 Rhode Island Avenue, NW,
Washington, DC 20036-3278
202-628-4160 (voice)
202-347-5323 (fax)
202-216-1572 (TTY)
www.hrc.org

National Gay and Lesbian Task Force
1325 Massachusetts Avenue, NW, Suite 600
Washington, DC 20005
202-393-5177 (voice)
202-393-2241 (fax)
202-393-2284 (TTY)
www.thetaskforce.org

Gay and Lesbian Advocates and Defenders (GLAD)

30 Winter Street, Suite 800

Boston, MA 02108

617-426-1350 (voice)

617-426-3594 (fax)

www.glad.org

American Civil Liberties Union (ACLU)

Lesbian & Gay Rights and AIDS Projects

125 Broad Street, 18th Floor

New York, NY 10004

212-549-2627 (voice)

www.aclu.org

Legal Referrals for People With HIV

If you need legal assistance and don't know where to turn, check your local telephone directory or the Internet for an HIV-specific legal organization, a legal aid or legal services office, or your city or county's bar association. Many of those groups can provide HIV-related legal referrals. You should also check with the national and regional LGBT legal associations listed in the previous section. The American Bar Association maintains a clearinghouse for legal information about AIDS and HIV. Here is the contact information:

ABA AIDS Coordination Project

750 15th St., NW

Washington, DC 20005-1009

202-662-1025 (voice)

www.abanet.org/AIDS/home.html

Using the Interactive Forms

Editing RTFs 408

List of Forms 409

T his book comes with interactive files that you can access online at www.nolo.com/back-of-book/LG16.html. To use the files, your computer must have specific software programs *installed*. The files provided for this book are in RTF format. You can open, edit, print, and save these form files with most word processing programs such as Microsoft *Word*, Windows *WordPad*, and recent versions of *WordPerfect*.

TIP

Note to Macintosh users. These forms were designed for use with Windows. They should also work on Macintosh computers; however Nolo cannot provide technical support for non-Windows users.

Editing RTFs

Here are some general instructions about editing RTF forms in your word processing program. Refer to the book's instructions and sample agreements for help about what should go in each blank.

- **Underlines.** Underlines indicate where to enter information. After filling in the needed text, delete the underline. In most word processing programs you can do this by highlighting the underlined portion and typing CTRL+U.
- **Bracketed and italicized text.** Bracketed and italicized text indicates instructions. Be sure to remove all instructional text before you finalize your document.
- **Optional text.** Optional text gives you the choice to include or exclude text. Delete any optional text you don't want to use. Renumber numbered items, if necessary.
- **Alternative text.** Alternative text gives you the choice between two or more text options. Delete those options you don't want to use. Renumber items, if necessary.
- **Signature lines.** Signature lines should appear on a page with at least some text from the document itself.

Every word processing program uses different commands to open, format, save, and print documents, so refer to your software's help documents for help using your program. Nolo cannot provide technical support for questions about how to use your computer or your software.

CAUTION

In accordance with U.S. copyright laws, the forms provided for this book are for your personal use only.

List of Forms

To download the following forms go to:

www.nolo.com/back-of-book/LG16.html

File Name	Form Name
Renting Together Agreement	RentingTogether.rtf
Moving-In Agreement	MovingIn.rtf
Agreement to Jointly Raise Our Child	RaiseChild.rtf
Parenting Agreement	Parenting.rtf
Nomination of Guardian for a Minor	GuardianNomination.rtf
Donor Insemination Agreement	Donor.rtf
Contract Regarding Child Support and Custody	ChildSupport.rtf
Temporary Guardianship Agreement	TemporaryGuardian.rtf
Authorization to Consent to Medical, Surgical, or Dental Examination or Treatment of a Minor	MedicalAuthorization.rtf
Will	Will.rtf
Codicil	Codicil.rtf
Mediation-Arbitration Clause #1	Mediation1.rtf
Mediation-Arbitration Clause #2	Mediation2.rtf
Agreement to Keep Income and Accumulations Separate	SeparateIncome.rtf

File Name	Form Name
Agreement to Combine Income and Accumulations	CombineIncome.rtf
Agreement for Joint Outright Purchase	JointPurchase.rtf
Agreement Regarding Jointly Owned Item Purchased on Credit in One Partner's Name	CreditPurchase.rtf
Contract for Long-Term Couples	LongTerm.rtf
Living Together Agreement—Keeping Things Separate	SeparateAgreement.rtf
Living Together Agreement—Sharing Most Property	SharingAgreement.rtf
Agreement for Sharing Household Expenses	SharingHousehold.rtf
Joint Project Agreement #2	JointProject2.rtf
Agreement Allowing Alternating Time Off	TimeOff.rtf
Agreement for Educational Support	EducationalSupport.rtf
Agreement for Compensating a Homemaker	Homemaker.rtf
Contract for Equal Ownership of Real Property	EqualOwnership.rtf
Contract for Ownership of Real Property and Payments Split Unequally	UnequalOwnership.rtf
Promissory Note for Down Payment Money	PromissoryNote.rtf
Contract When One Owner Does Not Live on the Premises #1	AbsentOwner1.rtf
Contract When One Owner Does Not Live on the Premises #2	AbsentOwner2.rtf
Contract for Sale of a Share of House	ShareSale.rtf
Postseparation Agreement Regarding Housing	HousingAgreement.rtf
Settlement Agreement	SettlementAgreement.rtf
Agreement Regarding Mediation and Arbitration	MediationAgreement.rtf
Postseparation Parenting Agreement	SeparateParenting.rtf

Index

A

AB trusts, 238
Adopting a child
  agency adoptions, 141–144
  "black market" adoptions, 144–145
  international adoptions, 145–148
  joint adoptions, 106
  legal requirements, 139–140
  open and closed adoptions, 141
  overview, 138–139, 140
  private adoptions, 144–145
  second parent legal adoption, 106, 107–112
  state bans on, 31
  stepparent adoptions, 108–109
  Virginia ruling on, 14
  See also Birth certificates; Parenting, second
    parent protections
Adopting your partner, 30–31, 81
Adoption fraud, international, 146
Advance Health Care Directives, 166, 177
Advance planning in case of separation/
  divorce, 338–339
AIDS and custody battles, 386
Airline companies, 20–21
Alabama, 31, 389
Alaska, 14
Alimony, 44, 379
Alternate attorney-in-fact, 182
Alternatives to Marriage Project website, 18, 71
American Law Institute, 14
Andorra, 24
Annuities, 192–193, 245

Anonymous sperm donors, 122–123
Antidiscrimination ordinance, 86–87
Appraisals
  appointment of, 328–329
  of business value, 277
  of home value, 303, 355
  for jointly owned goods, 265
Arbitration, 258, 347–350
Arbitration and mediation agreement, 348,
  349–350
Arbitration and mediation clause of living
  together contracts, 257–260, 270–271,
  272–273
Arkansas, 149–150, 361
Attorney-in-fact
  for finances, 181–182, 183, 185, 187–189
  for health care decisions, 173, 174–175
  powers portion of document, 189–194
Attorney-mediators, 258
Attorneys. *See* Lawyers, consulting with
Australia, 24, 29, 83
Austria, 24
Auto insurance, 21, 72–73. *See also* Vehicles

B

Baehr v. Miike, 23, 26
Banks
  and durable power of attorney for finances,
  191
  joint accounts, 62–63, 339, 340, 359
  pay-on-death bank accounts, 231–232
  See also Credit accounts; Durable power of
    attorney for finances; Mortgages

Belgium, 83

Beneficiaries

alternate beneficiary, 219, 220

of life insurance, 223

reciprocal beneficiaries, 23, 54

of retirement plan, 243–244, 245

survivorship period, 222

of trusts, 230

See also Wills

Benefits outside employment, 20–21

Benefits related to employment, 17–20

Bigamy, 40–41

Birth certificates

for adopted children, 140, 147–148

completing the birth certificate, 134–136

for lesbians and gay men parenting together, 136, 138

new birth certificate after second-parent adoption, 112–113, 136

"Black market" adoptions, 144–145

Brazil, 83

Breaking up. *See* Ending a relationship; Separation process

Burial and body disposition, 177–180

Business interests and durable power of attorney for finances, 191–192

Business partnership model of marriage, 61

Buying a home together

contracts for home purchase and ownership, 309–310

and ending the relationship, 354–359

equal ownership agreement, 310–312, 313

finding a house, 289–292

historical perspective, 289

overview, 288–289

ownership models, 305–309

selling your home, 357–358

See also Mortgages; Real estate

Buying a home, unequal shares ownership agreement

complicated contributions contracts, 320–323

group ownership, not all owners live in the house, 323–330

moving into a home owned by your lover, 330–333

one person buys the house, the other fixes it up, 317–320

overview, 313

two-third/one-third ownership, 313–315

unequal ownership with provision for equal ownership, 316

Buyout of home share when ending the relationship, 354–357

C

California

employer requirements, 17

fight for same-sex marriage, 43

foster care placement of gay kids, 152–153

fostering parenting in, 149

mortgage lenders disclose consumer's credit score, 293

overview, 21–22, 125

paid family leave, 11

parentage law, 361–362

property transfers at death of one partner, 206–207

same-sex adult adoptions, 30

San Francisco, 2004, 4, 8, 43

stepparent procedures for adoptions, 109

and transgender partners, 29

unemployment benefits, 10

workers' compensation death benefits, 11

See also Domestic partnerships; Marriage-equivalent states

California court cases
  on adoption agency discrimination, 143
  discrimination by country club, 14
  emotional distress award for unmarried partner, 13
  on fertility clinic discrimination, 122
  on parent-child relationships, 114, 133
  on same-sex marriage, 43
  on sperm donor rights, 125
  and Uniform Parentage Act, 113
California Franchise Tax Board, 70
California's domestic partnership law
  ending a relationship, 45–48
  inheritance rights of your partner, 200–201
  and name change, 75
  overview, 41
  rights and responsibilities, 44–45
Cambodia, 146
Canada, 26–27, 83, 114
Cars. *See* Vehicles
Cases, researching, 401. *See also* California court cases; Court cases and legislative action
Cash and credit
  buying and investing together, 67–68
  joint accounts, 61–66, 339
  overview, 60
  and taxes, 68–70
  See also Banks; Buying a home together; Credit accounts; Durable power of attorney for finances
Challenges to wills, 202
Charitable trusts, 239
Child custody and support
  both legal parents, 366
  child's best interests, 128, 384, 391
  coming out after straight marriage, 388–391
  court decision on, 375
  custody battles, 384–385, 390
  foster care mother fights for, 150
  guardians, 115, 120, 153, 158, 203–204, 205
  leaving your children with other parent, 383
  legal parent's right to visitation or, 102, 103, 105, 366
  negotiating as a couple, 340
  one legal parent, 367–370
  overview, 360–361, 381
  and parentage law, 361–366
  parenting agreements on, 117, 118–119, 137, 138
  and sexual orientation when leaving a straight marriage, 388–391
  and sperm donors, 126, 129
  transgender parents, 381–382
  types of custody, 383
  visitation, 385–386
  See also Child support
Children
  agreements with teenagers, 158–160
  and California's domestic partnership law, 44
  clause in will, 212–213, 218
  considering feelings of, 367–368
  and ending a relationship, 109, 121
  gifts of property to, 204–205
  and marriage choice, 58
  in marriage-equivalent states, 36–37
  providing for in a will, 203–205
  and tax filing status, 70
  See also Birth certificates; Child custody and support; Child support; Guardians and guardianships; entries beginning with "Parenting"
Child's trust, 205
Child support
  federal income taxes on, 380
  overview, 386–387

prepartnership agreements not used for, 53
and sperm donors, 126, 129, 130, 137
See also Child custody and support
China, 145
Citizenship of children adopted abroad, 148
Civil Code, 399–400
Civil unions
domestic partnership vs., in New Jersey, 51
effects of marriage-equivalent systems, 52
and employee benefits, 17
inheritance rights of your partner, 201
LGBT-friendly rulings, 11
marriage-equivalent state laws, 49–52
not available in right-to-marry states, 22
overview, 21–22
in Vermont, 26
See also Prepartnership agreements
Clinton, Hilary, 11
"Closed" and "open" adoptions, 141
Closing costs, 303–305
Club membership discounts, 21
Club membership discrimination, 14
COBRA coverage, 20
Codicils, 233–226
Cohabitation laws and alimony, 379
Collaborative practice, 346–347, 380
College domestic partnership benefits, 21
Colorado
ban on adoption by same-sex couples, 31
marriage lite, 53–54
overview, 21–22
parentage law, 362
sick leave to care for partner, 12
on sperm donor rights, 125
Columbia, 24
Comfort care, 171
Coming out in a divorce situation, 387–391
Community property laws, 44, 56, 69, 299

Compromise, 374
Conditional durable power of attorney, 174
Connecticut, 21–22, 52, 126. *See also* Marriage equality states
Contracts
historical perspective, 9
implied, 63, 93, 250, 251–252, 371–372
importance of, 249
for jointly acquired items, 255, 265–267
modifying, 285
oral contracts, 200, 250, 251–252, 371–373
simplicity of, 323
and taxes, 285
See also Living together contracts
Cooling off clause of living together contracts, 256–257, 270, 272
Coparenting agreements, 115–119, 121
Corporate Equality Index, 18
Costa Rica, 146
Cotenants, 89, 93, 94, 97
Counseling, 257
Court case decisions, researching, 401
Court cases and legislative action
child custody while coming out, 388–391
on discrimination based on religion, 86
on discrimination by adoption agencies, 143
on genetic mother's rights, 133
government benefits, 10–11
on marriage with sex change, 29–30
on parental rights of sperm donor, 124–125, 126
on same-sex marriage, 23, 26, 37, 43
same-sex partnership recognition, 12–15, 23, 26
on second-parent adoption, 107–108, 112, 113, 361
on third-parent adoptions, 114
on transgender parents, 381–382

on unmarried couples, 13, 249, 250
See also California court cases; Federal laws
Court hearings
for adoptions, 140, 142–143
formal guardianships, 153, 158
public nature of, 352
for visitation rights, 385–386
Court order for a name change, 74–77
Credit accounts
closing when relationship ends, 360
and credit score, 293
joint accounts, 63–64, 339, 340
purchasing a jointly-owned item on one
partner's card, 266–267
See also Mortgages
Credit bureaus, 65–66
Credit discrimination, 65–65
Credit score, 293
Cremation, 179–180
Croatia, 24
Custody. *See* Child custody and support
Czech Republic, 24

D

Defense of Marriage Act, federal (DOMA)
conflict between state marriage laws and, 38,
40, 68–69, 377–378
and divorce, 377–378
and employer benefits, 40
and estate taxes, 235
and foreign service officers, 11
and marriage-based visa, 79
and military service, 36
overview, 23, 26, 32
and public benefits, 99
and social security disability benefits for
children, 11
tax issues related to, 68–69, 377, 380

Defense of marriage acts, state, 23, 26, 38–39
Delaware
employer requirements, 17
marriage-equivalent laws, 48–52
overview, 21–22
parentage law, 362
same-sex adult adoptions, 30
See also Marriage-equivalent states
Denmark, 24, 83
Direct discussions, 344–345
Disability benefits, 44, 98
Disability insurance, 71
Discrimination
by adoption agencies, 142, 143
and coming out when leaving a straight
marriage, 388–391
credit, 65–65
by landlord, 86–88
of lenders, 301–302
at retirement community, 14
Disinheriting (except spouses) in a will, 209
Dispute resolution
arbitration, 258, 347–350
arbitration and mediation agreement, 348,
349–350
collaborative practice, 346–347, 380
direct discussions, 344–345
litigation, 352–353
overview, 343–344
settlement agreement, 350–352
See also Mediation
District of Columbia
employer requirements, 17
overview, 21–22
on sperm donor's rights, 123
surviving partner as "next of kin," 12
See also Marriage equality states
Diversity Immigrant Visa Lottery, 81–82

Divorce
  alimony, 379
  and bequests in your will, 224
  in California, 42
  dividing property and assets, 376–378
  overview, 39, 41, 336–338, 337, 373–375
  separation or "no-fault" divorce, 375–376,
    379
  state laws on, 50, 375–376
  state of residence at time of, 39, 56, 377–378
  from straight marriage, 387–391
  tax problems, 379–380
  See also Ending a relationship; Separation
    process
DNR (do not resuscitate) orders, 169
Doctor-assisted suicide, 176
DOMA. *See* Defense of Marriage Act, federal
Domestic abuse or violence, 339, 392
Domestic Partner Rights and Responsibilities
  Act (CA—2005), 42
Domestic partnership forms, employer-
  provided, 20
Domestic Partnership Organizing Manual for
  Employee Benefits (NGLTF Policy Institute),
  18
Domestic partnerships
  benefits outside employment, 20–21
  and bigamy, 40–41
  civil union vs., in New Jersey, 51
  employee benefits for, 17–20
  formal termination of, 32
  and gift taxes, 242
  and health care decisions, 163
  history of, 16
  and home mortgages, 299–300
  marriage-equivalent state laws, 49–52
  marriage lite, 53–55
  not available in right-to-marry states, 22

  overview, 15–18, 21–22
  See also California's domestic partnership
    law; Civil unions; Parenting, second parent
    protections; Prepartnership agreements
Donor insemination
  anonymous donor, 122–123
  donor insemination agreements, 127–131
  known donor, 124–125, 127–131
  legal cases involving sperm donors, 126
  overview, 121–122
  and public benefits, 132
Down payment for a home, 295–296
Durable power of attorney for finances
  attorney-in-fact, 181–182, 183, 185, 187–189
  expiration at your death, 180
  overview, 181–184
  sample document, 185–196
Durable power of attorney for health care, 166,
  167, 172–173, 174

E

Ecuador, 24
Education and living together contracts,
  281–282
Egg donation/ovum sharing, 106–107,
  132–133
Electronic wills, 210
Employer-recognized partnerships, 16–17
Employer requirements, 17
Employment-based green cards, 82
Employment benefits
  and California's domestic partnership law,
    44
  contractor requirements, 12
  and federal DOMA, 40
  overview, 17–20
  and same-sex marriage, 40
  sick leave, 12

Ending a relationship
domestic partnership or civil union, 45–48,
50
home ownership agreement clause, 311,
314–315, 317–318, 322, 334
and joint tenancy ownership of a home, 331
leaving your children with other parent, 383
legal marriage, 39, 41
overview, 31–32, 336–338
and rental unit you've lived in, 90, 91, 97–98
See also Child custody and support;
Separation process
Equal Benefits Law (New York), 12
Equal Credit Opportunity Act, 65
Escrow and closing costs, 303–305
Estate planning
estimating value of your property, 228, 229,
234, 235–236
joint tenancy with right of survivorship,
233–234, 235
life insurance, 234, 240–241
overview, 180–181, 198–199, 227
probate avoidance, 228, 230–234
resources, 246
retirement accounts, 234, 243–245
tax-saving trusts, 238–239
See also Durable power of attorney for
finances; Wills
Estate taxes
avoiding or reducing, 238–241
federal, 58, 234–236, 237–238
gifts and gift taxes, 233, 241–242
and life insurance, 240–241
overview, 234
state inheritance taxes, 234, 236–237
Eviction, 87–88, 92
Exchange visitor visas, 83

Executor of your estate, 206–207, 213–214,
220
Expenses clause of living together contracts,
255–256
Experts. See Lawyers, consulting with; Tax
professionals, consulting with
Expert witnesses for child custody cases, 390

F
Fair Credit Reporting Act, 65
Family
defining, 8, 9
maintenance of, 193–194
paid family leave, 11
values, 2
See also Children; entries beginning with
"Parenting"
Fault issues in divorces, 375–376
FDA (Food and Drug Administration), 127
Federal court
LGBT-friendly rulings, 13, 40, 43, 112
Supreme Court, 23, 26–27, 165
unfriendly rulings, 86
Federal estate taxes, 58, 234–236, 237–238
Federal income taxes, 230, 239, 283, 380
Federal laws
on citizenship of children adopted abroad,
148
Equal Credit Opportunity Act, 65
Fair Credit Reporting Act, 65
and marriage-based visas, 79–80
Pension Protection Act, 245
and property transfers at death of one
spouse, 56, 58
See also Defense of Marriage Act, federal;
Taxes, federal
Fertility clinics, 122, 132–133
Film wills, 210

Financial institution forms for durable power
  of attorney, 183
Financial matters. *See* Money issues
Financial statement, 294–295
Finland, 24, 83
Florida
  ban on adoption by same-sex couples, 31
  lesbian refused access to dying lover, 15
  parentage law, 362
  pension rights denied, 14–15
  and transgender partners, 29
Food and Drug Administration (FDA), 127
Formal (court-appointed) guardians, 153, 158
Forms, about, 6, 408–410. *See also* Health care
  documents; specific forms
Foster parenting, 149–153
France, 24, 83
FSBO ("for sale by owner") property, 291–292
Funeral parlors, 179
Funerals, 178–179, 180

G

Generation-skipping transfer tax, 238–239
Generation-skipping trusts, 239
Georgia, 389
Germany, 24, 83
Gifts
  alimony considered to be, for federal tax
    purposes, 380
  clause of a will, 213, 219–220
  life insurance policy as, 240–241
  received by one partner, 255, 270, 272, 279
Gift taxes
  for adding partner's name to a deed, 309
  gifts and, 233, 241–242
  and income pooling of partners, 256
  overview, 285

and paying your partner for extra work at
  home, 283
Government-arranged contractual
  relationships, 248, 253. *See also* Marriage
Government benefits
  and durable power of attorney for finances,
    194
  overview, 9
  paid family leave, 11
  partner benefits for diplomats, 11
  pension benefits, 11
  Social Security benefits, 11
  unemployment benefits for caretakers, 10
  unemployment benefits for relocation, 10–11
  workers' compensation death benefits, 11
  See also Public agencies
Grantor of a trust, 230
Group ownership of a home, contracts for,
  323–330
Guardians and guardianships
  foster parenting, 149–153
  for incapacitated adults, 162, 193
  nominating in your postseparation parenting
    agreement, 370
  nominating in your will, 115, 116, 119, 120,
    203–204, 205, 212–213
  overview, 153–158
  and sperm donor agreement, 130
  standby guardian, 218

H

Hague Adoption Convention, 146
Handwritten wills, 210
Hawaii
  employer requirements, 17
  marriage-equivalent laws, 48–52
  overview, 21–22
  reciprocal beneficiaries, 23

See also Marriage-equivalent states

Health care decisions
  and California's domestic partnership law, 44
  for children, 115
  and informal guardianships, 155, 157
  marriage-equality states, 49
  marriage-like states, 54–55
  overview, 162–164, 164–165
  terminology, 174
Health care documents
  attorney-in-fact, 173, 174–175
  body disposition instructions, 177–178
  DNR orders, 169
  durable power of attorney, 166, 167, 172–173, 174
  expiration of, 163
  filling out the forms, 168–173
  finalizing, 175–176
  living will, 165, 167
  overview, 165–167
  reasons for having, 163
  state forms, 167–168
Health insurance, 71
Historical perspectives
  on divorce, 337
  parenting, 103
  political struggle, 9, 103
  real property ownership, 289
HIV, legal referrals for people with, 405
Holographic wills, 210
Home inspections, 300–301
Homemaker contract, 282–284
Homeowner's insurance, 72
Home values, 292
Household expense and chore-share contracts, 274, 275
Human Rights Campaign website, 18
Hungary, 24

I

ICE (U.S. Immigration and Customs Enforce), 79–80
Iceland, 83
Idaho, 389
Illinois
  employer requirements, 17
  marriage-equivalent laws, 48–52
  overview, 21–22
  on sperm donor rights, 125
  and transgender partners, 29, 381–382
  See also Marriage-equivalent states
Immigration issues
  and domestic partnership registration, 36
  employment-based green cards, 82
  exchange visitor visas, 83
  international residency rights, 83
  marriage-based visas, 79–80
  "marriage of convenience" to a U.S. citizen, 80
  moving to the United States, 79–84
  overview, 77
  political asylum, 81
  student visas, 83
  temporary employment visas, 82–83
  visa lottery, 81–82
  visiting the United States, 77–78
Implied contracts, 63, 93, 250, 251–252, 371–372
Incapacity, defining, 166, 174, 186–187
Income, alimony as, for federal tax purposes, 380
Income taxes
  federal, 230, 239, 283, 380
  state, 45, 68, 70
Indiana, 126, 363
Informal domestic partnerships, 15–16

Informal guardianships, 153, 154–158

Inheritance laws

and California's domestic partnership law, 44

in marriage-equality states, 50

in marriage-like states, 54–55

property inherited during a relationship, 255, 270, 272, 279

state inheritance taxes, 234, 236–237

Insurance

auto insurance, 21, 72–73

and California's domestic partnerships, 44

COBRA coverage, 20

disability insurance, 71

and durable power of attorney for finances, 192–193

health insurance, 71

homeowner's insurance, 72

"insurable interest," 240

life insurance, 71–72

overview, 70

renter's insurance, 96–97

secondary auto coverage, 73

Internal Revenue Code tax credit for adoption expenses, 109

Internal Revenue Service (IRS), 76

International laws, 24–25, 26–27, 83

Internet resources

domestic partnership employment benefits information, 18

for domestic violence issues, 392

legal aspects, 57

for legal research, 402

for legal updates, 32

parentage law, 366

for tax filing information, 69

Intestate succession laws, 180, 308

Intravenous feeding, 171–172

Investments and durable power of attorney for finances, 190–191

Iowa, 21–22, 236–237. *See also* Marriage equality states

IRAs, 244

Ireland, 24

Irrevocable charitable remainder trusts, 239

IRS (Internal Revenue Service), 76

Israel, 83

Italy, 24

J

Joint and several liability for rent, 89

Joint legal custody, 383

Jointly acquired items contract, 255, 265–267

Joint projects contracts, 274, 276–278

Joint tenancy with right of survivorship

and estate planning, 233–234, 235

federal laws affecting transfer at death, 235–236

for home purchase, 306–308

overview, 67–68, 233–234

simultaneous death of joint tenants, 223

Joint wills, 211

Justice Department (DOJ), 11, 79

K

Kansas, 29, 126

Kentucky, 363, 382

L

Lambda Legal Defense and Education Fund website, 18

Lawyers, consulting with

for child adoptions, 138–139

for conditions on gifts given in a will, 219

for contracts, 28

for custody battles, 385

for divorce/separation, 352, 353, 373, 375, 380

for home purchase with one partner on deed, 306, 307

for immigration issues, 84

for implied or oral contract enforcement, 372

for lesbians and gay men parenting together, 136

and mediation process, 346

for prenuptial or preregistration agreements, 35–36

for prepartnership agreements, 52, 53

for protecting the validity of your will, 202, 221

for reviewing legal documents, 260–261, 350, 398

for second-parent adoptions, 112

for surrogacy agreements, 134, 135

for third and fourth parent adoptions, 114

for transsexual name and gender changes, 76

Lawyers, hiring, 394–398

Lease or rental agreement provisions, 88

Legal custody, 383

Legal encyclopedias, 401

Legal organizations, 403–405

Legal parent, defining, 104–105, 366

Legal research, 398–402

LGBT community

and gay kids (or kids of gays) needing homes, 152–153

lesbians and gay men parenting together, 136–138

views, 3–4, 57

Liability of non-livein owner of a home, 330

Library research, 398–401

Life insurance

and estate planning, 234, 240–241

and estate taxes, 240–241

home ownership agreement clause, 311

overview, 71–72

and simultaneous death of owner and beneficiary, 223

Life-prolonging medical treatments, 170–172

Limited partnerships, 330

Litigation for divorce/separation, 352–353

Living arrangement when separating, 338–339, 341–342

Living together

Alternatives to Marriage Project website, 18

and auto insurance, 72–73

and children, 134–136

and club membership, 14

court cases and legislative action, 13, 249, 250

death of one partner, 199–200

emotional distress claim, 13

and employment benefits, 19, 71

ending your relationship, 371–373

loss of consortium claim, 13

and property laws, 56

and public benefits, 98–100

tax benefits for married couples vs., 56, 58

Unmarried Couple Adoption Ban (Arkansas), 150

See also Buying a home together; Renting a home together

Living together contracts

adopting your partner, 30–31, 81

arbitration and mediation clause, 257–260, 270–271, 272–273

contents of, 253–260

cooling off clause, 256–257, 270, 272

for giving a partner "time off," 278–280

income and accumulations combined, 264, 268–269, 272

income and accumulations separate,
  262–263, 269–271, 275, 284
for jointly acquired items, 255, 265–267
for joint projects, 274, 276–278
for long-term couples, 267–273
modifying, 285
moving into a home owned by your lover,
  330–333
overview, 27–28, 248–250
for people in school, 281–282
property and finances clauses, 254–256
reasons for, 252–253
sample contracts, 260–264
for sharing household expenses and chores,
  274, 275
sharing most property, 272–273
tax issues, 285
transgender partners, 28–30
validity of, 250–252
will vs., 199–200
for work done in the home, 282–284
Living trusts, 193, 230–231, 238–239
Living will, 165, 167
Local laws
  nondiscrimination ordinance, 86–87
  registration as domestic partners, 17
Long-term couples' contracts, 267–273
Loss of consortium claims, 13, 49
Louisiana
  child custody and coming out, 389
  laws of, and wills, 211, 216
  new birth certificate following adoption, 112
  parentage law, 363
  and transgender partners, 29
Luxembourg, 24

M
Maine
  marriage lite, 53–54, 55
  overview, 21–22
  same-sex adult adoptions, 31
Marital status clause of a will, 212, 217–218
Marriage
  burial and body disposition, 177–180
  business partnership model, 61
  choosing, 55–58
  financial responsibilities of partners, 62
  as government-arranged contractual
    relationship, 248, 253
  overview, 5
  prenuptial agreements, 28, 35, 54, 253, 261,
    309
  private contracts as secondary to, 56, 62, 90
  socialist model, 61
  splitsies model, 62
  Supreme Court on, 23, 26–27
  and tenancy by the entirety, 308
  traditional model, 61
  wills and surviving spouse, 56, 58
  See also Divorce; Same-sex marriage
Marriage-based visas, 79–80
Marriage equality states
  and auto insurance, 73
  employment-related issues, 40
  ending your marriage, 39, 41
  and home mortgages, 299–300
  inheritance rights of your spouse, 201
  license requirements, 37–38
  and marriage-equivalence in another state,
    50
  and name change, 74
  overview, 37

rights and responsibilities, 38–39

and tax issues, 285

in transition, 22

Marriage-equivalent relationships, 21–22, 34–37, 309. *See also* Civil unions; Domestic partnerships

Marriage-equivalent states

and California's domestic partnership law, 41–48

children born into relationship, 36–37

employers in, 17, 19

and home mortgages, 299–300

inheritance rights of your partner, 201

and outdated civil unions, 52

overview, 48–52

state COBRA coverage, 20

See also Civil unions; Domestic partnerships

Marriage-like relationships

overview, 21–22

prepartnership agreements, 35–36, 52–53, 248, 253, 261, 289

See also Civil unions; Domestic partnership; Living together; Same-sex marriage

Marriage-like relationship contracts

adopting your partner, 30–31, 81

overview, 27–28

transgender partners, 28–30

See also Living together contracts

Marriage lite, 53–55

"Marriage of convenience" to a U.S. citizen, 80

Marvin v. Marvin, 250–251

Maryland, 363

Massachusetts

legalization of same-sex marriage, 8

loss of consortium ruling, 13

overview, 21–22

parentage law, 363

state's DOMA law as violation of constitution, 26

See also Marriage equality states

Mediation

arbitration and mediation clause of living together contracts, 257–260, 270–271, 272–273

for child custody issues, 384

and cooling off period, 257, 270, 272

home ownership agreement clause, 311, 315, 317–318, 322–323, 325–326

overview, 258, 345–346

Medical issues

burial and body disposition, 177–180

determination of incapacity, 166, 174, 186–187

overview, 162–164

physician-assisted suicide, 176

See also Health care decisions; Health care documents

Mexico, 24

Michigan

adult adoption ban, 31

child custody and coming out, 389

parentage law, 363

public employer restrictions, 15

Miike, Baehr v., 23, 26

Military service members, 36

Minimum required withdrawals from IRAs, 244

Minnesota, 14, 23, 364

Mississippi, 31

Missouri, 389

Mitford, Jessica, 179

Money issues

buying and investing together, 67–68

and name changes, 74–77

See also Cash and credit; Durable power of attorney for finances; Insurance; entries beginning with "Taxes"

Montana, 364

Mortgages
    calculating your ability to pay, 296–298
    and credit score, 293
    escrow, loan fees, and closing costs, 303–305
    fees, 303–304
    interest on, 296
    and marital status of couple, 299–300
    overview, 301–302

Motor vehicles. *See* Vehicles

Moving your residence, 38

N

Name changes, 37, 74–77

Naming your child, 134

National Center for Lesbian Rights website, 69, 108, 366

National Gay and Lesbian Task Force (NGLTF) Policy Institute, 18

Nebraska, 31

Netherlands, 83

Net value of an estate, 228, 229, 234, 235–236

Nevada, 17, 21–22, 48–52. *See also* Marriage-equivalent states

New Hampshire, 21–22, 52. *See also* Marriage equality states

New Jersey
    domestic partnership and civil union in, 51
    employer requirements, 17
    fostering parenting in, 149
    LGBT-friendly rulings, 13
    marriage-equivalent laws, 48–52
    and name change, 75
    overview, 21–22
    paid family leave, 11
    and residency requirement for divorce, 378
    state inheritance tax, 236–237
    and transgender partners, 29
    See also Marriage-equivalent states

New Mexico
    loss of consortium claim, 13
    parentage law, 364
    on sperm donor's rights, 123, 126

New York
    adoption agency discrimination prohibited, 143
    Equal Benefits Law, 12
    fostering parenting in, 149
    overview, 21–22
    parentage law, 364
    and property settlement of couple married in Massachusetts, 13
    right to keep apartment, 12
    same-sex adult adoptions, 30
    state employee pension fund, 11
    state inheritance tax, 236–237
    and transgender partners, 382
    and transsexual name change, 76
    See also Marriage equality states

New Zealand, 24, 83

NGLTF (National Gay and Lesbian Task Force) Policy Institute, 18

No contest clause of a will, 214, 221–222

No-fault divorces, 375–376

Nondiscrimination ordinance, 86

Nonmarital agreements, 248

Nonmarital cohabitation contract laws, 250–252. *See also* Living together contracts

Nonmarital couple ending their relationship, 371–373

North Carolina, 364, 389

Norway, 24, 83

Notary public
for durable power of attorney, 183, 195–196
for health care documents, 175
for living together contracts with real estate, 261
Notice of Revocation of Termination of Domestic Partnership (CA), 48
Notice of Termination of Domestic Partnership (CA), 47–48

O

Office of Personnel Management, 12
Ohio
adult adoption ban, 31
parentage law, 364–365
on sperm donor's rights, 126
and transgender partners, 29, 30
"Open" and "closed" adoptions, 141
Oral contracts, 200, 250, 251–252, 371–373
Oregon
employer requirements, 17
marriage-equivalent laws, 48–52
overview, 21–22
on sperm donor rights, 125
on sperm donor's rights, 123
See also Marriage-equivalent states
Organ donation, 172
Organizations, legal, 403–405

P

Palliative care, 171
Parenting
agreements with teenagers, 158–160
becoming parents together, 105–107
completing the birth certificate, 134–136
coparenting agreements, 115–119, 121
egg donation/ovum sharing, 106–107, 132–133

foster parenting, 149–153
as guardian, 115, 153–158
historical perspective, 103
legal parentage, 102, 104–105, 366
lesbians and gay men parenting together, 136–138
naming the child, 134
overview, 102, 121
placing gay kids in gay homes, 152–153
prebirth judgments, 135
surrogacy, 133–134, 135
transgender parents, 381–382
See also Adopting a child; Donor insemination
Parenting, second parent protections
adoption and other court methods, 106, 107–112
becoming parents together, 105–107
international adoptions, 148
lack of, 367–370
legal parentage, meaning of, 104–105, 366
new birth certificate after second-parent adoption, 112–113, 136
overview, 102–105, 107
and private agreements, 114–121
and third and fourth parents, 113–114
Parenting time (visitation), 385–386
Partner benefits for diplomats, 11
Pay-on-death bank accounts, 231–232
Pay-on-death securities accounts, 232
Pennsylvania, 12, 74, 365
Pension benefits, 11
Pension Protection Act (2006), 245
Personal property and durable power of attorney for finances, 190
Physical custody, 383
Physician-assisted suicide, 176
Pick-up taxes (state estate taxes), 236–237

Political asylum, 81
Political struggle
  historical perspective, 9, 103
  successes, 2–3, 5, 8
  See also California court cases; Court cases
    and legislative action
Portugal, 83
Postpartnership agreements, 53
Postseparation agreement regarding housing,
  341–342
Postseparation parenting agreement, 369–370
Prebirth judgments of parentage, 135
Prenuptial agreements, 28, 35, 54, 253, 261,
  309
Prepartnership agreements, 35–36, 52–53,
  248, 253, 261, 289
Presbyterian retirement community, 14
Priorities for home purchase, 290, 296
Private agreements for second parent, 114–121
Probate, 199, 201, 206–207, 227, 230
Probate avoidance
  joint bank accounts for, 63
  overview, 228, 230–234
  pay-on-death bank accounts, 231–232
  for retirement plans, 244
  trusts, 193, 205, 230–232, 238–239
  See also Estate planning
Probate Code, 399–400
Property and finances clauses of living together
  contracts, 254–256
Property, estimating value of, 228, 229, 234,
  235–236
Property list, 228, 229
Property taxes, 70
Property transfers
  by attorney-in-fact, 184, 190
  and California domestic partnership law, 44
  county tax exemption, 17

and estate planning, 180
and gift taxes, 285
and living trust, 193
oral contracts invalid for real property, 200
overview, 56
probate for, 228, 230
taxes related to, 70
Public agencies
  adoptions through, 141–144
  foster care placements, 151, 152–153
  Justice Department, 11
  New York public employee pension fund, 11
  Office of Personnel Management, 12
  Social Security, 11
  State Department, 11
  Unemployment Appeals Board, 10–11
  Workers' Compensation Appeals Board, 11
  See also Court cases and legislative action;
    Government benefits; Social workers
Public benefits
  and children by donor insemination, 132
  and domestic partnership registration, 36
  and living together, 98–100
  and marriage, 56
  marriage-equality states, 49

R

Readoption in U.S. after international
  adoption, 147–148
Real estate
  and divorce or separation, 354–359
  and durable power of attorney for finances,
    184, 189–190
  and ending a relationship, 344
  as investment and tax shelter, 288
  selling your home, 357–358
  transfer-on-death deeds for, 232

See also Joint tenancy with right of survivorship; entries beginning with "Buying a home"
Real property transfers
and California's domestic partnership law, 44
federal taxes on, 56, 70
oral transfer invalid for, 200
Realtors, 291
Reciprocal beneficiaries, 23, 54
Registration
local registration as domestic partners, 17
preregistration agreements, 35–36
requirements in California, 41–42
Regulations and statutes, 399–400
Rental agreement or lease provisions, 88
Renting a home together
ending the relationship, 354
landlord discrimination, 86–88
legal obligations to landlord, 89
and public benefits, 98–100
renter's insurance, 96–97
rights and responsibilities of a housemate, 93
security deposits, 91, 92, 341, 354
sharing one partner's rented home, 92–96
tenant-subtenant situations, 94, 96, 97
written agreement, 88, 90–91, 94–96
Residue clause of a will, 213, 220
Restraining orders, 392
Retirement accounts, 234, 243–245
Retirement community discrimination, 14
Retirement plans
and durable power of attorney for finances, 194
Revocable living trusts, 230–231, 238–239
Revocation of Termination of Domestic Partnership (CA), 47–48
Revoking your will, 223, 227

Rhode Island
employer requirements, 17
marriage-equivalent laws, 48–52
overview, 21–22
recognition of marriages performed in other states, 13–14
See also Marriage-equivalent states
Right of survivorship, 233, 299, 306. *See also* Joint tenancy with right of survivorship

S
Same-sex adult adoptions, 30–31, 81
Same-sex marriage
and children, 58, 104, 105–106, 135
as family tie for immigrants, 80
federal rights, 35
and federal taxes, 40, 379–380
fight in California, 43
and gift taxes, 242
and health care decisions, 163
and inheriting retirement plans, 245
legal meaning of, 34–35
not recognized for federal taxes, 40, 285, 379–380
overview, 34–37
See also Divorce
Same-sex partners
countries with residency rights for, 83
problematic zoning ordinances, 290–291
San Francisco, 2004, 4, 8, 43
Schiavo, Terri, 162
School and living together contracts, 281–282
Secondary auto coverage, 73
Second parent. *See* Parenting, second parent protections
Security deposits, 91, 92, 341, 354
Selling a home, 357–358
Separation-based divorces, 375–376

Separation process
  advance planning, 338–339
  dividing other assets and debts, 359–360
  no legal relationship, 371–373
  overview, 336–338, 353–354
  and owned home, 354–359
  practical aspects, 339–342
  and rented home, 354
  See also Child custody; Ending a relationship
Settlement agreement, 350–352
Sex and contract validity, 251
Sick leave, 12, 19, 45
Signature and witnessing clause of a will, 214, 233
Simultaneous death clause of a will, 214, 222–223
62-or-over domestic partnerships in California, 42
Slovenia, 24
Small businesses, starting together, 274, 277–278
Small claims court, 89
Socialist model of marriage, 61
Social Security Administration and name change, 76
Social Security benefits, 11
Social services and second parent adoptions, 108
Social workers
  and adopting a child, 108, 140, 142–143, 145, 150
  for foster parenting, 150–151, 152
  and living with someone on public benefits, 99
Sole custody, 383
South Africa, 83
Spain, 24, 83

Sperm banks, 121–123, 125, 127. *See also* Donor insemination
Sperm donor legal rulings, 126
Sperm donors, known, 124–125, 127–131
Splitsies model of marriage, 62
Springing durable power of attorney, 174, 181
Standby guardian, 218
State Department, 11
State employees with domestic partnership benefits, 18
State estate taxes, 236–237
State forms
  for durable power of attorney for finances, 183
  for medical care, 167–168
State income taxes, 45, 68, 70
State inheritance taxes, 234, 236–237
State laws
  on adopting a child, 138, 139–140
  on child custody and visitation, 361–366
  defense of marriage acts, 23, 26, 38–39
  on divorces, 50, 376
  familiarizing yourself with, 55
  on gender changes, 75–76
  on guardianships, 158
  and informal domestic partnerships, 15–16
  on international adoptions, 147–148
  on intestate succession, 180, 308
  on lawyer required for real estate closings, 305
  and marriages made in Canada, 27
  nonmarital cohabitation contract laws, 250–252
  on prenuptial/prepartnership agreements, 261
  on real estate buyouts, 356–357
  on recognition of same-sex marriage of another state, 50

on same-sex marriage recognition, 38, 40, 377–378

on second parent adoptions, 110–111

state employee's domestic partner benefits, 18

transfer-on-death deeds, 232

transfer-on-death vehicle registration, 232

Uniform Child Custody Jurisdiction Enforcement Act, 390–391

Uniform Parentage Act, 113, 132, 133

Uniform Simultaneous Death Act, 222

Uniform Transfer-on-Death Securities Registration Act, 232

Uniform Transfers to Minors Act, 205

See also Taxes, state

State of residence at time of divorce, 39, 56, 377–378

Statutes and regulations, 399–400

Stepparent adoptions, 108–109

Stock certificates, 67–68

Strategic ambiguity, 261–262

Student visas, 83

Successor trustees, 230

Support groups, 390–391

Supreme Court, United States, 23, 26–27, 165

Surrogacy, 133–134, 135

Sweden, 24, 83

Switzerland, 24

T

Taxes, federal

claiming partner as a dependent, 69–70

and durable power of attorney for finances, 194

on employment benefits offered to domestic partners, 19, 46

generation-skipping transfer tax, 238–239

income taxes, 230, 239, 283, 380

living together contract tax issues, 285

and profits from selling a home, 288

same-sex marriage not recognized, 40, 285, 379–380

tax credit for adoption expenses, 109

tax issues related to DOMA, 68–69, 377, 380

See also Estate taxes; Gift taxes

Taxes, state

and California's domestic partnership law, 44

and durable power of attorney for finances, 194

filing joint returns, 68–69

income taxes, 45, 68, 70

inheritance taxes, 234, 236–237

in marriage-equality states, 50

See also Inheritance laws

Tax professionals, consulting with, 46, 69, 236, 242, 261

Tax-saving trusts, 238–239

Teenagers, agreements with, 158–160

Temporary Guardianship Agreement, 155, 156

Tenancy by the entirety, 49, 308

Tenancy-in-common, 67, 233, 307, 308

Tenant-subtenant situations, 94, 96, 97

Termination documents, 339

Terminology, 3

Texas, 29–30, 39, 365

Third and fourth parents, 113–114

Thompson, Karen, 162

"Time off" contract, 278–280

Title documents, 67–68, 73, 300, 305–309

Totten trusts, 231–232

Tourist visas, 78

Traditional model of marriage, 61

Transfer-on-death deeds for real estate, 232

Transfer-on-death vehicle registration, 232

Transgender Law Center, 29, 30, 76
Transgender people
  and child custody issues, 381–382
  and immigration, 80
  legal complications, 28–30
  name and birth certificate changes, 75–76
  overview, 5
Trustee of a trust, 230
Trusts, 193, 205, 230–232, 238–239
Tube feeding, 171–172

U

UCCJEA (Uniform Child Custody
  Jurisdiction Enforcement Act), 390–391
Unemployment Appeals Board, 10–11
Unemployment benefits, 10–11, 44
Uniform Anatomical Gift Act, 179
Uniform Child Custody Jurisdiction
  Enforcement Act (UCCJEA), 390–391
Uniform Parentage Act (UPA), 113, 132, 133
Uniform Simultaneous Death Act, 222
Uniform Transfer-on-Death Securities
  Registration Act, 232
Uniform Transfers to Minors Act (UTMA),
  205
United Kingdom, 24, 83
United States Supreme Court, 23, 26–27, 165
University domestic partnership benefits, 21
Unmarried Couple Adoption Ban (Arkansas),
  150
Unmarried couples. *See* Living together
UPA (Uniform Parentage Act), 113, 132, 133
Uruguay, 24
"Usage" method for changing your name, 75
U.S. Citizenship and Immigration Service, 30
U.S. Immigration and Customs Enforce (ICE),
  79–80

U.S. State Department, Visa Waiver Program,
  77–78
Utah, 31, 365
UTMA (Uniform Transfers to Minors Act),
  205

V

Validity of your will, 202–203
Vehicles
  auto insurance, 21, 72–73
  and name change, 76
  title documents, 67–68, 73
  transfer-on-death vehicle registration, 232
Vermont
  certification of civil union, 49
  outdated civil unions in, 52
  overview, 21–22
  parentage law, 365
  prohibiting same-sex marriage violates
    constitution, 26
  See also Marriage equality states
Video wills, 210
Virginia
  child custody and coming out, 389
  new birth certificate following adoption, 112
  new birth certificates following adoptions,
    14
  parentage law, 365–366
Visa lottery, 81–82
Visa Waiver Program, U.S. State Department,
  77–78
Visitation, 385–386

W

Washington (state)
  employer requirements, 17
  legalization of same-sex marriage, 8
  marriage-equivalent laws, 48–52

overview, 21–22

paid family leave, 11

parentage law, 366

stepparent procedures for adoptions, 109

"superwill" statute and beneficiary designations, 244

and transgender partners, 382

See also Marriage-equivalent states

Welfare benefits

for court-appointed guardians, 153

and living together, 98–100

West Virginia, 150, 366

Wills

challenges to, 202

changing, 233–226

disinheriting in, 209

executor of, 206–207

for guardian nomination, 115, 116, 119, 120, 203–204, 205, 212–213

importance of, 198

living together contract vs., 199–200

and moving to another state, 211

nontraditional formats, 210–211

overview, 200–201

providing for children, 203–205

provisions, 207–208

and retirement plans, 244

revoking, 223, 227

sample, 211–215

storing and copying, 233

technical requirements, 208–209

validity of, 202–203

Wills and surviving spouse, 56, 58

Wills, preparing with Nolo form

children clause, 218

executor clause, 220

gifts of money or personal property clause, 219–220

marital status clause, 217–218

no contest clause, 221–222

overview, 216–217

residue clause, 220

revocation clause, 217

signature and witnessing, 214, 233

simultaneous death clause, 222–223

Wisconsin

marriage lite, 53–54, 55

overview, 21–22

parentage law, 366

probate laws, 207

Witnesses

for durable power of attorney for finances, 183–184

for health care documents, 176

signature and witnessing clause of a will, 214, 233

Witnesses for child custody cases, 390

Workers' Compensation Appeals Board, 11

Workers' compensation death benefits, 11

Wrongful death of a partner

and California's domestic partnership law, 44

District of Columbia ruling, 12

marriage-equality states, 49

marriage-like states, 54

Z

Zoning ordinances, 290–291 ●

 **NOLO** *Keep Up to Date*

 Go to Nolo.com/newsletters to sign up for free newsletters and discounts on Nolo products.

- **Nolo's Special Offer.** A monthly newsletter with the biggest Nolo discounts around.

- **Landlord's Quarterly.** Deals and free tips for landlords and property managers.

 Don't forget to check for updates. Find this book at **Nolo.com** and click "Legal Updates."

Let Us Hear From You

 Register your Nolo product and give us your feedback at Nolo.com/book-registration.

- Once you've registered, you qualify for technical support if you have any trouble with a download (though most folks don't).

- We'll send you a coupon for 15% off your next Nolo.com order!

LG16

⚖ NOLO *Online Legal Forms*

Nolo offers a large library of legal solutions and forms, created by Nolo's in-house legal staff. These reliable documents can be prepared in minutes.

Create a Document

- **Incorporation.** Incorporate your business in any state.
- **LLC Formations.** Gain asset protection and pass-through tax status in any state.
- **Wills.** Nolo has helped people make over 2 million wills. Is it time to make or revise yours?
- **Living Trust (avoid probate).** Plan now to save your family the cost, delays, and hassle of probate.
- **Trademark.** Protect the name of your business or product.
- **Provisional Patent.** Preserve your rights under patent law and claim "patent pending" status.

Download a Legal Form

Nolo.com has hundreds of top quality legal forms available for download—bills of sale, promissory notes, nondisclosure agreements, LLC operating agreements, corporate minutes, commercial lease and sublease, motor vehicle bill of sale, consignment agreements and many, many more.

Review Your Documents

Many lawyers in Nolo's consumer-friendly lawyer directory will review Nolo documents for a very reasonable fee. Check their detailed profiles at **www.nolo.com/lawyers/index.html**.

 **Lawyer Directory**

Find an Attorney

Qualified lawyers · In-depth profiles

When you want help with a serious legal problem, you don't want just any lawyer—you want an expert in the field who can give you and your family up-to-the-minute advice. You need a lawyer who has the experience and knowledge to answer your questions about personal injury, wills, family law, child custody, drafting a patent application or any other specialized legal area you are concerned with.

Nolo's Lawyer Directory is unique because it provides an extensive profile of every lawyer. You'll learn about not only each lawyer's education, professional history, legal specialties, credentials and fees, but also about their philosophy of practicing law and how they like to work with clients.

www.nolo.com